Applied Econometric Techniques

Applied Econometric Techniques

Keith Cuthbertson
Stephen G. Hall
Mark P. Taylor

Philip Allan

New York   London   Toronto   Sydney   Tokyo   Singapore

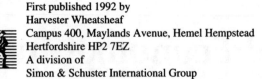

First published 1992 by
Harvester Wheatsheaf
Campus 400, Maylands Avenue, Hemel Hempstead
Hertfordshire HP2 7EZ
A division of
Simon & Schuster International Group

Typeset in 10/12 pt Times
by Keytec Typesetting Ltd, Bridport, Dorset, UK

Printed and bound in Great Britain by
BPCC Wheatons Ltd, Exeter

British Library Cataloguing in Publication Data

Cuthbertson, Keith
  Applied econometric techniques.
  I. Title II. Hall, Stephen III. Taylor, Mark
  330.01

  ISBN 0-7450-1244-2 (pbk)

3 4 5 96 95 94 93

Contents

Introduction

This book has a distinct philosophy and it is appropriate to make this explicit at the outset. In our view good applied econometrics can reveal important and useful insights about real-world behaviour; econometrics is not simply a body of abstract theory but a fundamental tool of the economic analyst. As with any tool it can easily be misused and its power lies at least partly in the skill of the practitioner. Many formal econometric courses leave the student with a detailed knowledge of the analytical tools of econometrics but often little feel for how it can be applied and of the practical dangers which face the applied econometrician. Our view is that good applied econometrics requires an amalgam of up-to-date statistical knowledge, good economic theory and a knowledge of real-world institutional factors. It is only when these diverse elements are successfully brought together that useful empirical results can be obtained.

The view expressed above is neither particularly new nor controversial, but there are several real problems which face any student nearing the end of an econometrics course. Most notably there has been a number of recent advances in econometrics which are often not covered comprehensively in the standard textbooks. However, some of these techniques are central to much current applied work. It is also true that the link between much textbook theory and what econometric modellers do often in practice, is not always apparent. This book then is designed to bridge the gap between a standard third-year undergraduate or a postgraduate econometric theory course and the practical work which will be asked of most applied economists, some of whom are employed in government or in large corporations.

We try to achieve this aim in two ways: We give a series of overviews of topics which we regard as particularly important; for example, general-to-specific modelling, cointegration, Kalman filters, maximum likelihood, etc. In each overview we attempt to concentrate on the implications of these concepts for practical work. Thus we do not generally dwell on formal proofs or a complete exposition of the theory. Instead we attempt to draw out important practical insights, give an intuitive feel for the techniques and show how these relate to other areas of econometrics. The second part of our approach is to illustrate the techniques discussed with actual examples of applied work. These examples are not constructed specially for this book but each one represents a genuine piece of economic research which has been undertaken on a real-world problem. So they contain many instances of the problems which arise constantly in real applied work; problems of data availability, problems of possible structural, institutional and policy changes, etc. This emphasis on illustrating techniques by real applications rather than by simple constructed examples is, in our view, important. It demonstrates that these techniques really do provide insights to real-world problems and that making them work is neither simple nor automatic. Applied econometrics can not be done mechanically: it needs understanding, intuition and skill. Much of the material in the book is based on our own practical experience of the Bank of England, H.M. Treasury, International Monetary Fund, The National Institute of Economic and Social Research, The London Business School and for private sector organisations. We hope that some will gain useful insights from the examples used and that passing it on in this way we may shorten the learning time of others.

One way to view the structure of this book is to contrast it with many standard textbooks. A common approach is to discuss basic estimation methodology and then devote much of the book to the problems which arise when the underlying assumptions fail; serial correlation, multicollinearity, heteroscedasticity, endogenous regressors, omitted variables, latent variables, etc. Often each of these is seen as a single isolated problem. The resulting undesirable effects of the problem are described and a 'solution' is offered, based usually on a rather simplified, stylised equation. There is nothing wrong with this approach; after all, the basic concepts of econometrics need to be understood fully before further progress can be made. However, for most of this book we are interested in developing the student's awareness of practical problems that require further development of these concepts. For example Kalman filtering provides an answer to the problem of latent variables and time-varying parameters. Cointegration deals with non-stationarity, and our approach to dynamic modelling allows us to deal with problems of serial correlation, multicollinearity and thorough testing of all aspects of a model. Thus much of this book is about practical solutions to problems, and how we proceed with 'real-world' econometrics despite the difficulties which always exist.

The opening Chapter is designed to provide a brief survey of the theoretical underpinnings of 'standard econometrics'. In most of the book we assume that the reader is familiar with this basic material and this Chapter is designed primarily as a 'refresher course'. We hope it will be useful as a reference source for background information for the later Chapters but we are aware that our exposition is probably too concise to be of use to students coming to econometrics for the first time.

Chapter 2 deals with the unifying principle which underlies much of the rest of the book, namely maximum likelihood. This provides the conceptual basis both for structural estimation and for classical inference which justify many of the techniques and procedures which are outlined later. In this Chapter perhaps even more than the later ones, we concentrate on an intuitive exposition and an understanding of the key results rather than detailed proofs. We illustrate both the power and generality of the maximum likelihood principle by outlining the way it may be applied to a range of models which would be particularly hard to deal with in any other way. These include discreet switching disequilibrium models, censored models (Tobit and Probit), and ARCH and GARCH models.

Chapter 3 gives an account of time series modelling techniques looking at both autoregressive and moving average representations and discussing the Box–Jenkins methodology. While we have only limited interest in pure time series analysis (our main interest being in structural economic modelling), the techniques of time series modelling are both useful and important for many aspects of structural economic modelling. For example, time series representations of data will be seen to be of considerable use when we come to deal with the modelling of expectations variables and for cointegration in later Chapters.

The next Chapter gives a broad exposition of the dynamic modelling strategy which has grown out of the work of Sargan and his former students at the London School of Economics. This has developed into a major theme within modern econometrics. We have found these techniques to be both powerful and intuitively appealing in many practical applications and this Chapter in some sense provides the basis for many of our practical examples. We begin by providing an overview of the methodology of general-to-specific modelling which is at the heart of this approach. We then consider the formulation and estimation of dynamic models in some detail and outline the broad range of econometric tests which are performed on such models. We conclude this Chapter with an illustration of modelling the demand for money for a number of countries.

Chapter 5 deals with the problem of non-stationarity and discusses the relatively new area of cointegration. This Chapter is strongly related to the previous one on dynamic modelling as developments in cointegration provide a sound theoretical underpinning for the dynamic modelling strategy. It also draws on some of the ideas developed within the 'time series' school of modelling which were outlined in Chapter 3. Cointegration is presented as a central concept for the econometric modelling of non-stationary data. It is an absolute prerequisite for the satisfactory modelling of most economic time series (e.g. output, consumption, interest rates, etc.) and thus testing for cointegration and the estimation of cointegrating relationships is a crucial element in economic modelling. This topic is still in its embryonic stage and we are aware that both the theory and practical techniques are developing at a rapid rate.

Chapter 6 considers how we may handle the important question of expectations of future economic variables. This is important both in terms of understanding the structure of the economy, as we believe that many structural relationships have important expectations effects, and in building models which are robust to structural change due to changing expectations formation procedures (the 'Lucas' critique). We concentrate principally on the limited information estimation techniques which have proved useful in applied work and we survey a range of methods for achieving both consistency in estimation and correct inference. This Chapter may be viewed as outlining one set of solutions to the problem of 'unobserved variables', namely agents expectations.

The next Chapter gives a different and, in many ways, complimentary approach to the problem of unobserved components, measurement error and time-varying coefficients by discussing the principle and application of the Kalman filter. This approach provides a general framework for estimating a wide range of models, including the ones mentioned above. We develop the Kalman filter as a generalisation of more conventional econometric techniques before giving a formal statement and derivation. We illustrate how a range of standard and non-standard models can be represented in state space form and estimated with the aid of the Kalman filter.

The final Chapter outlines a range of techniques which are rarely considered in econometrics courses or discussed in textbooks; these centre around the use of large models. Often one of the products from single-equation or small sub-system estimation is a collection of equations which together constitute a large non-linear econometric model. These models are used widely by governments in policy formation and analysis and by many forecasting organisations. A body of techniques has grown up which allows the model users to analyse and manipulate their models and this body of knowledge forms the core of the Chapter. The use of large models is a topic which does not usually receive much attention on most courses, which is unfortunate given that many applied economists in government and large corporations will often have to use such models during the course of their careers.

Econometrics at a formal level has a number of quite divergent views and philosophies, at a practical level these divergences become more marked. Three of the competing methodologies (although we do not claim to be exhaustive) are the Bayesian school, best typified by the work of Arnold Zellner, the non-structural modelling approach typified by the vector autoregressive models of Christopher Simms, and the dynamic modelling approach which has grown out of the work of Dennis Sargan and latterly David Hendry. There is also something of a divide at the practical level between those researchers who attempt to estimate and test a tightly defined theory and those who attempt to derive models which are broadly theory consistent but which are designed to characterise the actual data set used. We would not presume to attempt to judge between these views, but our background and experience give us competence to deal with only one of these approaches to our own satisfaction. We have been trained and we work within the framework which has been developed by the dynamic modelling approach. This book then sits firmly within that tradition which has developed out of Sargan's work at the LSE and which has been influenced profoundly by the many notable scholars who over recent years have contributed to this branch of the literature. The fact that this book does not attempt to give an exposition of some of the other modelling philosophies should not be taken as a criticism of these views but simply an admission of the limits of our own expertise.

1

Review of the general linear model

This chapter reviews some of the standard theory of estimation of econometric relationships which makes up many econometric courses. We show how a set of assumptions regarding the structure of the model lead ordinary least squares (OLS) to be an optimal estimator and how the failure of these assumptions can produce highly misleading results. This chapter sets the scene for much of the rest of the book as later chapters focus both on the problems which arise when these assumptions are violated and more importantly on the range of new techniques which have been developed for dealing with these problems.

1.1   Economic and statistical models

We may define an *economic* model as one that has some basis in economic theory. Economic theory usually (but not exclusively) yields static, or 'long-run' relationships. For example, in the simple Keynesian consumption function, consumption at time t, y_t say, is assumed proportional to income, x_t say. If we assume instantaneous adjustment of y to x, we may write

$$y_t = \beta_1 + \beta_2 x_t + \varepsilon_t \tag{1.1}$$

where ε_t is a random error term which encapsulates deviations from the model; we discuss various possible properties of ε_t below. It may be possible, however, to obtain a good approximation to the behaviour of y without recourse to *any* economic theory. A simple, pure time series model of consumption might be a univariate autoregressive model of order one – an AR(1):

1

$$y_t = \alpha_1 + \alpha_2 y_{t-1} + \varepsilon_t \tag{1.2}$$

It may be the case that *some* economic theory is consistent with equation (1.2), but a pure time series modeller need not be concerned with this. Although an 'economic modeller' and a 'time series modeller' may end up with similar statistical models, their aims will usually be subtly different. The time series modeller is aiming for a succinct summary of the time series behaviour of the variable. Typically, the applied economist will want to go further than this, to test some kind of *restrictions* on the time series model, as a test of an economic hypothesis. For example, the life-cycle theory of consumption under rational expectations would suggest that a univariate model of consumption of the form (1.2) should hold, with $\alpha_2 = 1$.

1.2   Time series and stochastic processes

A *stochastic process* is a sequence of random variables – any one element of the sequence may take on any of a range of values in any particular realisation. Thus, if I plan to roll a fair, six-sided die every morning before breakfast next week, then I can imagine seven random variables (each morning's score) associated with this activity which together form a stochastic process. If I denote the number of dots uppermost on the ith day as d_i then the sequence $(d_i)_{i=1...7}$ denotes a stochastic process. If a stochastic process has one element for each of a set of points in time, then any realisation of the stochastic process is a *time series*. Thus, if the number of dots uppermost on the die each morning was as follows: Monday 1, Tuesday 3, Wednesday 5, Thursday 5, Friday 2, Saturday 4, Sunday 4; then the sequence $(1,3,5,5,2,4,4)$ denotes a time series. Any element of a stochastic process is a *random variable*. Any element of a time series is a *number* which is referred to as an *observation*. In general, when econometricians speak of *modelling* a time series, they mean the act of postulating a *stochastic process* which may have generated the observed time series. Following standard practice, we shall, where there is no possibility of confusion, use the same notation to denote a stochastic process, a time series or an element of either.

1.3   Properties of stochastic processes

In the early morning die-rolling example given above, the *sample* mean is just the mean of the observed time series (which is 24/7); the *population* mean is the expected value of any element of the stochastic process (which is 21/6). Roughly speaking, if a process is *ergodic*, then its *moments* (i.e. mean, variance, etc.) can be estimated 'well' (or, to be precise, *consistently* – see below) by the corresponding moments of the observed time series over a long period of time. Consider the following AR(1) model for y:

$$y_t = \beta y_{t-1} + \varepsilon_t \tag{1.3}$$

where ε_t is a zero–mean random variable with constant variance σ^2, which is uncorrelated with any other variable in the sequence $(\varepsilon_t)_{t=-\infty}^{+\infty}$, i.e.

$$E(\varepsilon_t) = 0 \tag{1.4a}$$

$$\text{Var}(\varepsilon_t) = E(\varepsilon_t^2) = \sigma_\varepsilon^2 \tag{1.4b}$$

$$\text{Cov}(\varepsilon_t, \varepsilon_{t-j}) = 0, \text{ for all } j \neq 0 \tag{1.4c}$$

A stochastic process displaying these properties is often referred to as *white noise*. A white noise process is a special case of a more general class of stochastic processes, namely those which are *stationary*. A *covariance stationary* stochastic process, y_t say, has a constant mean and variance and the covariation between any two elements in the sequence is a function only of the distance in time between the two elements:

$$E(y_t) = \mu \tag{1.5a}$$

$$\text{Var}(y_t) = E[(y_t - \mu)^2] = \gamma(0) < \infty \tag{1.5b}$$

$$\text{Cov}(y_t, y_{t-j}) = \gamma(j) \quad \text{for all } j \tag{1.5c}$$

A stochastic process is *strictly stationary* if the joint probability of any consecutive r observations is always the same, for any integer r. In this book we shall generally use the term *stationary* to refer to *weak* or *covariance* stationarity. Note that, if a process is both covariance stationary and normally distributed, then it is also strictly stationary.

Equation (1.3) can be written in the form

$$(1 - \beta L)y_t = \varepsilon_t \tag{1.6}$$

where L is the lag operator, which has the property:

$$L^m y_t = y_{t-m}$$

and $(1 - \beta L)$ is thus a polynomial of order one in the lag operator. If we lag (1.3) by one period, we have

$$y_{t-1} = \beta y_{t-2} + \varepsilon_{t-1} \tag{1.7}$$

Substituting equation (1.7) into (1.3):

$$y_t = \beta^2 y_{t-2} + \varepsilon_t + \beta \varepsilon_{t-1} \tag{1.8}$$

If we now lag (1.3) twice [i.e. lag (1.7) once] and substitute into equation (1.8) we have an expression in y_{t-3}, ε_t, ε_{t-1} and ε_{t-2}. Continually substituting for lagged values of y in this fashion we have, after $n-1$ substitutions:

$$y_t = \beta^n y_{t-n} + \varepsilon_t + \beta \varepsilon_{t-1} + \beta^2 \varepsilon_{t-2} + \beta^3 \varepsilon_{t-3} + \ldots$$
$$+ \beta^{n-1} \varepsilon_{t-n+1} \tag{1.9}$$

If β is less than one in absolute value, $|\beta| < 1$, then as n gets bigger and bigger (tends towards infinity), β^n gets smaller and smaller (tends towards zero). Thus, for large n we can write:

$$y_t = \varepsilon_t + \beta \varepsilon_{t-1} + \beta^2 \varepsilon_{t-2} + \beta^3 \varepsilon_{t-3} + \ldots \tag{1.10a}$$

or

$$y_t = [1 + \beta L + (\beta L)^2 + (\beta L)^3 + \ldots] \varepsilon_t \tag{1.10b}$$

where we have again used the lag operator. Multiplying both sides of equation (1.10b) by βL and subtracting the resulting expression from (1.10a) gives

$$y_t (1 - \beta L) = \varepsilon_t \tag{1.11a}$$

or

$$y_t = (1 - \beta L)^{-1} \varepsilon_t \tag{1.11b}$$

Since ε_t is a white noise process, (1.10a) implies the following:

$$E(y_t) = E(\varepsilon_t) + \beta E(\varepsilon_{t-1}) + \beta^2 E(\varepsilon_{t-2}) + \ldots = 0 \quad (1.12a)$$

$$\text{Var}(y_t) = E(y_t^2) = (1 + \beta^2 + \beta^4 + \beta^6 + \ldots)\sigma_\varepsilon^2$$
$$= (1 - \beta^2)^{-1} \sigma_\varepsilon^2 \tag{1.12b}$$

$$\text{Cov}(y_t, y_{t-j}) = E[(\varepsilon_t + \beta \varepsilon_{t-1} + \beta^2 \varepsilon_{t-2} + \ldots)$$
$$\times (\varepsilon_{t-j} + \beta \varepsilon_{t-j-1} + \beta^2 \varepsilon_{t-j-2} + \ldots)]$$
$$= \beta^{j2} E(y_t^2) \tag{1.12c}$$

Comparing (1.12) with (1.5), we can see that the AR(1) process (1.3) is stationary for $|\beta| < 1$.

Virtually the whole of standard econometric theory is based on the assumption that the processes under examination are stationary. However many economic time series – particularly macroeconomic and financial time series – appear to be generated by non-stationary processes. Recently, however, a body of literature has developed which deals with non-stationary processes directly. This will be the subject matter of Chapter 5.

1.4   Properties of estimators

Econometrics is largely to do with estimating the parameters of economic relationships and testing hypotheses with respect to those parameters. For example, consider again the simple, linear Keynesian consumption function relating consumption, y, to income, x:

$$y_t = \beta_1 + \beta_2 x_t + \varepsilon_t \tag{1.13}$$

Economic theory suggests the form of the consumption function (Keynes's 'fundamental psychological law' – Keynes 1936), and may even suggest qualitative restrictions on the parameters. For example, since β_1 is equal to autonomous consumption and β_2 is the marginal propensity to consume, we can infer:

$$\beta_1 \geqslant 0, \, 0 \leqslant \beta_2 \leqslant 1 \tag{1.14a}$$

In general, however, economic theory will be silent on the *exact* values of the parameters of a model. Moreover, even when an exact value of a parameter *is* suggested by economic theory, an econometrician may still want to estimate it to see if the data is in accordance with the theory. Econometrics can thus be used to obtain estimates of unknown parameters in empirical economic models and to test hypotheses with respect to them.

For example, Davis (1952) uses annual data for the United States for the period 1929–40 (deflated for price and population changes) and estimates the parameters in (1.13) as:

$$y_t = 11.45 + 0.78 x_t \tag{1.14b}$$

Thus, Davis's estimate of β_1 ('autonomous consumption') is 11.45 and of β_2 (the 'marginal propensity to consume') is 0.78. These are numbers. To obtain these *estimates*, Davis used formulae suggested by econometric theory. These formulae are *estimators*.

There is an infinite number of estimators, all but a few of which are unacceptable to an econometrician. For example, a particularly silly estimator could be obtained simply by writing down the number of the day of the month. Whilst it may be *obvious* that such an estimator is silly, there are other estimators which are not obviously so. Thus, we need a formal set of criteria by which to judge an estimator.

Sampling distributions

Consider the model

$$y_t = \beta x_t + \varepsilon_t \qquad (1.15)$$

where ε_t is assumed to be white noise. Equation (1.15) defines an assumed data-generating process for y_t. Suppose we have observed time series for y and x. For any given estimator of β, β^* say, we can construct an estimate using these observed time series. But since time series are realisations of stochastic processes, it is equally possible that different realisations, i.e. time series, could have been obtained. Theoretically, we can consider how the estimate given by the estimator will vary according to different realisations – this is the basis for the *sampling distribution* of an econometric estimator. The sampling distribution simply allows us to calculate the probability of observing an estimate within a given interval, i.e. it is the frequency distribution of the estimator.

For concreteness, suppose that x is in fact non-stochastic – for example, it may be a time trend. Then we could carry out a *Monte Carlo* experiment whereby say, 2000 series for ε were generated using a random number generator. Given the series for x, equation (1.15) then implies 2000 time series for y – we simply *fix* β at a number, e.g. 2.5. Since the true value of β is known in the experiment, we can then see how the estimator behaves with respect to it in *repeated samples* by constructing, say, 2000 estimates of β (i.e. realisations of β^*). The manner in which these estimates differ is called the *empirical sampling distribution*, which could be approximated by constructing a histogram of the estimates. Monte Carlo studies are often used to construct empirical sampling distributions where the model or the estimator is particularly complex, or its behaviour is known only in very large samples. Often, however, we can deduce the properties of the sampling distribution from the assumptions we have made concerning the model.

Econometricians normally judge the quality of an estimator by considering the properties of its sampling distribution. In particular, an estimator will clearly be more attractive if there is a high, rather than a low probability that it will yield an estimate that is close to the true (but unknown) value of the parameter which is being estimated.

Unbiasedness

The first property we consider is *unbiasedness*. An estimator is unbiased if the mean of its sampling distribution is in fact the true value of the parameter being estimated. This *does not* mean that, 'on average' we should expect an unbiased estimator to yield the true value of the parameter vector, since the sampling distribution is continuous, the probability of this happening is in fact zero.

An alternative way of thinking about this property is to consider the *bias* of an estimator. The bias is the difference between the mean of the sampling distribution – the expected value of the estimator – and the true value:

$$B = E(\beta^*) - \beta \qquad (1.16)$$

Consider the sampling distributions of two univariate estimators: β^* which is unbiased but which has a large variance and $\tilde{\beta}$ which has a small degree of bias but with a very small variance. Because the variance of the sampling distribution of $\tilde{\beta}$ is smaller than the sampling distribution of β^*, $\tilde{\beta}$ is more *efficient* than β^*. Thus it is probable that $\tilde{\beta}$ will yield an estimate closer to β than β^* in any particular realisation. This example shows very clearly that the variance, as well as the mean of the sampling distribution should be considered when assessing the quality of an estimator.

Best unbiased

The preceding discussion illustrated the importance of considering the variance as well as the mean of the sampling distribution. In general, we should choose estimators which have 'low' variance. It is, however, almost meaningless to speak of a 'minimum variance' estimator. Suppose, for example that whenever a model with one parameter was being considered, we used the estimator $\beta^* = 103.9$ – *regardless* of the context, or the data, or whatever. Because this estimator never varies, its variance is zero, the smallest possible, notwithstanding its patent silliness. For this reason, it is necessary to qualify the search for low variance. Normally, this is done by considering only estimators which are unbiased. Consider the sampling distribution of two unbiased estimators, one of which, β^*, has lower variance than the other, $\tilde{\beta}$. Clearly, β^*, the more efficient estimator, is more likely to yield an estimate closer to the true value of the parameter than is $\tilde{\beta}$.

An estimator which has the lowest variance – is the most efficient – within a certain class of estimators is said to be the *best* estimator in that class. As we shall see in Chapter 2, there is a general principle for choosing estimators, the maximum likelihood principle, which will always give the best unbiased estimator, if it exists. Often, however, econometricians will want to restrict the analysis to consider only estimators which are linear functions of the errors. An estimator which is linear, unbiased and minimum variance among all linear unbiased estimators is termed the best linear unbiased estimator (BLUE).

Where we are considering estimating a parameter vector with more than one element, the discussion of efficiency has to be qualified somewhat. In general, if we are considering two $k \times 1$ estimators β^* and $\tilde{\beta}$, then we will be comparing the $k \times k$ covariance matrices of these estimators. If the matrix

$$\mathrm{Var}\,(\tilde{\beta}) - \mathrm{Var}\,(\beta^*)$$

is a positive semidefinite matrix, then β^* is said to be more efficient than $\tilde{\beta}$.

Asymptotic properties of estimators

The properties discussed above relate to an estimator's sampling distribution, regardless of the number of observations in the time series employed by the estimator. An unbiased estimator, for example, has an expected value equal to the true parameter, independently of how many data points, or observations are available. In many situations, however, an estimator with these desirable properties does not exist, and it is then necessary to inspect an estimator's *asymptotic* properties, i.e. to see how it behaves when very large samples of data are used. Sometimes, where an estimator's properties are known only asymptotically, Monte Carlo experiments are performed to try to simulate the behaviour of the estimator in small samples.

To get an intuitive idea of what asymptotic theory is about, consider again the Monte Carlo experiment with reference to equation (1.15). The independent variable, x, is assumed non-stochastic (e.g. a time trend) and the Monte Carlo procedure consists of generating a time series for the disturbance term and so, for a given value of β, of y. The estimator is then applied to this data to produce an estimate. Repeating this a large number of times then produces an estimate of the sampling distribution of the estimator.

Now, this will be for a given sample size – i.e. we generate series for ε and y which are a certain length, say 100 observations. Let us denote the sample size or number of observations by T, so initially $T = 100$. We could then repeat the Monte Carlo experiment for $T = 101$, then for $T = 102$, then for $T = 103$ and so on, letting T get bigger and bigger. For each value of T we would have a different empirical sampling distribution. If the estimator's properties do not depend on sample size, then the empirical sampling distribution will look very similar, regardless of the value of T. If, on the other hand, sample size does affect the estimator's behaviour, then the shape and/or the location of the empirical sampling distribution will tend to alter as T gets bigger and bigger. For many estimators, we do not in fact have to carry out such experiments to find out what its properties are when T is very large – we can work out mathematically how it behaves as T tends in the limit to infinity. The properties of an estimator as T tends to infinity are termed its *asymptotic properties*.

As we mentioned previously, however, the shape and location of the empirical sampling distribution for small values of T may be examined in order to assess the small-sample properties of the estimator if these cannot be determined mathematically. Note that the sequence $(\beta_T^*)_{T=k}^{\infty}$, where β_T^* denotes the estimator applied to a sample of size T, is itself a stochastic process since each element in the sequence is a random variable which can take on any of a range of values depending on the particular time series used.

The sampling distribution of an estimator as T tends to infinity is termed the *asymptotic distribution*. If the asymptotic distribution has a mean equal to the true value of the parameter being estimated, the estimator is said to be asymptotically unbiased. Often, however, we are more concerned with another asymptotic property – *consistency*. If the asymptotic distribution is concentrated on the true value of the parameter, then the estimator is said to be consistent. Formally, consistency requires that the probability of an estimate generated from an estimator being an arbitrarily small distance from the true value should be unity as the sample size tends to infinity:

$$\lim_{T\to\infty} \Pr\{|\beta_T^* - \beta| < \delta\} = 1 \qquad (1.17)$$

If an estimator is consistent, then its probability limit is equal to the true value of the parameter. If we are considering estimating a parameter vector then the estimator is said to be consistent if each element converges in probability to the corresponding element of the true parameter vector.

A shorthand way of writing equation (1.17) is:

$$\operatorname*{plim}_{T\to\infty} \beta_T^* = \beta \qquad (1.18)$$

Suppose we have two estimators applied to a sample of size T, α_T^* and β_T^* such that equation (1.18) holds and

$$\operatorname*{plim}_{T\to\infty} \alpha_T^* = \alpha \qquad (1.19)$$

Then the following properties of probability limits can be established:

$$\plim_{T\to\infty}(\alpha_T^* \pm \beta_T^*) = \plim_{T\to\infty}\alpha_T^* \pm \plim_{T\to\infty}\beta_T^* = \alpha \pm \beta \qquad \text{(1.20a)}$$

$$\plim_{T\to\infty}(\alpha_T^*\beta_T^*) = \{\plim_{T\to\infty}\alpha_T^*\}\{\plim_{T\to\infty}\beta_T^*\} = \alpha\beta \qquad \text{(1.20b)}$$

If $\beta_T^* \neq 0$ and $\beta \neq 0$:

$$\plim_{T\to\infty}(\alpha_T^*/\beta_T^*) = \{\plim_{T\to\infty}\alpha_T^*\}/\{\plim_{T\to\infty}\beta_T^*\} = \alpha/\beta \qquad \text{(1.20c)}$$

If $\beta_T^* \geqslant 0$ and $\beta \geqslant 0$:

$$\plim_{T\to\infty}\sqrt{\beta_T^*} = \sqrt{(\plim_{T\to\infty}\beta_T^*)} = \sqrt{\beta} \qquad \text{(1.20d)}$$

If γ is a constant:

$$\plim_{T\to\infty}\gamma = \gamma \qquad \text{(1.20e)}$$

If $\phi(\ )$ is a continuous function:

$$\plim_{T\to\infty}\phi(\beta_T^*) = \phi(\beta) \qquad \text{(1.20f)}$$

The last expression, (1.20f), is sometimes referred to as the Slutsky theorem.

A common source of confusion in econometrics concerns the relationship between the mean and variance of the asymptotic distribution, the asymptotic mean and variance and the probability limit of an estimator. The asymptotic mean and variance are the limits of the first and second moments of the sampling distribution:

$$\text{Asymptotic mean} = \lim_{T\to\infty} E(\beta_T^*)$$

$$\text{Asymptotic variance} = \lim_{T\to\infty} \text{Var}(\beta_T^*)$$

$$= \lim_{T\to\infty} E\{[\beta_T^* - \lim_{T\to\infty} E(\beta_T^*)]^2\}$$

There are circumstances in which the asymptotic mean and variance do not exist while the mean and variance of the asymptotic distribution do, so that the latter are often thought of as the more useful concepts. A sufficient condition for an estimator to be consistent is that the mean of the asymptotic distribution be equal to the true parameter value and that the variance of the asymptotic distribution be zero. The following example, however, demonstrates very clearly that this is not a necessary condition.

Suppose the sampling distribution of the estimator β_T^* is described as:

$$\Pr\left(|\beta_T^* - \beta| < \delta\right) = 1 - 1/T$$

$$\Pr\left(|\beta_T^* - T| < \delta\right) = 1/T$$

where δ is an arbitrarily small number. Clearly, such an estimator would be consistent since $1/T$ tends to zero as T tends to infinity. The asymptotic mean and variance, however, can be calculated as:

$$\lim_{T \to \infty} E(\beta_T^*) = \lim_{T \to \infty} [\beta(1 - 1/T) + T(1/T)]$$

$$= \beta + 1$$

and

$$\lim_{T \to \infty} E\{[\beta_T^* - \lim_{T \to \infty} E(\beta_T^*)]^2\}$$

$$= \lim_{T \to \infty} E[\beta^2(1 - 1/T) + T^2(1/T) - \{\beta(1 - 1/T) + 1\}^2]$$

$$= \infty$$

Thus, the asymptotic mean is not equal to the true value of the parameter and, moreover, its asymptotic variance is infinite. Nevertheless, it is still a consistent estimator.

1.5   The general linear model

In this section we begin to develop the core of econometrics – the general linear model. Starting from a well-defined set of assumptions we can develop the basic econometric estimator – the ordinary least squares estimator. Much of standard econometric theory can be viewed as adapting this estimator to deal with circumstances in which one or more of these so-called classical assumptions break down. In order to keep the discussion as general as possible, much of the discussion in the remainder of this chapter is in matrix notation.

The classical assumptions, the OLS estimator and the Gauss–Markov theorem

The starting point in our review of standard econometric theory is the general linear regression model. At its most basic, this asserts that the data generating process for an observed variable y_t is a linear combination of K known explanatory variables, x_{kt}, $k = 1, \ldots, K$, plus a stochastic disturbance term u_t:

$$Y_t = \beta_1 x_{1t} + \beta_2 x_{2t} + \beta_3 x_{3t} + \ldots + \beta_k x_{kt} + u_t \tag{1.21}$$

where the β_is are unknown. A basic objective of econometrics is to provide 'optimal' estimates of the unknown parameters in relationships such as (1.21). If we have available T observations on y_t and the x_{kt}, we can write them all in matrix notation as

$$Y = X\beta + u \qquad\qquad (1.22)$$

where

$$Y = (y_1 y_2 \ldots y_T)'$$

$$X = \begin{bmatrix} x_{11} & x_{21} & x_{31} & \cdots & x_{k1} \\ x_{12} & x_{22} & x_{31} & \cdots & x_{k2} \\ \vdots & \vdots & \vdots & & \vdots \\ x_{1T} & x_{2T} & x_{3T} & \cdots & x_{kT} \end{bmatrix}$$

$$\beta = (\beta_1 \beta_2 \ldots \beta_k)'$$

$$u = (u_1 u_2 \ldots u_T)'$$

Thus, Y is a $(T \times 1)$ vector of observations on the dependent variable (the 'regressand'), X is a $(T \times K)$ matrix of observations on the explanatory variables ('regressors'), β is a $(K \times 1)$ vector of unknown parameters and u is a $(T \times 1)$ vector of unobservable stochastic disturbances. X is sometimes termed the 'design matrix'.

The classical linear regression model makes certain assumptions in order to establish various properties of econometric estimators. These are:

1. The disturbances are uncorrelated with one another and each has mean zero and finite variance σ^2:

    $$E(u) = 0, \operatorname{Var}(u) = \sigma^2 I$$

2. The explanatory variables are non-stochastic and are thus independent of the disturbances:

    $$E(X'u) = 0$$

3. The explanatory variables are linearly independent:

    $$\operatorname{rank}(X'X) = \operatorname{rank}(X)$$

    $$= K$$

    and hence $(X'X)^{-1}$ exists.

Note that we have not yet made any assertions concerning the statistical distribution of the disturbances. Nor have we assumed that the disturbances are independently distributed (i.e. that their joint density function is just the product of their individual density functions), although this property follows from the zero correlation property under normality. Under assumptions 1–3, the best (i.e. minimum sampling distribution variance) linear unbiased estimator of β, $\hat{\beta}$ say, is given by minimising the sum of squared estimated disturbances, or residuals:

$$\min_{\hat{\beta}} S = (Y - X\hat{\beta})'(Y - X\hat{\beta}) \tag{1.23}$$

The first order conditions for equation (1.23) are:

$$\frac{\partial S}{\partial \hat{\beta}} = -2X'(Y - X\hat{\beta}) = 0$$

which can be expressed as the 'normal equations':

$$X'Y = X'X\hat{\beta} \tag{1.24}$$

and since we know by assumption 3 that $(X'X)$ is non-singular, we have the ordinary least squares (OLS) estimator:

$$\hat{\beta} = (X'X)^{-1} X'Y \tag{1.25}$$

That equation (1.25) solves (1.23) is clear since the second order conditions are satisfied:

$$\frac{\partial^2 S}{\partial \hat{\beta} \partial \hat{\beta}'} = 2X'X$$

which is positive definite.

Since the elements of X are fixed, $(X'X)^{-1}X'$ can be interpreted as a linear function which maps ('projects') any vector in T-dimensional space (Y) into a vector in K-dimensional space (β):

$$(X'X)^{-1}X': R^T \rightarrow R^K$$

Thus the matrix $(X'X)^{-1}X'$ is often referred to as the *projection matrix* P_X, with the useful result that $P_X X = I$ and $\hat{\beta} = P_X Y$. Since $\hat{\beta}$ is a linear function of Y, it is a linear estimator. It is also unbiased in the sense that the expected value of $\hat{\beta}$ is the true parameter vector β:

$$E(\hat{\beta}) = E[(X'X)^{-1}X'Y]$$
$$= E[(X\ X)^{-1}\ X'(X\beta + u)]$$
$$= \beta + (X'X)^{-1}E(X'u)$$
$$= \beta \tag{1.26}$$

where we have used $P_X X = I$ and assumption 2 (non-stochastic regressors). It is clear from equation (1.26) that $\hat{\beta}$ is also a linear function of the errors u.

The variance–covariance matrix for $\hat{\beta}$ is easily established using, $\hat{\beta} = \beta + P_X u$:

$$\text{Var}(\hat{\beta}) = E[(\hat{\beta} - \beta)(\hat{\beta} - \beta)']$$
$$= E[P_X uu' P_X]$$
$$= (X'X)^{-1} X'(\sigma^2 I) X(X'X)^{-1}$$
$$= \sigma^2 (X'X)^{-1} \tag{1.27}$$

where assumptions 1 and 3 have been used.

If β^* is any other linear unbiased estimator of β, it is straightforward to show that the variance of β^* exceeds that of $\hat{\beta}$ in the sense that $[\text{Var}(\beta^*) - \text{Var}(\hat{\beta})]$ is a positive semidefinite matrix (the Gauss–Markov theorem). Since β^* is a linear estimator, we can write it as:

$$\beta^* = AY$$

where A is a $K \times T$ matrix of constants. If we define

$$C = A - (X'X)^{-1} X'$$

then clearly

$$\beta^* = [(X'X)^{-1} X' + C]Y$$
$$= [(X'X)^{-1} X' + C](X\beta + u)$$
$$= \beta + CX\beta + [(X'X)^{-1} X' + C]u$$

Thus

$$E(\beta^*) = \beta + CX\beta$$

Hence, if β^* is to be unbiased, $CX = 0$. Thus,

$$\text{Var}(\beta^*) = E(\beta^* - \beta)(\beta^* - \beta)'$$
$$= E[(X'X)^{-1} X' + C]uu'[(X'X)^{-1} X' + C]'$$
$$= \sigma^2[(X'X)^{-1} + CC']$$

where the property $CX = 0$ has been used. Hence,

$$\text{Var}(\beta^*) - \text{Var}(\hat{\beta}) = \sigma^2 CC'$$

So $\text{Var}(\beta^*)$ exceeds $\text{Var}(\hat{\beta})$ by a positive semidefinite matrix. In particular, note that the diagonal elements of $\sigma^2 CC'$ must be non-negative, so that

$$\text{Var}(\beta_i^*) - \text{Var}(\hat{\beta}_1) > 0, \ i = 1, \ldots, K.$$

Thus, under assumptions 1–3, the OLS estimator $\hat{\beta}$ is the best (minimum variance) linear unbiased estimator (BLUE).

Goodness of fit: coefficient of determination and error variance

Given $\hat{\beta}$, we can divide the Y vector into the sum of an 'explained' part $\hat{Y}$ and an unexplained part $\hat{u}$:

$$Y = X\hat{\beta} + \hat{u} = \hat{Y} + \hat{u} \tag{1.28}$$

One way of determining how well an estimated model fits is to calculate the proportion of the variation in Y which is 'explained' by variation in $\hat{Y}$, and how much is unexplained, due to variation in $\hat{u}$. One measure of variability is the sum of squared $y_t's$, $Y'Y$. Using equation (1.28):

$$Y'Y = \hat{\beta}'X'X\hat{\beta} + \hat{u}'\hat{u} + 2\hat{\beta}'X'\hat{u} \tag{1.29}$$

The OLS estimator constructs the residual vector $\hat{u}$ so that it is orthogonal to the regressors:

$$\begin{aligned}
X'\hat{u} &= X'(Y - X\hat{\beta}) \\
&= X'[I - X(X'X)^{-1}X']Y \\
&= 0
\end{aligned}$$

so that the last term in equation (1.29) is zero. Hence, $Y'Y$ is partitioned into two components, one due to the explanatory variables and one unexplained by the model:

$$\begin{aligned}
Y'Y &= \hat{\beta}'X'X\hat{\beta} + \hat{u}'\hat{u} \\
&= \hat{Y}'\hat{Y} + \hat{u}'\hat{u}
\end{aligned} \tag{1.30}$$

It is, however, more usual to measure variation in a variable around its mean. If we denote the total sum of squares (TSS):

$$\text{TSS} = \sum_{t=1}^{T} (y_t - \bar{y})^2$$

where

$$\bar{y} = T^{-1} \sum_{t=1}^{T} y_t$$

or

$$\text{TSS} = Y'Y - T\bar{y}^2$$

Thus, subtracting $T\bar{y}^2$ from (1.30):

$$\text{TSS} = (\hat{Y}'\hat{Y} - T\bar{y}^2) + \hat{u}'\hat{u} \tag{1.31}$$

If the model contains an intercept, then $x_{1t} = 1$ for all t (see Note 1) and so the first row of the normal equations, (1.24), is:

$$x_1'Y = x_1'X\hat{\beta}$$
$$= \bar{T}\hat{y}$$

where

$$x_1 = (x_{11}, x_{12}, \ldots, x_{1T})'$$
$$= (1, 1, \ldots, 1)'.$$

Thus,

$$\sum y = T^{-1}x_1'X\hat{\beta}$$
$$= T^{-1}\sum_{t=1}^{T}\hat{y}_t$$

Thus, the first bracketed term in equation (1.31) measures the variation in the 'explained' part of Y, that is $\hat{Y}$, around its mean, or the explained sum of squares (ESS). It is trivial to demonstrate that the OLS residuals have mean zero, hence the second term in (1.31) measures the unexplained (or residual) sum of squares (USS):

$$\text{TSS} = \text{ESS} + \text{USS} \tag{1.32}$$

The coefficient of determination, or R^2, measures ESS as a proportion of TSS:

$$R^2 = \frac{\text{ESS}}{\text{TSS}} = 1 - \frac{\text{USS}}{\text{TSS}} \tag{1.33}$$

Clearly, $0 \leqslant R^2 \leqslant 1$. The closer R^2 is to unity, the better the fit of the regression. Since the R^2 cannot fall, and will usually rise, as the number of regressors is expanded, an allowance is sometimes made for the degrees of freedom lost in constructing the R^2. K degrees of freedom are used up in constructing ESS (corresponding to the K estimated parameters) and 1 in constructing TSS (corresponding to $\bar{y}$). Hence, the degrees-of-freedom corrected R^2, $\bar{R}^2$, is

$$\bar{R}^2 = 1 - \frac{\hat{u}'\hat{u}/(T - K)}{(Y'Y - T\bar{y}^2)/(T - 1)} \tag{1.34}$$

or

$$\bar{R}^2 = 1 - [(T - 1)/(T - K)](1 - R^2)$$

Error variance

An unbiased *estimator* of the error variance σ^2 is often written as s^2 given by:

$$s^2 = \hat{u}'\hat{u}/(T - K)$$

We can demonstrate that s^2 is an unbiased estimator of σ^2 as follows. Note that if we define $M = I - X(X'X)^{-1}X'$, then

$$\hat{u} = Y - X\hat{\beta} = (X\beta + u) - (X\beta + XP_X u) = (I - XP_X)u$$

So $\hat{u} = Mu$.

It is easily seen that M is symmetric $(M = M')$ and idempotent $(M'M = MM' = M)$ hence using $\hat{u} = Mu$:

$$s^2 = u'[M'M]u/(T - K) \tag{1.35}$$

Since s^2 is a scalar, it is trivially equal to its own trace. The properties of trace can be exploited usefully on the right-hand side of equation (1.35), however, in determining the expected value of s^2 (see Notes 2 and 3):

$$\begin{aligned}
E(s^2) &= E[\text{trace}\,[u'(I - X(X'X)^{-1}X')u]/(T - K)] \\
&= \text{trace}\,[[I - X(X'X)^{-1}X']E(uu')]/(T - K) \\
&= \text{trace}\,[[I - X(X'X)^{-1}]I\sigma^2]/(T - K) \\
&= \sigma^2\,(T - K)/(T - K) \\
&= \sigma^2 \tag{1.36}
\end{aligned}$$

hence s^2 is an unbiased estimator of σ^2.

It can be shown that, given two regression models, one of which is assumed to be true, the expected value of s^2 for the true model is less than or equal to the expected value for the alternative model. To see this, let

$$Y = X\beta + u$$

be the true model and

$$Y = Z\gamma + u$$

be the alternative, where X and Z are $T \times K_x$ and $T \times K_z$ matrices and X contains at least one variable not included in Z. Then we can write the s^2 for the two models using:

$$\hat{u} = Y - X\hat{\beta} = Y - X(P_x Y) = (I - XP_X)Y = M_x Y$$

Hence $s_x^2 = Y'M_x Y/(T - K_x) \quad s_z^2 = Y'M_z Y/(T - K_z)$

where $M_x = I - X(X'X)^{-1}X'$; $M_z = I - Z(Z'Z)^{-1}Z'$. It follows that

$$(T - K_z)E(s_z^2) = E(Y'M_zY)$$
$$= E[(X\beta + u)'M_z(X\beta + u)]$$
$$= \beta'X'M_zX\beta + E(u'M_zu)$$
$$= \beta'X'M_zX\beta + (T - K_z)\sigma^2$$
$$> (T - K_z)\sigma^2$$

Thus $E(s_z^2) > \sigma^2$ or, using the unbiasedness result (1.36) for the 'true model' s_x^2, we then have

$$E(s_z^2) > E(s_x^2) \tag{1.37}$$

Relation (1.37) is sometimes used to justify specification search strategies which maximise the R^2, since, from (1.33):

$$R^2 = 1 - (T - K)s^2/(T - 1)s_y^2 \tag{1.38}$$

where s_y^2 is the sample variance of y_t. Hence, loosely speaking, searching over alternative variables to minimise s^2 also maximises R^2.

Imposing linear restrictions

Suppose that we wished to impose a set of linear restrictions on our estimate of the parameter vector β, in accordance with some underlying economic theory for example. Linear restrictions can always be written in the form

$$R\hat{\beta} = r \tag{1.39}$$

where R is a $(q \times K)$ matrix, q being the number of restrictions, and r is a $K \times 1$ vector. Suppose, for example, that the vector of parameter estimates was 3×1:

$$\hat{\beta} = (\hat{\beta}_1\hat{\beta}_2\hat{\beta}_3)'$$

and we wished to impose the restrictions

$$\hat{\beta}_1 = 1; \ \hat{\beta}_2 + \hat{\beta}_3 = 1 \tag{1.40}$$

To write the restrictions (1.40) in the form of (1.39) let

$$R = \begin{bmatrix} 1 & 0 & 0 \\ 0 & 1 & 1 \end{bmatrix}$$

and

$$r = (1\ 1)'$$

The method of obtaining the restricted least squares estimator should be familiar to an economist: constrained optimisation. We minimise the sum of squared residuals subject to the restrictions. One way of doing this is by unconstrained minimisation of a Lagrangean:

$$\min_{\beta} \pounds = (Y - X\beta)'(Y - X\beta) + 2\lambda'(R\beta - r) \qquad (1.41)$$

where 2λ is a $q \times 1$ vector of Lagrange multipliers, scaled by 2 in order to simplify some of the following algebra. The first-order conditions for expression (1.41) are:

$$\frac{\partial \pounds}{\partial \beta} = -2X'Y + 2X'X\beta + 2R'\lambda = O \qquad (1.42)$$

$$\frac{\partial \pounds}{\partial \lambda'} = R\beta - r = O \qquad (1.43)$$

Premultiply (1.42) by $R(X'X)^{-1}$:

$$[R(X'X)^{-1}R']\lambda = R(X'X)^{-1}X'Y - R\beta$$
$$= R\hat{\beta} - r$$

using (1.43). Thus:

$$\lambda = [R(X'X)^{-1}R']^{-1}(R\hat{\beta} - r) \qquad (1.44)$$

where

$$\hat{\beta} = (X'X)^{-1}X'Y \qquad (1.45)$$

i.e. $\hat{\beta}$ is the unconstrained OLS estimator. Substituting (1.44) back into (1.42), premultiplying by $(X'X)^{-1}$ and using (1.45), we derive the restricted least squares (RLS) estimator:

$$\tilde{\beta} = \hat{\beta} - (X'X)^{-1}R'[R(X'X)^{-1}R']^{-1}(R\hat{\beta} - r) \qquad (1.46)$$

If the restrictions were true and all the other classical assumptions were satisfied, then the vector $(R\hat{\beta} - r)$ should be small – the OLS estimates should be close to satisfying the restrictions. From equation (1.46), the RLS estimates will then be close to the OLS estimates. Moreover, the bigger the difference between the OLS and RLS estimates, the less faith we might have in the restrictions. In order to formalise this intuition, however, we need to make some further assumptions.

The distribution of the OLS estimator and linear hypothesis testing

In an earlier section we stated the three classical assumptions which have been used up until now to establish certain properties of the OLS estimator. The first of these assumptions was that the disturbance vector has a zero mean $[E(u) = 0]$ and a scalar covariance matrix $[\text{Var}(u) = \sigma^2 I]$. In order to go further, for example to establish the distribution of the OLS estimator and discuss hypothesis testing, we now need to make some assumptions concerning the statistical distribution of the disturbances.

It is usual to assume that u has a multivariate normal distribution as well as being mean zero and having a scalar covariance matrix:

$$u \sim N(0, \sigma^2 I) \tag{1.47}$$

that is u_t is a Gaussian white noise process. Since, by classical assumption 2, the elements of X are non-stochastic, we can also infer the distribution of Y from (1.47):

$$Y \sim N(X\beta, \sigma^2 I) \tag{1.48}$$

Since the OLS estimator $\hat{\beta}$ is a linear function of Y, it too must be normally distributed, with mean and variance as given by (1.26) and (1.27):

$$\hat{\beta} \sim N[\beta, \sigma^2(X'X)^{-1}] \tag{1.49}$$

Hence, under the classical assumptions plus the assumption of normally distributed disturbances, the OLS estimator is normally distributed with mean β, the true parameter vector, and covariance matrix $\sigma^2(X'X)^{-1}$. Although the error variance σ^2 will usually be unknown, we derived above an unbiased estimator of this quantity, s^2 in equation (1.35), which can be used to construct an unbiased estimate of the covariance matrix:

$$\text{Var}(\hat{\beta}) = s^2(X'X)^{-1} \tag{1.50}$$

We can now apply this framework to derive statistical tests of linear restrictions of the kind considered above. In particular, suppose we wished to test the null hypothesis

$$H_0: R\beta - r = O \tag{1.51}$$

where R is an $q \times K$ matrix, r is an $q \times 1$ vector and O is an $q \times 1$ null vector. As we suggested above, if the restrictions (1.51) are correct, then we should expect the vector $(R\hat{\beta} - r)$ to be close to the origin. Given the distribution of the OLS estimator, (1.49), we can infer the distribution of $(R\hat{\beta} - r)$:

$$(R\hat{\beta} - r) \underset{H_0}{\sim} N(0, \sigma^2 R(X'X)^{-1}R') \tag{1.52}$$

where '$\underset{H_0}{\sim}$' is to be read 'is distributed under the null hypothesis as'. If $R\hat{\beta} - r$ is close to the origin, then the following quadratic form should be close to zero:

$$F' = (R\hat{\beta} - r)'[R(X'X)^{-1}R']^{-1}(R\hat{\beta} - r)\sigma^{-2} \tag{1.53}$$

Now,

$$\hat{\beta} = (X'X)^{-1}X'Y = P_X(X\beta + u) = \beta + P_X u$$

where we have used $P_X X = I$ and $P_X = (X'X)^{-1}X'$ is a $K \times T$ 'projection matrix' of constants. Hence, under the null hypothesis,

$$R\hat{\beta} - r = RP_x u$$

Since u is, by assumption, a vector of independent, normally distributed random variables, $RP_x u$ is a vector of q independent, normally distributed random variables and so, given (1.52) and (1.53), F' is the sum of $-q$ squared independent standard normal variates; it is therefore a chi-square variate with q degrees of freedom:

$$F' \underset{H_0}{\sim} \chi^2(q) \tag{1.54}$$

Since, however, we do not, in general, know the value of σ^2, expression (1.53) is non-operational. Intuitively, one might be tempted to use an unbiased estimator of σ^2, such as s^2 in (1.53). Since s^2 is itself an estimator then (1.54) would no longer be true. However we can obtain the distribution of s^2 as follows. We have seen that

$$\hat{u} = [I_T - X(X'X)^{-1}X']u = Mu$$

where M is symmetric and idempotent and the subscript in 'I_T' is to make clear the dimensions of this identity matrix. From expression (1.47), we know

$$u\sigma^{-1} \sim N(0, I)$$

A standard result in statistics is that:

$$\frac{\hat{u}'\hat{u}}{\sigma^2} = \frac{u'Mu}{\sigma^2} \sim \chi^2(\text{rank } M)$$

Moreover, by the properties of idempotent matrices:

$$\text{rank } M = \text{trace } M$$
$$= \text{trace } I_T - \text{trace } X(X'X)^{-1}X'$$
$$= T - \text{trace}\,(X'X)^{-1}X'X$$
$$= T - \text{trace } I_K$$
$$= T - K$$

Thus, given $s^2 = \hat{u}'\hat{u}/(T - K)$ we have:

$$(T - K)s^2/\sigma^2 \sim \chi^2(T - K) \tag{1.55}$$

From expressions (1.53), (1.54) and (1.55) we can therefore write:

$$\frac{(R\hat{\beta} - r)'\ [R(X'X)R'](R\hat{\beta} - r)/q}{s^2} \underset{H_0}{\sim} F(q,\ T - K) \tag{1.56}$$

Expression (1.56) contains no unknown quantities; it can therefore be used to test linear restrictions on the model under the relevant assumptions. Although (1.56) may appear rather cumbersome, it can in fact be computed in a relatively straightforward fashion, as the following demonstrates.

From the definition of the RLS estimator $\tilde{\beta}$, (1.46), we have:

$$X'X(\hat{\beta} - \tilde{\beta}) = R'[R(X'X)^{-1}R^1]^{-1}(R\hat{\beta} - r) \tag{1.57}$$

Now, $\tilde{\beta}$ must satisfy the restrictions, so that $R\tilde{\beta} = r$, hence:

$$(R\hat{\beta} - r)' = (R\hat{\beta} - R\tilde{\beta})'$$
$$= (\hat{\beta} - \tilde{\beta})'R'$$

So, premultiplying (1.57) by $(\hat{\beta} - \tilde{\beta})'$:

$$(\hat{\beta} - \tilde{\beta})'X'X(\hat{\beta} - \tilde{\beta})$$
$$= (R\hat{\beta} - r)'[R(X'X)^{-1}R']^{-1}(R\hat{\beta} - r) \tag{1.58}$$

Now consider the restricted sum of squared residuals $(e_r'e_r)$ and the unrestricted sum of squared residuals $(e_u'e_u)$:

$$e_r'e_r = (Y - X\tilde{\beta})'(Y - X\tilde{\beta}) \tag{1.59}$$
$$e_u'e_u = (Y - X\hat{\beta})'(Y - X\hat{\beta})$$
$$= (T - K)s^2 \tag{1.60}$$

Developing equation (1.59):

$$e_r'e_r = (Y - X\hat{\beta} + X\hat{\beta} - X\tilde{\beta})'(Y - X\hat{\beta} + X\hat{\beta} + X\tilde{\beta})$$
$$= (Y - X\hat{\beta})'(Y - X\hat{\beta}) + (\hat{\beta} - \tilde{\beta})'X'X(\hat{\beta} - \tilde{\beta}) \tag{1.61}$$

where we have used the orthogonality property $X'\hat{u} = X'(Y - X\hat{\beta}) = 0$ to eliminate some terms. From (1.60) and (1.61) we then have:

$$e_r'e_r - e_u'e_u = (\hat{\beta} - \tilde{\beta})'X'X(\hat{\beta} - \tilde{\beta})$$

or, using (1.58):

$$e_r'e_r - e_u'e_u = (R\hat{\beta} - r)'[R(X'X)^{-1}R']^{-1}(R\hat{\beta} - r)$$

Hence, (1.56) may be expressed alternatively:

$$\frac{(e_r'e_r - e_u'e_u)/q}{e_r'e_r/(T - K)} \underset{\widetilde{H_0}}{\sim} F(q, T - K) \tag{1.62}$$

The formulation (1.62) is quite intuitive. Since the unrestricted OLS estimator minimises the sum of squared residuals, imposing the restrictions must increase the sum of squares. The left-hand side of (1.62) thus gives the increase in the sum of squares per restriction. We would want to reject restrictions that led to a 'large' increase in the sum of squares; exactly how large 'large' is can be determined from the tables for the F distribution once we choose a specific probability of making an error.

Confidence intervals

Consider expression (1.56) again. Under the null hypothesis, (1.51), $r = R\beta$ (where β is the true parameter vector), so that (1.56) may be expressed alternatively:

$$\frac{(\hat{\beta} - \beta)'R'[R(X'X)^{-1}R']^{-1}R(\hat{\beta} - \beta)}{s^2} \underset{\widetilde{H_0}}{\sim} F(q, T - K)$$

$$\tag{1.63}$$

Now let $F_\alpha(q, T - K)$ denote the critical value for the upper 100α per cent of the distribution (or 'test size'), i.e. it is the point on the horizontal axis such that the area under a graph of the central $F(q, T - K)$ distribution to the right of this point is α (or, since the total area under the graph must sum to unity, 100α per cent). This allows us to construct a $100(1 - \alpha)$ per cent confidence ellipsoid:

$$\Pr\left\{\frac{(\hat{\beta} - \beta)'R'[R(X'X)^{-1}R']^{-1}R(\hat{\beta} - \beta)}{s^2} \leqslant F_\alpha(q, T - K)\right\}$$

$$= 1 - \alpha \tag{1.64}$$

What is the interpretation of expression (1.64)? Suppose we were given repeated samples of the data – that is to say, given the true model (1.22), suppose that we generated many Y vectors using the same values for the design matrix, X, and the same coefficients, β, but a different disturbance vector, u, for every case. This would allow us to derive a sampling distribution for $\hat{\beta}$, since there will generally be a different $\hat{\beta}$ for each sample. The statements concerning the unbiasedness and efficiency of the OLS estimator discussed earlier in this chapter are in fact statements about the mean and variance of this sampling distribution. Now suppose that, for each repeated sample we constructed the region in m-dimensional Euclidean space described by the term inside the braces on the left-hand side of (1.64). Expression (1.64) tells us that in $100(1 - \alpha)$ per cent of repeated samples the region considered will contain the true value of $R\beta$.

A special case of interest is where R is a $K \times K$ identity matrix. Expression (1.64) then becomes

$$\Pr\left\{\frac{(\hat{\beta} - \beta)'(X'X)(\hat{\beta} - \beta)/K}{s^2} \leqslant F_\alpha(K, T - K)\right\} = 1 - \alpha$$

(1.65)

This says that in $100(1 - \alpha)$ per cent of repeated samples, the ellipsoid in K-dimensional Euclidean space described by the term in braces will contain the true parameter vector β.

Another interesting case is where R is a K-dimensional row vector with unity in the ith element and zeros elsewhere. Expression (1.64) then becomes

$$\Pr\left\{\frac{(\hat{\beta}_i - \beta_i)^2}{s^2(X'X)_{ii}^{-1}} \leqslant F_\alpha(1, T - K)\right\} = 1 - \alpha \qquad (1.66)$$

where '$[\ ]_{ii}$' denotes the (i, i)th (i.e. ith diagonal) element of the matrix inside the brackets. Using the fact that the square root of an $F(1, T - K)$ variate is distributed as $t(T - K)$, this can be written

$$\Pr\left\{-t_{\alpha/2}(T - K) \leqslant \frac{(\hat{\beta} - \beta)}{s[(X'X)_{ii}^{-1}]^{1/2}} \leqslant t_{\alpha/2}(T - K)\right\}$$
$$= 1 - \alpha$$

or

$$\Pr\{\hat{\beta}_i - t_{\alpha/2}(T - K)se(\hat{\beta}_i) \leqslant \beta_i \leqslant \hat{\beta}_i + t_{\alpha/2}(T - K)se(\hat{\beta}_i)\}$$
$$= 1 - \alpha \qquad (1.67)$$

In moving from (1.66) to (1.67) we have used the notation '$se(\hat{\beta}_i)$' to denote the square root of the ith diagonal element of $s^2(X'X)^{-1}$, the estimated standard error of $\hat{\beta}_i$ and have moved to a two-sided confidence region because the square root may be either positive or negative. Suppose, for example, that $T - K = 60$; then since $t_{0.025}(60) = 2$, equation (1.67) would mean that in 95% of repeated samples, a region consisting of the point estimate of β_i plus or minus two estimated standard errors would contain the true value of β_i.

Note that a distinction should be made between testing a number of restrictions individually, and testing all of them jointly. Consider, for example, the individual null hypotheses

$$H_a{:}\beta_i = 0$$
$$H_b{:}\beta_j = 0$$

and the *joint* null hypothesis

$$H_c{:}(\beta_i, \beta_j) = (0, 0)$$

Suppose that the $100(1 - \alpha)$ per cent confidence regions for β_i and β_j each contain zero. Then we would not be able to reject either H_a or H_b at the 100α per cent significance level. It may be, however, that the two-dimensional $100(1 - \alpha)$ per cent joint confidence ellipse for β_i and β_j does not contain the origin, so that H_c may be rejected at the 100α per cent level (i.e. although we cannot reject a hypothesis that one of these coefficients is zero, we can reject the joint hypothesis that they are both zero).

In order to construct the joint confidence ellipse for β_i and β_j, let R be a $2 \times k$ matrix with unity in the $(1, i)$-th and $(2, j)$-th elements and zeros elsewhere. Let the estimated covariance of $\hat{\beta}_i$ and $\hat{\beta}_j$, the (i, j)-th element of the (symmetric) matrix $s^2(X'X)^{-1}$, be denoted $\text{Cov}(\beta_i, \beta_j)$ and let $se(\hat{\beta}_i)$ and $se(\hat{\beta}_j)$ denote the positive square roots of the ith and jth diagonal elements of this matrix. Then, with R as just defined, expression (1.64) becomes:

$$\begin{aligned} \Pr\{(1/2)(\hat{\beta}_i - \beta_i)^2 se(\beta_i)^2 + (1/2)(\hat{\beta}_j - \beta_j)se(\beta_j)^2 \\ + (\hat{\beta}_i - \beta_i)(\hat{\beta}_j - \beta_j)\text{Cov}(\hat{\beta}_i, \hat{\beta}_j) \\ \leqslant F_\alpha(2, T - K)\} = 1 - \alpha \end{aligned} \tag{1.68}$$

The region described by the term in braces on the left-hand side of (1.68) is an ellipse with centre $(\hat{\beta}_i, \hat{\beta}_j)$. If we make the assumption that $\text{Cov}(\hat{\beta}_i, \hat{\beta}_j) = 0$, then the region defined by (1.68) would be a rectangle centred on $(\hat{\beta}_i, \hat{\beta}_j)$, with sides equal to the individual $100(1 - \alpha)$ per cent confidence intervals for $\hat{\beta}_i$ and $\hat{\beta}_j$ derived from expressions analogous to (1.67). However, if we know that $\hat{\beta}_i$ and $\hat{\beta}_j$ have positive covariance, then we know that an over-estimate (under-estimate) of β_i is likely to be accompanied by an over-estimate (under-estimate) of β_j. This allows us to rule out the corner areas of the rectangle and so we derive an ellipse which is appropriate in forming a joint $100(1 - \alpha)$ per cent confidence region.

It is also straightforward to construct a confidence region for σ^2, the (constant) variance of the disturbance. From expression (1.55), we know that $(T - K)s^2/\sigma^2$ has a χ^2 distribution with $(T - K)$ degrees of freedom. Let $\chi^2(T - K, 1 - \alpha/2)$ and $\chi^2(T - K, \alpha/2)$ denote, respectively, the lower and upper $100\alpha/2$ per cent critical values of the $\chi^2(T - K)$ distribution. Then

$$\Pr[\chi^2(T - K, 1 - \alpha/2) < (T - K)s^2/\sigma^2 < \chi^2(T - K, \alpha/2)]$$

$$= 1 - \alpha$$

which implies:

$$\Pr\left\{\frac{(T - K)s^2}{\chi^2(T - K, 1 - \alpha/2)} \leqslant \sigma^2 \leqslant \frac{(T - K)s^2}{\chi^2(T - K, \alpha/2)}\right\} \tag{1.69}$$

1.6   Departures from the classical assumptions

In this section we consider the consequences of and possible remedies to various breakdowns in the classical assumptions.

Omitted variables

So far, our analysis has been conducted under the assumption that the assumed model is correctly specified as in section 1.5. Suppose, however, that we have omitted some important explanatory variables, so that the true model is in fact as in equation (1.70):

$$Y = X\beta + Z\gamma + u \tag{1.70}$$

where Z is a $T \times r$ matrix of observations and γ is an $r \times 1$ parameter vector. Thus, we have omitted r explanatory variables.

The residual vector obtained from the regression $Y = X\hat{\beta} + \hat{v}$, that is excluding Z, may be written

$$\hat{v} = M_X Y$$

Substituting the true expression for Y

$$\hat{v} = M_x(X\beta + Z\gamma + u)$$

$$= M_X Z\gamma + M_X u$$

where we have used

$$M_X X = (I - X(X'X)^{-1}X')X = 0 \quad \text{Thus,}$$

$$E(\hat{v}) = M_x Z\gamma \tag{1.71}$$

Expression (1.71) means that the residual vector $\hat{v}$, where we have omitted the variables Z will have an expected value equal to the residual vector obtained by regressing $Z\gamma$ on to X. Thus, the residuals $\hat{v}$ should be of use in checking for misspecification – this will be developed further in Chapter 4.

Now consider the bias in the OLS estimator, $Y = X\hat{\beta} + \hat{v}$

$$\hat{\beta} = (X'X)^{-1}X'Y = P_xY$$

Given that the true model is (1.70), and $P_xX = I$, it is easy to show that

$$E(\hat{\beta}) = \beta + P_xZ\gamma \neq \beta$$

and therefore 'omitted variables' will generally lead to biased estimates. However there is no omitted variable bias when X and Z are orthogonal, i.e.

$$X'Z = 0$$

Non-scalar covariance matrix

The first of the classical assumptions which we listed in section 1.5 was that the disturbance terms in the regression model were mean zero and uncorrelated with one another and that each has a constant, finite variance:

$$E(u) = 0, \text{Var}(u) = \sigma^2 I$$

The violation of the assumption of zero-mean disturbances causes no major problems – this effect will simply be picked up by including an intercept term among the regressors. The violation of the assumption that the variance–covariance matrix is a diagonal matrix with a constant term on the main diagonal (i.e. a 'scalar matrix') is, however, quite important.

Each element on the main diagonal of the variance–covariance matrix gives the variance of the distribution from which that element is assumed to be drawn. If the elements of the main *diagonal* of the disturbance variance–covariance matrix differ from observation to observation, then the series is said to be *heteroscedastic* – as opposed to the case of *homoscedastic disturbances*, where the variance is constant. This means that each element in the disturbance vector can be thought of as being drawn from a different distribution.

Each off-diagonal element of the variance–covariance matrix gives the covariance between the disturbances associated with two of the sample observations (for example, the element in the third row, second column gives the covariance between the third observation and the second observation). If all of the off-diagonal terms are zero, the disturbances are said to be uncorrelated; otherwise they are serially correlated.

If the disturbance vector is characterised by either heteroscedasticity or serial correlation, or both, then the variance–covariance matrix will no longer be a scalar matrix:

$$E(uu') = \Omega \neq \sigma^2 I \tag{1.72}$$

Since the proof of unbiasedness of the OLS estimator relied only on the first-moment properties of the model, the OLS estimator will still be unbiased and consistent in this case. The distribution of the OLS estimator will, however, be affected:

$$\begin{aligned}
\mathrm{Var}\,(\beta) &= E[(\hat{\beta} - \beta)(\hat{\beta} - \beta)'] \\
&= E[(X'X)^{-1}X'uu'X(X'X)^{-1}] \\
&= (X'X)^{-1}X'\Omega X(X'X)^{-1}
\end{aligned} \tag{1.73}$$

Thus, the standard formula for the variance–covariance matrix of the estimator, $s^2(X'X)^{-1}$ is incorrect and hence is biased and inconsistent.

There are two possible ways of remedying this problem. One way is to transform the model so that the disturbance variance–covariance matrix is transformed to a scalar matrix and then to apply OLS to the transformed equation. This is generalised least squares (GLS). Note that this method assumes an exact knowledge of the changing covariance structure of the model. Another method, which is becoming increasingly popular, is to use the OLS point estimates for β, since they are unbiased and consistent, but to use a consistent estimate of Ω in equation (1.73) to obtain a consistent estimate of the variance –covariance matrix of the OLS estimator. Since information with respect to Ω is not used in the latter approach, it will result in a less efficient estimator than if the transformation approach is taken. Recently, however, authors have developed methods of estimating Ω consistently without specifying in detail the form of the heteroscedasticity or serial correlation, so that the latter approach can be seen as more general.

Generalised least squares

The 'generalised' linear regression model is

$$Y = X\beta + u \tag{1.74}$$

$$E(u) = 0, \ E(uu') = \sigma^2 \Omega$$

where we assume that β and σ^2 are unknown and Ω is known. We have scaled the covariance matrix by the unknown σ^2 in order to reinforce the idea that GLS requires that the form of the covariance matrix need only be known up to a scalar multiple.

Since Ω is a positive definite matrix, it can be shown that there exists a non-singular matrix P which has the property that

$$P \Omega P' = I$$

from which it follows that

$$P' P = \Omega^{-1}$$

Premultiplying (1.74) by P, we have:

$$PY = PX\beta + Pu$$

or

$$Y^* = X^*\beta + u^* \tag{1.75}$$

where $Y^* = PY$, $X^* = PX$, $u^* = Pu$. The covariance matrix of u^* is given by

$$E(u^*u^{*\prime}) = E(Puu'P')$$
$$= \sigma^2 P \Omega P'$$
$$= \sigma^2 I$$

Thus, applying OLS to (1.75) will yield the best, linear, unbiased estimator of β:

$$\hat{\beta}_{GLS} = (X^{*\prime}X^*)^{-1}X^{*\prime}Y^*$$
$$= (X'P'PX)^{-1}X'P'PY$$
$$= (X'\Omega^{-1}X)^{-1}X'\Omega^{-1}Y \tag{1.76}$$

Equation (1.76) gives the GLS estimator. Intuitively, the GLS estimator works because it *weights* the data – for example, in the case of heteroscedasticity, an observation associated with a disturbance whose variance is thought to be especially large would receive less weight than one whose disturbance variance was thought to be small.

Note that, as it stands, the GLS estimator is non-operational because it requires that Ω be known. In general, researchers have to estimate Ω in advance before substituting it in to an equation such as (1.76). This results in the *feasible generalised least squares estimator*. The way in which it is estimated will depend on whether or not the researcher is assuming heteroscedasticity, or autocorrelation, or both.

Heteroscedasticity

Consider again the simple Keynesian consumption function where consumption, y_t, is assumed to depend on current income, x_t:

$$y_t = \beta_1 + \beta_2 x_t + \varepsilon_t \qquad (1.77)$$

It may well be the case that the variance of the disturbance term varies as income rises, since the bigger one's income, the more room there is for acts of caprice in consumption, rather than sticking fairly closely to a basic consumption bundle. Suppose, for example, that the variance of the disturbance was assumed to vary with the *square* of income:

$$\text{Var}(\varepsilon_t) = \sigma_t^2 = \alpha x_t^2 \qquad (1.78)$$

Deflating (1.77) by x_t yields:

$$y_t^* = \beta_1 z_t^* + \beta_2 + \varepsilon_t^* \qquad (1.79)$$

where $y_t^* = y_t/x_t$, $z_t^* = 1/x_t$, $\varepsilon_t^* = \varepsilon_t/x_t$. The variance of the tth transformed disturbance is

$$\text{Var}(\varepsilon_t^*) = \text{Var}(\varepsilon_t)/x_t^2 = \alpha x_t^2/x_t^2 = \alpha$$

which demonstrates that it is homoscedastic, so that OLS can be applied to the *transformed equation* (1.79) to yield an optimal estimator.

In terms of the more general discussion of the previous subsection, we can write, in matrix notation:

$$Y^* = X^*\beta + \varepsilon^* \qquad (1.80)$$

$$\Omega = \alpha \begin{bmatrix} x_1^2 & & & & \\ & x_2^2 & & 0 & \\ & & x_3^2 & & \\ & & & \cdot & \\ & 0 & & & \cdot \\ & & & & x_T^2 \end{bmatrix} \qquad (1.81)$$

$$P = \begin{bmatrix} 1/x_1 & & & & \\ & 1/x_2 & & 0 & \\ & & 1/x_3 & & \\ & & & \cdot & \\ & 0 & & & \cdot \\ & & & & 1/x_T \end{bmatrix}$$

It is easily seen that $P\Omega P' = \alpha I$ – a scalar matrix – hence the GLS estimator (i.e. OLS applied to (1.79)) will have the desired properties.

A more general method, suggested by White (1980) is to obtain unbiased point estimates of β using OLS and then to estimate Ω as a diagonal matrix with the ith squared OLS residual as the (i,i)th element in Ω:

$$\hat{\Omega} = \begin{bmatrix} \hat{\varepsilon}_1^2 & & & & \\ & \hat{\varepsilon}_2^2 & & 0 & \\ & & \hat{\varepsilon}_3^2 & & \\ & & & \cdot & \\ 0 & & & \cdot & \\ & & & & \hat{\varepsilon}_T^2 \end{bmatrix} \qquad (1.81a)$$

White then shows that

$$\plim_{T \to \infty} (X'X)^{-1} X'\hat{\Omega}X(X'X) = (X'X)^{-1}X'\Omega X(X'X)^{-1}$$

so that the formula

$$\text{Var}(\hat{\beta}_{\text{OLS}}) = (X'X)^{-1}X'\hat{\Omega}X(X'X)^{-1}$$

can be used as a consistent estimator of the variance–covariance matrix of the OLS estimator – regardless of the precise form of the heteroscedasticity. Many regression packages will now calculate heteroscedasticity-consistent, or 'robust' estimated standard errors using this formula or some variant of it. They have also been widely used in estimating equations containing expectations terms (see Chapter 6).

Autocorrelation

A particularly simple case of serially correlated disturbances is where the disturbance is assumed to follow a first-order autoregressive, or AR(1) process. For example:

$$y_t = \beta_1 + \beta_2 x_t + \varepsilon_t \qquad (1.82)$$

$$\varepsilon_t = \rho \varepsilon_{t-1} + v_t \qquad (1.83)$$

where v_t is assumed to be a white noise process and, in order to ensure the stationarity of ε_t, $|\rho| < 1$:

$$E(v_t) = 0, \qquad (1.84a)$$

$$E(v_t^2) = \sigma_v^2, \qquad (1.84b)$$

$$E(v_t v_{t-j}) = 0, \text{ for all } j \neq 0 \qquad (1.84c)$$

If we lag (1.82) once, multiply it by ρ and subtract the result from (1.82), we have:

$$y_t^* = \beta_1(1 - \rho) + \beta_2 x_t^* + v_t \tag{1.85}$$

where $y_t^* = (y_t - \rho y_{t-1})$, $x_t^* = (x_t - \rho x_{t-1})$. Since v_t is white noise, OLS applied to (1.85) will be optimal. (See Note 4.)

To see that this is equivalent to the general form for the GLS estimator discussed above, we need to derive the variance–covariance matrix of the autoregressive disturbance term.

We have already discussed the AR(1) model. In particular, equation (1.83) can be written as:

$$\varepsilon_t = v_t + \rho v_{t-1} + \rho^2 v_{t-2} + \rho^3 v_{t-3} + \rho^4 v_{t-4} + \ldots$$

$$= \sum_{i=0}^{\infty} \rho^i v_{t-i}$$

By substituting (1.85) into (1.82) we can see that y_t is influenced by past error terms – with geometrically declining weights. Thus, the data-generating process for y is *dynamic*; a fact which is not obvious in (1.82).

From (1.83) we have

$$E(\varepsilon_t) = \sum_{i=0}^{\infty} \rho^i E(v_{t-1}) = 0$$

which follows from the assumption that v is a white noise process (1.84a). Thus, the assumption of zero-mean disturbances is unaffected.

Now construct the variance–covariance matrix for $\varepsilon = (\varepsilon_1 \varepsilon_2 \varepsilon_3 \ldots \varepsilon_T)'$. Using (1.84b):

$$E(\varepsilon_t^2) = E(v_t^2 + \rho^2 v_{t-1}^2 + \rho^4 v_{t-2}^2 + \rho^6 v_{t-3}^2 + \ldots$$

$$+ \rho v_t v_{t-1} + \rho^2 v_t v_{t-2} \ldots)$$

$$= E(v_t^2) + \rho^2 E(v_{t-1}^2) + \rho^4 E(v_{t-2}^2) + \rho^6 E(v_{t-3}^2) + \ldots$$

$$= \sigma_v^2 [1 + \rho^2 + \rho^4 + \rho^6 + \ldots]$$

$$= \sigma_v^2/(1 - \rho^2) \tag{1.86}$$

Note that the cross-product terms in (1.86) disappear because v is an uncorrelated process (1.84c).

By a similar procedure used to derive (1.86), the covariance between two disturbances j periods apart is given by:

$$E(v_t v_{t-j}) = E(v_t v_{t+j}) = \rho^j \sigma_v^2/(1 - \rho^2) \tag{1.87}$$

Thus, the variance–covariance matrix can be written:

$$\Omega = E(\varepsilon\varepsilon') = \frac{\sigma_v^2}{1 - \rho^2} \begin{bmatrix} 1 & \rho & \rho^2 & \cdots & \rho^{T-1} \\ \rho & 1 & \rho & \cdots & \rho^{T-2} \\ \rho^2 & \rho & 1 & \cdots & \rho^{T-3} \\ \rho^3 & \rho^2 & \rho & \cdots & \rho^{T-4} \\ \cdot & & & \cdots & \\ \cdot & & & \cdots & \\ \rho^{T-1} & \rho^{T-2} & \rho^{T-3} & \cdots & 1 \end{bmatrix}$$

$$(1.88)$$

We now need to find a matrix P such that $P'P = \Omega^{-1}$. It can be shown that this matrix is given by:

$$P = \begin{bmatrix} \surd(1 - \rho^2) & 0 & 0 & \cdots & 0 \\ -\rho & 1 & 0 & \cdots & 0 \\ 0 & -\rho & 1 & \cdots & 0 \\ 0 & 0 & -\rho & \cdots & \cdot \\ \cdot & & & \cdots & \\ 0 & 0 & 0 & \cdots & 1 \end{bmatrix} \qquad (1.89)$$

If (1.82) is written in matrix form as

$$Y = X\beta + \varepsilon$$

then premultiplying by P yields

$$Y^* = X^*\beta + \varepsilon^*$$

where

$$Y^* = \begin{bmatrix} \surd(1 - \rho^2)y_1 \\ y_2 - \rho y_1 \\ \vdots \\ y_T - \rho y_{t-1} \end{bmatrix} \qquad (1.90a)$$

$$X^* = \begin{bmatrix} \surd(1 - \rho^2) & \surd(1 - \rho^2)x_1 \\ 1 - \rho & x_2 - \rho x_1 \\ \vdots & \vdots \\ 1 - \rho & x_T - \rho x_{T-1} \end{bmatrix} \qquad (1.90b)$$

$$\varepsilon^* = \begin{bmatrix} \surd(1 - \rho^2)\varepsilon_1 \\ v_2 \\ v_3 \\ \cdot \\ v_T \end{bmatrix} \qquad (1.90c)$$

It is straightforward to show that $\surd(1 - \rho^2)\varepsilon_1$ has variance σ_v^2 and is uncorrelated with v_t for $t \geq 2$, so:

$$E(\varepsilon^*\varepsilon^{*'}) = \sigma_v^2 I$$

Thus, applying OLS to the transformed data, i.e. GLS, will yield the optimal GLS estimator. This method only differs from the intuitive procedure for correcting for AR(1) disturbances in the treatment of the first observation.

In practice, of course, ρ is not known *a priori*, and hence Ω is not (see Note 5). In practice, therefore, this parameter must be estimated. There exists a number of techniques for doing this. This first, the so called Hildreth–Liu technique, involves carrying out an exhaustive grid search for ρ over its admissible range, i.e. -1 to $+1$. For each value of ρ, the GLS estimator is calculated and the sum of squared residuals $(Y^* - X^*\beta)'(Y^* - X^*\beta)$ is computed. The value of ρ is then chosen which minimises this sum of squares.

The second algorithm is due to Cochrane and Orcutt (1949). The Cochrane–Orcutt technique starts by exploiting the fact that OLS will provide an unbiased and consistent estimate of the parameter vector in the presence of autocorrelation (see Note 6), and thus of the disturbance vector. The resulting estimates of ε can then be substituted into (1.83) and OLS applied to yield an estimate of ρ. This then can be used to find a GLS estimate of β, which yields a more efficient estimate of ε. OLS is then applied to the new set of residuals to find a more efficient estimate of ρ, which is again used to construct the GLS estimate, and so on. The procedure stops when successive estimated values of ρ are deemed to be sufficiently close – i.e. until the algorithm converges.

Finally, we should sound a note of caution in 'correcting' for autocorrelation in this fashion indiscriminately. In particular, it is important to distinguish between autocorrelation in the 'true' errors and autocorrelated regression residuals. The latter may be indicative of the former, but they may also indicate dynamic misspecification. One way of attempting to discriminate between the two is to apply a common factor test. For example, consider the dynamic model

$$y_t = \alpha_1 + \alpha_2 x_t + \alpha_3 x_{t-1} + \rho y_{t-1} + v_t \qquad (1.91)$$

Using the lag operator, (1.91) can be written:

$$(1 - \rho L)y_t = \alpha_1 + \alpha_2[1 + (\alpha_3/\alpha_2)L]x_t + v_t \qquad (1.92)$$

If the restriction $-\rho = (\alpha_3/\alpha_2)$ holds, or equivalently:

$$\rho\alpha_2 + \alpha_3 = 0 \qquad (1.93)$$

then we can divide (1.92) through by the common factor $(1 - \rho L)$ to obtain the AR(1) disturbance model (1.82), (1.83). Thus, estimating a static model with an AR(1) disturbance term is tantamount to imposing the common factor restrictions (1.93) on the dynamic model with a white noise error, (1.92). If there is sign of serial correlation in the static regression residuals (such as from the Durbin–Watson statistic) but the AR(1) common factor restrictions are rejected, then the remedy is not to 'correct' for serially correlated residuals, but to improve the dynamic specification of the model. Testing non-linear restrictions of the kind (1.93) lies outside the scope of this introductory chapter but will be discussed in Chapter 2. The topic of dynamic specification is discussed at length in Chapter 4.

Stochastic regressors

The second classical assumption which we listed in section 1.5 was that the regressors are non-stochastic and are thus independent of the errors.

$$E(X'u) = 0$$

This assumption was required to derive the unbiasedness property of the OLS estimator. In general, however, the assumption that the regressors are non-stochastic – or fixed in repeated samples – can be seen to be quite restrictive. For example, we may have a lagged dependent variable, representing some degree of inertia in the behaviour of a variable. More generally, there seems to be little sense in asserting that some economic time series such as consumption are stochastic, while others such as income are not. Moreover, there may be random errors in the measurement of the regressors, i.e. 'errors in variables', or the equation we are considering may be part of a larger simultaneous system involving stochastic feedback between variables.

If the regressors are not considered to be non-stochastic, but it is considered safe to assume that they are distributed independently of the disturbance, then most of the desirable characteristics of the OLS estimator can in fact be recovered, although the algebra becomes considerably more complicated. This is the *conditional regression model* which is discussed briefly in Chapter 4. The small-sample properties of the OLS estimator under the assumption of stochastic regressors cannot, however, be retrieved, although consistency holds if the regressors are *contemporaneously* uncorrelated with the disturbances, i.e. the nth observation of the regressor is uncorrelated with the nth observation of the disturbance.

Consider the general linear model, where the design matrix is not assumed to be non-stochastic:

$$Y = X\beta + u \tag{1.94}$$

The covariance matrix is assumed to be scalar. If the following conditions hold:

$$\plim_{T\to\infty} T^{-1} X'X = \Sigma \tag{1.95a}$$

$$\plim_{T\to\infty} T^{-1} X'u = 0 \tag{1.95b}$$

where Σ is a non-singular matrix, then the OLS estimator $\hat{\beta}$ is consistent:

$$
\begin{aligned}
\plim_{T\to\infty} \hat{\beta} &= \plim_{T\to\infty} (X'X)^{-1} X'Y \\
&= \plim_{T\to\infty} (X'X)^{-1} X'(X\beta + u) \\
&= \beta + \plim_{T\to\infty} (X'X)^{-1} X'u \\
&= \beta + \plim_{T\to\infty} (T^{-1} X'X)^{-1} \plim_{T\to\infty} (T^{-1} X'u) \\
&= \beta + \Sigma 0 \\
&= \beta
\end{aligned}
$$

Assumptions (1.95a) and (1.95b) thus replace the second classical assumption. Assumption (1.95a) will hold if X consists of realisations from a stationary multivariate stochastic process with a non-singular contemporaneous variance–covariance matrix. It can also be shown that the standard estimators of the disturbance variance and of the variance–covariance matrix of the OLS parameters, $\hat{\beta}$, will also be consistent.

Errors in variables

Another reason that regressors may be stochastic is where there is stochastic measurement error in one or more of the regressors. In this case, however, the OLS estimator is no longer even consistent.

Say, for example, we believe Y and X are related by an exact linear relationship:

$$\widetilde{Y} = \widetilde{X}\beta \tag{1.96}$$

but instead of observing $\widetilde{X}$ and $\widetilde{Y}$ directly, we observe only measured data X and Y which may be contaminated by measurement error:

$$X = \widetilde{X} + \zeta \tag{1.97a}$$

$$Y = \widetilde{Y} + \mu \tag{1.97b}$$

where ζ and μ represent the measurement error. Often, there is no reason why measurement error should not be autocorrelated; for example, where x represents a stock (such as money supply for example), it may make sense to propose a first-order moving average representation for the measurement error:

$$\zeta_t = v_t - \partial v_{t-1} \tag{1.98}$$

This would imply that a proportion ∂ of measurement error tends to be reversed in the following period. For our purposes, however, we need only assume that the measurement errors are white noise stochastic processes.

Substituting from (1.97) and (1.96), we have:

$$Y = X\beta + \omega \tag{1.99a}$$

$$\omega = \mu - \beta\zeta \tag{1.99b}$$

If the measurement errors are assumed uncorrelated, then the covariance matrix for ω is:

$$E(\omega\omega') = \sigma_\mu^2 I + \beta^2 \sigma_\zeta^2 I = \sigma_\omega^2 I \tag{1.100}$$

where σ_μ^2 and σ_ζ^2 denote the variance of μ and ζ respectively. From equation (1.100) it is clear that ω has a scalar covariance matrix.

From equations (1.99a) and (1.99b), however, it is clear that the disturbance term in (1.99a), ω, is correlated with the regressor, X, which violates one of the classical assumptions which we discussed in section 1.5 and which was needed to derive the unbiasedness property of the OLS estimator. Moreover, the OLS estimator is no longer even consistent since, although condition (1.95a) may still be assumed to hold, condition (1.95b) is violated:

$$\text{plim}_{T\to\infty} T^{-1} X'X = \Sigma$$

$$\text{plim}_{T\to\infty} T^{-1} X'\omega = \text{plim}_{T\to\infty} T^{-1} (\tilde{X} + \zeta)'(\mu - \beta\zeta)$$

$$= -\beta\sigma_\zeta^2 I \neq 0$$

Thus:

$$\text{plim}_{T\to\infty} \hat{\beta} = \text{plim}_{T\to\infty} (X'X)^{-1} X'Y$$

$$= \text{plim}_{T\to\infty} (X'X)^{-1} X'(X\beta + \omega)$$

$$= \beta + \text{plim}_{T\to\infty} T(X'X)^{-1} \text{plim}_{T\to\infty} T^{-1} X'\omega$$

$$= \beta - \beta\sigma_\zeta^2 \Sigma^{-1}$$

$$\neq \beta$$

Simultaneous equations and instrumental variables

Another standard case where some of the independent variables in a regression are correlated with the errors is in a simultaneous equation system. In such a system there is a *contemporaneous* feedback between the endogenous variables of the system. OLS on any single equation therefore gives biased and inconsistent parameter estimates. Although it is possible to estimate the full system 'at one go' (see Chapter 2), frequently, applied economists only wish to estimate a single structural equation. Nevertheless they are aware that the equation of interest may be part of a larger simultaneous system and hence OLS is inappropriate. A consistent estimator is provided by the method of instrumental variables (IV) on a single equation although it is not always obvious how one chooses a particular set of instruments and whether they are independent of the error term. IV is a single equation estimation technique and does not consider all of the information in the rest of the system of equations, (although it may be generalised to a system estimator, three stage least squares, 3SLS, is a limited information estimator which can be compared to a full information estimator such as maximum likelihood (see Chapter 2).

The IV approach is very general and there is a wide variety of estimators within this general class. The approach is to take a set of variables ('instruments') which satisfy the classical assumption and use them to construct a 'proxy' for the variable which is endogenous. To delineate members of the class, one's choice of instrument set may determine the name given to a particular IV estimator. For example, the two stage least squares (2SLS) estimator is a specific form of IV estimator. To complicate matters the 2SLS estimator may also be interpreted as a two-step estimator; it is equivalent to doing two (particular) OLS regressions. However there are some subtle differences between 2SLS viewed as a special form of IV estimator and the two-step procedure.

The IV estimator is derived as follows. Suppose in the general linear model we have a subset of variables $X_1(1 \times k_1)$ that are uncorrelated with the error term u in large samples. But the subset of variables $X_2(1 \times k_2)$ are correlated with u

$$Y = X\beta + u = (X_1, X_2)\beta + u \qquad (1.101)$$

where

$$\text{plim } T^{-1}(X_1'u) = 0 \qquad (1.102a)$$

$$\text{plim } T^{-1}(X_2'u) \neq 0 \qquad (1.102b)$$

Without loss of generality assume $u \sim N(0, \sigma^2 I)$. Suppose there exists a set of k_2 variables denoted W_1 (the 'instruments') which have the properties:

$$\text{plim}_{T\to\infty} T^{-1}(W_1'u) = 0$$

$$\text{plim}_{T\to\infty} T^{-1}(W_1'X_2) \neq 0$$

(1.103)

Hence W_1 is uncorrelated in the limit with u and there is a non-zero correlation between W_1 and X_2 (with a constant asymptotic moment matrix, W'_1X_2).

The full matrix of instruments is

$$W = (W_1, X_1)$$

(1.104)

where X_1 acts, in effect, as its own instrument and W_1 has 'replaced' the variables X_2. Now we premultiply (1.101) by W' and take probability limits:

$$\text{plim}_{T\to\infty} T^{-1}(W'Y) = \text{plim}_{T\to\infty} T^{-1}(W'X)\beta + \text{plim}_{T\to\infty} T^{-1}(W'u)$$

(1.105)

Taking the sample moments as estimates of their population values (which we assume throughout this section) and using equation (1.103) above, it is easily seen that $\hat{\beta}_{IV}$ the *instrumental variable estimator* is

$$\hat{\beta}_{IV} = (W'X)^{-1}(W'Y)$$

(1.106)

Note that if all the X variables satisfy the classical assumptions then W is the same as X and this is simply the OLS estimator. The asymptotic covariance matrix of the IV estimator (which we simply denote as $\text{Var}(\hat{\beta}_{IV})$) may be derived as follows. Substituting (1.101) in (1.106) produces

$$\hat{\beta}_{IV} - \beta = (W'X)^{-1}(W'u)$$

(1.107)

Hence

$$\text{Var}(\hat{\beta}_{IV}) = \text{plim}_{T\to\infty} T(W'X)^{-1} \, \text{plim}_{T\to\infty} T^{-2}(W'uu'W)$$

$$\times \text{plim}_{T\to\infty} T(X'W)^{-1}$$

$$= \sigma^2(W'X)^{-1}(W'W)(X'W)^{-1}$$

(1.108)

Since $\hat{\beta}_{IV}$ is consistent (to see this take 'plims' of (1.107)) and using (1.102), (1.103) and (1.104) the residuals

$$\hat{u}_{IV} = Y - X\hat{\beta}_{IV}$$

(1.109)

can be used to obtain a consistent estimator for σ^2:

$$s_{IV}^2 = (\hat{u}_{IV}'\hat{u}_{IV})/T$$

(1.110)

Note that X and not W is used in (1.109) and that (1.108) would again be the OLS formula when X and W are identical.

We now turn to a simple two-equation simultaneous equation system to demonstrate the relationship between IV and 2SLS. (Because of space constraints we do not discuss the identification problem in simultaneous models, although we make the implicit assumption that the systems we are discussing are identified. This means that the order condition, that the number of predetermined variables excluded from any equation must at least equal the number of endogenous variables included on the *right-hand side*, and the rank condition, are met. We also require that there are at least as many instruments as endogenous variables.)

A simultaneous system

Our simple illustrative system is:

$$y_1 = \alpha y_2 + \beta x_1 + \varepsilon_1 \tag{1.111a}$$
$$= Q\delta + \varepsilon_1$$

$$y_2 = \gamma y_1 + \theta x_2 + \varepsilon_2 \tag{1.111b}$$

where $\varepsilon_i \sim N(0, \sigma_i^2 I)$

and $\plim_{T \to \infty} (x_i'\varepsilon_j)/T = 0 \ (i, j = 1, 2)$

$$E(\varepsilon_{1t}\varepsilon_{2t}) = E(\varepsilon_{1t}\varepsilon_{2t-j}) = 0$$

and we define $Q = (y_2, x_1)$, $\delta = (\alpha, \beta)$

Because we wish to isolate the issues that arise solely from simultaneity between the endogenous variables y_{1t} and y_{2t} we assume white noise errors in each equation and no contemporaneous correlation between the errors in different equations.

The reduced form equations of the system are:

$$y_{1t} = x_{1t}\pi_{11} + x_{2t}\pi_{12} + v_{1t} \tag{1.112a}$$

$$y_{2t} = x_{1t}\pi_{21} + x_{2t}\pi_{22} + v_{2t} \tag{1.112b}$$

where $\pi_{11} = (1 - \alpha\gamma)^{-1}\beta$, $\pi_{12} = (1 - \alpha\gamma)^{-1}\alpha\theta$, $\pi_{21} = (1 - \alpha\gamma)^{-1}\gamma\beta$,

$\pi_{22} = (1 - \alpha\gamma)^{-1}\theta$, $v_{1t} = (1 - \alpha\gamma)^{-1}(\varepsilon_{1t} + \alpha\varepsilon_{2t})$

$v_{2t} = (1 - \alpha\gamma)^{-1}(\varepsilon_{2t} + \gamma\varepsilon_{1t})$

In what follows, of crucial importance in (1.112a) and (1.112b) is that y_{1t} and y_{2t} depend on a linear combination of the structural errors $\varepsilon_{it}(i = 1, 2)$. This arises because of the simultaneity of the system and so the classical assumptions outlined in section 1.5 do not hold, also condition (1.95b) is violated and so by the proof given in section 1.6 OLS is neither unbiased nor consistent. An instrumental variable estimator may be used to provide consistent parameter estimates of either a part of the system or the complete system.

In most of what follows we assume the econometrician is only interested in estimating the structural equation (1.111a) but is aware that this equation is embedded in a simultaneous system which could consist of a number of additional equations. Also we could easily extend the analysis to consider y_2 to be a vector of endogenous variables, just as there could be many more than two x variables. However, for pedagogic reasons we assume for the moment the simple model outlined above.

The IV estimator of (1.111a) is consistent. We require an instrument for y_2, that is both independent of ε_1 in large samples and has some non-zero correlation with y_2. Call this variable w_1. The instrument matrix is then

$$W_1 = (w_1, x_1)$$

where x_1 may be thought of as acting as its own instrument. The IV estimator is,

$$\delta = (W_1'Q)^{-1}W_1'y_1 \tag{1.113}$$

An obvious question is how do we choose a particular variable to act as an instrument for y_{2t}? An obvious candidate is x_{2t} since by assumption this is independent of ε_{1t} and from (1.111b) is correlated with y_{2t}. But if we know the system we can do better than this.

Two-stage least squares (2SLS)

An alternative is to use a linear combination of *all* the predetermined variables in the system. To obtain our linear combination we perform the OLS regression

$$y_2 = x_1\hat{\pi}_{21} + x_2\hat{\pi}_{22} + \hat{v}_2 \tag{1.114}$$

and form $\hat{y}_2$ as the fitted values from this model, note that this is the true reduced form equation for y_2. The instrument matrix is then

$$W = (\hat{y}_2, x_1)$$

and

$$\delta^*(2\text{SLS}) = (W'Q)^{-1}(W'y_1) \tag{1.115}$$

When we use $\hat{y}_2$ as the instrument and apply IV then δ^* is known as the 2SLS estimator (a particular form of IV). The name originates because we obtain $\hat{y}_2$ in the 'first-stage' regression and use this in the IV (second stage) formula. For the moment we assume that plim $T^{-1}(\hat{y}_2'\varepsilon_1) = 0$. Intuitively we might expect $\hat{y}_2$ to be uncorrelated with ε_1 because it is a linear combination of x_1 and x_2 which are both assumed to be independent of ε_1.

Other IV estimators

More often than not applied economists are interested only in estimating one structural equation although they are aware that this equation may form part of a larger simultaneous system. If we are interested only in (1.111a) we will still obtain biased parameter estimates because of the existence of (1.111b) even if we do not explicitly formulate this second equation. So whenever the possibility of simultaneity (or the failure of weak exogeneity, see Chapter 4) exists we must be prepared to consider an IV estimation strategy. However we may have only a hazy idea of the form of the rest of the model and of the set of weakly endogenous variables in the complete system. We may therefore try a number of alternative instruments sets for y_{2t}. We could choose any one x_i variable from the potentially large set of X ($X = (x_1, \ldots, x_k)$). Alternatively we can choose one of many essentially arbitrary sub-sets of X, $X^j \subset X$ and perform the OLS regression of y_2 on X^j. We could then form

$$\hat{y}_2^j = X^{j'}\hat{\Pi} \tag{1.116}$$

where $\hat{y}_2^j$ may be used as an instrument for y_2. Clearly many such instruments may be constructed depending on the choice of X^j and they will all differ and give somewhat different parameter estimates in finite samples. By assumption, however, all of these IV estimators are consistent. This is a practical problem with IV estimation: results are not invariant to the choice of instrument set. Ideally one should report a sensitivity analysis with respect to alternative instrument sets. As a general guideline in small samples there is also a trade-off between efficiency and consistency. Choosing a very small set of instruments will ensure consistency but may yield very inefficient estimates but, in a small sample, as the number of instruments grows the IV parameter estimate will converge on the OLS estimator and will be inconsistent. One way of checking the validity of the instrument set is to use a test due to Sargan which tests for the orthogonality of the instrument set and the structural residual; this test is discussed in Chapter 4.

Two-step and two-stage least squares

We will now consider the 2SLS estimator from a slightly different angle, namely as *two applications of OLS*. Suppose we have a fixed set of instruments $X = \{x_1, x_2\}$ where x_1 are the k^* predetermined variables in the structural equation of interest and x_2 are the k^{**} predetermined variables excluded from the equation. The OLS regression of y_2 on X is the first stage regression and we may construct the instrument:

$$\hat{y}_2 = x_1\hat{\pi}_1 + x_2\hat{\pi}_2 = X\hat{\Pi} \tag{1.117}$$

Now let us replace the endogenous variable y_2 with $\hat{y}_2$ in (1.111a) and then estimate the resulting equation by OLS

$$y_1 = \alpha\hat{y}_{2t} + \beta x_1 + \omega_1 \tag{1.118}$$

$$= \hat{Q}\delta + \omega_1$$

Then the '2-step least squares estimator' (OLS done twice) is

$$\hat{\delta}_p = (\hat{Q}'\hat{Q})^{-1}(\hat{Q}'y_1) \tag{1.119}$$

The OLS formula for the covariance matrix $\mathrm{Var}(\hat{\delta}_p)$ and the variance of the equation s_p^2 produced by standard regression packages on (1.118) will be:

$$\mathrm{Var}(\hat{\delta}_p) = s_p^2(\hat{Q}'\hat{Q}) \tag{1.120}$$

$$s_p^2 = (y_1 - \hat{Q}\hat{\delta}_p)'(y_1 - \hat{Q}\hat{\delta}_p)/(T - K) \tag{1.121}$$

How do these formulae compare with the ones given for the 2SLS estimator? For 2SLS the instrument matrix is:

$$W = (\hat{y}_2, x_1) = \hat{Q} \tag{1.122}$$

which is the same as that used above in the second stage of the two-stage estimation. So (1.115) reduces to δ^* (2SLS) $= (\hat{Q}'Q)^{-1}(\hat{Q}'y_1)$. However, it may be shown that

$$(\hat{Q}'Q) = \hat{Q}'\hat{Q}) \tag{1.123}$$

and therefore the 2SLS estimator gives exactly the same numerical value as the two-step estimator for the estimated parameters. Also, using $(\hat{Q}'Q) = (\hat{Q}'\hat{Q})$, $W = \hat{Q}$, and noting that $X \equiv Q$ then (1.108) gives:

$$\mathrm{Var}(\delta_{2SLS}) = s_{2SLS}^2(\hat{Q}'\hat{Q})^{-1} \tag{1.124}$$

The difference in the two formulae (1.120) and (1.124) lies in the estimate of s^2. Equation (1.124) constructs s^2 from the IV/2SLS residuals defined by $u_{2SLS} = y_1 - Q\hat{\delta}_{2SLS}$ where $Q = (y_2, x_1)$ while s_p^2 is constructed using the residuals defined in (1.121) using $\hat{Q} = (\hat{y}_2, x_1)$; these are not the same. Thus the two-step procedure constructs the residuals using $\hat{y}_2$ while the 2SLS procedure uses y_2, the actual value of y_2. Hence, while the two-step procedure provides consistent parameter estimates it does not calculate correctly the variance of the equation or the covariance matrix of the parameters; for these the IV/2SLS formulae must be used.

Consistency of the two-step estimator $\hat{\delta}_p$

We have already implicitly established the consistency of the two-step procedure by appealing to its numerical equivalence with the IV estimator but given the use we will make of the two-step procedure in Chapter 6 on rational expectations it is useful to establish this result and outline a complication. If we take (1.111a) and add and subtract $\alpha\hat{y}_2$ from it we may restate it as

$$y_1 = \alpha\hat{y}_2 + \beta x_1 + \omega_1 \tag{1.125}$$

where

$$\omega_1 = \varepsilon_1 + \alpha(y_2 - \hat{y}_2) \tag{1.126}$$

Consistency of the two-step estimator then requires:

$$\plim_{T\to\infty} T^{-1}(x_1'\omega_1) = \plim_{T\to\infty} T^{-1}(\hat{y}_2'\omega_1) = 0$$

We have:

$$\plim_{T\to\infty} T^{-1}(x_1'\varepsilon_1) = 0 \quad \text{by assumption}$$

$$\plim_{T\to\infty} T^{-1}(x_1'(y_2 - \hat{y}_2)) = \plim_{T\to\infty} T^{-1}(x_1'\hat{v}_2) = 0 \quad \text{by OLS}$$

$$\plim_{T\to\infty} T^{-1}(\hat{y}_2'\varepsilon_1) = 0 \quad \text{by equation (1.117)}$$

$$\plim_{T\to\infty} T^{-1}(\hat{y}_2'(y_2 - \hat{y}_2)) = \plim_{T\to\infty} T^{-1}(\hat{y}_2'\hat{v}_2) = 0 \quad \text{by OLS}$$

which establishes the consistency of the estimator. Note that a complication is that this proof rests on the assumption that x_1 and $\hat{y}_2$ are uncorrelated with $\hat{v}_2$; this is correct by construction given our specification of (1.117), but if we had omitted x_1 from the specification this would no longer be valid. So if we define $\hat{y}_2^*$ from OLS on:

$$\hat{y}_2^* = x_2\hat{\pi}^* \tag{1.127}$$

then

$$x_1'(y_2 - \hat{y}_2^*) \neq 0$$

if x_1 has any influence on y_2. In this case the two-step estimator using $\hat{y}_2^*$ is inconsistent. This arises in expectations models (see Chapter 6). However if $\hat{y}_2^*$ is used *as an instrument* for y_2,

$$W = (\hat{y}_2^*, x_1)$$

then the IV formulae yield consistent estimates of δ, s^2 and Var(α), Var(β).

1.7 Conclusion

In this chapter we have given an account of the standard econometric results which underlie single equation estimation by OLS, we have shown that under a fairly stringent set of assumptions OLS is an optimal estimator and we have outlined how the failure of these assumptions leads to a poor performance on the part of this technique. So far we have said little about systems estimation and ways in which we can deal with the problems which arise when the classical assumptions are violated. Much of the rest of the book is aimed at dealing with these problems. Chapter 2 introduces the notion of maximum likelihood and this allows systems of equations to be treated effectively. The failure of the assumption of stationarity is the central issue of Chapter 5 on cointegration and correct conditioning and testing of the underlying dynamic specification is the heart of dynamic modelling, treated in Chapter 4.

Notes

1. Of course, the intercept need not be placed first in the regression. If it were placed in the ith position, then we would examine the ith row of the normal equations.
2. The *trace* of a matrix is defined as the sum of the elements on the leading diagonal.
3. An idempotent matrix, M, has the property that $MM = M$. If M is non-singular (i.e. if its inverse exists), then it follows immediately that M is the identity matrix. In general, an idempotent matrix is singular.
4. Note that we have not stated explicitly what should be done with the first observation – y_t^* is defined only for $t \geq 2$. One option is simply to drop this observation. A more satisfactory alternative will become clear below.
5. The variance of v_t need not be known because, as we noted above, the variance–covariance matrix of the disturbance need be known only up to a scalar multiple.
6. Provided there are no lagged dependent variables. If there were, this would in any case violate the assumption of non-stochastic regressors, which we consider below.

2
Maximum likelihood estimation

In many ways the maximum likelihood (ML) approach forms the cornerstone of classical statistical methodology. The conceptual approach underlying maximum likelihood procedures is an appealing one which is much less '*ad hoc*' than other estimation procedures. To emphasise this point Hendry (1976) shows that many of the conventional estimation techniques, such as three-stage least squares, two-stage least squares, etc. can be interpreted as approximations to the maximum likelihood estimator. Generally speaking, an appropriate maximum likelihood estimation technique is both consistent and asymptotically efficient, so the ML approach forms a useful point of comparison for judging other estimators. We present the general issues behind maximum likelihood estimation and the associated test procedures (LR, Wald and LM) in section 2.1. Next we discuss numerical optimisation procedures and in section 2.3 we outline two special forms of the likelihood function frequently encountered in the empirical literature: the discrete switching model and various forms of the ARCH model. In section 2.4 we present two empirical examples, a model of the mortgage market and a model of time-varying risk premia in the foreign exchange markets.

2.1   The conceptual approach

ML is a very general procedure with the following common features. First we assume a particular probability distribution and calculate the probability of observing a particular outcome. This generally depends on some unknown parameters. Given our data set we then choose those parameter estimates which maximise the probability of the observed outcome. These parameter estimates are then the maximum likelihood estimate of the unknown true parameter values.

An example may help to clarify this. Suppose we wish to test a consignment of goods for quality, we might take a *sample* of ten items and test these and find that five fail the quality check. What then is our estimate of the proportion of total goods which are faulty? The intuitive answer is, of course 0.5, but the ML procedure would approach the question rather differently. Consider first the probability distribution for the problem at hand. Suppose we draw a random sample of size n and the (unknown) probability of each item being defective is Π in the population. If we actually find B bad items, then the probability P of finding B bad items in our sample of n is given by the binomial formula (i.e. our probability distribution)

$$P = \frac{n!}{B!(n - B)!} \Pi^{B}(1 - \Pi)^{n-B} \tag{2.1}$$

In the example above $n = 10$, $B = 5$. Given fixed n and B, from our *sample*, if we arbitrarily set $\Pi = 0.1$ then (2.1) yields $P = 0.0015$, if $\Pi = 0.2$ then $P = 0.0254$, etc. So in principle we could search over the whole range of Π and we would discover that P is maximised when we chose $\Pi = 0.5$ (which gives $P_{max} = 0.264$). The value of Π which maximises the probability of getting the *observed* sample outcome (i.e. $B = 5$ for $n = 10$) is therefore $\Pi = 0.5$. This is the ML estimate of the *true* population value of Π. We could of course maximise (2.1) analytically by setting its first derivative equal to zero.

$$\frac{\partial P}{\partial \bar{\Pi}} = B\left[\frac{\bar{\Pi}!}{B!(n - B)!} n^{B-1}(1 - \bar{\Pi})^{n-B} \right]$$

$$- (n - B) \frac{n!}{B!(n - B)!} \bar{\Pi}^{B}(1 - \bar{\Pi})^{n-B-1} = 0$$

$$B\bar{\Pi}^{B-1}(1 - \bar{\Pi})^{n-B} = (n - B)\bar{\Pi}^{B}(1 - \bar{\Pi})^{n-B-1}$$

$$B\bar{\Pi}^{-1} = n - B(1 - \bar{\Pi})^{-1}$$

$$\bar{\Pi} = \frac{B}{n} \tag{2.2}$$

$\bar{\Pi}$ is the ML estimator and in our case $\bar{\Pi} = B/n = 5/10 = 1/2$.

There are many cases where we can define the probability density function but where the problem is too complex for analytical maximisation. In these cases some numerical technique for locating the maximum must be used but even in the most complex cases the conceptual approach remains that discussed above.

A general statement

Suppose we have a sample of $(X_1, X_2 \ldots X_n)$ which is drawn from a probability distribution $P(X|A)$ where A is a set of parameters which, together with the assumed structural form, define the density function of X. We further assume that the X_i are independent, each with probability distribution $P(X_i|A)$ and so the joint probability distribution of the whole set $X_1 \ldots X_n$ is given by:

$$P(X_1, X_2 \ldots X_n|A) = P(X_1|A).P(X_2|A) \ldots P(X_n|A)$$

$$= \prod_{i=1}^{n} P(X_i|A) \tag{2.3}$$

We assume that the X_i are sample values, and therefore fixed. If we now ask what value of A maximises the probability of observing the sample values X_i we may restate (2.3) as the likelihood function

$$L(A) = \prod_{i=1}^{n} P(X_i|A) \tag{2.4}$$

It is often convenient to work in terms of the log of the likelihood function, which is simply

$$\log[L(A)] = \sum_{i=1}^{n} \log[P(X_i|A)] \tag{2.5}$$

The advantage of the ML approach is that it is a very general specification which can be applied to a wide range of models. It generally gives consistent parameter estimates which are asymptotically efficient. The main disadvantages are essentially practical. ML often produces highly complex non-linear optimisation problems and it also assumes an exact knowledge of the form of the probability distribution involved (up to a set of unknown parameters). This means that ML may be particularly sensitive to any structural misspecification in the model.

The likelihood function for a general non-linear model

If we write a non-linear model with N endogenous variables Y and M exogenous variables X, as

$$e = Y - f(X, \beta) \tag{2.6}$$

where β is a set of parameters and $e \sim N(0, \Theta)$ is a set of error terms which are normally distributed with zero mean and covariance matrix Θ, then the likelihood function evaluated for one period may be written as

$$L(\beta, \phi) = \frac{1}{(2\pi)^{1/2}|\Theta|^{1/2}} \exp\{(-1/2)[Y - f(X, \beta)]'$$
$$\times \Theta^{-1}[Y - f(X, \beta)]\} \tag{2.7}$$

or the log form may be written (after dropping the constant and multiplying through by 2):

$$\log[L(\beta, \phi)] = -\log|\Theta| - [Y - f(X, \beta)]'\Theta^{-1}[Y - f(X, \beta)] \tag{2.8}$$

In the special case where the diagonal elements of Θ are constant and the off-diagonal elements are zero, that is all covariances are zero, then $\Theta = \sigma^2 I$ and (2.8) is maximised by setting B at the value which minimises the squared errors of the model. We see therefore that under the assumption that the model errors are independent and normally distributed then the least squares estimator for β, is equivalent to the maximum likelihood estimator. (The variance–covariance matrix for β is however different in the two cases, in small samples.)

If we now return to the general form of the log likelihood function (2.5), there are two particularly important matrices which can be derived from it. The first of these is the *efficient score* for A, defined as

$$\frac{\partial \log(L(A))}{\partial A} = S(A) \tag{2.9}$$

So at the maximum likelihood estimate of A the efficient score is zero. The second matrix is the *information matrix*. It is defined:

$$E\left[-\left(\frac{\partial^2 \log(L(A))}{\partial A \partial A'}\right)\right] = I(A) \tag{2.10}$$

Where E is the expectations operator, $I(A)$ is a measure of the (average) curvature of the likelihood function. Under a suitable set of regularity conditions it may be shown that the variance of the ML estimator of A is given by the inverse of the information matrix.

$$\mathrm{Var}(\hat{A}_{\mathrm{ML}}) = [I(\hat{A})]^{-1} \tag{2.11}$$

Equation (2.11) is a statement of the Cramer–Rao lower bound. As the ML estimator normally attains the Cramer–Rao lower bound in large samples, it is said to be asymptotically efficient.

Concentrating the likelihood function

In (2.5) the parameter vector A contains both the parameters associated with the equation and the unknown moments of the error distribution (in the case of (2.8) these are the elements of the covariance terms). It is often possible to deal with subsets of the total parameter vector however and this is termed 'concentrating the likelihood function'. This can be both analytically and numerically convenient.

Let A consist of two subvectors A_1 and A_2, then (2.5) can be written as $L(A_1, A_2)$. Now suppose we knew a value for A_1, then it is possible that we could derive an analytical formula for the maximum of $L(A_1, A_2)$ with respect to A_2 for that given value of A_1. If this formula can be represented by a function of the form $A_2 = g(A_1)$ then we could write the likelihood function as $L(A_1, g(A_1))$ which could be restated as $L^*(A_1)$, the concentrated likelihood function. As an example consider the single-equation version of (2.8). The likelihood function for the non-linear model evaluated over T periods now is given by

$$L(A) = -T\log(\sigma^2) - e'e/\sigma^2$$

where e is the $T \times 1$ vector of errors $e_t = Y_t - f(X_t, \beta)$ and A consists of both β and σ^2. We may concentrate this likelihood function with respect to σ^2 in the following way. The FOC for a maximum with respect to σ^2 is given by

$$\partial L/\partial\sigma^2 = -T/\sigma^2 + e'e/(2\sigma^2)^2 = 0$$

and so we can derive an expression for σ^2 which is dependent on β, that is $\sigma^2 = e'e/T$, (where e_t depends on the unknown β). The concentrated log likelihood function which depends only on β becomes

$$L^*(\beta) = -T - T\log(e'e/T)$$

The prediction error decomposition

In the likelihood functions specified above, [e.g. in (2.5) and (2.8)] we make the assumption that the observations are independent of each other over time. This assumption will not generally be true when we are dealing with dynamic time series models which include lagged dependent variables. The maximum likelihood approach may still be used, even in this case, by adopting the following factorisation called the prediction error decomposition (Harvey 1981). From the basic definition of conditional probability we know that

$$\Pr(\alpha, \beta) = \Pr(\alpha|\beta)\Pr(\beta) \tag{2.12}$$

That is the unconditional probability of event α occurring is given by the probability of α conditional on β, multiplied by the unconditional probability of β.

This condition may be applied directly to a general form of likelihood function, which is after all simply a particular form of probability function. Suppose we have a general log likelihood function $\log[L(Y)] = \log[L(Y_1, Y_2 \ldots Y_T)]$ where the observations at each time period are not independent due to the dynamic structure of the model. Then by using the log of (2.12) we may write

$$\log[L(Y)] = \log[L(Y_T|Y_1, Y_2 \ldots Y_{T-1})]$$
$$+ \log[L(Y_1, Y_2 \ldots Y_{T-1})] \tag{2.13}$$

The first term is simply the conditional probability of the final period Y_T given the past realisations of Y. The second term is the unconditional probability of $Y_1 \ldots Y_{T-1}$ occurring. This second term can of course be factorised again to give the conditional likelihood function for Y_{T-1} and the unconditional function for $Y_1 \ldots Y_{T-2}$. This process may be repeated for all periods to give

$$\log[L(Y)] = \sum_{i=0}^{T-2} \log[L(Y_{T-i}|Y_1, \ldots Y_{T-1-i})] + \log[L(Y_1)] \tag{2.14}$$

This decomposes the likelihood function into a set of one step ahead prediction errors, v_t.

$$v_t = Y_t - E(Y_t|Y_1 \ldots Y_{t-1}) \tag{2.15}$$

That is the prediction error is defined as actual Y_t minus the models forecast of Y_t conditional on all information up to period $t-1$. For the general non-dynamic model (2.8), $v_t = Y - f(X, \beta)$. Then the likelihood function may be restated for the dynamic case as

$$\log[L(\beta, \Theta)] = -\log|\Theta| - (v'\Theta^{-1}v) \tag{2.16}$$

where Θ is the covariance matrix of the residuals, which is here assumed to be time invariant.

Constructing asymptotic hypothesis tests

In general, the purpose of hypothesis testing is to construct a test statistic which has a well-defined distribution under both the null

(H_0) and the alternative (H_1) hypotheses but which does not depend on the set of *unknown* parameters A.

There are three major classes of test statistic available which allow the construction of such tests: the Wald test, the Lagrange multiplier test and the likelihood ratio test. All three tests rely on the ML procedure and may be regarded as utilising different transformations of the score function. The three procedures are asymptotically equivalent but there small sample properties differ (except when the likelihood function is quadratic in the unknown parameters). One difference between the three tests lies in the point estimate which is used to calculate the test statistics. The Wald test is evaluated using only an unrestricted estimate of the model, the Lagrange multiplier test is evaluated using only the restricted estimate of the model (i.e. under the null) and the likelihood ratio test uses information from both the restricted and unrestricted estimates. In practice therefore the choice between the procedures is often made on the grounds of which set of estimates is actually easiest to compute. All three test procedures are frequently used when the estimated system is non linear because they may give different inferences in small samples.

Suppose the *unrestricted* ML estimate of the true vector A is $\hat{A}$ then we may wish to test the general restriction $H_0:g(A) = 0$ against the alternative $H_1:g(A) \neq 0$. The function $g(A)$ must be a function for which all the restricted parameters can be estimated; $g(A)$ must also be continuously differentiable and $(\partial g/\partial A)$ must have full rank in the neighbourhood of A. Gallant and Holly (1984) give a full set of conditions on g. The simplest forms for $g(A)$ for a single parameter are $a_1 = 0$ or $a_1 = 1$, etc. A linear restriction involving two parameters might be $g(A) = a_1 + a_2 - 1 = 0$ or a joint hypothesis might be $a_1 = 0$ *and* $a_2 - 1 = 0$. A non-linear restriction would be $g(A) = a_1^2 - 4(a_2^2/a_1) = 0$, for example.

The likelihood ratio test

The likelihood ratio test (LR) is the oldest of the three procedures, originating from the work of Neyman and Pearson (1928). It relies on the comparison between the value of the likelihood function at the unrestricted estimate $\hat{A}$ and the restricted estimate $[A^r|g(A) = 0]$. It is clear that

$$\text{LR} = \frac{L(A^r)}{L(\hat{A})} < 1 \tag{2.17}$$

since by definition $L(\hat{A}) > L(A^r)$. We need now to express this term in a form which will have a well-defined asymptotic distribution. This is done by taking a Taylor series expansion of $\log[L(A)]$ around the unrestricted estimate $\hat{A}$. (A suitable set of regularity assumptions is needed to justify this procedure.)

$$\log[L(A)] = \log[L(\hat{A})] + (\hat{A} - A)\left[\frac{\partial \log[L(A)]}{\partial A}\right]$$

$$+ \tfrac{1}{2}(\hat{A} - A)'\left[\frac{\partial^2 \log[L(A)]}{\partial A \partial A'}\right](\hat{A} - A) + 0(1)$$

$$(2.18)$$

Where $O(1)$ refers to a set of terms which is asymptotically negligible. At $\hat{A}$:

$$\frac{\partial \log[L(A)]}{\partial A} = S(A) = 0 \tag{2.19}$$

and

$$\frac{\partial^2 \log[L(A)]}{\partial A \partial A'} \xrightarrow{P} I(A) \tag{2.20}$$

Dropping the term $O(1)$ we may state (2.18) (following Serfling 1980) as

$$\log[L(A)] = \log[L(\hat{A})] + \tfrac{1}{2}(\hat{A} - A)'I(\hat{A})(\hat{A} - A) \tag{2.21}$$

From (2.17) we have that

$$-2\log(\text{LR}) = 2\{\log[L(\hat{A})] - \log[L(A')]\} \tag{2.22}$$

and so from (2.21), replacing the 'unknown' A by A',

$$-2\log(\text{LR}) = (\hat{A} - A')'I(\hat{A})(\hat{A} - A') \tag{2.23}$$

Also, under a reasonable set of regularity conditions it is known that asymptotically an ML estimate gives

$$\sqrt{n}(\hat{A} - A) \sim N(0, I(A)^{-1}) \tag{2.24}$$

and that $(\hat{A} - A)'I(A)(\hat{A} - A)$ is $\chi^2(m)$, where m is the number of constraints. Hence using (2.23) we may write the likelihood ratio test statistic as LRT.

$$\text{LRT} = 2\{\log[L(\hat{A})] - \log[L(A')]\} \sim \chi^2(m) \tag{2.25}$$

This is the usual form of the likelihood ratio test and simply states that the difference in the log-likelihoods (multiplied by 2) is $\chi^2(m)$. If the test statistic, LRT, exceeds the chosen critical value then we reject the restriction.

Three test procedures

The three general forms of test procedure used are the (LR) test (as described above), the Wald test (W) and Lagrange multiplier (LM) test. To illustrate the relationship (Buse 1982) between these three test procedures, suppose we wish to test the simple hypothesis on the scalar parameter A, namely $H_0: A = A_0$ against $H_1: A \neq A_0$. The LR test computes the value of the likelihood under *both* H_0 and H_1 and directly computes the distance $(1/2)$LR (Figure 2.1). The distance $(1/2)$LR depends on the distance $(\hat{A} - A_0)$, and the curvature of the log likelihood function which we define as $R(\hat{A}) = |(\mathrm{d}^2 \log L)/\mathrm{d}A^2|$ evaluated at $A = \hat{A}$. For a given distance $(A - A_0)$ the greater the curvature or 'steepness' of the likelihood function the larger is the distance $(1/2)$LR. Thus the 'precision' of the ML estimate $\hat{A}$ is greater for likelihood function L^1 (Figure 2.1) than for likelihood L^*. With the likelihood function L^1, we would tend to reject $A = A_0$ more often than with likelihood L^*. If the curvature $R(\hat{A})$ is large then the variability of A around its ML estimate is small: somewhat loosely the variance is inversely related to the curvature.

The Wald test uses only the unrestricted ML estimates. Intuitively in the Wald test we estimate the distance $(1/2)$LR by standing at point X, measuring the distance $(\hat{A} - A_0)$ and estimating the position of P_1 (or P_2) using the curvature $R(\hat{A})$ evaluated at the maximum point X. Thus we might define the Wald statistic for $H_0: A = A_0$ by

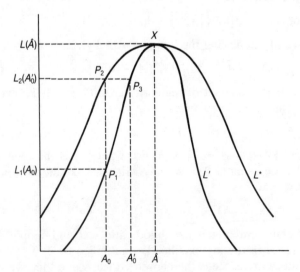

Figure 2.1 The three test procedures.

$W = (\hat{A} - A_0)^2 R(\hat{A})$. However, the Wald statistic uses the *average* curvature, as measured by the information matrix:

$$W = (\hat{A} - A_0)^2 I(\hat{A})$$

where $I(\hat{A})$ is defined in (2.10).

We can now generalise the above for a set of g non-linear restrictions $g(A) = 0$ on the k parameters $g < k$, and the Wald statistic (Wald 1943) is

$$W = [g(\hat{A})]'\{G(I(\hat{A}))^{-1}G'\}^{-1}g(\hat{A}) \tag{2.26}$$

Where G is the $g \times k$ matrix of partial derivatives $\partial g(A)/\partial A$ evaluated at $\hat{A}$. Large values of W are generated by large deviations of $g(\hat{A})$ from zero and the deviations are 'weighted' by the average curvature of the log-likelihood. Hence for large values of W we reject H_0. The Wald statistic is distributed $\chi^2(m)$ where m is the number of restrictions in the vector g. For example, the hypothesis $H_0: A = A_0$ (where $A_0 = 1$ say) is a special case and here $g(A) = (A - A_0)$. Hence G is the identity matrix. It is easily seen that the standard t-test for a restriction on a single parameter in a linear regression is a particularly simple form of Wald test. Suppose we wish to test the restriction $\hat{\beta} = 0$ in a linear regression. Then $g(\beta) = \beta - 0$, the Wald test is:

$$W = \hat{\beta}(I(\hat{A}))^{-1}\hat{\beta} = \hat{\beta}^2/(\text{Var } \hat{\beta}) \sim \chi^2(1) \tag{2.27}$$

where we have noted that the inverse of the information matrix is the ML estimate of the variance. The Wald test in this case is therefore simply the square of the standard t-test (and gives the same inference asymptotically as applying the χ^2 distribution as in (2.27)).

The Lagrange multiplier test, suggested by Aitchison and Silvey (1938) and a closely related test, the Rao statistic (Rao 1948) are both based solely on the restricted estimate of the model. The Lagrange multiplier test is sometimes referred to as the efficient score test as it is based on the asymptotic distribution of the score function

$$\frac{1}{\sqrt{n}} S(A) \sim N(0, I(A)) \tag{2.28}$$

Intuitively the LM test *estimates* the distance $(1/2\text{LR}_2)$ (Figure 2.1) but uses P_2 as its starting point. First the likelihood function is evaluated with the restriction $A = A_0$ imposed, that is, at point P_2. We then estimate the point X based on the curvature of L^* at P_2. The unrestricted ML estimate $\hat{A}$ satisfies the equation $S(\hat{A}) = \partial \log L/\partial A = 0$ where S is the score function. At $A = A_0$ the score function is *not* zero and $[S(A_0)]^2$ therefore gives a measure of the departure of A_0 from $\hat{A}$. However, two likelihoods can generate the same value for $[S(A_0)]^2$ but one has A_0 closer to the maximum. We therefore weight the 'squared slope' by the curvature of L^*. In fact the greater the curvature (i.e. L' as opposite to L^* in Figure 2.1) for any value of $\log[L(A_0)]$ the closer is the restricted estimate to $\hat{A}$ (compare points P_2 and P_3 in Figure 2.1, where A_0' is clearly closer to $\hat{A}$, and the curvature of L' is larger than that for L^*). We therefore weight by the inverse of the (expected value) of the curvature $[I(A_0)]^{-1}$ evaluated at the *restricted estimate A_0*. Our simple LM test statistic is therefore

$$\text{LM} = [S(A_0)]^2[I(A_0)]^{-1}$$

The generalised version is

$$\text{LM} = [S(A_0)]'[I(A_0)]^{-1}[S(A_0)] \sim \chi^2(m) \qquad \textbf{(2.29)}$$

where m is again the number of restrictions.

The intuition behind the test is that if the restrictions hold exactly (i.e. $A^r = \hat{A}$) then $S(A^r) = 0$ as this is the first order condition for an unconstrained maximum. The departure of $S(A^r)$ from zero therefore measures the strength of the effect of the restriction, on the maximum likelihood value.

The relationship between the three procedures depends on how good an approximation the second derivative is able to give of the value of the likelihood function at the restricted or unrestricted estimates. If we are testing a simple linear restriction, as in the example above, and the likelihood function is quadratic then the second derivative would provide a perfect estimate of the global shape of the likelihood function. In this case all three test procedures produce exactly the same numerical value, $\text{w} = \text{LM} = \text{LR}$. When, however, the second derivative is not known with certainty but must be estimated, this equality disappears and instead we have that $\text{w} \geqslant \text{LR} \geqslant \text{LM}$ as demonstrated by Berndt and Savin (1977).

A transformation of the LM test

The formula presented in (2.27) for the Lagrange multiplier test is not a particularly useful one in practice as it requires estimates of both the information matrix and the score matrix, evaluated with the restrictions imposed. Following Breusch and Pagan (1980) a transformation of (2.27) which is particularly easy to calculate and which is applicable to a wide class of problems may be performed. Suppose the model takes the form of the non-linear regression

$$Y_t = f(x_t; A) + e_t \equiv f_t + e_t \qquad t = 1 \ldots T \qquad (2.30)$$

where the errors, e_t, are identically and independently normally distributed as $N(0, \sigma^2)$ and f_t is independent of all e_t. The parameter set A is split into two subsets: A_1, which will be restricted (fixed) and A_2 which are unrestricted. The log-likelihood function will have the general form of (2.8) and the information matrix will be block diagonal between the terms in A and σ^2 and so we can concentrate solely on the term due to A. The non-linear restrictions are $g(A) = 0$. Now to evaluate (2.29) we need

$$S = \frac{\partial \log L}{\partial A} = \sigma^{-2} G' e \qquad (2.31)$$

and

$$V = E\left[\frac{\partial^2 \log (L)}{\partial A^2}\right]^{-1} = (\sigma^2 E(G'G))^{-1} \qquad (2.32)$$

where G is a matrix of partial derivatives of g with respect to the parameter A. We may then write (2.29) as

$$\tilde{\sigma}^{-2} \tilde{e}' \tilde{G} [\tilde{\sigma}^{-2} \tilde{E}(G'G)]^{-1} \tilde{\sigma}^{-2} \tilde{G}' \tilde{e} \qquad (2.33)$$

where $\sim$ denotes an estimate formed at the restricted parameter set $A_1 = \tilde{A}$. If $\tilde{E}(G'G)$ is estimated as $\tilde{G}'\tilde{G}$ then (2.33) may be simplified to

$$\tilde{\sigma}^2 \tilde{e}' \tilde{e} \qquad (2.34)$$

which may be interpreted as TR^2 where R^2 is the coefficient of determination in the regression of $\tilde{e}$ on $\tilde{G}$.

This procedure has found a range of applications, the most popular of which is the Lagrange multiplier test for serial correlation.

Suppose the unrestricted model is

$$Y = X\beta + u \qquad (2.35)$$

$$u_t = \rho_i u_{t-i} + \varepsilon_t \qquad (2.36)$$

This model may be transformed to give

$$Y_t = \rho_i Y_{t-i} + (X_t - X_{t-i}\rho_i)\beta + e_t \equiv f(\rho, \beta) + e_t \qquad (2.37)$$

which puts it into the notation given above. Now if we wish to construct the LM test for $\rho_i = 0$ we proceed as above by identifying $\rho_i = 0$ with $A_1 = A$ and β as A_2. For $\rho_i = 0$ the restricted estimates of $\hat{\beta}$ are given by an OLS regression of Y on X. The residuals from this OLS regression $\hat{u} = Y - X\hat{\beta}$ may then be associated with $\tilde{e}$. To derive the elements of $\tilde{G}$ we note that

$$\frac{\partial f}{\partial \rho_i} = (Y_{t-1} - X_{t-i}\beta)' = \hat{u}'_{-i} \tag{2.38}$$

$$\frac{\partial f}{\partial B} = (X_t - X_{t-i}\rho)' \tag{2.39}$$

so that $\tilde{G} = (\hat{u}_{-i}, X_t)$.

Now under the null hypothesis that $\rho_i = 0$ and that X is strictly exogenous it may be shown that the LM statistic becomes Tr_i^2 where

$$r_i = (\hat{u}'\hat{u})^{-1}\hat{u}'_{-1}\hat{u}$$

An alternative form of this test may also be constructed by performing the regression

$$\hat{u}_t = X_t\delta + \sum_{i=1}^{m} \gamma_i\hat{u}_{t-i} \tag{2.40}$$

The R^2 from this regression may then be used to form an LM statistic as $TR^2 \sim \chi^2(m)$. This test may be constructed either for individual lagged errors or for a number of lagged errors considered jointly. If TR^2 exceeds $\chi^2(m)$ then we reject the null hypothesis that the restrictions are valid (i.e. that there is no serial correlation of order $1, 2, \ldots m$).

Both of these forms of the LM test have the same intuitive interpretation. On the assumption that $\rho_i = 0$ the correlation between u_t and u_{t-i} should be zero. The first test looks at this correlation directly and its interpretation is obvious. In the second test, because $\hat{u}_t$ are the OLS residuals, the R^2 of $\hat{u}_t$ regressed on X_t is zero, (recall that the normal equations for OLS imply $\hat{u}'X = 0$). So the R^2 of the auxiliary regression (2.40) measures the extra explanatory power given by the terms $\hat{u}_{t-i}(i = 1, 2, \ldots m)$. If R^2 from (2.40) is low then there is a low correlation between $\hat{u}_t$ and $\hat{u}_{t-i}$ and hence autocorrelation is unlikely to be present.

2.2   Non-linear optimisation procedures

In general the log-likelihood function is a non-linear function of the parameters of the model and often $\log(A)/\partial A = 0$ is not amenable to an analytical solution. There are, of course, exceptions to this statement the most important of which is the case of the general linear model where the ML estimate of β can be derived analytically and is numerically equal to the OLS estimator. If an analytic solution is not possible we must use some numerical method for finding the maximum likelihood parameter values. The techniques which may be used are applicable to maximising any objective function which is a non-linear function of a set of control variables and we will discuss them within this general framework.

We therefore view the parameters (A) of the model as a set of control variables, C, and similarly the likelihood function itself is viewed simply as any general non-linear function of those control variables. Our objective may then be described without loss of generality as

$$\text{Min } H(C) = -\log[L(A)] \tag{2.41}$$

where C is a vector of all the parameters of the system – such as Π in (2.1) and, in some cases, any unknown variance or covariance terms.

Practical computation

The numerous methods of solving a minimisation problem, such as (2.41), proceed along a broadly similar set of steps and may all be classified under the general heading of hill-climbing algorithms. From an initial, and arbitrary, guess of the optimal solution C^*, say C_1, they attempt to construct a sequence of vectors $C_1, C_2 \ldots, C_N$ such that at every point on the sequence $H(C_J) < H(C_{J-1}) < H(C_{j-2}) < \ldots$ etc. and as $N \to \infty$, $C_N \to C^*$.

The broad steps of achieving this sequence may be outlined as follows:

1. Set an arbitrary initial value for C_i.
2. Determine a *direction of movement* for C_i which will decrease the value of $H(C_i)$.
3. Determine a 'step length' for the change C_i and evaluate the objective function of C_{i+1}.
4. Examine a terminal criterion; if it is fulfilled, stop. If it is not fulfilled, set $i = i + 1$ and repeat the procedure from step 2.

A usual criterion for termination would be that $H(C_{i-1}) - H(C_i) < \varepsilon$ where ε is some small tolerance. Because of the possibility of the algorithm 'jamming' at some non-optimal point we might also examine

$$\frac{\partial H}{\partial C'_K} \qquad K = 1, 2, \ldots J$$

or

$$\left(\left\| \frac{\partial H}{\partial C'} \right\| \right)' \left(\left\| \frac{\partial H}{\partial C'} \right\| \right)$$

to see that both of these are close to zero.

Among the hill-climbing algorithms by far the most important group are those which base the optimisation procedure on the calculation of derivatives of the objective function. These algorithms are known collectively as gradient methods for example, the Newton method, Davidson-Fletcher-Powell, steepest descent, and quadratic hill climbing. The non-gradient, or derivative free methods, are generally of most use when the function to be minimised is extremely irregular. This class includes, for example, the Powell algorithm, the non-linear Simplex method and grid search methods.

Gradient methods

Given a current value C_i the gradient methods all proceed by constructing a sequence where

$$H(C_{i+1}) < H(C_i) \tag{2.42}$$

where C_{i+1} is defined as follows

$$C_{i+1} = C_i + s\,\text{d}(C) = C_i + s[V(C).\partial(C)] \tag{2.42a}$$

s = the *step length* (a positive scalar), $\partial(C)$ is the *gradient*, (we use '∂' as shorthand below) a vector of first-order partial derivatives of H with respect to the control variables (i.e. $\partial = \partial H/\partial C$). $V = V(C)$ is a function which varies depending on the gradient method used. $\text{d}(C)$ is the direction vector and depends on the gradient *and* the function $V(C)$. The evaluation of both the first and indeed the second derivatives (see below) may be done either analytically or numerically. For analytical calculation the actual formulae for the derivatives must be coded into the computer program (for example, if $H(C) = 2C^2 - 4C$, $\partial H/\partial C = 4C - 4$, $\partial^2 H/\partial C^2 = 4$). In the case of complex functions it is often impossible to calculate derivatives analytically. In practice it is often satisfactory to use a numerical *approximation* to the derivatives, so that for the first derivative we use:

$$\frac{\partial H}{\partial C_K} = \frac{H(C_1 C_2, C_K + \Delta, C_{K+1}, C_J) - H(C_1, C_2, C_J)}{\Delta} \tag{2.43}$$

where Δ is a suitably small number. To illustrate the calculation of the numerical derivative (2.43) consider the simple quadratic

$$H(C) = 2C^2 - 4C$$

In this simple case we can solve analytically for the first derivative, ∂, and second derivatives, $\partial^{(2)}$

$$\partial = \partial H / \partial C = 4C - 4$$

The numerical approximation ∂_a for arbitrary values $C_1 = 0.5$, $C_2 = 0.52$ and hence $\Delta = 0.02$ is

$$\partial_a = [H(C_2) - H(C_1)]/0.02 = [(-1.5392) - (-1.5)]/0.02$$

$$= -1.96$$

We can check this approximation by evaluating the 'true' slope using $\partial = 4C - 4$. For $C_1 = 0.5$, $\partial_1 = -2$, while for $C_2 = 0.52$, $\partial_2 = -1.92$, so the approximation ∂_a lies between the two analytic values as one would expect. Similarly the second derivative $\partial_a^{(2)}$ can be approximated by

$$\partial_a^{(2)} = (\partial_{a2} - \partial_{a1})/(C_2 - C_1)$$

Equation (2.43) is a 'one-sided' derivative calculation; improved accuracy can be achieved, at extra cost, by using a two-sided approximation. The choice of Δ embodies two considerations: an accurate derivative requires a small Δ, but if there is any inaccuracy in the objective function evaluation $H(C)$ itself then Δ must not become so small that the inaccuracy significantly affects the calculation of ∂.

The Newton method

The Newton (sometimes called Newton–Raphson) method is perhaps the most fundamental of the gradient methods. Many of the other methods are developments of it, or approximations to it, and are often called quasi-Newton methods. The Newton method makes use of the matrix of second derivatives of the objective function with respect to the control variables (the Hessian matrix) for V:

$$V = \left(\frac{\partial^2 H}{\partial C \partial C'} \right)^{-1} \tag{2.44}$$

and $s = 1$. If the function H were quadratic the Newton step procedure would reach the optimum point in one iteration. In essence the algorithm works by making a series of local quadratic approximations of H, solving this problem and then recomputing the approximation.

In order to give some intuitive understanding of the procedure consider the one control variable case where the minimum is given by C^*. A Taylor series expansion of $H(C)$ around the minimum C^* gives

$$H(C) = H(C^*) + (C - C^*)\partial(C^*)$$
$$+ (1/2)(C - C^*)^2\partial^{(2)}(C^*)$$

Differentiating with respect to C and noting that

$H(C^*)$, $\partial^{(2)}(C^*)$ are constants (for a given $C = C^*$) then

$$\partial(C) = \partial(C^*) + (C - C^*)\partial^{(2)}(C^*)$$

Rearranging and noting that at the minimum $\partial(C^*) = 0$, we have

$$C^* = C - [\partial^{(2)}(C)]^{-1}\partial(C) \tag{2.45}$$

If $H(C)$ is quadratic then C could be set at *any* initial value and C^* would be given *exactly* by the RHS of (2.45) (see below). For more general functions the latter does not hold but (2.45) suggests an iterative scheme

$$C_2 = C_1 - [\partial^{(2)}(C_1)]^{-1}\partial(C_1) \tag{2.46}$$

In this single parameter case $V(C) = [\partial^2(C_1)]^{-1}$, the general case is shown in (2.44).

To illustrate some of the above points consider our quadratic example $H(C) = (2C^2 - 4C)$. Analytically the minimum is given by $\partial(C) = 4C - 4 = 0$, and hence $C^* = 1$. How would our iterative scheme handle this problem starting with an arbitrary starting value $C_1 = 2$ and the *analytic* derivatives $\partial = 4C - 4$ and $\partial^{(2)} = 4$ so that $\partial(C_1) = 4$, $\partial^{(2)}(C_1) = 4$, hence

$$C_2 = 2 - (1/4)4 = 1$$

The minimum is achieved in one iteration when $H(C)$ is quadratic and we utilise analytic derivatives. (This is because the curvature $\partial^{(2)}$ is constant for any quadratic.) Consider next a cubic for $H(C)$:

$$H(C) = C^3 - 3C^2 + 7$$

hence

$$\partial(C) = 3C^2 - 6C$$
$$\partial^{(2)}(C) = 6C - 6$$

If we begin with $C_1 = 1.5$, then $\partial = -2.25$, and $\partial^{(2)} = 3$, hence

$$C_2 = (1.5) - (-2.25)/3 = 2.25$$

The next iteration is

$$C_3 = (2.25) - (0.168)/7.5 = 2.02$$

Analytically we know the solution namely $\partial(C) = 0$, which implies $C^* = 2$ so our second iteration is close to the optimum. One problem with the Newton–Raphson method is that it may move *away from* the minimum if $\partial^{(2)}$ is not positive definite. For example if we had chosen $C_1 = 0.5$ then $\partial^{(2)} = -3$ (i.e. negative) and $C_2 = 0.5 - (-2.25)/(1.3) = -0.25$ and we move in the wrong direction. Some techniques modify the basic Newton–Raphson procedure to ensure that the gradient $\partial(C)$ is always multiplied by a positive definite matrix (see below).

Method of steepest descent

At the current point C_i, the direction which will improve the objective function most rapidly is given by the vector of first derivatives, ∂. The method of steepest descent therefore simply sets V equal to the identity matrix (or minus the identity matrix if the problem is being maximised). The important choice therefore becomes the determination of the step size. In this case some variant of the Armijo (1966) step procedure is generally used. This works as follows: a succession of steps is generated using

$$s_i = \lambda B^i i \qquad = 0, \ldots$$

where λ is some given maximum step size and B is a constant $0 < B < 1$. Some form of grid search may then be used over these step sizes to check for the best step size at each iteration.

The method of steepest descent avoids the costly computation of the Hessian matrix but its disadvantage is that convergence can often be slow and there are well-known examples where the algorithm will not reach a maximum.

Method of quadratic hill climbing

The method of quadratic hill climbing (Goldfeld *et al.* 1966) is a slight extension of the standard Newton algorithm to include a variable step size and to ensure a positive definite matrix. The iterative scheme is $C_2 = C_1 - sQ\partial$ where $Q = (V + uI)^{-1}$, with u a positive scalar. This may improve the performance of the algorithm when the function is non-concave or is not close to quadratic.

Quasi-Newton methods

In order to calculate the Hessian matrix required by the Newton method, either an expensive numerical procedure must be repeated at each iteration or the analytical second derivatives must be calculated and supplied by the user. The quasi-Newton methods are a family of algorithms which avoid this necessity by calculating an *approximation* to the Hessian matrix and continually update it and hence improve on the approximation (to the true matrix of second derivatives).

From (2.42) we can see that for iteration $i + 1$, the inverse of the second derivative matrix at iteration i was

$$\left(\frac{\partial^2 H}{\partial C \partial C'} \right)_i^{-1} = (C_{i+1} - C_i)(\partial_{i+1} - \partial_i) \tag{2.47}$$

so by comparing the parameter estimates (C_{i+1}, C_i) and the derivatives $(\partial_{i+1}, \partial_i)$ at two *succeeding iterations* we can estimate the Hessian at the last iteration. This may be compared with the estimate at iteration i, namely, E_i and then some correction based on the error can be made so that

$$E_{i+1} = E_i + f\left(E_i, \frac{\partial^2 H}{\partial C \partial C'} \right) \tag{2.48}$$

where 'f' is a function of the Hessian evaluated at iteration i, the precise form of the correction determines the form of the quasi-Newton algorithm under consideration. One of the most common algorithms in this class is the Davidson–Fletcher–Powell method. Himmelblau (1972) presents a number of correction formulae.

Scoring

It is sometimes easier to obtain a numerical approximation to the *expectation* of the matrix of second derivatives, that is the *information* matrix, $I(C)$

$$I(C) = -E[\partial^2 H / \partial C \partial C']$$

The iterative scheme is then

$$C_{i+1} = C_i + [I(C)]^{-1} \partial(C)$$

and the procedure is known as the *method of scoring*. It is likely to have a slower rate of convergence than Newton–Raphson since $I(C)$ is only an approximation to the Hessian. However, the information matrix is easier to compute and will be estimated more quickly. A variable step length is also often incorporated. If the model is identified then $I(C)$ is always positive definite.

Derivative-free techniques

Generally speaking, optimisation techniques which employ derivatives are fast and reliable when the function being maximised is well behaved. However the derivative-free techniques are recommended for highly non-linear functions or functions which are subject to discontinuities. In principle the reason for this is simple to understand: the gradient-based techniques work by examining the first and second derivatives at a single point and drawing an inference about the whole surface based on some simple regularity conditions. When a function is either discontinuous or highly non-linear the information given at a single point can be very misleading. (Consider trying to find the direction of Everest, based on the slope of a minor peak in the foot-hills of the Himalayas.) The derivative-free techniques generally derive their 'working information' by examining a larger area around a current point on a surface and so they are less likely to draw very fragile inferences about the shape of the surface being climbed. (Derivative-free techniques maybe likened to having a powerful pair of binoculars at the top of a local peak from which one can see Everest in the distance, although, of course, there is no guarantee of this.)

The two widely used algorithms in this class are the conjugate gradient method of Powell (1964) and the non-linear Simplex method suggested by Spendley, Hext and Himsworth (1962). The Powell technique works essentially by carrying out a set of linear searches in orthogonal pairs and deriving a direction of movement from this information. The Simplex technique constructs a simplex around some initial point and evaluates the objective function at the vertices of the simplex. A simplex is the simplest shape which has positive area in any given dimension; in the two-dimensional plane it is simply a triangle. The algorithm works by starting from an arbitrary simplex in the hill-climbing space and examining the value of the objective function at each corner; it then drops the least desirable corner and calculates a point which is a weighted average of the other corners. A line search is then conducted from the least desirable corner in the direction of the weighted point. The best point along this line then forms one of the corners of a new simplex which is completed by using the corners of the old simplex with the exception of the worst one which has already been dropped. The algorithm then repeats itself, thus moving the simplex around the n-dimensional space until the maximum is bracketed within the simplex and then collapsing the simplex around the maximum until all the corners lie arbitrarily close to the optimal point.

Inequality-constrained optimisation

In many cases we may wish to maximise an objective function $H(C)$ while obeying a set of inequality constraints (for example, that the probability of default in a loan is always greater than zero). This complicates the maximisation algorithm substantially. There are basically two approaches to dealing with this problem: the first involves adapting the objective function so as to penalise any violations of the constraint; the second adapts the optimisation algorithm.

When we adapt the objective function the technique is generally known as a barrier method. The idea is to define a barrier function which heavily penalises violation of the constraint but has a near-zero effect when the constraint is satisfied. If we have the following set of inequality constraints

$$G(C) \geq 0 \tag{2.49}$$

we create a set of barrier functions such as

$$B[G(C)] \tag{2.50}$$

Where $B[G(C)]$ is near zero for $G(C) \geq 0$ and is large for $B[G(C)] < 0$, a typical function for iteration i, might be

$$B_i[G(C)] = -\gamma \ln [G_i(C)]$$

where γ is a suitably chosen weighting factor. Since as $G(C) \to 0$ the log approaches minus infinity, this severely penalises moving $G_i(C)$ towards zero.

Disadvantages of this technique are: (a) a good barrier function should be highly non-linear and therefore makes the optimisation more difficult; (b) if the unconstrained optimum were near or on the constraint the barrier function will tend to distort the final solution. If a barrier function is to be used it is often advisable to experiment by sequentially dropping some or all of the constraints, to check which individual constraints do not hold in the unconstrained optimisation.

The second main approach to inequality constraints is to adapt the direction finding procedure so that the algorithm does not move in directions which violate the inequality constraints. This amounts to deriving a value '$V(C)\partial(C)$' in (2.42a) in such a way that it will not cause steps out of the feasible region. Algorithms which implement such procedures are collectively termed methods of feasible direction and a detailed survey of these techniques may be found in Polak (1972). A typical procedure would be to derive the gradient vector and then calculate the derivatives of any close inequality constraints. A linear-programming problem may then be formed which maximises the change in the objective function, given from the gradient vector, subject to non-violations of the constraints.

2.3   Special forms of likelihood functions

Qualitative response models

The basic idea which lies behind the qualitative response (QR) model (sometimes referred to as limited dependent variable model) is that there are times when we either have only partial information on a variable or the information is not continuous. For example in Tobin (1958), a model of the demand for cars is constructed using disaggregated data. The basic idea is that expenditure on cars is related to an individual's income. The problem is that some individuals choose not to buy cars at all, and so individuals are divided into two groups, G_1, those who had bought a car and G_2, those who did not. Hence we have only partial information. If we simply remove the group G_2 from the sample we would get a biased estimate of the income elasticity. Consider the second case where we have a non-continuous variable, in the simplest case 1 or 0 say. For example, we might know when an incomes policy is on '1' or off '0' but we have no continuous measure of the strength of the policy. Finally, a classic example from the field of biology is the testing of the effect of poison on insects. The hypothesis is that more poison increases the probability of death, but the observations on the individual insect come in the form of survivors '0' or deaths '1'.

The general approach to this class of problem is to assume a linear regression model:

$$Y_t = \beta X_t + u_t$$

We observe Y_t only if $Y_t > 0$, so that the model becomes

$$Y_t = \beta X_t + u_t \qquad \text{if } \beta X_t + u_t > 0$$

$$Y_t = 0 \qquad \text{otherwise}$$

If we attempt to estimate this equation by OLS using only the G_1 observations when $Y_t > 0$ then the resulting estimates would be biased and inconsistent since we cannot assert that the $E(u_t) = 0$ for all t. The approach in the QR model is to define the likelihood function for the model on the assumption that the error term follows a particular distribution. The assumption made by Tobin (1958) was that u_t has a normal distribution with zero mean and variance σ^2, this gives rise to the Tobit (or Tobin's probit) model. We may then write the likelihood function L for the model as

$$
L = \prod_{Y \varepsilon G_1} \left\{ \frac{1}{\sigma(2\pi)^{1/2}} \exp\left[-\frac{1}{2\sigma^2} (Y_t - \beta X_t)^2 \right] \right\}
$$

$$
\times \prod_{Y \varepsilon G_2} \left\{ \int_{-\infty}^{0} \frac{1}{\sigma(2\pi)^{1/2}} \exp\left[-\frac{1}{2\sigma^2} (Y_t - \beta X_t)^2 \right] dy \right\}
$$

(2.51)

This may be maximised to give estimates of σ and β using the numerical techniques discussed earlier in this chapter.

Variations on the QR model generally involve alternative assumptions about the distribution of the error term. We can therefore present a compact form of the likelihood function by defining $f(.)$ to be a given density function and $F(.)$ to be the cumulative density function. Using this notation we may restate the likelihood function as

$$
L = \prod_{Y \varepsilon G_1} \left[\frac{1}{\sigma} f[(Y_t - \beta X_t)/\sigma] \right] \prod_{Y \varepsilon G_2} [F(-\beta X_t/\sigma)] \qquad (2.52)
$$

An important alternative QR model arises when $F(.)$ is defined as the logistic function

$$
F(w) = \frac{e^w}{1 + e^w}
$$

This model is then known as a *logit model*. Its main advantage over the Tobit model is the ease of numerical calculation, as the logistic function is much easier to calculate than the cumulative normal function. (Amemiya, 1981 discusses the relative merits of the two functions at some length.)

In the case where we have only discrete observations on the dependent variable, then the likelihood function is a simplification of the general QR model. For example, suppose $Y = 1$ when a government is operating an incomes policy and $Y = 0$ if the policy is inoperative. If G_1 is the group when $Y = 0$ then the likelihood function involves only the cumulative density function of the following form:

$$
L = \prod_{Y \varepsilon G_1} F(-\beta X_t) \prod_{Y \varepsilon G_2} [1 - F(-\beta X_t)] \qquad (2.53)
$$

The likelihood function would then represent a Probit model, when $F(.)$ is the cumulative normal (density) function and a logit model when it is in the logistic function.

Discrete switching disequilibrium models

A model closely related to the qualitative responses QR model is the discrete switching disequilibrium model. The link between them lies in the form of the likelihood function. Both the QR and disequilibrium model contain terms in the cumulative density function of the error terms of the model. The disequilibrium model contains equations for the 'notional' or 'desired' demand Y^d and supply Y^s of the good Y. These typically have the form

$$Y_t^d = \alpha_1 P_t + \beta_1' X_t + u_{1t} \tag{2.54}$$

$$Y_t^s = \alpha_2 P_t + \beta_2' X_t + u_{2t} \tag{2.55}$$

where P_t is the real price of the good, X_t is a vector of exogenous variables, β_1, β_2 are vectors of parameters and u_{1t} and u_{2t} are normally distributed error processes. Equations (2.54) and (2.55) are standard to any single market model. The distinguishing feature of the disequilibrium model is given by the method of determining Q_t the *actual* quantity of the good Y_t which is to be traded in each time period. The standard equilibrium model makes the assumption that $Q_t = Y_t^D = Y_t^S$ that is, the actual quantity Q_t is given by the intersection of demand and supply. Other assumptions which are sometimes made are, $Q_t = Y_t^d$, that is demand side dominance only, or $Q_t = Y_t^S$, supply side dominance only. The assumption made in disequilibrium models is $Q = \min(Y^d, Y^s)$, that is the *traded quantity* is determined by the smaller of the notional demand or supply.

The justification for this approach is based on the idea of voluntary exchange. A notional demand or supply curve may be thought of as defining the maximum amount of a good which will be exchanged voluntarily at any given price. If someone is offered a smaller quantity than he demands at a given price, he will generally accept this trade as profitable, but an individual will not generally purchase a larger quantity than indicated by his demand curve.

In order to close the disequilibrium model it is necessary to make some assumption about the determination of prices. The typical assumption is:

$$P_t = P_{t-1} + \gamma(Y_t^d - Y_t^s) + u_{3t}, \qquad \gamma > 0 \tag{2.56}$$

If demand is greater than supply, the real price will rise and vice-versa. Equations (2.54)–(2.56) then constitute a full statement of the single market disequilibrium (SMDM) model. Over time, the real price will tend to adjust to the market clearing price and the speed at which it does this is governed by γ. If γ becomes very large the disequilibrium model will closely approximate the equilibrium model. Alternatively, if γ is small the disequilibrium will persist for a considerable time. One of the advantages of using an empirical model based on (2.54)–(2.56) is that the estimate of γ will give us an indication of how closely the model approximates a market clearing model.

An early attempt to estimate a model of this type is due to Fair and Jaffee (1972). However, their work is not based on the maximum likelihood approach but makes the simplifying assumption that $u_{3t} = 0$ and utilises instrumental variable estimation of the model. The likelihood function for SMDM was developed by Maddala and Nelson (1974).

The derivation of the likelihood function begins by defining:

$$g(Y_t^D, Y_t^S) \tag{2.57}$$

as the joint probability density function of the unobserved random variables (Y_t^d, Y_t^s) and $h(Q_t)$ as the probability density function of Q_t, the *traded* quantity. We can then relate

$$h(Q_t) \text{ to } g(Y_t^D, Y_t^S) \tag{2.58}$$

in the following way:

$$
\begin{aligned}
h(Q_t) = &\ f(Q|Y_t^D < Y_t^S)\Pr(Y_t^D < Y_t^S) \\
&+ f(Q_t|Y_t^S \leqslant Y_t^D)\Pr(Y_t^S \leqslant Y_t^D)
\end{aligned} \tag{2.59}
$$

That is to say, the PDF of Q_t is given by (a) the conditional PDF of Q_t when Q is demand constrained, multiplied by the probability of being demand constrained *plus* (b) the PDF of Q_t when Q_t is supply constrained, multiplied by the probability of being supply constrained. Now:

$$
f(Q_t|Y_t^D < Y_t^S) = \int_{Q_t}^{\infty} g(Q_t, Y_t^S|Y_t^D < Y_t^S)\,\mathrm{d}Y_t^S
$$

$$
= [1/\Pr(Y_t^D < Y_t^S)] \int_{Q_t}^{\infty} g(Q_t, Y_t^S)\,\mathrm{d}Y_t^S \tag{2.60}
$$

and similarly $f(Q_t|Y_t^S \leqslant Y_t^D)$ may be expressed as

$$
[1/\Pr(Y_t^S \leqslant Y_t^D)] \int_{Q_t}^{\infty} g(Y_t^D, Q_t)\,\mathrm{d}Y_t^D
$$

The PDF of Q_t may therefore be written as

$$h(Q_t) = \int_{Q_t}^{\infty} g(Q_t, Y_t^s)\, dY_t^s + \int_{Q_t}^{\infty} g(Y_t^d, Q_t)\, dY_t^d \qquad (2.61)$$

the likelihood function may then be specified as

$$L = \prod_t h(Q_t) \qquad (2.62)$$

'L' is a function of all the parameters of the system and the covariance matrix of the errors, u_{1t}, u_{2t} and u_{3t}.

ARCH and GARCH likelihood functions

Our general statement of the likelihood function of the non-linear model (2.7) assumed that the error terms had a constant covariance structure Θ. In fact it is not obvious that the covariance matrix will always be constant over time and it is easy to further generalise (2.7) to take account of this. If the covariance matrix is known over time, that is Θ_t is a known series, then Θ_t may simply be entered into (2.7). If Θ_t is assumed to vary over time but its value is unknown then the problem is more complex and we cannot simply estimate all the elements of Θ_t as there can never be sufficient degrees of freedom to allow this.

One approach to estimating Θ_t lies in a suggestion made by Engle (1982) to model the expected (or conditional) covariance matrix as a function of observed past squared errors, this model is termed the autoregressive conditional heteroskedasticity (ARCH) model. The basic assumption is that H_t is a conditional expectation of Θ_t based on past information, thus

$$H_t = E(\Theta_t : \Omega_{t-1}) \qquad (2.63)$$

where Ω_{t-1} is the relevant known information set. The specific assumption of the ARCH model is that

$$\text{Vech}(H_t) = \gamma_0 + \sum_{i=1}^{N} \gamma_i \, \text{Vech}(e_{t-i} e_{t-i}') \qquad (2.64)$$

where $\text{Vech}(H)$ denotes column-stacking the lower triangular elements of a symmetric matrix H and γ_0 and γ_1 are suitably dimensioned vectors of parameters. A scalar version of (2.64) is simply $h_t = \alpha_0 + \sum \alpha_i e_{t-i}^2$; the conditional variance h_t depends on past squared forecast errors. H_t may then be substituted into (2.7) in place of Θ to produce the ARCH likelihood function.

A further extension to the ARCH model is the generalised autoregressive conditional heteroscedasticity model (GARCH) (due to Bollerslev 1986) which basically allows other terms to enter the ARCH equation beyond simply the lagged errors. One particularly useful form of GARCH model is when the lagged conditional expectation of the covariance term enters the equation. In this case

$$\text{Vech}\,(H_t) = \gamma_0 + \sum_{i=1}^{P} \gamma_{1i}\,\text{Vech}\,(H_{t-i}) + \sum_{j=1}^{N} \gamma_{2j}\,\text{Vech}\,(e_{t-j}e'_{t-j})$$

(2.65)

In its general form this would be termed a GARCH(N, P) model, denoting the number of lags in H and ee' which feature in the model. Once again H_t can simply be substituted into (2.7) to produce the GARCH likelihood function. A simple scalar version of the above is e_{t-1}^2, which would be a GARCH(1, 1) model.

A final further elaboration of this type of model is due to Engle, Lilien and Robins (1987) who point out that many theoretical models, especially in finance theory, include terms in 'risk' which can be modelled by including conditional elements of the covariance matrix into the specification of the model. Thus (2.6), the structural equations of the model may include any elements of H_t as 'risk' terms: $y_t = f(x, \beta) + \delta H_t + e_t$. When this is done the models are then generally termed ARCH-in-mean (ARCH-M) or GARCH-in-mean (GARCH-M) models.

2.4 Empirical applications using maximum likelihood

A discrete switching disequilibrium model of the market for building society loans

In this section we present an example of maximum likelihood estimation of a disequilibrium model for mortgage lending from building societies (taken from Hall and Urwin 1989). The model involves formulating equations for the demand and supply for mortgage lending and the determination of mortgage interest rates. The model is estimated on the assumption that the short side of the market dominates and uses the discrete switching model discussed above.

The demand for mortgages

The demand for mortgages may be derived from a fairly simple utility maximisation problem. Suppose a representative household has a utility function $U(H, G)$ where H is housing services and G is an aggregate of other goods (in real terms). The household maximises this function subject to a total limit on disposable income of the form:

$$g(r^m, P^H)H + GP = DY \tag{2.66}$$

Where $g(r^m, P^H)$ is a cost function of servicing a mortgage which will provide housing services H. The cost function depends on r^m the rate of interest on mortgages and P^H the price of houses. DY is (nominal) disposable income and P is the general price level (of goods). Maximising $U(H, G)$ subject to (2.66) yields a demand function of the form:

$$H = f(r^m, P^H, DY, P) \tag{2.67}$$

Hall and Urwin then relate the demand for mortgages (M^D) to this basic function by introducing the number of owner-occupied houses (NOH). They then invoke adjustment costs to introduce lagged actual mortgage borrowing and a term for the effects of banks moving into the mortgage market (ZBL). This then gives the general demand function:

$$\begin{aligned}
\log(M^D/P) = {} & A_0 + A_1 \log(r^m) + A_2 \log(P^H/P) \\
& + A_3 \log(NOH) + A_4 \log(DY/P) \\
& + A_5 \log(P) + A_6 \Delta \log(P) \\
& + A_7 \log(ZBL) + A_8 \log(M/P)_{t-1}
\end{aligned} \tag{2.68}$$

where $A_1, A_7 < 0$; $A_2, A_4, A_8 > 0$

The supply of mortgage lending The supply of mortgages depends on two main factors. First, the supply of building society shares and deposits (primarily) from the personal sector and second the action of the building society when it carries out its role as an intermediary between depositors and lenders.

The supply of deposits is given by a fairly simple application of portfolio theory. The supply of deposits to building societies is given by the demand function of the personal sector for building society deposits. Deposits will therefore vary with income and relative returns between building society deposits and other assets (r^D/r^1).

They then introduce terms in the loan to value ratio of first time buyers (LV) and the loan to income rate of first time buyers (LY) as proxies for the willingness of societies to lend. To capture changes in the supply of mortgages they introduce a term for building societies borrowing in the wholesale money markets (ZWB). Lags are introduced to model adjustment costs giving the supply equation:

$$\log(M^S/P) = B_0 + B_1 \log(r_D/r^1) + B_2 \log(DY/P)$$
$$+ B_3 \Delta \log(P) + B_4 \log(LV) + B_5 \log(LY)$$
$$+ B_6 \log(ZWB) + B_7 \log(M/P)_{t-1} \qquad (2.69)$$

where $B_1, B_2, B_5, B_6, B_7 > 0$

The interest rate adjustment equation   Finally, in order close the model we need an interest-rate adjustment equation. We assume the change in $\log(r_D/r^1)$ is a function of excess demand or supply to which is added a set of other relevant interest rates. This part of the model is really of only minor interest. A simple '*ad hoc*' equation involves the change in the long-term consol rate $(20YC)$, the change in the treasury bill yield (r^1) and a lagged dependent variable:

$$\Delta \log(r^D/r^1) = C_0 + C_1 \Delta \log(20YC) + C_2 \Delta \log(r^1)$$
$$+ C_3 \Delta \log(r^D/r^1)_{t-1} + C_4 \log(M^D/M^S)$$

$$(2.70)$$

Estimation of the model

The likelihood function for the discrete switching disequilibrium model is an extremely complex one. It is not available as part of any of the standard econometric computer programs and it is sufficiently ill-conditioned to present serious problems for any of the standard numerical maximisation procedures. Numerical optimisation is therefore achieved by the combined use of a non-linear simplex algorithm and a conventional quasi-Newton algorithm using analytical first derivatives. The non-linear simplex algorithm is used first as it is relatively robust to the presence of local maxima and discontinuities; its final convergence on the maximum point is, however, slow. When we are close to the maximum the quasi-Newton algorithm takes over the optimisation problem from the simplex procedure and it then efficiently pinpoints the true maximum. Verifying that a true maximum has actually been located is of course difficult. One check is to use a graphical search around the final solution, resulting in a set of line searches across the likelihood space, and these may be used to detect a failure to find a true maximum.

We outlined above the general form of the model to be estimated, but there is of course scope within this general framework for a wide range of dynamic specifications. In a 'general-to-specific' modelling exercise we start from a general model and 'test down' on the dynamics until a parsimonious form of the model is achieved. This is not a practical procedure for this type of system estimation as the general form would involve far too many parameters for successful optimisation. Even in the final form to be reported here the model involved maximising the likelihood function with respect to 26 parameters. The estimation procedure is therefore less systematic than one might like. It is also worth pointing out that the standard battery of diagnostic test procedures on the error process are not applicable to this model. The reason for this is that the observed error, $Q - \hat{Q}$ (where Q is the traded quantity of mortgages), cannot be uniquely associated with any of the structural error terms in the model. The observed error will be a combination of the errors on the notional supply and demand curves and as such it provides no formal evidence about the properties of the structural errors. We do not make the assumption that $Q - \hat{Q}$ is white noise and uncorrelated and so there is no point in testing this assumption. Residual tests may however be constructed in a number of complex ways, see Hall, Henry and Pemberton (1991).

Maximising the log likelihood then produces the results detailed in Table 2.1 which gives the parameter estimates of the preferred model

Table 2.1 Parameter estimates for the model (Asymptotic t statistics in parenthesis)

	Model 1		Model 2		Model 3	
A_0	−6.86	(5.1)	−6.92	(5.8)	−1.13	(5.5)
A_1	−0.045	(8.1)	−0.046	(8.8)	−0.08	(8.3)
A_2	0.03	(2.4)	0.03	(2.9)	0.005	(0.34)
A_3	0.75	(5.2)	0.78	(6.1)	−	
A_4	0.06	(1.8)	0.04	(1.7)	0.11	(3.4)
A_5	−0.12	(5.2)	−0.12	(6.0)	0.005	(0.6)
A_6	−0.79	(8.1)	−0.82	(10.6)	−0.73	(5.6)
A_7	−0.087	(3.7)	−0.09	(3.9)	−0.07	(1.6)
A_8	0.94	(23.1)	0.95	(27.7)	1.01	(85.9)
B_0	−1.03	(4.0)	−1.08	(5.2)	−0.99	(5.1)
B_1	0.003	(0.7)	0.002	(0.4)	0.003	(1.2)
B_2	1.10	(3.9)	0.13	(4.4)	0.11	(2.0)
B_3	−1.1	(16.7)	−1.1	(18.6)	−1.1	(2.0)
B_4	0.11	(3.6)	0.10	(4.2)	0.09	(1.9)
B_5	0.06	(3.2)	0.06	(3.5)	0.06	(2.9)
B_6	0.38	(2.3)	0.54	(2.2)	0.82	(1.9)
B_7	0.91	(44.1)	0.88	(35.0)	0.91	(16.9)
C_0	0.007	(0.9)	0.007	(0.8)	0.007	(0.9)
C_1	0.35	(2.2)	0.42	(3.0)	0.36	(2.2)
C_2	−0.95	(14.3)	−0.97	(15.4)	−0.955	(15.1)
C_3	−0.13	(2.1)	−0.06	(1.11)	−0.13	(2.2)
C_4	0.0004	(0.00002)	0.00004	(0.0)	0.00003	(0.0)
$\sigma(Q - \hat{Q})$	0.0031		0.0026		0.0034	
Likelihood	510.006		462.03		505.04	
Data period	6902–8601		6902–8401		6902–8601	

(model 1). This model estimated excluding the last eight data points which are then used the test structural stability (model 2). In model 3 we combine the terms in the stock of housing and the price of housing and use the *value* of owner-occupied housing. The term $\sigma(Q - \hat{Q})$ is the standard error of the observed forecast of the model which may be compared with the standard error of the Anderson and Hendry (1984) model of 0.0029 and the Wilcox (1985) model of 0.0029.

The preferred model 1 conforms with our prior views about the signs of the parameters. It produces a model which tracks the data reasonably well even in comparison with conventional OLS models. This is indicated by the standard deviation of the observed error which is of a size similar to that found in other studies of mortgage lending (although the data periods are quite different). The tendency of the models to move towards equilibrium is measured by the size of C_4, ($C_4 = 0$ implies equilibrium is never reached, $C_4 = \infty$ implies continuous market clearing) this parameter estimate suggests that there is only very slow adjustment and that for practical purposes disequilibrium may persist indefinitely. This conforms well with the conventional view of building society prior to 1986. Nevertheless the market for mortgages is not characterised by a very large degree of disequilibrium. Figure 2.2 shows the model's forecast for the stock of

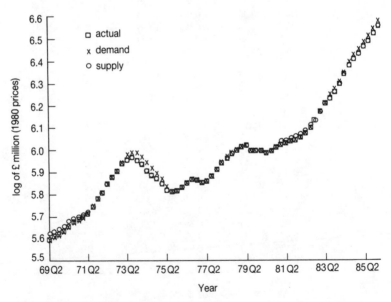

Figure 2.2 Demand and supply of mortgages.

mortgage demand and supply in contrast with the actual level of lending. It is quite clear from this figure that, by and large, the building societies are able to equate the demand and supply of mortgages fairly effectively.

However, this is not to suggest that disequilibrium is insignificant in this market. Figure 2.3 shows the deterministic model estimates of excess demand over the period 1969 Q2–1986 Q1. The degree of disequilibrium peaks in 1974 at around 4% of the mortgage stock. This represents a sizeable constraint on households borrowing. For example, in 1985 this would have implied a constraint in excess of £1,000 million. The overall pattern of excess demand corresponds remarkably closely with that estimated by Wilcox, although this model does not detect such strong excess demand in the period 1979–80. Unfortunately there is no time series available for the size and duration of mortgage queuing to compare with Figure 2.3.

Figure 2.3 also suggests that the incursions into the mortgage market of non-building society lenders, particularly the banks, have had a very significant impact on either the degree of excess supply or demand. The three periods (the start of the 1970s, 1981–3 and 1986–7) in which the banks' market share rose very rapidly are estimated to have been those in which the extent of rationing fell substantially, or even that conditions of excess supply prevailed. The

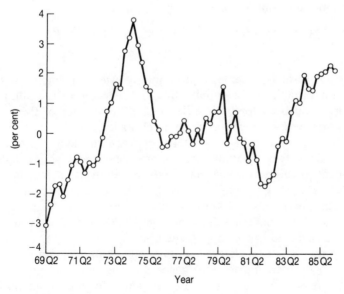

Figure 2.3 Excess demand for mortgages.

fact that lenders did not attempt to reduce their lending standards in order to eliminate excess supply suggests that competitive forces have had a relatively weak impact on such standards and that lenders have attempted to retain the appropriate prudential criteria. It is perhaps surprising that the degree of rationing is estimated to have been greater in 1984–5 than in the second half of the 1970s, as in the later period building societies were thought to have adopted a more flexible interest-rate policy. While this finding may not be consistent with general perceptions of the way of the mortgage market operated at that time, the results do indicate that over the period as a whole, societies' propensity to use interest rates to equilibriate the demand for and supply of mortgage was greater when competitive pressures were more intense.

The long-run properties of the demand and supply equations are fairly sensible. The long-run solution to the demand equation is:

$$\log(M^D/P) = -0.75 \log(r^m) + 0.5 \log(P^H/P)$$
$$+ 12.5 \log(NOH) + 1.0 \log(DY/P)$$
$$- 2.0 \log(P) - 1.4 \log(ZBL)$$

These parameter estimates are all quite reasonable with the possible exception of the elasticity on the number in owner-occupied housing, *NOH*, which will be discussed further below.

The long-run solution for the supply equation is:

$$\log(M^S/P) = 0.03 \log(r^D/r^1) + 1.11 \log(DY/P)$$
$$+ 1.2 \log(LV) + 4.2 \log(ZWB)$$

Rather surprisingly, the level of liquidity was not found to be a significant variable in the supply equation. Because of the non-linear transformation used for both *ZBL* and *ZWB* neither of these coefficients may be interpreted as a simple elasticity.

There is an interesting asymmetry between the long-run effect of prices in these two equations. Real mortgage *demand* shows a strong permanent price effect while the *supply* equation has a zero long-run response. This may be explained in terms of the fact that all existing mortgages are reduced, in real terms, by a rise in the price level leading to a permanent fall in mortgage demand. No such effect would be expected in the supply equation.

The only unrealistic elasticity is the effect of the number of houses, *NOH*, on the demand for mortgages. A long-run elasticity of 12 is clearly unreasonable. It would be quite plausible to have an elasticity greater than one and we would certainly expect the elasticity on the number of houses to be larger than that on house prices, as almost all houses which are additions to the owner-occupied stock have associated mortgages. None the less, a long-run figure of 12 is clearly implausible. There would seem to be two possible explanations. First, we may have failed to pick up the full dynamic effect and so we may have a plausible short-run effect from housing but a very poorly defined long-run. Second, there may be a trend factor in mortgage demand which we have failed to model but which is highly collinear with the housing stock. In this case, part of our long-run effect on *NOH*, may be due in part to this unidentified component.

In an attempt to investigate these possibilities we performed a number of experiments. First, lags in the housing stock were introduced to allow for the possibility of more complex dynamics. This did not change the long-run elasticity on *NOH*, to any great extent. However, it is possible that more complex dynamics are required but our data, which span less that 20 years, are simply not long enough to analyse a market where the average term to maturity of loans is about 7 years. Second, model 3 in Table 2.1 considers the effect of restricting the housing terms to be the *value* of the owner-occupied housing stock. This restriction when applied to the model has a number of undesirable features. In particular, the demand equation is dynamically unstable and so the long-run solution is no longer defined. We therefore conclude that this real-world application of the smdm has yielded useful insights but clearly specification problems still remain.

Measuring the risk premium in the forward exchange rate market

A simple ARCH-M example

Under the assumptions that economic agents are risk neutral, there are no transaction costs, expectations are formed rationally and the market is efficient, the forward exchange rate should be an unbiased predictor for the future spot rate. There is now considerable empirical evidence which rejects this proposition however; for example, Hansen and Hodrick (1980), Hakkio (1981) and Taylor (1987). As the assumption of zero transaction costs seems reasonable in this case, we might question either rationality or market efficiency. However in neither case do we have a readily acceptable alternative and clearly another extreme assumption is that agents are risk neutral. Much recent work has concentrated on a search for the 'risk premium' such as Frankel (1982), Domowitz and Hakkio (1985), Fama (1984),

Hodrick and Srivastava (1984), Nelson (1985), and Taylor (1987). An important element of this research has been the recognition that, in principle, the risk premium will vary over time depending on the degree of uncertainty in the system.

Our example will assume that the existence of a risk premium causes a differential between the forward rate and the expected future spot rate in accordance with a simple ARCH-M model.

If the log of the forward exchange rate i periods ahead is denoted as f_{t+i}, and the log of the spot exchange rate is denoted s_t then the risk premium ρ_t may be defined as

$$\rho_t = f_{t+i} - s^e_{t+i} \tag{2.71}$$

where s^e_{t+i} is the market expectation of the spot exchange rate at period $t + i$, based on information at time $t(\Omega_t)$. Under the rational expectations hypothesis

$$s^e_{t+i} = E(s_{t+i}|\Omega_t) = s_{t+i} + \varepsilon_{t+i} \tag{2.72}$$

where ε_{t+i} is the RE forecast error, hence

$$\rho_t = f_{t+i} - (s_{t+i} + \varepsilon_{t+i}) \tag{2.73}$$

A formal derivation of the risk premium is complex and will not be given here (see Grauer, Litzenberger and Stehlf 1976, or Stockman 1978). The important feature of the derivation which holds irrespective of the specific form of the model, is that the risk premium is determined by the degree of risk aversion of the market agents and the variances and covariances of the assets in the system. It is perhaps reasonable to assume that the degree of agents risk aversion is constant but the idea that *uncertainty* about asset returns and in particular exchange rate movements is constant is rather hard to accept.

As a simple first step towards recognising the importance of the time-varying nature of the risk premium, suppose that ε_{t+i} has zero mean but a time varying conditional variance, so that $\varepsilon_t \sim N(0, h_t)$. Agents form an expectation of the variance, h_t based on available information. A simple assumption is that the risk premium ρ_t is positively related to the conditional variance of the RE forecast errors $\rho_t = A_0 + A_1 h_t$. Using (2.73) we have,

$$(f_{t+i} - s_{t+i}) = A_0 + A_1 h_t + \varepsilon_t \tag{2.74}$$

This is a simple ARCH-M model. To complete the model we need to make h_t an explicit function of the information set, again a simple approach is to assume that the expected variance is a linear function of recent lagged squared errors:

$$h_t = B_0 + B_1\left(\sum C_i \varepsilon_{t-i}^2\right) \tag{2.75}$$

Then, conditional on the initial values of the data, the log likelihood function may be expressed as

$$\log(L) = \sum_{t=1}^{T} (-\log h_t - \varepsilon_t^2/h_t) \tag{2.76}$$

In order to simplify the estimation we assume that the weights C_i, decline linearly over eight months to zero and this leaves four parameters to be estimated: B_0, B_1, A_0, A_1. Note that if $B_0 \neq 0$ and $B_1 = 0$ then the risk premium is not time varying, so this model has the constant risk premium as a special case.

Estimation may be carried out using a numerical maximisation technique as described above, t statistics may be derived for the parameters of the system from the inverse of the Hessian of the likelihood function and standard likelihood ratio tests may be used to test special versions of the model.

Estimation results

The model outlined above was estimated using monthly data from 1973 M2 to 1987 M6 for the sterling-dollar spot rate and three-month forward rate. The parameter estimates are given below

$A_0 = 0.034$ (1.63)

$A_1 = -7.655$ (1.61)

$B_0 = 0.002$ (5.01)

$B_1 = 0.431$ (3.30)

Log likelihood $= -806.22$

$SEE(\varepsilon_t) = 0.059$

Normality test (see Chapter 4)$\chi^2(2) = 0.85$

The coefficient B_1 has a reasonable size and sign and is significantly different from zero, which suggests that there is an important ARCH component to the error process. The coefficients A_0 and A_1 both have sensible magnitudes but are not strictly significant; this suggests that either term may be dropped from the model and hence the risk premium may not be time varying. On balance there is *weak* evidence in favour of a time-varying risk premium (i.e. $A_1 \neq 0$) and clearly there is an ARCH process in the error term ($B_1 \neq 0$). This suggests that a more complex relationship determining the conditional variance is required, perhaps of the form

$$h_t = B_0 + B_1 h_{t-1} + B_2 \varepsilon_{t-1}^2 + B_3 Z_t \tag{2.77}$$

This GARCH(1, 1) process allows 'shocks' ε_{t-1} to have an impact on the conditional variance h_t in all future periods (but with declining weights). Z_t consists of other information which might influence the conditional variance (such as domestic and foreign interest rates or current account factors).

Although ARCH and GARCH type models have proved useful in modelling time-varying risk premia in financial markets (e.g. Chou 1988, or Hall *et al*. 1989), nevertheless the exact formulation of the ARCH equation (2.77) is often not well based in a formal framework where agents optimise some explicit objective function.

2.5 Summary

We have explained the basis of maximum likelihood estimation and discussed testing using the likelihood ratio test, the Wald test and the LM test. We have outlined several numerical optimisation techniques and demonstrated how certain 'non-standard' models may be examined in the maximum likelihood framework.

3
Time series modelling

In Chapter 1 we discussed briefly the relationship between the purely statistical approach to time series modelling and an approach which may be more appropriately thought of as economic modelling. In this chapter we discuss the purely statistical approach to time series modelling in more detail. Time series modelling is, of course, a discipline in its own right but our interest is more in the use which has been made of time series techniques in other branches of econometrics. So basic time series representations of data are often useful in modelling expectations (see Chapter 6); the cointegration analysis of Chapter 5 also grew out of this approach.

While good applied econometrics is much more than time series analysis the techniques of time series analysis are now widely seen to be a basic building block of econometrics.

3.1　Autoregressive time series models

Perhaps the simplest, purely statistical time series model is the first-order autoregression, or AR(1) process:

$$x_t = \rho x_{t-1} + \xi_t \tag{3.1}$$

where $|\rho| < 1$ and ξ_t is a white noise error process. Equation (3.1) states that the time series behaviour of x_t can be approximated by assuming that it is determined largely by its own value in the preceding period.

More generally, an nth order autoregressive process, or AR(n) can be written as

83

$$x_t = \rho_1 x_{t-1} + \rho_2 x_{t-2} t \ldots + \rho_n x_{t-n} + \xi_t \tag{3.2}$$

So that n lags of x are deemed to be important in determining the time series behaviour of x_t.

The concept of stationarity was introduced in Chapter 1. In (3.1) we imposed the condition $|\rho| < 1$ specifically in order to guarantee stationarity of the AR(1) process. If we had $|\rho| > 1$, then x would tend to get bigger and bigger each period, in absolute value, and so would be an explosive series. We can write the AR(n) process (3.2) using the lag operator as

$$x_t(1 - \rho_1 L - \rho_2 L^2 \ldots - \rho_n L^n) = \xi_t$$

or

$$\Phi(L)x_t = \xi_t \tag{3.3}$$

The stationarity of an AR(n) process is guaranteed only if the n roots of the polynomial equation

$$\Phi(z) = 0 \tag{3.4}$$

(where z is a real variable) are greater than one in absolute value. For the AR(1) equation (3.1), this condition reduces to the roots of

$$(1 - \rho z) = 0$$

being greater than one in absolute value. If this is so, and if the first root is λ, then the condition is

$$|\lambda| = |1/\rho| > 1$$

which is the same as

$$|\rho| < 1.$$

A necessary, but not sufficient requirement for an AR(n) process to be stationary is that the sum of the n autoregressive coefficients should sum to less than unity:

$$\sum_{i=1}^{n} \rho_i < 1 \tag{3.5}$$

3.2   Moving average time series models

A second kind of pure time series model which is frequently applied is one where the stochastic process under consideration is postulated to be a moving average of current and lagged values of a white noise process. For example, a first-order moving average, MA(1), model would be written:

$$x_t = \xi_t + \theta\xi_{t-1} \tag{3.6}$$

where ξ is a white noise process. More generally, an MA(n) process would be written

$$x_t = (1 + \theta_1 L + \theta_2 L^2 + \ldots \theta_n L^n)\xi_t \tag{3.7}$$

or

$$x_t = \Theta(L)\xi_t \tag{3.8}$$

Because any MA(n) process is, by definition, an average of n stationary white noise terms, it follows that every moving average is stationary.

A property which is often discussed in relation to moving average processes is *invertibility*. Consider the MA(1) process (3.6), rewritten using the lag operator:

$$x_t = (1 + \theta L)\xi_t$$

Equivalently

$$x_t/(1 + \theta L) = \xi_t \tag{3.9}$$

if $|\theta| < 1$, then the left-hand side of (3.9) can be considered as the sum of an infinite geometric progression:

$$x_t(1 - \theta L + \theta^2 L^2 - \theta^3 L^3 + \ldots) = \xi_t \tag{3.10}$$

Alternatively, (3.9) could be derived by substituting repeatedly for lagged values of ξ_t in (3.6). Thus, the MA(1) process has been inverted into a high-order autoregressive process with geometrically declining weights. For the MA(1) model to be invertible, we require $|\theta| < 1$.

In general, the MA(n) process (3.7) is invertible if the roots of the polynomial

$$\Theta(z) = 0 \tag{3.11}$$

are greater than one in absolute value.

It is often useful to consider, at least in theory, infinite-order moving average representations. Such a process would take the form:

$$x_t = \sum_{i=0}^{\infty} \theta_i \xi_{t-i} \tag{3.12}$$

If ξ is a white noise process with constant variance σ_ξ^2, then the variance of x_t is given by

$$x_t = \sigma_\xi^2 \sum_{i=1}^{\infty} \theta_i^2 \tag{3.13}$$

Clearly, although all finite-order moving average processes are stationary, in the infinite-order case it is necessary to place some restrictions on the moving average parameters in order to ensure that the process has finite variance. From (3.13), these restrictions are easily seen to be

$$\sum_{i=0}^{\infty} \theta_i^2 < \infty \tag{3.14}$$

Any model which can be written in the form (3.12) where (3.14) holds is said to be an indeterministic process. An alternative terminology, motivated by (3.14), is to say that it is an infinite-order, square-summable process. Note that any finite-order moving average process can be thought of as an indeterministic process with coefficients on lags beyond a certain point identically equal to zero.

3.3 ARMA and ARIMA process

Sometimes, as we shall discuss later in the chapter, it may be appropriate to model a time series as a combination of both autoregressive and moving average components. Such a process is termed, not unnaturally, an autoregressive moving average, or ARMA, process. An ARMA(p, q) process can be written

$$x_t = \phi_1 x_{t-1} + \phi_2 x_{t-2} \ldots + \phi_p x_{t-p} + \xi_t + \theta_1 \xi_{t-1} + \ldots$$
$$+ \theta_q \xi_{t-q}$$

or, more generally:

$$\Phi(L)x_t = \Theta(L)\xi_t \tag{3.15}$$

The stationarity of an ARMA process depends entirely upon its autoregressive component, and requires that all the roots of

$$\Phi(z) = 0$$

lie outside the unit circle (i.e. greater than one in absolute value). Similarly, invertibility of an ARMA process requires that all the roots of the characteristic equation associated with the moving average polynominal, i.e.

$$\Theta(z) = 0$$

lie outside the unit circle.

In Chapter 5 we will discuss integrated processes. An integrated process of order d must be differenced d times before it has a stationary, invertible ARMA representation. If this ARMA representation is of order (p, q) then the original, undifferenced process is said to have an autoregressive integrated moving average representation of order (p, d, q), i.e. it is ARIMA(p, d, q). If a process, x say, has an ARIMA(p, d, q) representation, then $\Delta^d x_t$ has an ARMA(p, q) representation:

$$(1 - \phi_1 L - \ldots - \phi_p L^P)\Delta^d x_t = (1 + \theta_1 L + \ldots + d_q L^q)\, \xi_t$$

$$(3.16)$$

3.4 Wold's decomposition

An important result in time series analysis, known as Wold's decomposition theorem, states that any covariance stationary process, x say, can be represented as the sum of a deterministic component, $\bar{x}_t$ say, and an indeterministic component:

$$x_t = \bar{x}_t + \sum_{i=0}^{\infty} \theta_i \xi_{t-i}$$

$$(3.17)$$

Note that the deterministic component $\bar{x}_t$ need not be constant but it must be non-stochastic – it may for example be a trigonometric function of t (e.g. $\cos \lambda t$). Often, however, $\bar{x}_t$ is in practice thought of as a constant.

Wold's decomposition can be thought of as a central motivation for considering pure time series models. If we believe or know that a certain time series is covariance stationary, then Wold's decomposition tells us that it can be decomposed into deterministic and indeterministic components. We can then take out the deterministic component by assuming that it takes a particular form, such as a constant. This leaves a potentially infinite-order, square-summable component. If the coefficients of this component are very small beyond a certain lag, then it may be convenient to approximate the indeterministic component by a finite-order moving average process. Alternatively, it may be better to approximate the process by an ARMA process of finite orders.

This can be illustrated by means of the following examples. Consider the following indeterministic process:

$$x_t = \xi_t(1 + L + 0.5L^2 + 0.25L^3 + 0.125L^4 + 0.0625L^5$$
$$+ 0.03125L^6 + \ldots)$$

$$(3.18)$$

This is clearly a square-summable process since the coefficients are geometrically declining:

$$\sum_{i=0}^{\infty} \theta_i^2 = [1 + 1 + (0.5)^2 + (0.25)^2 + \ldots)$$

$$= 1/[1 - (0.5)^2] + 1 = 2\tfrac{1}{3} < \infty$$

The fact that the moving average coefficients are geometrically declining gives us a clue that (3.18) can be written as a stationary, invertible ARMA process of finite orders.

Consider the ARMA(1, 1) process:

$$x_t = 0.5x_{t-1} + \xi_t + 0.5\xi_{t-1} \tag{3.19}$$

This can be written

$$x_t (1 - 0.5L) = \xi_t(1 + 0.5L)$$

or

$$x_t = \xi_t(1 + 0.5L)(1 - 0.5L)^{-1}$$

$$= \xi_t(1 + 0.5L)(1 + 0.5L + 0.25L^2 + 0.125L^3 + \ldots)$$

$$= \xi_t(1 + L + 0.5L^2 + 0.25L^3 \ldots)$$

So that (3.18) and (3.19) are in fact equivalent. In practice, of course, there is no reason why the indeterministic component should have coefficients which decline in such an exact geometric pattern; but even if they do so only approximately, then an ARMA representation of finite orders may yield a sufficiently close approximation to the time series behaviour of the process.

As another example, consider the indeterministic process:

$$x_t = \xi_t(1 + 0.7L + 0.34L^2 + 0.068L^3 + 0.0136L^4$$

$$+ 0.00272L^5 + \ldots) \tag{3.20}$$

The reader should verify that, providing the coefficients beyond the fifth lag are very small, this process would be well approximated by an ARMA(1, 2) process of the form

$$x_t(1 - 0.2L) = \xi_t(1 + 0.5L + 0.2L^2) \tag{3.21}$$

3.5 Autocovariance and autocorrelation functions

The covariance between two random variables, w, z, is defined to be

$$\text{Cov}(w, z) = E\{(w - E[w])(z - E[z])\}$$

Thus, since any two elements of a stochastic process x_t, x_{t+i} say, are themselves random variables, we have:

$$\text{Cov}(x_t, x_{t+i}) = E\{(x_t - E[x_t])(x_{t+i} - E[x_{t+i}])\} \tag{3.22}$$

This is called the autocovariance function. The autocovariance function is an extremely useful tool in characterising the properties of stochastic processes. For example, in Chapter 1 we defined a white noise stochastic process to be one which had constant mean and finite variance and for which the autocovariance function was always zero.

Consider the first-order autoregressive process

$$x_{t+1} = \rho x_t + \xi_{t+1} \tag{3.23}$$

where $|\rho| < 1$ and where ξ_{t+1} is white noise and is, in particular, uncorrelated with x_t. From (3.23), substituting repeatedly for lagged x, we have:

$$x_{t+1} = \rho^t x_0 + (\rho^t \xi_1 + \rho^{t-1} \xi_2 + \dots \xi_{t+1}) \tag{3.24a}$$

Since $|\rho| < 1$, ρ^t will be close to zero for large t. Thus, we have:

$$E(x_{t+1}) = E(\rho^t \xi_1 + \rho^{t-1} \xi_2 + \dots \xi_{t+1}) = 0 \tag{3.24b}$$

Since $E(\xi_i) = 0$ for all i. Also,

$$\begin{aligned} \text{Var}(x_{t+1}) &= E[\rho^{2t} \xi_1^2 + \rho^{2t-2} \xi_2^2 + \dots \xi_{t+1}^2] \\ &= \sigma_\xi^2 (\rho^{2t} + \rho^{2t-2} + \dots 1) \end{aligned} \tag{3.25}$$

where σ_ξ^2 is the variance of ξ_{t+1}. For large t, the geometric progression (3.25) can be summed:

$$\text{Var}(x_{t+1}) = \sigma_\xi^2/(1 - \rho^2) \tag{3.26}$$

Now consider the autocovariance function for the autoregressive process:

$$\begin{aligned} \text{Cov}(x_t, x_{t+k}) &= E(x_t x_{t+k}) \\ &= E[x_t(\rho x_{t+k-1} + \xi_{t+k})] \\ &= \rho E(x_t x_{t+k-1}) + E(x_t \xi_{t+k}) \\ &= \rho E(x_t x_{t+k-1}) \\ &= \rho E[x_t(\rho x_{t+k-2} + \xi_{t+k-1})] \\ &= \rho^2 E(x_t x_{t+k-2}) \end{aligned}$$

Continuing in this fashion it is easily seen:

$$\begin{aligned} \text{Cov}(x_t, x_{t+k}) &= \rho^k \text{Var}(x_t) \\ &= \rho^k \sigma_\xi^2/(1 - \rho^2) \end{aligned} \tag{3.27}$$

If we write

$$\text{Var}(x_t) = \sigma_x^2$$

and

$$\text{Cov}(x_t, x_{t+k}) = \gamma_k$$

then (3.27) becomes

$$\gamma_k = \rho^k \sigma_x^2 \qquad\qquad\qquad \textbf{(3.28)}$$

Moreover, it is clear that, for all k,

$$\gamma_k = \gamma_{-k}$$

so that it is only necessary to consider non-negative k. The sequence $\{\gamma_k\}_{k=0}^{\infty}$ is the autocovariance function. Note that $\gamma_0 = \sigma_x^2$.

Note that the autocovariance function is not expressed as a pure number – its units of measurement are dependent upon the underlying units of measurement of the x process. Thus, the size of γ_k would differ, for example, if x were measured in pounds rather than pence, or dollars rather than cents (by a factor of 10000). In order to circumvent this problem, it is sometimes more convenient to consider the *autocorrelation function* rather than the autocovariance function, since the former is expressed in terms of pure numbers, and is independent of the units of measurement of the underlying process. The autocorrelation function is obtained simply by dividing each of the γ_k by $\gamma_0 = \sigma_x^2$, thereby cancelling out the units of measurement:

$$\rho_k = \gamma_k/\gamma_0, \; k = 0, 1, 2, \ldots \qquad\qquad \textbf{(3.29)}$$

Note that $\rho_0 = 1$, by definition.

For the autoregressive, AR(1) process considered above, for example, we have:

$$\rho_k = \gamma_k/\gamma_0 = \rho^k \sigma_x^2/\sigma_x^2 = \rho^k \qquad\qquad \textbf{(3.30)}$$

As another example, consider the first-order moving average, MA(1) model:

$$y_t = \xi_t + \theta \xi_{t-1} \qquad\qquad\qquad \textbf{(3.31)}$$

where ξ_t is again white noise. We have:

$$\begin{aligned}
\gamma_0 &= E[(\xi_t + \theta\xi_{t-1})(\xi_t + \theta\xi_{t-1})] \\
&= E(\xi_t^2) + \theta^2 E(\xi_{t-1}^2) + 2\theta E(\xi_t \xi_{t-1}) \\
&= (1 + \theta^2)\sigma_\xi^2 \qquad\qquad\qquad \textbf{(3.32)}
\end{aligned}$$

Similarly

$$\gamma_1 = E[(\xi_t + \theta\xi_{t-1})(\xi_{t-1} + \theta\xi_{t-2})]$$
$$= E(\xi_t\xi_{t-1}) + \theta E(\xi_{t-1}^2) + \theta^2 E(\xi_{t-1}\xi_{t-2})$$
$$= \theta\sigma_\xi^2 \tag{3.33}$$

Since ξ_t is serially uncorrelated, it also easily seen that

$$\gamma_k = 0, \; k > 1 \tag{3.34}$$

Thus, the autocorrelation function for an MA(1) process is given by:

$$\rho_0 = 1, \; \rho_1 = \theta/(1 + \theta^2), \; \rho_k = 0, \; k > 1 \tag{3.35}$$

3.6 The correlogram

In general, when a researcher is analysing a time series, he or she will have to estimate the autocovariance function by using the sample moments. This estimate is termed the *correlogram*. A commonly used estimator for ρ_k is

$$\gamma_k = c_k/c_0$$

where

$$c_k = \frac{1}{T} \sum_{t=1}^{T-k} (x_t - \bar{x})(x_{t+k} - \bar{x}) \text{ for } x = 0, 1, 2 \ldots \tag{3.36}$$

and where

$$\bar{x} = \frac{1}{T} \sum_{t=1}^{T} x_t \tag{3.37}$$

and where T is the sample size. Sometimes, especially where the sample size is relatively small, T is replaced in the denominator in (3.36) by $(T - k)$ to correct for lost degrees of freedom.

Under the null hypothesis that the x process consists of independent drawings from identical populations, it can be shown that, for large T, c_k will be approximately normally distributed with mean zero and variance $1/T$ under weak conditions:

$$c_k \sim N(0, 1/T) \tag{3.38}$$

Thus, the 95% confidence interval for c_k is given approximately by

$$c_k - 2/\sqrt{T}, \; c_k + 2/\sqrt{T} \tag{3.39}$$

Hence, if this interval does not contain zero, the null hypothesis

$\rho_k = 0$ can be rejected at a nominal significance level of approximately 5%.

If the series is not white noise, then the appropriate formula for the large-sample variance of c_k is

$$\frac{1 + 2(\rho_1^2 + \rho_2^2 + \ldots \rho_n^2)}{T} > \frac{1}{T} \text{ for } n > 0 \qquad (3.40)$$

where n is such that $\rho_k \neq 0$ for $k \leq n$ and $\rho_k = 0$ for $k > n$. Thus, the fact that $1/T$ is only an approximation to the sample autocorrelation variance suggests that, even when the sample autocorrelations are apparently insignificant when using $1/T$ as an estimate of the variance, one should still look for apparent regularities in the *shape of* the correlogram.

3.7 The partial autocorrelation function

The correlogram is useful for identifying a pure moving average model, since there will tend to be a cut-off of significant points on the correlogram after the appropriate lag depth. For autoregressive or mixed processes, however, the order of the autoregressive component may be harder to determine from the correlogram. For this reason, it is usual to use a complementary procedure which involves plotting the estimated coefficient of x_{t-k}, from an OLS estimate of an AR(k) model for x_t, against k. If the observations are generated by an AR(p) process, then the theoretical partial autocorrelations are zero at lags beyond p. Since any invertible MA process can be represented as an AR process with geometrically declining coefficients, the partial autocorrelation function for an MA process should decay slowly.

The identification of the orders of a mixed model may be more difficult to determine, and a good deal of skill must be exercised.

3.8 Common factors

A simple approach to econometric modelling involves deliberate over-parameterisation – more than enough variables and lags are included in a fitted equation, with the objective of eliminating those with poor explanatory power (i.e. insignificant coefficients). In the context of pure time series modelling, such deliberate over-parameterisation will often prove disastrous, because of the presence of common factors. As an example, suppose that the 'true' model is an ARMA(1, 1):

$$x_t = \phi x_{t-1} + \xi_t + \theta \xi_{t-1} \tag{3.41}$$

Multiplying the right-hand side of (3.41) by $(1 + \gamma L)/(1 + \gamma L) = 1$:

$$x_t = \frac{(1 + \gamma L)}{(1 + \gamma L)} (\phi x_{t-1} + \xi_t + \theta \xi_{t-1}) \tag{3.42}$$

$$x_t = (\phi - \gamma)x_{t-1} + \gamma \phi x_{t-2} + \xi_t + (\theta + \gamma)\xi_{t-1} + \gamma \theta \xi_{t-2} \tag{3.43}$$

(3.42) is in the form of an ARMA(2, 2):

$$x_t = \beta_1 x_{t-1} + \beta_2 x_{t-2} + \xi_t + \lambda_1 \xi_{t-1} + \lambda_1 \xi_{t-2} \tag{3.44}$$

with

$$\beta_1 = (\phi - \gamma), \ \beta_2 = \gamma \phi, \ \lambda_1 = (\theta + \gamma), \ \lambda_2 = \gamma \theta$$

Thus, if an ARMA(1, 1) model such as (3.41) is correct, then an ARMA(2, 2) model such as (3.44) will fit well. Moreover, this will be true for *any* value of γ. Thus, (3.44) is in fact unidentified.

This example therefore illustrates the pitfall in over-parameterisation of a pure time series model. A much more subtle approach to model selection is required.

3.9   Model selection: the Box–Jenkins approach

Box and Jenkins (1976) suggest a three-stage approach to pure time series modelling, the three stages being *identification, estimation* and *diagnostic checking*.

At the *identification* stage, a tentative ARIMA model is specified that may approximate the data-generating process for the given sample, through examination of the correlogram and the partial autocorrelation functions. This stage is discussed in more detail below.

Once a model has been tentatively identified, the next stage is to *estimate* its parameters. The estimation stage is also discussed further in a following section.

Once the tentative model has been estimated, a set of estimated residuals are automatically generated. For example, for an AR(1) model we would have the estimated residuals:

$$\hat{\xi}_t = x_t - \hat{\phi} x_{t-1}$$

(where a circumflex denotes a fitted value), while for an ARIMA(0, 1, 1), we have:

$$\hat{\xi} = \Delta\hat{\xi}_{t-1}$$

(where one would normally set $\hat{\xi}_0 = 0$). If the fitted model is correct, then this residual series should be approximately white noise. One test of the adequacy of the model thus includes testing for the whiteness of the fitted reiduals using diagnostic checks such as the Box–Pierce or Ljung–Box portmanteau statistics (see Chapter 4).

If the estimated parameters of the fitted model are significantly different from zero and the fitted residuals appear to be approximate white noise, then the fitted ARIMA model may be held to be adequate. If the model fails on either of these counts, then the identification stage should be returned to.

The Box–Jenkins approach to model selection thus involves three stages: identification, estimation and diagnostic checking. The procedure is summarised by the flow chart presented as Figure 3.1.

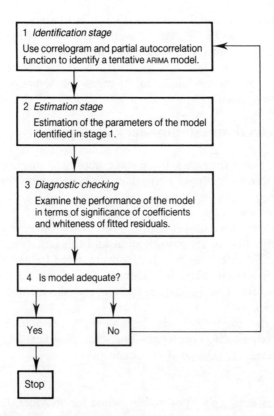

Figure 3.1   Flow diagram for the Box-Jenkins model selection procedure.

3.10 Model identification

The theoretical autocorrelation function for an AR(1) process was shown above to be given by

$$\rho_k = \phi^k \tag{3.45}$$

where ϕ is the first-order autoregressive coefficient. Stationarity of the process requires

$$|\phi| < 1$$

Thus, non-stationarity of a first-order process will be revealed by a correlogram which shows no sign of decay in the absolute magnitude of the estimated autocorrelations. This is, in fact true more generally: if the estimated autocorrelations to not die out or show signs of decay, the data must be transformed to induce stationarity. A common stationarity-inducing transformation with economic data is to take logarithms and then to first difference once. This will induce stationarity, for example, if the data exhibits a fairly consistent average growth rate.

Once apparent stationarity has been achieved, the next step is to identify the orders of the ARIMA process. For a pure moving average process of order q, MA(q), the correlogram will tend to show estimated autocorrelations which are significantly different from zero only up to lag q, while the partial autocorrelation function will tend to taper off. For a pure autoregressive process of order p, the estimated partial autocorrelations will tend to be insignificantly different from zero beyond lag p while the correlogram will show the estimated autocorrelations tapering off.

If neither the correlogram nor the partial autocorrelation function show a definite cut off, then a mixed process is suggested. In seeking to identify the orders of the moving average and autoregressive parts, it then may be useful to think of the correlogram and partial autocorrelation functions of the pure MA and AR processes being superimposed upon one another. For example, if both the correlogram and the partial autocorrelation function show signs of a slow tapering off, then an ARMA(1, 1) process may be identified. Similarly if the correlogram has two spikes at lags one and two and then exponential decay, while the partial autocorrelation function shows either exponential decay or damped sinewave behaviour, then an ARMA(1, 2) may be identified. Table 3.1 lists other possible combinations for low-order ARMA processes.

Table 3.1   Correlogram and partial autocorrelation patterns for low-order ARMA models

Correlogram pattern	Partial autocorrelation pattern	Underlying model
Single spike at lag 1	Exponential decay or damped sinewave	MA(1)
Exponential decay or damped sinewave	Single spike at lag 1	AR(1)
Spike at lag 1 followed by exponential decay or damped sinewave	Spike at lag 1 followed by exponential decay or damped sinewave	ARMA(1, 1)
Spikes at first two lags followed by exponential decay or damped sinewave	Spike at lag 1 followed by exponential decay or damped sinewave	ARMA(1, 2)
Spike at lag 1 followed by exponential decay or damped sinewave	Spikes at first two lags followed by exponential decay or damped sinewave	ARMA(2, 1)
Spikes at first two lags followed by exponential decay or damped sinewave	Spikes at first two lags followed by exponential decay or damped sinewave	ARMA(2, 2)

In general however, identifying mixed processes involves a fair degree of trial and error, and this is why the estimation and diagnostic checking stages are important to see if the tentatively identified model 'flies'.

3.11   Estimation

Estimation of pure time series models can be carried out by maximum likelihood methods, which were discussed in general in Chapter 2.

For a pure autoregressive AR(p), process, maximum likelihood estimation is in fact little different from an ordinary least squares regression applied to x_t on p lags, $x_{t-1}, \ldots, x_{t-p}$.

For moving average and mixed processes, non-linear techniques must be used. In nearly all cases, maximum likelihood estimation can be approximated closely by minimising a sum of squares function. This is because, as we showed in Chapter 2, the likelihood function can always be broken down into a form involving only squared one-step-ahead prediction errors. But the one-step-ahead prediction errors are in fact the residuals of the model.

Consider, for example, the AR(1) model:

$$x_t = \phi x_{t-1} + \xi_t$$

Conditional on information (i.e. observations on x) at time $t - 1$, the model predicts x_t as

$$\hat{x}_t = \phi x_{t-1}$$

Thus the prediction error is

$$x_t - \hat{x}_t = \hat{\xi}_t$$

Thus, for any given value of ϕ, the prediction error is just the fitted residual. One could then form the sum of squared residuals function:

$$S(\phi) = \sum \hat{\xi}_t^2$$

and ϕ could be chosen by minimising it – which is, of course, exactly what OLS does.

For an ARMA(p, q) model, the residuals can be generated recursively by an equation of the form:

$$\hat{\xi}_t = x_t - \phi_1 x_{t-1} - \ldots - \phi_p x_{t-p} - \theta_1 \hat{\xi}_{t-1} - \ldots - \theta_q \hat{\xi}_{t-q}$$

with $\hat{\xi}_p = \hat{\xi}_{p-1} = \hat{\xi}_{p-q+1} = 0$. The conditional sum of squares function would then be:

$$S(\phi_1, \ldots, \phi_p, \theta_1, \ldots, \theta_q) = \sum_{t=p+1}^{T} \hat{\xi}_t^2$$

In general, the covariance matrix of the estimates can also be obtained from an approximation of the information matrix and applying standard maximum likelihood properties (see Chapter 2).

3.12 Conclusion

We have discussed how data may be categorised and described purely in terms of their time series properties; this is an important and useful technique which has a wide range of applications. In Chapter 4 we will discuss dynamic structural models; the time series representation is often a useful benchmark against which to measure a structural model. In Chapter 5 we will discuss cointegration; this analysis rests heavily on recognising the importance for structural modelling of the univariate properties of the data we are dealing with. Chapter 6 considers rational expectations; here again time series modelling is used widely as a way of capturing the expectations formation procedure for variables which are not of central interest to the model at hand.

4

Dynamic modelling – the general to specific methodology

In this chapter we give an account of one particular approach to econometric modelling. This approach has been developed largely by individuals associated with the London School of Economics and we will term it the LSE tradition. This approach does not of course enjoy universal support; alternative modelling frameworks have for example been proposed by Leamer (1978), Sims (1980) or Zellner (1971), to name but a few. Nonetheless, we regard the LSE tradition to be of sufficient importance that it warrants a detailed exposition. The founder of the LSE tradition is without a doubt Sargan who both through his own research Sargan (1964) and through the work of his students, Davidson *et al*. (1978), Davidson and Hendry (1981), Hendry and Von Ungern-Sternberg (1981), Hendry and Mizon (1978), Mizon and Richard (1986), etc. have had an enormous influence on applied econometrics.

In the first section we will outline the conceptual approach of the LSE tradition. Section 4.2 will examine a range of test procedures which have come to play a central role in applying the approach. The final section will give an example of the practical application of the approach using the demand for money.

4.1 The conceptual approach

At the centre of the LSE approach lies the concept of the data generation process (DGP), see Hendry Pagan and Sargan (1984), which represents a totally general statement of the joint probability distribution of all variables. As such it is too general to have any direct practical use but its importance lies in providing a benchmark against which more simple models may be measured. It also allows us to formalise the assumptions and steps we need to make when we construct actual models for estimation.

Suppose x_t is a vector of observations on all variables in period t, and $X_{t-1} = (x_{t-1} \ldots x_1)'$, then the joint probability of the sample x_t, the DGP, may be stated as

$$\prod_{t=1}^{t} D(x_t | X_{t-1}; \Theta) \tag{4.1}$$

where Θ is a vector of unknown parameters. The process of econometric modelling then consists of simplifying this very general formulation by imposing a set of restrictions. We therefore 'simplify' the DGP to yield a set of explicit equations complete with numerical parameter estimates. These simplifying assumptions may be categorised into four types.

1. Marginalise the DGP. The full DGP contains far more variables than we are normally interested in, or can possibly deal with. We therefore select a subset of 'variables of interest' and relegate the rest to a set of variables which are of no interest given the problem at hand.
2. Conditioning assumptions. Given the choice of 'variables of interest' we must now select a subset of these variables to be the endogenous variables (Y_t). These are then 'conditioned' or determined by the remaining variables (Z_t) of interest. The Z_t should be, at least, weakly exogenous for this 'conditioning' to be valid.
3. Selection of functional form. The full DGP is a general functional specification and before any estimation can be done a specific functional form for the model must be assumed.
4. Estimation. Finally, the unknown parameters in the assumed functional form must be replaced by a set of estimated numerical values.

It is wrong to think of these stages as being sequential. As Spanos (1986) has emphasised, the early stages of marginalising and conditioning are often done with a sharp eye on how the data perform at stage 4. It is therefore best to view the process of applied econometrics as an interaction among these stages until an adequate model is achieved.

Given the general DGP in (4.1) we may represent the first two assumptions by the following factorisation, where the function 'B' represents what one might usually refer to as the structural equations of interest.

$$D(x_t|X_{t-1}; \Theta) = A(W_t|X_t:\alpha) \, B(Y_t|Y_{t-1}, Z_t: \beta)$$
$$\times \, C(Z_t|Y_{t-1}, Z_{t-1}: \gamma) \tag{4.2}$$

The first component, A, specifies the determination of W, the variables of *no* interest, as a function of all the variables X_t. The second term B gives the endogenous variables of interest Y_t as a function of lagged Y and the exogenous variables Z_t. The final term C gives the determination of the exogenous variables Z_t as a function of the lagged endogenous and exogenous variables.

For the conditioning assumptions of the model to be valid we require that the Z_t variables are at least weakly exogenous. This means that Z_t is independent of Y_t, as is assumed in term 'C' in (4.2). It also requires that the parameters of interest of the model to be finally estimated (Θ) are a function of β only and the β and γ are variation free.

Other, more general, forms of exogeneity are strong exogeneity and super exogeneity: Strong exogeneity is given by the assumption that the third term in (4.2) takes the form $(Z_t|Z_{t-1}: \gamma)$ that is, the exogenous variables are determined without any reference to any lagged values of the endogenous variables Y_t. The strong exogeneity assumption therefore amounts to the assumption of weak exogeneity plus the assumption that Y does not 'Granger cause' Z. Super exogeneity is related to the Lucas (1976) critique. Lucas points out that when we model expectations by functions of lagged variables then the parameters of these functions may vary as the regime for determining the expectation variable changes. Super exogeneity rules out this possibility by assuming that the parameter vectors β and γ are independent. Under this assumption a change in the β vector will not influence γ. Super exogeneity is strong exogeneity plus this assumption of independence of β and γ. In general, weak exogeneity is all that is needed for estimation and testing, strong exogeneity is necessary for forecasting and super exogeneity for policy analysis.

Having made our assumption about the conditioning and marginalisation we may then state a partial log likelihood function for our model as

$$\log[L(\Theta)] = \sum_{t=1}^{t} L(\Theta; y_t|z_t, y_{t-1}) \tag{4.3}$$

and this may form the basis for estimation. It is important to realise, at this stage, that the assumptions needed to produce (4.3) are virtually never satisfied, in particular the chance of producing a correct and complete marginalisation of the data set is vanishingly small. As a result we can characterise the situation reached by equation (4.3) by the statement that 'all models are false'. We do not therefore want to determine whether our model is the true model but rather we want to test the model to see if it is an 'adequate' model. A model derived as above cannot be regarded as correct or valid in an absolute sense but rather as a useful tentative hypothesis. A good model will be congruent with all the evidence, that is to say it will be a statistically acceptable representation of the data which cannot be unambiguously outperformed by any other known model.

The LSE tradition in practice

Given an economic variable to be explained, say Y, the first step is to use economic theory to determine a set of m explanatory variables $X_t = (X_1 \ldots X_m)_t$. This is the marginalisation of the complete set of all variables into the set of variables to be considered $(Y, X)_t$. The conditioning of the data is determined by which, if any, elements of X_t are deemed not to be weakly exogenous. Given that agents will normally be operating within an inherently dynamic environment, it is likely that the X_{it} will influence Y_t with a certain lag structure. Let n be the maximum lag with which an element of X influences the current value of Y, and suppose also that Y_t be a function of its own lagged values. (In practice, n will be determined on such considerations as the available degrees of freedom and the nature of the data, for example four lags perhaps for seasonally unadjusted quarterly data.) The real-world process generating Y_t is then assumed to be contained or nested within the linear model:

$$Y_t = \alpha_0 + \sum_{i=1}^{n} \alpha_i Y_{t-1} + \sum_{k=1}^{m} \sum_{i=0}^{n} \beta_{ki} X_{kt-i} + u_t \qquad \textbf{(4.4)}$$

where u_t is a white noise disturbance. Since economic theory generally has little to say about short-run dynamics, the LSE tradition starts with the general unrestricted form (4.4) as the maintained hypothesis. Having estimated (4.4) the next step is to sequentially impose economically meaningful restrictions on the maintained hypothesis, each restriction being tested for significance against the slightly less restricted specification which precedes it in the sequence.

Hendry *et al.* (1984) provide a typology of the various dynamic specifications which are nested within (4.4), an exposition of which can be given in terms of the simplest form of (4.4), when $m = n = 1$:

$$Y_t = \alpha_0 + \alpha_1 Y_{t-1} + \beta_0 X_t + \beta_1 X_{t-1} + u_t \qquad \textbf{(4.5)}$$

Imposing $\alpha_1 = \beta_1 = 0$ in (4.5) yields a static regression model, while setting $\beta_1 = 0$ yields the standard partial adjustment form. Setting $\alpha_1 = \beta_0 = 0$ indicates that X acts as a 'leading indicator' for Y_t. Imposing $\alpha_1 = 0$ makes Y depend on a finite distributed lag of X. If both of the restrictions $\alpha_1 = 1$ and $\beta_0 + \beta_1 = 0$ are accepted, then (4.4) can be reduced to a first difference formulation (if Y and X are logarithms, this yields an equation in the growth rates of Y and X). Setting $\beta_0 = 0$ in (4.5) yields Y_t as a function of lagged values of itself and X_t, and is termed by Hendry *et al.* a reduced form or 'dead start' equation, for obvious reasons.

An interesting reparameterisation of (4.5) may be used to show how the above dynamic equation can be represented as a 'static equation' with an AR(1) error. This is the basis of the so called 'common factor' test. If one believes that a static equation has an AR(1) error, one cannot simply perform Cochrane–Orcutt (1949) estimation and accept the ensuing parameter estimates; one must also 'pass' the common factor test. To illustrate the latter, rewrite (4.5) as:

$$[1 - \alpha_1 L]Y_t = \alpha_0 + \beta_0[1 + (\beta_1/\beta_0)L]X_t + u_t \qquad (4.6)$$

If the restriction $\alpha_1 = -\beta_1/\beta_0$ is not rejected by the data, then the polynomial in the lag operator (in square brackets) contains a common element (factor) namely the coefficient in front of 'L'. Multiplying (4.6) by $(1 - \alpha_1 L)^{-1}$ and assuming the common factor restriction holds, we have

$$Y_t = \alpha_0^* + \beta_0 X_t + \varepsilon_t \qquad (4.7)$$

where

$$(1 - \alpha_1 L)^{-1}u_t = \varepsilon_t \quad \text{or} \quad \varepsilon_t = \alpha_1\varepsilon_{t-1} + u_t \qquad (4.8a)$$

$$(1 - \alpha_1 L)^{-1}\alpha_0^* = \alpha_0 \quad \text{or} \quad \alpha_0^* = \alpha_0/(1 - \alpha_1) \qquad (4.8b)$$

Hence, imposing the non-linear restriction $\alpha_1\beta_0 + \beta_1 = 0$ in (4.5) is equivalent to assuming a first-order serially correlated error AR(1) in the static model (4.7). Equations (4.7)–(4.8) contain one less parameter than (4.5) and it is in this sense that serial correlation can be a convenient simplification rather than a nuisance (Hendry and Mizon 1978). To present the argument in a different vein, if the naïve researcher runs a highly restricted equation (4.7) and finds evidence of first-order serial correlation and performs Cochrane–Orcutt, the results from the latter cannot be accepted unless the researcher also runs equation (4.5) and tests the common factor restriction. The Cochrane–Orcutt regression is

$$(Y_t - \alpha_1 Y_{t-1}) = \alpha_0(1 - \alpha_1) + \beta_0(X_t - \alpha_1 X_{t-1}) + v_t$$

$$(4.8c)$$

with α_1 being the AR(1) parameter – obtained from the residuals in (4.7). The common factor likelihood ratio test is then

$$\text{LR}(k) = T \ln [\text{RSS}(4.8c)/\text{RSS}(4.5)]$$

where RSS is the residual sum of squares, k is the number of restrictions in (4.8c) – in this case 1 – and T is the number of observations.

$\text{LR}(k) < \chi_k^2$ leads to non-rejection of the common factor restriction and supports (4.7) and (4.8a). If the common factor restriction is rejected, then even if α_1, α_0^*, β_0 are statistically significant, they are inconsistent estimates. In the latter case we must assume some other form of serial correlation in (4.7), say MA(q), AR(p); $p > 1$, or accept (4.5), the dynamic equation as our new maintained model rather than (4.7) + (4.8).

Another reparameterisation of (4.5) introduces an error correction mechanism (ECM).

$$\Delta_1 Y_t = \alpha_0 + \beta_0 \Delta_1 X_t - (1 - \alpha_1)(Y_{t-1} - X_{t-1})$$
$$+ \gamma X_{t-1} + u_t \tag{4.9}$$

where

$$\gamma = \alpha_1 + \beta_0 + \beta_1 - 1 \tag{4.9a}$$

Equations (4.9) and (4.5) are just different ways of expressing the same equation. However, proponents of the LSE tradition would probably argue that (4.9), a form of error correction model (ECM), is more intuitively appealing than (4.5). To illustrate this point, note that the static equilibrium solution from either equation is given when $\Delta Y_{t-j} = \Delta X_{t-j} = 0$, and $Y_{t-j} = Y$; $X_{t-1} = X$ are constant (and $u_t = 0$):

$$Y = [\alpha_0/(1 - \alpha_1)] + [(\beta_0 + \beta_1)/(1 - \alpha_1)]X$$

However if $\gamma = 0$ in (4.9), then $\beta_0 + \beta_1 = (1 - \alpha_1)$ and the long-run static equilibrium solution is

$$Y = [\alpha_0/(1 - \alpha_1)] + X$$

Hence a t-test on γ in (4.9) provides a very simple way of testing for a long-run unit elasticity. Suppose $\gamma = 0$ is not rejected in (4.9), the dynamic equation then becomes

$$\Delta Y_t = \beta_0 \Delta X_t - (1 - \alpha_1)(Y_{t-1} - Y_{t-1}^*) \tag{4.10}$$

where

$$Y_{t-1}^* = \alpha_0/(1 - \alpha_1) + X_{t-1} \tag{4.10a}$$

If $(1 - \alpha_1) > 0$ then if actual Y_{t-1} is above its long-run equilibrium value Y^*_{t-1}, we expect ΔY_t to fall in the next period, which brings actual Y_t closer to Y^*. Also, in (4.10) the growth in Y_t depends on the growth in X_t with a coefficient β_0. Hence $\beta_0 \Delta X_t$ and the ECM terms are 'sensible' dynamic decision variables given the long-run equilibrium condition of a unit elasticity.

In estimation the constant term in the equation for Y^*_{t-1} (4.10) would be estimated 'separately':

$$\Delta Y_t = \alpha_0 + \beta_0 \Delta X_t + \beta_1 (Y - X)_{t-1} + u_t \qquad \textbf{(4.11)}$$

where $\beta_1 = -(1 - \alpha_1)$. Equation (4.11) *imposes* the long-run unit elasticity for any (non-zero) value of β_1 (and for dynamic stability $-2 < \beta_1 < 0$). One can use the ECM formation in a number of useful ways; for example, consider the following two equations:

$$\Delta Y_t = \beta_0 \Delta X_t - \beta_1 (Y - 0.9X)_{t-1} \qquad \textbf{(4.12a)}$$

$$\Delta Y_t = \beta_0 \Delta X_{1t} + \beta_1 \Delta X_{2t} - \beta_3 (Y - X_1)_{t-1}$$
$$- \beta_4 (Y - X_2)_{t-1} \qquad \textbf{(4.13a)}$$

with long-run static equilibrium solutions

$$Y = 0.9X \qquad \textbf{(4.12b)}$$

$$Y = [\beta_3/(\beta_3 + \beta_4)] X_{1t} + [\beta_4/(\beta_3 + \beta_4)]X_{2t} \qquad \textbf{(4.13b)}$$

Thus equation (4.12a) *imposes* long-run elasticity of 0.9 while equation (4.13) imposes homogeneity between Y and X_1 *plus* X_2 (since the coefficients in square brackets *sum* to unity for *any* non-zero values of β_3 and β_4). The latter might represent a production function with constant returns to scale or a price mark-up equation on wage costs (X_{1t}) and raw materials costs (X_{2t}). Note that the restrictions apply to the long run and the dynamic response in the estimated equations (4.12) and (4.13) is reasonably general. To *test* for the above restrictions one merely adds γX_{t-1} to (4.12) and either $\gamma_1 X_{1t-1}$ or $\gamma_2 X_{2t-1}$ to (4.13) and performs a simple t-test on the appropriate γ.

Let us now consider 'growth effects' in the auto-regressive distributed lag (ADL) framework, our unrestricted ADL model is

$$Y_t = \alpha_0 + \sum_{i=1}^{4} \alpha_i Y_{t-1} + \sum_{i=0}^{4} \beta_1 X_{t-1} + u_t \qquad \textbf{(4.14)}$$

and this unrestricted ADL form embodies 'growth effects': that is the level of Y depends not only on the *level of the* X *variables* but also on the *rate of growth* of X. To illustrate this point suppose we sequentially test and impose the restrictions on (4.14), namely

$$\alpha_i = 0, \qquad i = 2, 3, 4$$

$$\beta_i = 0, \qquad i = 3, 4$$

$$\alpha_1 + \beta_0 + \beta_1 = 1$$

then the restricted form of (4.14) is

$$\Delta_1 Y_t = \alpha_0 + \beta_0 \Delta_1 X_t - (1 - \alpha_1)(Y_{t-1} - X_{t-1}) + u_t \quad \textbf{(4.15)}$$

The steady-state 'growth solution' for (4.15) is obtained by using

$$\Delta X_t = g_x, \ \Delta Y_t = g_y, \ X_{t-1} = X_t - g_x, \ \text{etc. in (4.15)}$$

$$Y_t = \frac{\alpha_0}{1 - \alpha_1} + X + \left[\frac{\beta_0 - (1 - \alpha_1)}{(1 - \alpha_1)} \right] g_x - \left(\frac{\alpha_1}{1 - \alpha_1} \right) g_y \quad \textbf{(4.16)}$$

Taking first differences of (4.16) and noting that by assumption $\Delta g_x = \Delta g_y = 0$, we obtain $g_y = g_x$ and hence (4.16) becomes

$$Y_t = \frac{\alpha_0}{(1 - \alpha_1)} + X + \left[\frac{(\beta_0 - 1)}{(1 - \alpha_1)} \right] g_x \quad \textbf{(4.17)}$$

Unless $(\beta_0 - 1)/(1 - \alpha_1) = 0$ then Y depends on the growth in X, in steady state. The impact of g_x on Y can often be large empirically. Although growth effects are usually not implied by economic theory, however, if we impose the restriction of a zero growth effect we may severely distort the lag structure. In our extremely simple illustrative example a zero growth effect implies $\beta_0 = 1$, that is the short-run and long-run response is the same: a strong restriction compared with the lagged effects in the unrestricted ECM, (4.15). In practice, growth effects are often ignored and in any case one would not expect a 'constant growth solution' from an equation estimated over data that is quite short and volatile to yield very precise estimates of 'growth effects'.

The ECM specification can be justified theoretically within (finite or infinite horizon) quadratic costs of adjustment framework (Hendry and von Ungern-Sternberg 1981; Nickell 1985). Less formally, the specification captures the idea that agents alter their behaviour according to 'signals' that they are out of equilibrium. For example, if Y is the logarithm of (real or nominal) money stock and X is the logarithm of (réal or nominal) income, then the error correction term $(Y_{t-1} - X_{t-1})$ is the logarithm of the money income ratio lagged once. Deviation in the money–income ratio from its long-run value will lead to future changes in money holdings by agents, in order to move closer to their desired long-run position.

The ECM specification has worked well in a number of empirical

studies of the demand for money in the UK, both for broad definitions (Hendry and Mizon 1978) and a narrow definition (Hendry
1980) and also for the US demand for money (Baba *et al.* 1987). An
ECM consumption function (Davidson *et al.* 1978, Hendry 1983) for
the UK also performs well statistically.

Two further points should be noted about the econometric
methodology outlined in this section. Firstly, general-to-specific methodology will inevitably involve a certain amount of 'data mining' (or
'lag mining' perhaps). For this reason it has become customary to
subject the final 'preferred' equation to a number of diagnostic
checks. Whilst these checks will usually have greatest power against a
specific alternative hypothesis (higher-order serial correlation, heteroskedasticity, etc.), they will usually also give some idea of the general
adequacy of the specification.

Secondly, when agents have forward-looking expectations, the
parameters of dynamic models of this kind will generally be functions
of the parameters of agents' objective functions and of the historically
given stochastic environment (see Hansen and Sargent 1980; Sargent
1981; Cuthbertson and Taylor 1987). They may therefore be subject
to the Lucas (1976) critique.

4.2　Testing the dynamic model

Clearly when we move from the general dynamic model (4.4) to a
restricted parameterisation of it such as (4.15) it is important to test
the model in a number of ways. It is important to test the general
unrestricted model for a homoscedastic serial uncorrelated error process at an early stage since all further testing is (usually) dependent
on white noise errors in the maintained hypothesis. We must test the
restrictions directly and we must also check that the assumptions
made about the residuals are not violated in the restricted model.

A range of test statistics is used to assess the validity of a model
and this section will outline some of the most common. The underlying theoretical derivation of these statistics will not be given here as
Chapter 2 discusses the construction of the three main classes of test
procedures and the relationship between them. Often an ECM model
is contructed or 'designed' so that one ensures it passes a set of
diagnostic 'tests'. Tests for parameter constancy and encompassing
tests then become of increasing importance in testing competing models.

Testing the restrictions (F-test)

At each stage in moving from our general equation to our 'best' equation we need to test the acceptability of the restrictions we are imposing on the model. In the case of a simple exclusion restriction this can be done using the standard t test. In the case of a combination of restrictions or a set of linear restriction involving more than one parameter we must use a more general procedure. The most commonly used test is the F-test which is a special version of the likelihood ratio test. Suppose we have a general 'unrestricted' model $Y_t = \beta_0' X_t + u_t$ and a restricted set of parameters β which gives $Y_t = \beta_1' X_t + v_t$, where β_0 contains fewer non-zero coefficients than β_1. Then we may construct a test of these restrictions by estimating both the unrestricted and the restricted models (as both are needed for the construction of the test it is a likelihood ratio test).

We define RSS_1 to be the residual sum of squares from the unrestricted regression and RSS_2 to be the residual sum of squares from the restricted regression. The F-test may then be most conveniently calculated as

$$F(m, T - k) = \left[\frac{\text{RSS}_2 - \text{RSS}_1}{\text{RSS}_1} \right] \left(\frac{T - k}{m} \right) \tag{4.18}$$

where T is the total sample size, k is the number of parameters in the unrestricted model and m is the number of restrictions. This is then distributed as $F(m, T - k)$. This test allows a wide range of restrictions and combinations of restrictions to be tested although it must be remembered that when a number of restrictions are tested jointly, rejection may be due to only one of the restrictions being invalid.

The intuition behind this test is simple; if the restriction is valid then we would expect RSS_2 to be only slightly larger than RSS_1. We are therefore testing for an increase in RSS_2 which is 'too' large to be due to chance.

The Durbin–Watson statistic (DW)

One of the earliest tests for serial correlation in the error process is due to Durbin and Watson (1950); this test is still used widely so we present it here, although it does have a number of disadvantages. In particular it is known to be inappropriate when the model contains a lagged dependent variable and also the rejection criteria consists of a region rather than an actual point. The formula for the DW statistic is

$$\text{DW} = \frac{\sum_{t=2}^{T} (u_t - u_{t-1})^2}{\sum_{t=1}^{T} u_t^2} \tag{4.19}$$

where u_t is the residual from the estimated equation, $Y_t = \beta' X_t + u_t$. It may easily be shown that

$$\text{DW} \simeq 2 - 2\rho$$

where ρ is the first-order serial correlation coefficient in the residual process $u_t = \rho u_{t-1} + v_t$. When there is no serial correlation, $\rho = 0$ and the DW statistic takes a value of 2. Positive serial correlation ($\rho_{\max} = 1$) produces a DW < 2 while negative serial correlation produces a DW > 2. We set up the null hypothesis H_0: $\rho = 0$, and a DW value sufficiently far away from 2 rejects this hypothesis (in favour of the assumption that serial correlation is present). The DW statistic can be generalised to tests of higher-order serial correlation but other tests are more frequently used in such cases.

The Lagrange multiplier (LM) test for serial correlation

A more satisfactory test for serial correlation may be constructed using the Lagrange multiplier approach discussed in Chapter 3. This test has an asymptotically exact distribution and is valid in the presence of lagged dependent variables. It can also be constructed to test for any order of serial correlation. We begin by setting up two general models of the error process, an AR(m) model.

$$u_t = \rho_1 u_{t-1} \ldots + \rho_m u_{t-m} + \varepsilon_t \tag{4.20}$$

and a MA(m) one

$$u_t = v_t + \rho_1 v_{t-1} \ldots \rho_m v_{t-m}$$

where ε_t and v_t are white noise errors and u_t is the error term from the structural equation $y_t = \Sigma \alpha_i y_{t-i} + \beta' X_t + u_t$. The null hypothesis H_0: $\rho_1 \ldots \rho_m = 0$, is that there is no serial correlation. The LM statistic is based on the R^2 from the auxiliary regression.

$$\hat{u}_t = \gamma_1 \hat{u}_{t-1} \ldots + \gamma_m \hat{u}_{t-m} + \sum_{i=1}^{K} \alpha_i y_{t-i} + \beta' X_t \tag{4.21}$$

where $\hat{u}_t$ is the residual from the structural equation; $\hat{u}_t$ is the residual utilising consistent parameter estimates ($\hat{\alpha}_i$, $\hat{\beta}$).

The LM test statistic with m degrees of freedom is then given by LM(m) = TR^2, where T is the sample size, and this is asymptotically distributed as $\chi^2(m)$, under the null. Intuitively if H_0 is true we expect γ_i in (4.21) to be zero, for the R^2 from (4.21) to be low and hence LM(m) to be 'small' and less than $\chi^2(m)$.

One difficulty with tests of this form, based on the LM procedure using an auxiliary regression, is that they are valid only when the estimation procedure is OLS. If any form of IV estimation is used then this LM test (and the Breusch–Pagan, Arch or Reset tests given below) is invalid. Breusch and Godfrey (1981) have however suggested a generalisation of the auxiliary regression LM procedure in the case of instrumental variable estimation. The null hypothesis is H_0: $\rho_1 = \ldots \rho_m = 0$, and the modified LM(MLM) test is then given as

$$\text{MLM} = T(R_1^2 - R_2^2)$$

where R_1^2 is the R^2 statistic of the OLS regression of $\hat{u}_t$ on the full set of instruments used in the estimation process (and $\hat{u}_t$ are the structural errors generated by (4.4) with $\hat{\alpha}_0$, $\hat{\alpha}_1$ and $\hat{\beta}_{ki}$ the IV estimates). R_2^2 is the R^2 statistic of the OLS regression of q_t on the same set of instruments (where q_t is the residuals generated by (4.4) when $\hat{u}_{t-1}$ $\ldots \hat{u}_{t-m}$ is also added to the set of explanatory variables in (4.4)). This test is again disributed as $\chi^2(m)$.

Instrument validity test

Much of this chapter has proceeded on the assumption that the estimation technique being used is OLS; section 1.6 (Chapter 1) demonstrated that when the right-hand side variables are not all weakly exogenous then a suitable estimation strategy is instrumental variables (IV). The choice of a correct set of instruments in the absence of a complete knowledge of the system is difficult and even if we know the full system the full set of instruments may be too large given the available data set, so a subset may have to be used. We would then naturally wish to test our chosen set of instruments to see if they are independent of the structural error term ε_1. Under the null hypothesis that the instruments are independent of the error term, the IV/2SLS residuals are consistent (see Chapter 1). Define the instruments as

$$W = (w_1, x_1)$$

where x_1 is the weakly exogenous variables in the equation and w_1 are the instruments for the endogenous variables. If W is independent of ε_1 we would expect a regression of ε_1 on W to yield a low R^2. This intuitive argument is consistent with the Sargan instrument validity test. In place of the unobservable ε_{1t}, we use the IV residuals $\hat{\varepsilon}_{1t}$.

The required OLS regression is:

$$\hat{\varepsilon}_{1t} = W\hat{\alpha}$$

The R^2 from this regression is then used to form the Sargan test:

$$\text{SARG} = (T - k)R^2 \sim \chi^2(r)$$

where

T = number of observations

k = number of parameters in the structural equation

r = number of over-identifying restrictions (the number of instruments in w_1 minus the number of endogenous variables on the right-hand side of the equation)

Under the null(H_0) of independence of the instruments and errors SARG is asymptotically distributed as $\chi^2(r)$ and hence for SARG $< \chi_c^2$ we 'accept' H_0. If SARG is greater than the chosen critical value then we conclude that at least one of the instruments is correlated with the error term and the IV estimates are invalid. The Sargan test may be written in an alternative form which often appears in the literature:

$$\text{SARG} = (\hat{\varepsilon}_1' P_w \hat{\varepsilon}_1)/s^2$$

where P_w = projection matrix of instruments = $W(W'W)^{-1}W'$

$$s^2 = (\hat{\varepsilon}_1'\hat{\varepsilon}_1)/(T - k)$$

These two forms of the test may easily be shown to be equivalent.

The Box–Pierce and Ljung–Box test

Clearly an important source of information in detecting the presence and form of serial correlation, for example AR(1) versus MA(1), is the correlogram, discussed in Chapter 3. Qualitative examination of the correlogram is an important diagnostic tool but it does not constitute a formal statistical test. The Box–Pierce and its related test the Ljung–Box test are both portmanteau tests which allow us to test the hypothesis that the first m points on the correlogram are random with a true value of zero. If we define r_i as the ith autocorrelation coefficient (or point on the correlogram) then it may be shown that asymptotically, r_i is approximately $N(0, T^{-1/2})$ under the null of no serial correlation of order i. Hence for $T = 64$ observations any individual $|r_i| > 0.23$ is indicative of serial correlation of order i (this test is very approximate for $i = 1 \ldots 4$ and more precise for $i > 4$).

Box–Pierce test (generally denoted Q) is defined as

$$Q = T \sum_{i=1}^{m} r_i^2$$

and asymptotically this will be distributed as $\chi^2(m)$. In fact it has been noted that the Q statistic has rather poor small sample properties and a better small sample statistic is given by Ljung–Box (often denoted Q^*) statistic which is defined as

$$Q^* = T(T + 2) \sum_{i=1}^{m} (T - i)^{-i} r_i^2 \tag{4.23}$$

This is again distributed as $\chi^2(m)$ under the null hypothesis of no serial correlation. Intuitively, if a subset of r_i^2 are 'large' then Q (or Q^*) will be 'large' indicating the presence of serial correlation. For both LM and $Q(Q^*)$ acceptance of H_0 for say $m = 8$, requires one to check the individual r_i to see if a large number of r_i close to zero do not mask the presence of a highly significant individual or subset of r_i.

Heteroscedasticity

The general Breusch–Pagan procedure

The most general forms of heteroscedasticity considered in the econometric time series literature usually take the form

$$\sigma_t^2 = \sigma^2 \alpha' X_t = \sigma^2(\alpha_0 + \alpha_1 X_{1t} + \alpha_2 X_{2t} + \ldots) \tag{4.24}$$

$$\sigma_t^2 = \sigma^2(\alpha' X_t)^2 = \sigma^2 [\alpha_0^2 + \alpha_1^2 X_{1t}^2 + \ldots$$

$$+ \sum_{i \neq j} \sum \alpha_i \alpha_j X_{it} X_{jt}] \tag{4.25}$$

$$\sigma_t^2 = \sigma^2 \exp(\alpha' X_t)^2 = \sigma^2 \exp[\alpha_0^2 + \alpha_1^2 X_{1t}^2 + \ldots$$

$$+ \sum_{i \neq j} \sum \alpha_i \alpha_j X_{it} X_{jt}] \tag{4.26}$$

where X_t is a vector of variables which is assumed to be associated with the changing variance of the errors u_t. (The first element of X_t is a constant, and α is a suitably dimensioned vector of parameters.) Often X_t consists of a *subset* of the variables of the 'structural equation' $Y_t = \beta X_t + u_t$ (where X_t may contain lagged dependent variables but this is not necessary for the procedure to be valid).

Breusch and Pagan (1979) point out that the assumption of homoscedastic errors is equivalent to the null hypothesis

$$H_0: \alpha_1 = \alpha_2 = \ldots \alpha_m = 0$$

Under H_0, $\sigma_t = k\sigma^2$ (where k is a constant) and is therefore constant and homoscedastic. They propose a standard LM test of this hypothesis based on the auxiliary regression for (4.24) for example:

$$(\hat{u}_t^2/\hat{\sigma}^2) = \alpha_1 + \alpha_2 X_{2t} + \ldots \alpha_m X_{mt} \tag{4.27}$$

where $\hat{\sigma}^2$ is the standard error of the structural equation $Y_t = \beta' X_t + u_t$. Once again the LM test in this case is $HT(m) = TR^2$, where the R^2 is from equation (4.27). Under H_0, $HT(m)$ is asymptotically distributed as $\chi^2(m)$. The intuition behind this test is as follows. Under the null $\alpha_2 = \ldots \alpha_m = 0$ and so the R^2 of this regression should be zero. If the R^2 is high then it says there is a systematic movement in u_t^2 which is highly correlated with one or more of the X variables and so $E(u_t^2) \neq \sigma^2$ (a constant).

Testing for an ARCH process

An alternative form of heteroscedasticity is termed auto-regressive conditional heteroscedasticity (ARCH). Instead of relating σ_t^2 to a vector of variables (X) as above, u_t^2 is assumed to depend on past squared errors u_{t-1}^2, $u_{t-2}^2 \ldots$ The ARCH process is autoregressive in the second moment. Engle (1982) proposed a LM test for the presence of an ARCH process. The appropriate auxiliary regression in this case is:

$$\hat{u}_t^2 = \alpha_0 + \alpha_1 \hat{u}_{t-1}^2 + \ldots + \alpha_m \hat{u}_{t-m}^2 \tag{4.28}$$

and again the test statistic $\text{ARCH} = TR^2$ from (4.28). Under $H_0: \alpha_1 = \alpha_2 = \ldots = \alpha_m = 0$ ARCH is asymptotically distributed as $\chi^2(m-1)$. The most common form of this test considers only the first order autoregressive model $(m = 1)$.

Parameter stability tests

Two types of Chow test (denoted c_1 and c_2 below) are used to test for statistical parameter stability, that is whether parameters remain stable given that they are always estimated with error. The general idea of parameter stability tests is that we have some known data T_1, after which we believe a structural break may have occurred in the model. So there is the possibility that the general model has the form

$$Y_t = B'_1 X_t + u_t, \quad u_t \sim N(0, \sigma_1^2): t < T \tag{4.29}$$

and

$$Y_t = B_2'X_t + u_t, \qquad u_t \sim N(0, \sigma_2^2): t \geq T_1 \qquad (4.30)$$

The total number of observations is $T = T_1 + T_2$. $T_1 = 1 \ldots T_1$ $T_2 = T_1 + 1 \ldots T$

The null hypothesis that the model is structurally stable is H_0: $B_1 = B_2$ *and* $\sigma_1^2 = \sigma_2^2$. This of course involves two separate hypotheses H_0^1: $B_1 = B_2$ and H_0^2: $\sigma_1^2 = \sigma_2^2$ where we are generally more interested in testing H_0^1 than H_0^2.

A complication which arises in constructing tests of this hypothesis lies in the choice of T_1. In order to estimate both of the models (4.29) and (4.30) we require $T_1 > k$ and $T - T_1 > k$, where k is the number of regressors in the model. This is simply a requirement that there are sufficient degrees of freedom in both sub-samples to estimate the models. We need to consider a test statistic for the case where both $T_1 > k$ and $T - T_1 > k$ holds, and when it does not.

Case A: $T_1 > k$ and $(T - T_1) > k$

This is an analysis of variance (ANOVA) test. In this case we can estimate the model over the whole period and each of the sub-samples. We define RSS$_T$ as the residual sum of squares for the model estimated over the whole period, RSS$_1$ as the residual sum of squares over the period with T_1 observations, and RSS$_2$ as the residual sum of squares for the second period with T_2 observations. Then under the null H_0 (the joint hypothesis), the statistic c_1:

$$c_1 = \left(\frac{\text{RSS}_T - (\text{RSS}_1 - \text{RSS}_2)}{\text{RSS}_1 + \text{RSS}_2} \right) \left(\frac{T - 2k}{k} \right) \qquad (4.31)$$

is distributed as $F(k, T - 2k)$. c_1 is commonly called the Chow test (Chow 1960). We can also separately test H_0^2, namely $\sigma_1^2 = \sigma_2^2$ using the statistic

$$V_1 = \frac{s_2^2}{s_1^2} \equiv \left(\frac{\text{RSS}_2}{\text{RSS}_1} \right) \frac{(T_1 - k)}{(T_2 - k)} \qquad (4.32)$$

where s_i is the standard error of the appropriate regression in periods T_1 and T_2 $s_i = \text{RSS}_i/(T_i - k)$. V_1 is distributed as $F(T_2 - k, T_1 - k)$ under the null that $\sigma_1^2 = \sigma_2^2$. Intuitively the test (V_1) for equality of variances in the two sub-samples is straightforward. If we have equal variances across sub-samples then $V_1 = 1$ and it will be less than the critical value of the F distribution.

Since c_1 tests for the *joint* hypothesis H_0 it is useful to first test V_1. If V_1 is not rejected (i.e. $\sigma_1^2 = \sigma_2^2$) then we test c_1. Rejection of c_1 then implies $B_1 \neq B_2$. If V_1 is rejected we would also expect c_1 to be rejected but we cannot say whether the latter implies that $B_1 \neq B_2$. Inference on $B_1 = B_2$ in such circumstances must remain inconclusive.

Case B: $T_2 < k$

It is usual to consider only the case where $T_2 < k$ since the case of $T_1 < k$ may be dealt with in an exactly analogous fashion. When there are not enough degrees of freedom to estimate B_2 or RSS$_2$ directly, a second version of the Chow test is possible:

$$C_2 = \left(\frac{\text{RSS}_T - \text{RSS}_1}{\text{RSS}_1} \right) \left(\frac{T_1 - k}{T_2} \right) \tag{4.33}$$

This is distributed as $F(T_2, T_1 - k)$ under the null that $B_1 = B_2$ against the alternative that $B_1 \neq B_2$ *and* $\sigma_0^2 = \sigma_2^2$. C_2 is a joint hypothesis and to test separately for constant error variance $\sigma_1^2 = \sigma_2^2$ we proceed as follows. Estimate over the first T_1 observations to obtain $\hat{B}'$. If we denote the values of (Y_t, X_t) over the second period as Y_t^2, X_t^2, then the one-step-ahead forecast errors (using $\hat{B}'$) are $\tilde{u}_{2t} = Y_t^2 - \hat{B}' X_t^2$ (there are T_2 of these) under the null $\sigma_1^2 = \sigma_2^2$, the variance of these one-step-ahead forecast errors in the second period, should equal those in the first period – as measured by $s_1^2 = \text{RSS}_1/(T_1 - k)$. Under the null that $\sigma_1^2 = \sigma_2^2$,

$$\text{HF}(T_2) = (s_1^2)^{-1} \sum \tilde{u}_{2t}^2 \tag{4.34}$$

is distributed as $\chi^2(T_2)$. This test is sometimes referred to as the Hendry forecast test. Again, the sequence of testing should be first to use HF to check that $\sigma_1^2 = \sigma_2^2$ cannot be rejected, and then C_2 to check that $B_1 = B_2$ cannot be rejected.

Although HF is a test of constant error variances, it may also be viewed either as an indicator of *numerical* parameter constancy or equivalently as a test of the *relative* accuracy of out-of-sample point forecasts. s_1^2 is a measure of the *within* sample variance of the errors or *within sample* forecast accuracy since $\hat{u}_t^1 = y_t^1 - \hat{y}_{2t}'$. The $\tilde{u}_{2t}$ series measure out-of-sample forecast errors (using the estimate of B based on the first T_1 observation.) If B is numerically the same in T_1 and T_2 periods we would expect $\tilde{u}_{2t}$ to be of the same order of magnitude as $\hat{u}_{1t}$. Hence HF would be unity for each of the T_2 periods, and HF $< \chi_c^2$, that is we do not reject numerical parameter constancy. A word of caution: if the equation fits badly within sample (s_1^2 large) then one may have HF $< \chi_c^2$ but the *absolute* value of the out-of-sample forecast errors $\tilde{u}_{2t}$ may be large. Here we have a 'bad' fit within the sample and equally poor predictions out-of-sample. It is therefore worth looking at individual $\tilde{u}_{2t}$ values.

These structural stability tests may be used more powerfully in a recursive setting by computing a sequence of tests where the 'break' period moves through time (see below). Another useful test procedure is the Salkever (1976) test which is similar in approach to the Chow tests. In this test a set of dummies (DV$_i$ = 00 ... 0100, each with unity in the ith period) are added to the equation for j subperiods. Then a joint F-test of the significance of the set of dummies is constructed to test for a structural break over the sub-period. The size of each dummy coefficient is equal to the out-of-sample forecast error and the 't' statistics on individual coefficients indicate those periods for which the equation undergoes a statistically significant shift in its parameters.

Recursive estimation and testing structural stability

Recursive estimation may be viewed as a special case of the Kalman filter and as such it is a powerful and interesting technique of its own right. In this section, however, we will be considering the more limited use of recursive estimation in testing the stability of structural models. One of the difficulties of the formal stability tests presented above is that we make the assumption that a possible break point is known '*a priori*' and we simply wish to test this known point. In general, however, we have no strong prior knowledge of specific structural breaks and so it is useful to have a general framework to investigate the stability of a model. Recursive estimation provides such a framework.

Recursive estimation may be thought of as a series of conventional OLS estimation of the same model where the data period is increased successively by one period in each estimate. It therefore produces a time series of estimates of β, $\hat{\beta}_t$ from the estimated equation:

$$Y_i = \hat{\beta}_t X_i + \hat{u}_i \qquad i = 1 \ldots t; \quad t = k \ldots T \qquad (4.35)$$

It must be stressed that while $\hat{\beta}_t$ varies, the underlying β is assumed to be constant, so this is not a time-varying parameter model. We simply derive varying estimates of the constant β from different data sets. It is intuitively clear that if our model is structurally stable the variation in $\hat{\beta}_t$, as we move through time, should be small and random. So sudden large changes in $\hat{\beta}_t$ may indicate periods of structural break, while non-random or trend movements in $\hat{\beta}_t$ may indicate some underlying misspecification. Once a specific period of instability is detected we could then turn to one of the structural tests above. However, the usefulness of recursive estimation does not end with the estimation of $\hat{\beta}_t$ as we see below. The recursive residuals are defined as:

$$v_t = Y_t - \hat{\beta}'_{t-1} X_t \qquad t = k + 1 \ldots T$$

This amounts to the one-step-ahead forecasting error made by the

OLS estimation procedure. Under the null hypothesis that β is constant and $u_t \sim N(0, \sigma^2)$ then $v_t \sim N(0, \sigma^2 d_t^2)$ where $d_t = (1 + x_r'(X_{r-1}'X_{r-1})^{-1}x_r)^{-1}$ defining $X_{r-1}' = (x_1, \ldots, x_{r-1})$, and so we may define the *standardised recursive residuals* as

$$w_t = v_t/d_t \sim N(0, \sigma^2)$$

While the standardised recursive residuals follow the same distribution as the OLS residuals they have a number of advantages. The first is that the OLS residuals are constrained (when a constant is included in the regression) to sum to zero. So, by definition there can be no overall departure of the residuals from zero. This is not true of the recursive residuals and so they will often show systematic departures from zero if there is any misspecification of time variation in the parameters. The second important property of the recursive residuals is that it may be shown that

$$\text{RSS}_t = \text{RSS}_{t-1} + w_t^2$$

That is, the residual sum of squares for an OLS estimation over period 1 to t is given by the residual sum of squares for an OLS estimation over the period 1 to $(t-1)$ plus the squared standardised recursive residual for time t. So given w_t it is possible to construct a wide variety of alternative Chow tests. For example, we could construct a series of one-period Chow tests, each testing the hypothesis that a structural break occurs in a successively later period.

Two test procedures which take special advantage of the properties of the recursive residuals are the CUSUM and CUSUMSQ tests of Brown, Durbin and Evans (1975). Both tests consist of a series of statistics, defined as:

$$\text{CUSUM}_t = (1/s) \sum_{i=k+1}^{t} w_i$$

where s is the full sample estimate of the standard error of the regression

$$\text{CUSUMSQ}_t = \left(\sum_{i=k+1}^{t} w_i^2 \right) \Big/ \left(\sum_{j=k+1}^{T} w_j^2 \right) = \frac{\text{RSS}_t}{\text{RSS}_T}$$

The CUSUM test is therefore simply the sum of the recursive residuals normalised by the standard error of the residuals. If the residuals are random we would expect the CUSUM statistic to remain close to zero; any systematic departure from zero would suggest misspecification. The CUSUMSQ statistic is simply the sum of the *squared* recursive residuals normalised by the residual sum of squared errors for the full period, so at T, CUSUMSQ $= 1$. Both of these tests are used generally in the form of a plot of either the CUSUM or CUSUMSQ statistics against time and critical values may be found in Harvey (1981). It is generally recognised however that the formal power of the tests is rather low and in practice they are often used as an informal diagnostic tool.

It is perhaps finally worth noting that the CUSUMSQ test may be put into the form of a recursive Chow test since the Chow (c_2) test given in (4.33) may be written as

$$c_{2t} = \left(\frac{1}{\text{CUSUMSQ}_t} - 1 \right) \left(\frac{T_1 - K}{T - T_1} \right)$$

Hence the CUSUMSQ test may be interpreted as a particular form of sequential Chow test.

Testing functional form

An important simplification in the move from the *general* DGP to an actual maintained hypothesis that is estimable is the assumption of a particular functional form. The Box–Cox (1964) procedure provides one method of assessing functional form, but a simple yet fairly general test is that due to Ramsey (1974). In Ramsey's test the alternative model involves a high-order polynomial to represent a different functional form. The RESET test (Ramsey 1974) in its most common form consists of the following regression

$$Y_t = \beta' X_t + \alpha_1 \hat{Y}_t^2 + \alpha_2 \hat{Y}_t^3 + \ldots + \alpha_m \hat{Y}_t^m \tag{4.36}$$

where $\hat{Y}_t = \hat{\beta} X_t$ are the predictions from the preferred structural model. The higher order powers in $\hat{Y}_t$ implicitly involve higher order terms in X_t as well as cross terms (such as $X_{1t} X_{2t}$) and hence embody a functional form different from $Y = B'X$.

Subtracting $\hat{\beta}' X_t$ from both sides of (4.36) we obtain

$$\hat{u}_t = \gamma' X + \sum_{i=1}^{m} \alpha_i \hat{Y}_t^{i+1} \tag{4.37}$$

where $\gamma' = (B' - \hat{B})'$. Under the null H_0: $\alpha_1 = \alpha_2 = \ldots \alpha_m = 0$, the RESET test is RESET(m) = TR^2 and is distributed as $\chi^2(m)$.

Testing for normality

An important assumption underlying the use of OLS, and most test statistics, is that the residuals of the model are normally distributed. When this assumption and the others regarding marginalisation and conditioning are valid then OLS is the maximum likelihood estimator. There are several non-parametric tests for normality (the Kolmogorov–Smirnov test and the Shapiro–Wilk test are examples) which we will not discuss here. The most widely used parametric test is based on testing the third and fourth moments, skewness and kurtosis, for departures from normality. Skewness is given by the formula

$$\text{SK} = \left(\frac{1}{T}\sum_{t=1}^{T} u_t^3\right)\bigg/\left(\frac{1}{T}\sum_{t=1}^{T} u_t^2\right)^{3/2} \tag{4.38}$$

SK is centred on zero and, when standardised by $T^{0.5}$ has a variance of 6. Kurtosis is given by

$$\text{EK} = \left(\frac{1}{T}\sum_{t=1}^{T} u_t^4\right)\bigg/\left(\frac{1}{T}\sum_{t=1}^{T} u_t^2\right)^{2} \tag{4.39}$$

When this is standardised by $T^{1/2}$ it has a mean value of 3 and a variance of 24. Given those properties it is possible to construct the following test for normality, due to Bera and Jarque (1982):

$$\text{BJ} = \left[\frac{T}{6}\,\text{SK}^2 + \frac{T}{24}\,(\text{EK} - 3)^2\right] \tag{4.40}$$

and under the null that the error term is normally distributed this will be distributed as $\chi^2(2)$.

While testing for normality is obviously important in practical applications the BJ test is perhaps even more useful as a test of outliers. It is very sensitive to the presence of outlier observations and so failing the BJ test is often simply a signal to look for one or two large errors and see if there are data problems or specific effects (such as strikes, incomes policy periods) which can be 'eliminated' with dummy variables.

Encompassing test

The idea of a model being adequate in the sense of being congruent with the data is an important one. It involves passing all the tests outlined above, but it also involves the model being one which cannot be dominated in all senses by some other model. To implement the latter point we need a framework for testing models against each other; this is the encompassing principle, see Mizon and Richard (1986). In general terms the notion of encompassing is a simple one. A model M_1 may be said to encompass another model M_2 if it can explain the results of that model. As an example, suppose M_1 contains an important weakly exogenous variable which behaves erratically at some point in time. If M_1 represents the DGP fairly well and M_2 excludes this variable we might expect to see structural instability of M_2 at the point in the data set where the omitted variable changes. In this case M_1 would predict the structural failure of M_2 and we would say that M_1 encompasses M_2. More formally we may follow the definition of Mizon and Richard. Let $\tilde{\Theta}$ denote some statistic which we are using to assess M_2 and let $\Theta_1 = E_1(\tilde{\Theta})$ denote the expectation of Θ when it is applied to M_1. Then under a suitable set of exogeneity assumptions we may consider the statistic.

$$\phi = \tilde{\Theta} - \Theta_1$$

which compares the *observed* value of $\tilde{\Theta}$ with its expectation under M_1. It may be shown that M_1 encompasses M_2 with respect to $\tilde{\Theta}$ if ϕ does not differ significantly from zero. Clearly in order to implement this we must derive forms of ϕ with a known distribution. One of the advantages of the encompassing principle is that it provides a framework for linking many existing test procedures. In particular, when we are dealing with nested pairs of models (i.e. when either $M_1 \subset M_2$ or $M_2 \subset M_1$) then Mizon and Richard show that the standard test procedures may be given an encompassing interpretation. So we may use F-tests or likelihood ratio tests in the usual way, giving the results an encompassing interpretation. Similarly in a non-nested framework (when neither M_1 is contained in M_2 nor M_2 is contained in M_1) then many of the non-nested tests may be applied as encompassing tests, for example the J test of Davidson and Mackinnon (1981) or the Hausman (1978) specification test.

To illustrate the case of *variance encompassing* consider the following two competing explanations of Y:

$$M_1: Y = X\alpha + u \qquad u \sim (0, \sigma_u^2) \tag{4.41}$$

$$M_2: Y = ZB + w \qquad w \sim (0, \sigma_w^2) \tag{4.42}$$

For any given sample of data we have the following relationship between the variables X and Z

$$X = Z\gamma + v \tag{4.43}$$

On the assumption that M_1 is true we would expect M_2 to be estimated as

$$Y = Z(\gamma\alpha) + (v\alpha + u) \tag{4.44}$$

Comparing (4.44) and (4.42) under M_1 we expect

$$\sigma_w^2 = \sigma_u^2 + \alpha^2 \sigma_v^2 \tag{4.45}$$

and $\sigma_u^2 < \sigma_w^2$, asymptotically. Hence if M_1 is true we expect it to have a lower standard error than a competing model M_2; this is a variance-encompassing test.

In the case where one model M_2 is nested within another larger model M_1 (i.e. $Z \subset X$) the M_1 will automatically encompass M_2. This means that a model can always be made to encompass rival models simply by adding variables so as to nest the rival models. This approach is of little value and to rule out this trivial form of encompassing the concept of *parsimonious* encompassing is used. A model is said to be parsimonious when it uses the minimum number of estimated parameters to adequately represent the DGP. So we may say that M_2 parsimoniously encompasses M_1 if and only if M_2 encompasses M_1 and M_2 is nested within M_1. (Note that it is possible for both M_1 to encompass M_2 and M_2 to encompass M_1.)

Where we are dealing with two non-nested hypotheses the encompassing principle offers a new approach to the standard non-nested tests which is intuitively appealing. Hendry and Richard (1987) demonstrate that if we define a model M_c as an artificial model which nests both M_1 and M_2 within it, then M_1 encompasses M_2 if and only if M_1 encompasses M_c. So a conventional F-test against the artificial nesting model M_c may be given an encompassing interpretation. The Hendry and Richard result is however based on a moderately strong set of assumptions including fixed regressors and strong exogeneity.

4.3 An application to the demand for M2 in three European countries

In this section we will illustrate the general to specific and ECM modelling strategy discussed above using an example taken from Taylor (1986) of the estimation of broad money (M2) demand functions for three European Countries – West Germany, France and the Netherlands.

The data

A common problem encountered in investigating money demand in European countries is that data definitions, particularly for the broader measure of the money stock, are not consistent across the various countries concerned (OECD 1977). Partly in order to attenuate this problem, and partly because some of the required data series are not available in published sources, Den Butter and Fase (1981)

(BF) asked the Central Banks of eight European countries to provide data on the relevant variables. The data series published in BF therefore constitute a fairly consistent data bank which is highly desirable in comparative studies of this kind. Even within this data bank, however, unbroken series on all variables for the whole of the sample period is available for only three countries: West Germany, the Netherlands and France. Also, all series on these three countries start at 1960(1) and terminate at 1978(4).

The series used were nominal M2, nominal GNP (GDP for France), the implicit GNP (GDP) deflator (1970 = 100), the long-term interest rate, the short-term interest rate (for West Germany and the Netherlands only, the three-month interbank rate for the former, the local authority three-month rate for the latter), and a business cycle indicator (derived from industrial output indices for France and West Germany and from the labour utilisation rate for the Netherlands). All data except those for M2 are seasonally adjusted.

The implications of using seasonally adjusted/unadjusted data should be pointed out at this point. For ease of exposition, consider a two-variable relationship using polynomials in the lag operator L(i.e. $L^i x_t = x_{t-i}$), and suppress the constant term:

$$\alpha(L)y_t = \beta(L)x_t + u_t \tag{4.46}$$

where

$$\alpha(L) = 1 - \alpha_1 L - \alpha_2 L^2 - \ldots - \alpha_n L^n$$
$$\beta(L) = \beta_0 + \beta_1 L + \beta_2 L^2 + \ldots + \beta_n L^n$$

Suppose that y_t is seasonally adjusted to y_t^a by means of the filter $\lambda(L)$ (a scalar polynomial in the lag operator):

$$y_t^a = \lambda(L)y_t \tag{4.47}$$

and similarly, x_t is seasonally adjusted by applying the filter $\mu(L)$ (a scalar polynomial in the lag operator):

$$x_t^a = \mu(L)x_t \tag{4.48}$$

Substituting (4.47) and (4.48) in (4.46):

$$\alpha(L)y_t^a = \beta(L)x_t^a + v_t \tag{4.49}$$

where

$$v_t = [\lambda(L) - \mu(L)]\beta(L)x_t + \lambda(L)u_t \tag{4.50}$$

From this we can note the following (see also Hendry and Mizon 1978). Firstly, if u_t in (4.46) is 'seasonally serially correlated and is 'whitened' by applying the filter $\lambda(L)$ and if, further, the same filter is applied to both y_t and x_t i.e. $\lambda(L) = \mu(L)$, then the disturbance in (4.49) will be white noise. Secondly, seasonal adjustment does not alter the appropriate lag structure for the equation. Thirdly, although it may seem odd to adjust seasonal variables such as interest rates, the above algebra makes clear that this is reasonable in the context of estimation since the whole equation is seasonally adjusted. Fourthly, problems may arise when (as in the present context) the same filter has *not* been applied to both the left- and right-hand side variables $(\lambda(L) \neq \mu(L))$. As expression (4.50) makes clear, this may introduce serial correlation into the disturbance term and distort the testing and estimation procedures. Since all the data used in this section are obtained from the BF data base and are not readily available elsewhere, this appears to be an insuperable problem.

However, the following method was applied in mitigation. Suppose the seasonal filter for the x variables, $\mu(L)$, can be approximated closely by the standard method of regressing the unadjusted variable on to seasonal dummies and using the residual as the adjusted series. Since, as is well known, including seasonal dummies in a regression is identically equivalent to adjusting all of the (left- and right-hand side) variables prior to estimation, this will have the effect of seasonally adjusting the dependent variable in the same fashion as the right-hand side variables (see Frisch and Waugh 1933; Malinvaud 1970, pp 486–9). Accordingly, seasonal dummies were included in all regressions. It should be noted, however, that previous empirical applications in the LSE tradition to money demand often use seasonally adjusted data.

Estimation results

Since the data on M2 was seasonally unadjusted and all series were quarterly, we decided to set the length of the lag structure for the maintained hypothesis at four periods. The maintained hypothesis for each of the countries was therefore:

$$m_t = \alpha_0 + \sum_{i=1}^{4} \alpha_i m_{t-i} + \sum_{i=0}^{4} \beta_i P_{t-i} + \sum_{i=0}^{4} \gamma_i y_{t-i}$$

$$+ \sum_{i=0}^{4} \sigma_i r_{t-i}^l \sum_{i=0}^{4} k_i r_{t-i}^s + \sum_{i=0}^{4} \lambda_i c_{t-i} + u_t \qquad (4.51)$$

where m denotes M2, p the price level, y real income, r^l the long interest rate, r^s the short interest rate, and c the business cycle indicator. All variables are in natural logarithms except r^s and r^l.

The business cycle indicator was included, following BF, on the argument that precautionary balances should rise as economic activity
slows down. The short-term interest rate was included for the Netherlands and West Germany, again following BF, in order to pick up
switching between components of M2 and less liquid assets that
occurred in these countries during the 1970s. As in BF, r^s is entered
as zero up to the fourth quarter of 1969 and a dummy variable taking
the value one for 1960 (1)–1969 (4) and zero otherwise was included
to adjust for the discontinuity. The short rate was entered in levels in
order to allow its elasticity to vary, since switching becomes more
likely as short rates rise. Three seasonal dummies were also included
in all regressions (but are not reported) as well as a dummy in the
French equations to account for the student riots of May 1968 (see
BF).

The first four observations of each series were lost because of lags
in (4.51). In common with BF, we reserved the last eight observations
for post-estimation stability tests. The specification search therefore
took place using data for 1961 (1)–1976 (4), a total of sixty-four observations. We used ordinary least squares for estimation purposes, and
tested for the validity of this procedure rather than use an estimator
such as instrumental variables (see below). In what follows we use a
nominal test size of five per cent (unless stated to the contrary).

Our final, parsimonious short-run money demand functions are
listed in Table 4.1, together with a set of diagnostic statistics for each
equation. The equation for demand for M2 in the Netherlands is
particularly encouraging. It relates short-run growth in real M2
demand to an error correction term of the kind discussed above (with
one lag), implying a highly significant 'inverse velocity' effect on
short-run money balances. The current rate of inflation ($\Delta_1 p_t$) and
lagged values of the long and short rates are also found to be
significant explanatory variables and have coefficients of the expected
signs. This indicates significant switching between components of M2
and less liquid securities and real assets over the period. The current
value of the cyclical indicator also was high explanatory power and
indicates a significant level of precautionary demand. These and the
other terms in the Netherlands equation allow an extremely rich
pattern for the short-run dynamics of money demand.

Turning to the diagnostic for the Netherlands equation, 'RESET' is
the F-statistic for the restrictions imposed on the general unrestricted
form (4.51) in order to arrive at the final specification, and is highly
insignificant – as one should expect given the data-based nature of
the specification search (see Note 1). We can see that the equation
explains nearly ninety per cent of the variation in real money growth

Table 4.1 Final parsimonious equations for money demand

Netherlands:

$$\Delta_1(m - p)_t = 4.99 \quad - 0.26(m-p-y)_{t-1}- 0.95\Delta_1 p_t \quad - 0.059 r_{t-3}$$
$$(6.52) \qquad\qquad (7.34) \qquad\qquad (8.43) \qquad\qquad (4.34)$$
$$-0.082\Delta_1^2 r_{t-2}^1 + 0.0043 r_{t-1}^s \quad - 1.13 c_t \quad + 5.17\Delta_1 c_t$$
$$(2.40) \qquad\qquad (5.75) \qquad\qquad (6.74) \qquad\qquad (6.01)$$
$$- 5.38\Delta_1^2 c_{t-1}$$
$$(3.21)$$

$R^2 = 0.88$, DW $= 2.09$, BP(12) $= 8.23$, SER $= 0.010$,
RESET(21, 30) $= 0.38$, SK $= -0.07$,
EK $= -0.42$, BJ(2) $= 0.42$, LM4(4, 43) $= 1.02$, Q(16) $= 13.47$,
ARCH(1) $= 0.13$, RESET(4, 47) $= 2.17$, EX(1, 50) $= 1.44$,
CHOW(7, 44) $= 0.48$, HF(5, 51) $= 2.00$

Germany:

$$\Delta_1(m - p)_t) = -0.17 \quad + 0.23\Delta_2 y_t \quad - 0.15(m-p-y)_{t-1}- 0.40\Delta_4 P_t$$
$$(2.11) \qquad\qquad (2.67) \qquad\qquad (3.6) \qquad\qquad (3.20)$$
$$- 0.056 r_t + 0.052 r_{t-4} + 0.0031 r_t^s \qquad -0.38\Delta_1(m - p)_{t-3}$$
$$(2.92) \qquad (3.18) \qquad\qquad (3.55) \qquad\qquad (3.43)$$

$R^2 = 0.81$, DW $= 2.12$, SER $= 0.012$, RESET(21, 20) $= 1.15$,
SK $= -0.36$, EK $= 0.39$, BJ(2) $= 1.55$, BP(10) $= 12.40$,
LM(44, 45) $= 1.48$, Q(16) $= 15.77$, ARCH(1) $= 0.032$,
RESET(4, 45) $= 2.22$, EX(4, 49) $= 1.17$,
CHOW(7, 46) $= 1.47$, PF(6, 53) $= 1.64$.

France:

$$\Delta_1(m - p)_t = 0.64 \quad + 0.13 y_t \quad + 0.17\Delta_4 y_t \quad + 0.52\Delta_2 y_{t-1}- 0.20(m-p-y)_{t-4}$$
$$(1.96) \qquad (2.78) \qquad (2.59) \qquad\qquad (3.98) \qquad\qquad (3.56)$$
$$-0.34\Delta_1 p_t \quad - 0.11\Delta_1^2 r_t^1 + 0.052 rl_{t-1} + 0.11\Delta_1 r_{t-3}^1 + 0.29\Delta_1(m - p)_{t-2}$$
$$(1.91) \qquad\qquad (2.21) \qquad (1.61) \qquad\qquad (1.91) \qquad\qquad (2.20)$$
$$0.21 c \quad - 0.67\Delta_2 c_{t-1}$$
$$(2.46) \qquad (4.49)$$

$R^2 = 0.73$, DW $= 2.08$, SER $= 0.009$, RESET(13, 33) $= 0.43$,
SK $= -0.61$, EK $= 0.65$, BJ(2) $= 3.84$, LM4(4, 40) $= 2.40$,
Q(16) $= 22.89$, ARCH(1) $= 0.047$, RESET(4, 44) $= 0.53$,
EX(4, 44) $= 1.30$, CHOW(12, 36) $= 1.73$, HF(5.48) $= 1.34$.

Note: Figures in parentheses below coefficient estimates denote *t*-ratios.

($R^2 = 0.88$) with an equation standard error (SER) of one per cent. DW is the Durbin–Watson statistic which, together with the Lagrange multiplier statistic for up to fourth-order (moving average or autoregressive) serial correlation (LM4), indicates that the non-systematic dynamics of the equation are white noise (see Note 2). This impression is echoed by the value of the Box–Pierce portmanteau statistic for sixteen lagges ($Q(16)$). SK and EK are the moment coefficients of skewness and excess kurtosis and should be approximately zero for normally distributed errors. Their size should also give an indication of any significant outliers in the residuals. BJ tests for the joint significance of SK and EK and is thus a test for normality of the residuals.

In order to examine possible heteroskedasticity in the residuals, we computed a test for a non-scalar covariance matrix due to Breusch and Pagan (1979) (BP), which was found to be insignificant. We also calculated a Lagrange multiplier test for possible first-order auto-regressive conditional heteroscedasticity (ARCH) effects in the residuals and this statistic (ARCH) was also insignificant. Since the equation was estimated by ordinary least squares, we implicitly assumed the econometric exogeneity of the current-dated, right-hand side variables. This hypothesis was tested using a test due to Hausman (1978) (EX) and we were unable to reject the hypothesis of exogeneity of the right-hand side variables (see Note 3). The general test for misspecification of the model, (RESET) is insignificant at the five per cent level.

Finally, we performed two tests for parameter stability on the model. CHOW is the analysis of covariance test for parameter stability due to Chow (1960), and tests for a structural break from the first quarter of 1970 onwards; it is insignificant. HF tests for the predictive accuracy of the equation of the model over the period 1977 (1)–1978 (4), which was not included in the estimation period. We used the indicator variable method due to Salkever (1976) and Pagan and Nicholls (1984) to perform this test. This essentially involves defining a dummy variable for each of the post-estimation data points and testing the joint significance of these dummies when the equation is run over the whole sample including the prediction period. Salkever (1976) shows that the coefficients of these dummies are the prediction errors with confidence intervals which can be calculated from the estimated standard errors.

A major advantage of this method is that it controls for sampling variations in the parameter estimates. It was found, however, that some of these dummies were individually significant when added into the general unrestricted form (5) when the whole sample was used. This indicates that the maintained hypothesis itself is incapable of explaining these observations and may be indicative of extraordinary circumstances in these periods or that the maintained hypothesis is itself incorrect (Baba *et al.* 1985, for example, include variables to control for items such as risk to long-term bond holding). Since there was some degree of overlap in the significance of the dummies in the maintained hypothesis for each of the three countries (1977 (3), 1978 (3) and 1978 (4) for the Netherlands, 1977 (1) and 1978 (4) for

West Germany, and 1977 (1), 1978 (2) and 1978 (3) for France) and because the maintained hypothesis could not readily be expanded because of data limitations, the predictive failure tests were computed without testing for the significance of dummies which were found to be individually significant in the unrestricted form. The resulting value of HF for the Netherlands is insignificant.

Similar comments apply to short-run equations obtained for West Germany and France. Good fits were obtained and all of the diagnostic statistics are insignificant at nominal test sizes greater than five per cent. In particular, both equations pass the Chow test for in-sample parameter stability. In the German equation, the short-term interest rate again showed the significant explanatory power and yielded a coefficient of the expected sign. However, the business cycle indicator dropped out of the German regressions during the sequential specification search, indicating the absence of any significant precautionary elements in German money demand over the period.

Following BF, the short interest rate was not included in the French regressions, but the business cycle indicator does appear with a significant coefficient of the expected sign in the final equation. Another interesting feature of the French equation is that the error correction term appears with a lag of four periods, indicating a slower response to the 'inverse velocity effect' than in the other two countries. Also, the French equation includes a significant value of the current level of real income. As discussed above, this destroys the property of long-run unit elasticity of money demand with respect to real income.

The long-run or steady-state solutions to the short-run demand functions are given in Table 4.2. Long-run unit real income elasticities are found for the Netherlands and West Germany. This contrasts with the results of BF (and also of Boughton 1979) who find real income elasticities in excess of unity for these countries – 1.19 and 1.21 respectively for the Netherlands and Germany (see Note 4). On the

Table 4.2 Steady-state solutions for money demand equations

Netherlands:	$m_t = \kappa_1 + p_t + y_t - 0.23r_t^l + 0.017r_t^s - 4.34c_t$
	$(\kappa_1 = 19.20 + 0.92g_p - 1.71g_y)$
Germany:	$m_t = \kappa_2 + p_t + y_t - 0.026r_t^l + 0.02r_t^s$
	$(\kappa_2 = -1.11 - 2.67g_p - 0.27g_y)$
France:	$m_t = \kappa_3 + p_t + 1.64y_t - 0.26r_t^l - 1.02c_t$
	$(\kappa_3 = 3.19 - 0.43g_p + 1.33g_y)$

Note: g_p and g_y denote the annualised steady-state growth rates of prices and real income respectively.

other hand, we estimated the long-run income elasticity for France to be 1.64, which is very close to BF's estimate of 1.61. The steady-state, long-term interest rate elasticity for France is indentical to BF's long-run elasticity at −0.26, and the long-run coefficients of the business cycle indicator are also very close (−1.02 on our estimate against −1.05 on BF's).

In the Netherlands long-run equation the long-term interest elasticity of −0.23 is very slightly lower than BF's estimate of −0.30, and the size of our long-run coefficient on the business cycle indicator (−4.34) compares with that of BF (−3.61). In the German steady-state equation, on the other hand, our long-term interest state elasticity of −0.026 is much smaller than the value reported by BF (−0.20), and we found the business cycle indicator to be insignificant altogether in explaining German money demand.

We find a long-run elasticity of 0.02 for the short interest rate in the German equation. This translates into an elasticity of 0.12 at the mean interest rate of about six per cent, and compares with the corresponding figure reported by BF of 0.15. In the Netherlands steady-state equation, at a mean short interest rate of approximately six per cent over the period, the semi-elasticity of 0.017 becomes 0.102, comparing with 0.13 reported by BF.

Overall, therefore, our steady-state money demand equations compare well with the long-run solutions to the transfer functions estimated by BF. A major difference between the two sets of results being that we find long-run real income elasticities of unity for West Germany and the Netherlands, in contrast to BF who find long-run elasticities or real income substantially in excess on unity. We believe that this may be due to the arbitrary (and untested) restrictions which BF impose on the lag structure of their equations.

4.4   Conclusion

In this chapter we have developed the methodology of dynamic modelling which has grown out the LSE tradition of econometrics and we have illustrated its power and usefulness by presenting a study of the demand for money. Dynamic modelling is a flexible tool which allows a complex interaction of economic theory and time series data so that both theory coherence and data coherence can be achieved. We would end on a note of warning, as dynamic modelling is sometimes presented as an almost mechanical rule for model building; this is almost never the case. Dynamic modelling is a framework for bringing together data and economic theory which requires skill and understanding on the part of the user; if this is absent then dynamic modelling can be little more use than step-wise regression and it is unlikely to yield insights into the real world.

Notes

1. Test statistics which appear in Table 4.1 with two figures in brackets (e.g. REST (21, 30)) should be referred to the F-distribution with the indicated degrees of freedom, while those appearing with one figure (e.g. BJ(2)) should be referred to the chi-square distribution with the indicated degree of freedom.
2. We calculated the Langrange multiplier statistic for serial correlation as an F rather than a chi-square statistic in the light of the Monte Carlo evidence of Kiviet (1983).
3. The Hausman exogeneity test requires an estimator which is consistent even under the alternative hypothesis of exogeneity of the current-dated right-hand-side variables. For this purpose we used an instrumental variables estimator with the once-lagged 'foreign' values of the putative endogenous variables as instuments (e.g. the French and German lagged inflation rates were used as instruments for the Netherlands inflation). In each case the instruments set was tested and accepted on the basis of Sargan's (1964) test for the validity of the instruments.
4. We refer to BF's estimates of real money demand (1981, Table 3).

5
Non-stationarity and cointegration

Cointegration analysis, carefully applied, allows the analysis of long-run economic relationships. In some ways, this work parallels the work on error correction mechanisms which we discussed in Chapter 4 on dynamic modelling. As we shall see, there is a close relationship between cointegration and error correction models.

The basic insight of cointegration analysis is that, although many economic time series may tend to trend up or down over time in a non-stationary fashion, groups of variables may drift together. If there is a tendency for some linear relationships to hold between a set of variables over long periods of time, then cointegration analysis helps us to discover it. If an economic theory is correct we would expect the specific set of variables suggested by the theory to be related to each other (usually with constant parameters). So there should be no tendency for the variables to drift increasingly further away from each other as time goes on. If, however, there is *no* (linear) relationship between the variables they are said *not* to cointegrate and severe doubt must be cast on the usefulness of the underlying theory. This cointegration can be used to test the validity of an economic theory if the latter involves variables which in the data set exhibit strong (stochastic) trends.

5.1   Stationarity

A key concept in the discussion of this chapter is that of stationarity. In general, we shall be concerned with the idea of *weak* stationarity (see Spanos, 1986). A weakly stationary series has a constant mean and constant, finite variance. Thus, a time series (x_t) is stationary if its mean, $E(x_t)$, is independent of t, and its variance, $E[x_t - E(x_t)]^2$ is bounded by some finite number and does not vary systematically with time. Thus it will tend to return to its mean and fluctuations around this mean will have a broadly constant amplitude. A non-stationary series, on the other hand, will have a time-varying mean (or variance) and so we cannot in general refer to it without reference to some particular time period.

The simplest example of a non-stationary process is a random walk (without drift):

$$x_t = x_{t-1} + e_t$$

where e_t is independent and normal, denoted $\sim \text{IN}(0, \delta^2)$ so that, if $x_0 = 0$

$$x_t = \sum_{i=1}^{t} e_i$$

The variance of x_t is $t\delta^2$ and this becomes infinitely large as $t \to \infty$. It is also clear that the concept of a mean value for x_t has no meaning. In fact, if at some point $x_t = c$ then the expected time until x_t again returns to c is infinite.

A stationary series tends to return to its mean and fluctuate around it within a more-or-less constant range. A non-stationary series would have a different mean at different points in time. One of the characteristics of a stationary series then is that it tends to return to, or cross, its mean values repeatedly and this property is the one which is exploited by most stationarity tests. As we discussed in Chapter 3, a stationary series will in general have an ARMA representation.

5.2 Unit roots and orders of integration

If a series must be differenced d times before it becomes stationary, then it is said to be integrated of order d, denoted $I(d)$. Thus, a series x_t is $I(d)$ if x_t is non-stationary but $\Delta^d x_t$ is stationary, where $\Delta x_t = x_t - x_{t-1}$ and $\Delta^2 = \Delta(\Delta x_t)$, etc. An alternative way of stating this is to say that a series is $I(d)$ if it has a stable, invertible non-deterministic ARMA representation after differencing d times – that is, if it is ARIMA (p, d, q) for some p, q. This means that the series can be written as

$$(1 - L)^d \phi(L) x_t = \theta(L) e_t \tag{5.1}$$

where L is the lag operator $(L^n x_t = x_{t-n})$, $\phi(L)$ and $\theta(L)$ are polynomials in the lag operator and e_t is a stationary process. If x_t is ARIMA (p, d, q), then we would have

$$\phi(L) = \sum_{i=0}^{p} \phi_i L^i \quad \text{and} \quad \theta(L) = \sum_{i=0}^{q} \theta_i L^i$$

Now consider the roots of the polynomial associated with the autoregressive part in (5.1), that is, the solutions to

$$(1 - L)^d \phi(z) = 0 \tag{5.2}$$

where z is a real variable. Clearly, this has d roots (i.e. solutions) of $z = 1$, or in other words, d *unit roots*. It is for this reason that testing for the order of integration of a series is often referred to as testing for unit roots.

In general, if we take a linear combination of two series; each integrated of a different order, then the resulting series will be integrated at the highest of the two orders of integration. This can be easily demonstrated. Suppose

$$x_t \sim I(d), \quad y_t \sim I(e) \tag{5.3}$$

where $e > d$. Now form the linear combination, z_t:

$$z_t = \alpha x_t + \beta y_t \tag{5.4}$$

If we difference z_t d times, we have:

$$\Delta^d z_t = \alpha \Delta^d x_t + \beta \Delta^d y_t \tag{5.5}$$

Now the first term on the right-hand side of (5.5) is stationary, since $x_t \sim I(d)$, but the second term is not, since $y_t \sim I(e)$ and $e > d$ – it requires further differencing. As the sum of a stationary series $(\alpha \Delta^d x_t)$ and a non-stationary series $(\beta \Delta^d y_t)$ is non-stationary then $\Delta^d z_t$ is non-stationary. Suppose we now continue differencing up to a total of e times:

$$\Delta^e z_t = \alpha \Delta^e x_t + \beta \Delta^e y_t \tag{5.6}$$

Now, $\alpha \Delta^e x_t$ is simply $\alpha \Delta^d x_t$ differenced $(e - d)$ times, and differencing a stationary series will always produce another stationary series. Thus, the first term on the right-hand side of (5.6) is stationary. The second term on the right-hand side is stationary since $y_t \sim I(e)$. Thus, $\Delta^e z_t$, as the sum of two stationary series must be stationary. This illustrates the general principle that, given (5.3) and (5.4), any linear combination has an order of integration equal to the highest order of the component series:

$$z_t \sim I[\max(d, e)]$$

Although this discussion has been in terms of two time series, it could easily be generalised to the case of three or more.

There are, however, exceptions to this general rule. Indeed, it is the exceptions of this rule which are of interest in cointegration analysis.

5.3   Cointegration

The important exception to this rule is where the low-frequency (or stochastic trend) components to two or more variables exactly offset each other to give a stationary linear combination. This is the case with a set of cointegrating variables. The basic idea is that if, *in the long run*, two or more series move closely together, even though the series themselves are trended, the difference between them is constant. We may regard these series as defining a long-run equilibrium relationship and, as the difference between them is stationary, the error term in a regression will have well-defined first and second moments. So traditional OLS regression becomes feasible in this case. The term *equilibrium* has many meanings in economics, and its use in the cointegration literature is rather different from most definitions of equilibrium. Within the cointegration literature all that is meant by equilibrium is that it is an *observed relationship* which has, on average, been maintained by a set of variables for a long period. Cointegration may be formally defined as: The components of the vector X_t are said to be cointegrated of order d, b [denoted $x_t \sim CI(d, b)$] if:

(i)   all components of X_t are $I(d)$
and
(ii)   there exists a vector $\alpha(\neq 0)$ such that $Z_t = \alpha' X_t \sim I(d - b)$, $b > 0$.

Thus if a set of $I(d)$ variables yields a linear combination that has a lower order of integration $(d - b < d$, for $b > 0)$ then the vector α is called the cointegrating vector.

An important implication of this definition is that if we have *two* variables which are integrated of *different* orders then these two series cannot possibly be cointegrated. This is an intuitively clear result; it would be very strange to propose a relationship between an $I(0)$ series x_t and and $I(1)$ series y_t. The $I(0)$ series would have a constant mean while the mean of the $I(1)$ series would tend to drift over time. Thus, the 'error' $(y_t - \alpha x_t)$ between them would be expected to become infinitely large over time.

It is, however, possible to have a mixture of different order series when there are *three or more* series under consideration. In this case, a subset of the higher-order series must cointegrate to the order of the lower-order series. For example, suppose $Y_t \sim I(1)$, $X_t \sim I(2)$ and $W_t \sim I(2)$. If X_t and W_t cointegrate then $V_t = aX_t + cW_t$ will be $I(1)$. V_t is now a potential candidate to cointegrate with the remaining $I(1)$ series Y_t. If so, then $Z_t = eV_t + fY_t$, will be $I(0)$. We could summarise this set of circumstances as (i) X_t, $W_t \sim CI(2, 1)$; (ii) V_t, $Y_t \sim CI(1, 1)$ and hence (iii) $Z_t \sim I(0)$.

5.4   The Granger representation theorem

One of the most important results in cointegration analysis is the Granger representation theorem (Granger 1983, Engle and Granger 1987). This theorem states that if a set of variables are cointegrated of order 1, 1 $[CI(1, 1)]$, then there exists a valid error-correction representation of the data. Thus, if X_t is an $N \times 1$ vector such that $X_t \sim (1, 1)$ and α is the cointegrating vector [i.e. $\alpha' X_t \sim I(0)$], then the following general error-correction representation may be derived:

$$\Phi(L)(1 - L)X_t = -\alpha' X_{t-1} + \Theta(L)e_t \qquad (5.7)$$

where $\Phi(L)$ is a finite order polynomial with $\Phi(0) = I_N$, $\Theta(L)$ is a finite order polynomial, 'L' is the lag operator and at least one element of X is non-zero.

Equation (5.7) is a statistical model containing only stationary variables and so the usual stationary regression theory applies. This supplies a complete theoretical basis for the error-correction model when the 'levels terms' in X_t cointegrate. The Granger representation theorem also demonstrates that if the data generation process is an equation such as (5.7) then X_t must be a cointegrated set of variables. The practical implications of this for dynamic modelling are profound: in order for an error-correction model to be immune from the 'spurious regression problem' it must contain a set of levels terms which cointegrate to give a stationary error term. The danger with dynamic estimation is that the very richness of the dynamic structure may make the residual process appear to be white noise in a small sample when in fact the levels terms do not cointegrate and the true process is non-stationary.

There are a number of other, more minor, implications which follow from a set of variables (X_t, Y_t) being cointegrated. First, if X_t and Y_t are cointegrated then because Y_t and Y_{t-i} will be cointegrated for all i, then X_t and Y_{t-i} will be cointegrated. Second, if X_t and Y_t are cointegrated and individually $I(1)$, then either X_t must

Granger cause Y_t or Y_t must Granger cause X_t. This follows essentially from the existence of the error correction model (5.7) which suggests that, at the very least, the lagged value of one variable must enter the other determining equation.

5.5   Estimating the cointegrating vector

One approach to estimating the cointegrating vector would be to work with (5.7), the error-correction representation of the data. This, however, is not an easy procedure to implement as it must be remembered that (5.7) is a complete system of equations determining *all* of the elements of X_t. Further, there is the cross-equation restriction that the same parameter should occur in the levels parts of all the equations. So it would in principle, need to be estimated as a full system subject to this non-linear constraint. In fact, consistent estimates may be achieved much more easily following a suggestion made by Engle and Granger (1987) which relies on two theorems given in Stock (1987).

We discussed in Chapter 1 the property of *consistency*. A related concept is that of and order of convergence. If $\hat{\beta}$ is the OLS estimator in a regression model which satisfies the classical assumptions, then $\hat{\beta}$ converges in probability to the *true* parameter vector β as the *square root* of the sample size T tends to infinity, denoted $0(T^{1/2})$. Stock (1987) demonstrates that, if a set of variables are cointegrated of order $(1, 1)$ with cointegrating vector α, then if $\hat{\alpha}$ is the OLS estimator of α, then $\hat{\alpha}$ is $0(T)$, i.e. $\hat{\alpha}$ converges in probability to α as T tends to infinity. Since T goes to infinity faster than $T^{1/2}$, this means that OLS estimates of the cointegrating vectors will generally be better, in some sense, than usual. This result is sometimes termed 'super consistency'.

The intuition behind the super consistency result is quite straightforward. Say, for example, we have two variables X_t, $Y_t \sim CI(1, 1)$. Consider the regression model

$$Y_t = \hat{\alpha} \, X_t + Z_t$$

where Z_t is the residual and $\hat{\alpha}$ is the OLS estimator. For the true value of α, $Y_t - \alpha X_t \sim I(0)$. Clearly, for $\hat{\alpha} \neq \alpha$, the OLS residual Z_t will be non-stationary and hence will have a very large variance in any finite sample. For $\hat{\alpha} = \alpha$, however, the estimated variance of Z_t will be much smaller. Since the ordinary least squares estimator essentially chooses $\hat{\alpha}$ to minimise the variance of Z_t, it will be extremely good at 'picking out' an estimate close to α.

However, offsetting this super consistency result is another result, also due to Stock (1987) which shows that there is a small-sample bias present in the OLS estimator of the cointegrating vector and that its limiting distribution is non-normal with a non-zero mean. Banerjee *et al.* (1986) suggest that this small-sample bias may be important in some cases and they show that for certain simple models the bias is related to $1 - R^2$ of the regression, so that a very high R^2 is associated with very little bias.

It is important to note that the proof of the consistency of the OLS estimator of the cointegrating vector does not require the assumption that the regressors are uncorrelated with the error term. In fact, any of the cointegrating variables may be used as the dependent variable in the regression and the estimates remain consistent. This means that problems do not arise when we have endogenous regressors or when these variables are measured with error. The reason for this may be seen quite easily at an intuitive level, the error process in the regression is $I(0)$ while the variables are $I(1)$ (or higher) so the means of the variables are time-dependent and will go to infinity. In effect what happens is that the growth in the means of the variables swamps the error process.

Engle and Granger (1987) demonstrate that once OLS has been used to estimate the cointegrating vector then the other parameters of the error correction model may be consistently estimate by imposing the first-stage estimates of the cointegrating vector in a second-stage regression. This is done simply by including the residuals from the first-stage regression in a general error correction model. This procedure is sometimes referred to as the two-step Granger and Engle estimation procedure. They also demonstrate that the OLS standard errors obtained at the second stage are consistent estimates of the true standard errors.

The advantages of the two-step procedure are that it allows us to make use of the super consistency properties of the first-stage estimates and that at the first stage it is possible to test that the vector of variables properly cointegrates. Thus, we can be sure that the full error correction model is not a spurious regression.

5.6 Testing for cointegration and drawing inference

Testing for cointegration

Suppose that we have an OLS estimate of the cointegrating vector $\hat{\alpha}$ and we may define the OLS residuals from the cointegrating regression as

$$Z_t = \hat{\alpha}' X_t$$

Now suppose Z_t follows an AR(1) process so that

$$Z_t = \rho Z_{t-1} + u_t$$

Then cointegration would imply stationary errors and hence that $\rho < 1$. The latter suggests testing the null hypothesis that $\rho = 1$ (i.e. that the error process is a random walk). The Dickey–Fuller test and the use of the Durbin–Watson statistic proposed by Sargan and Bhargava (1983) can both be used to test this hypothesis. There is, however, a further complication: if α is not known, the problem is much more complex: under the null hypothesis that $\rho = 1$ we cannot estimate α in an unbiased way. Because OLS will seek to produce the minimum squared residuals this will mean that the Dickey–Fuller tables will tend to reject the null too often. So we have to construct tables of critical values for each data generation process *individually* under the null hypothesis. Engle and Granger present some sample calculations of critical values for some simple models. We will discuss three of their proposed test procedures which have been most commonly used, namely the Dickey–Fuller, augmented Dickey–Fuller and cointegrating regression Durbin–Watson tests.

Consider the following autoregressive representation of a variable x_t:

$$x_t = \lambda_0 + \lambda_1 x_{t-1} + \lambda_2 x_{t-2} + \ldots \lambda_{n+1} x_{t-n-1} + u_t \tag{5.8}$$

where v_t is a white noise, stationary error term.

Now reparameterise (5.8):

$$\Delta x_t = \lambda_0 + \left(\sum_{i=1}^{n+1} \lambda_i - 1 \right) x_{t-1} - \sum_{z=1}^{n+1} \left[\left(\sum_{i=z}^{n+1} \lambda_i \right) \Delta x_{t-z} \right] + u_t \tag{5.9}$$

Consider the regression

$$\Delta x_t = \beta_0 + \beta_1 x_{t-1} + \sum_{i=1}^{n} \alpha_i \Delta x_{t-1} + u_t \tag{5.10}$$

Comparing (5.8), (5.9) and (5.10), for stationarity we require $\beta_1 < 0$, while if x_t is non-stationary, we would have $\beta_1 = 0$ and the sum of the autoregressive parameters λ_i in (5.8) would be unity (i.e. the series would have a unit root).

Thus, one way of testing for (non) stationarity of x_t would be to estimate a regression of the form (5.10) and to test the null hypothesis $\beta_1 = 0$. Intuitively, this could be done using the ratio of $\hat{\beta}$, to its estimated standard error. This 't-ratio' is termed the augmented Dickey–Fuller statistic (ADF). Unfortunately, under the null hypothesis of non-stationarity, the distribution of the ADF is not Student's t.

Fuller (1976), however, has tabulated approximate critical values of this statistic by Monte Carlo methods. The number of lags of Δx in (5.10) is normally chosen to ensure that the regression residual is approximately white noise. If *no* lags of Δx are required, then the '*t*-ratio' is termed the (non-augmented) Dickey–Fuller (DF) statistic. The critical values for the DF and ADF statistics, for a *single variable*, are the same and can be found in Fuller (1976). The DF and ADF statistics thus provide a method of testing for the order of integration of a variable.

Suppose, for example, $x_t \sim I(1)$, then in a regression of the form (5.10) we would be *unable* to reject the null hypothesis $\beta_1 = 0$. If we were then to run the regression

$$\Delta^2 x_t = \gamma_0 + \gamma_1 \Delta x_{t-1} + \sum_{i=1}^{n-1} \Psi_i \Delta^2 x_{t-i} + u_t \qquad (5.11)$$

we should be able to reject the hypothesis $\gamma_1 = 0$ against the alternative $\gamma_1 < 0$.

Dickey and Pantula (1988) suggest testing for higher-order unit roots and then 'testing down'. For example, estimate (5.11) first, then (5.10).

If a set of variables is cointegrated of order 1, $1 \sim CI(1, 1)$, then the residual from the cointegrating regression should be $I(0)$. It would therefore seem that one could test for cointegration by subjecting the cointegrating *residuals* to the DF and ADF tests, and this is indeed the case. There is, however, and additional complication in testing cointegrating residuals for non-stationarity using DF or ADF tests, which does not arise when applying these tests to single economic time series. This is because the OLS estimator 'chooses' the residuals in the cointegrating regression to have as small a sample variance as possible, even if the variables are *not* cointegrated, the OLS estimator will make the residuals *look* as stationary as possible. Thus, if we then use the DF or ADF tests on these residuals, we may reject the null hypothesis (non-stationarity) rather more than the nominal significance level would suggest. To correct for this test bias, the critical values have to be raised slightly. Engle and Granger (1987) have tabulated critical values for tests of this kind, generated by Monte Carlo methods.

Another test for the cointegrating residuals to contain a unit root, suggested by Bhargava (1980) and Sargan and Bhargava (1983), is to test the cointegrating regression Durbin–Watson (CRDW) statistic against a value of zero. This provides a useful complement to the two-step DF or ADF test, and the Monte Carlo results reported by Engle and Granger (1987) appear to show that it is quite powerful.

Intuitively, since CRDW $\simeq 2(1 - \rho)$, where ρ is the first-order autocorrelation coefficient, CRDW $\simeq 0$ when $\rho = 1$.

Mackinnon (1988) lists the critical values for the CRDW, DF and ADF statistics for a number of cases and degrees of freedom.

5.7 Inference on parameter values

It has been well known for some time that non-stationarity not only presents problems for the consistency of estimation techniques but that the problem of inference is also greatly complicated. The Dickey –Fuller statistics discussed above do not have a standard Student's t distribution even though they are calculated as standard t-tests. Stock (1987), and Engle and Granger (1987) point out that the standard errors produced by OLS when performing a static cointegrating regression are biased and so valid inference about the parameters of the cointegrating vector cannot be carried out in the usual way. This bias arises for two quite separate reasons. First and most simply, a static regression will generally be subject to considerable serial correlation in the error process and for conventional textbook reasons this will give rise to inconsistent estimates of the standard errors of the parameters. The second reason is more important and more complex. The non-stationarity in the data gives rise to 'nuisance' parameters in the asymptotic distribution of the parameter estimates which means that the distribution of the parameter estimates is not generally normal.

More recent work, notably by West (1988), Sims *et al.* (1986) and Park and Phillips (1988, 1989) has shown that the situation is even more complex in that the presence or absence of drift terms in the non-stationary variables can crucially affect the form of the distribution of the parameter estimates.

We will discuss this topic initially within a bivariate framework of only two non-stationary variables Y and X and one stationary variable W, whereby assumption Y and X cointegrate. So the model is

$$Y_t = \alpha X_t + \beta W_t + e_t$$

where Y_t, X_t are $I(1)$ and by assumption W_t, e_t are $I(0)$. Now we assume that X_t is generated by the following univariate process $X_t = X_{t-1} + \mu + u_t$, where μ is the drift term (in the random walk) which may be zero. Now the key point in understanding the way inference lies in noting the way the asymptotic sample moments alter as the drift term alters from zero to a non-zero (positive) value. Some of the key results are summarised below:

Case: $\mu = 0$ Case: $\mu \neq 0$

$T^{-1} M_{XX} \to$ RV $T^{-2} M_{XX} \to c$

$M_{Xe} \to$ RV $M_{Xe} \to$ NRV

Distribution of the OLS estimators

$T(\hat{\alpha} - \alpha)$ is NSRV $T^{3/2}(\hat{\alpha} - \alpha)$ is NRV

$T^{1/2}(\hat{\beta} - \beta)$ is NRV $T^{1/2}(\hat{\beta} - \beta)$ is NRV

where M_{Xe} is the moment matrix of X and e, etc., RV is a random variable, NSRV is a non-standard random variable and NRV is a normal random variable. Note that with zero drift $\mu = 0$, the distribution of α is non-standard while the presence of non-zero drift causes the distribution to become a normally distributed random variable. Also note that the presence of non-stationary variables does not affect the distribution of the stationary variable W_t, so that inference can proceed in the usual way for the stationary components of a dynamic regression.

The general point here is that a researcher cannot normally use t-statistics to draw inference about the significance of parameters on the non-stationary terms in a regression. One exception which can be made is that if X_t is strictly exogenous then the randomness in the distribution of the OLS estimators comes only from e_t which is, of course, asymptotically normal by virtue of the assumption of cointegration. Then the distribution of the OLS estimators becomes normal and standard t-tests can be used. A further complication is that the above results for the case $\mu \neq 0$ (i.e. presence of drift) apply only to the bivariate case. If there are three $I(1)$ variables with non-zero drift then only some linear combination of the drift terms will be normally distributed and this cannot be assigned uniquely to any of the parameters.

5.8 Exogeneity and cointegration

Engle and Yoo (1989) give a classification of the possible combinations of cointegration and exogeneity assumptions and their effects on the distribution of the OLS estimator of the cointegrating vector. If we again continue the bivariate example, suppose we have the general system

$$Y_t = \alpha X_t + \beta \Delta X_t + u_t \tag{i}$$

and

$$X_t = \gamma \Delta Y_{t-1} + \delta(Y_{t-1} - \alpha X_{t-1}) + v_t \tag{ii}$$

Note that in this general model the same cointegrating parameter α, appears in both equations. This has an important implication for the weak exogeneity property of both Y and X (the definition of weak exogeneity is given in Chapter 4). The key point is that even though X_t is a function of *lagged* Y (and not current Y_t), it is *not* weakly exogenous in (i) above. This arises because the *parameters* of the equation generating X are not independent of the parameters of the equation generating Y: this is obviously true because they both have α in common. The general properties of the estimators are now given for various restrictions on this general model:

1. No restrictions imposed. The model is equivalent to a general VAR model and the distribution of the estimators are non-standard.
2. $\beta = \gamma = \delta = 0$. X_t is strongly exogenous and so the FIML estimator of α may be obtained from equation (i) alone and the distribution of the parameter is asymptotically normal.
3. $\delta = 0$. X_t is weakly exogenous and again the FIML estimator of α is given by OLS on equation (i) and the distribution of the parameters is asymptotically normal.
4. $\beta = \gamma = 0$. X_t is predetermined but *not* weakly exogenous as α is common to both equations. In this case OLS estimation applied to either the Y or X equations alone will yield non-normal asymptotic distributions and both equations should be estimated using a systems technique (see below for the ML estimator for the unrestricted system).

5.9 Three-step estimation

Engle and Yoo (1989) have proposed a 'third step' to the Engle and Granger two-step estimation technique which is computationally tractable and overcomes two of the disadvantages of the two-step procedure. The full three-step procedure is actually given for an unresticted multivariate system. This general form is not, however, particularly relevant as it has no claim to priority over the maximum likelihood procedure given below. In the special case of a unique cointegrating vector and the assumption of weak exogeneity of the conditioning variables of the dynamic model, the procedure becomes particularly easy to implement and has some claim to being of relevance to practical work. We will discuss this special case.

The two problems of the two-step procedure are:

1. While the static regression gives consistent estimates of the co-

integrating vector these estimates are not fully efficient.

2. The distribution of the estimators of the cointegrating vector provided by the static regression is generally non-normal and so inference cannot be drawn about the significance of the parameters.

The third step provides a correction to the parameter estimates of the first stage, static regression which makes them asymptotically equivalent to FIML and provides a set of standard errors which allows the valid calculation of standard '*t*' tests.

The third stage consists simply of a further regression of the conditioning variables from the static regression multiplied by minus the error correction parameter, regressed on the errors from the second-stage error correction model. The coefficients from this model are the corrections to the parameter estimates while their standard errors are the relevant standard errors for inference.

The three steps are then: first estimate a standard cointegrating regression of the form

$$Y_t = \alpha X_t + Z_t$$

where Z_t is the OLS residual to give first-stage estimates of α, α^1. Then estimate a second-stage dynamic model using the residuals from the cointegrating regression to impose the long run constraint:

$$\Delta Y_t = \Phi(L)\Delta Y_{t-1} + \Omega(L)\Delta X_t + \delta Z_{t-1} + u_t$$

The third stage then consists of the regression

$$u_t = \varepsilon(-\hat{\delta} X_t) + v_t$$

The correction for the first-stage estimates is then simply

$$\alpha^3 = \alpha^1 + \varepsilon$$

and the correct standard errors for α_3 are given by the standard errors for ε in the third-stage regression.

We now turn to a practical example using the cointegration methodology.

5.10 Long-run purchasing power parity in the 1920s

Taylor and McMahon (1988) test for long-run purchasing power parity using cointegration techniques. Purchasing power parity (PPP) requires that the exchange rate between two currencies should be equal to the ratio of their price levels. If this is the case, then, at the going exchange rate, one unit of the domestic currency will have the same purchasing power in both countries. If we write

$$e_t - p_t \equiv u_t$$

where e_t is the (logarithm of the) nominal exchange rate (domestic price of foreign currency), p_t is the (logarithm of the) ratio of domestic to foreign prices, and u_t represents short-run deviations from PPP (logarithm of the real exchange rate), then *long-run* PPP would allow $u_t \neq 0$ in the short run, but would require $u_t = 0$ in the long run. At least a necessary condition for this to be the case is that u_t be a stationary process. If u_t is non-stationary, then it will tend to get larger over time and e_t and p_t will tend to diverge without bound. Thus, if e_t and p_t are $I(1)$, long-run PPP would require that they be cointegrated with a *unit* cointegrating parameter. Taylor (1988) uses simple models of mesurement error and transportation costs, to suggest that, even if long-run PPP holds, the cointegrating parameter may deviate from unity. Taylor and McMahon (1988) (TM) test for cointegration between exchange rates and relative prices for a number of exchange rates during the 1920s (i.e. under floating exchange rates). For illustrative purposes, we consider here only their results for the French franc–UK sterling exchange rate.

TM first test the exchange rate and relative price series for $I(1)$ behaviour. For franc–sterling they obtain ADF statistics of -0.71 and -0.78 for the exchange rate and relative prices respectively. The null hypothesis is that the series in question is $I(1)$. The rejection region is $\{\text{ADF} < c\}$ with $c = -3.58, -2.93$ or -2.60 at a significance level of 1%, 5% or 10% respectively (Fuller 1976). Thus, TM are unable to reject the hypothesis of $I(1)$ behaviour of exchange rates and relative prices.

Regressing the exchange rate on relative prices, they then obtain:

$$e_t = 3.272 + 1.061 \, p_t + \omega_t \tag{5.12}$$

where ω_t is the OLS residual. They then use ω_t to construct the ADF and CRDW statistics, and obtain values of -4.62 and 0.662 respectively. The 1% rejection regions for the ADF statistic (applied to the cointegrating residuals) and for the CRDW are:

ADF: $\{\text{ADF} < -3.77\}$

CRDW: $\{\text{CRDW} > 0.511\}$

Thus, TM clearly reject the null hypothesis of $I(1)$ cointegrating residuals (i.e. non-cointegration) and conclude that the exchange rate and relative prices are cointegrated.

Since the slope coefficient in (5.12) is close to unity, TM suspect that the cointegrating parameter may in fact be unity. They thus test the *real* exchange rate, $u_t \equiv e_t - p_t$, for non-stationarity, using the ADF statistic, and obtain a test statistic value of -4.15. Since the cointegrating parameter has been *imposed* rather than estimated, this is compared to the Fuller (1976) critical values and the $I(1)$ null hypothesis is easily rejected. TM thus concluded that exchange rates and relative prices are cointegrated with a unit cointegrating parameter, implying that – at least for the 1920s – long-run PPP held between the franc and sterling. TM then proceed to estimate an error correction model for the franc–sterling exchange rate and report the result:

$$\Delta e_t = \begin{array}{cccc} 0.857 & + \; 1.727\Delta p_t & - \; 0.803\Delta p_{t-1} & - \; 0.258(e - p)_{t-1} \\ (0.323) & (0.135) & (0.189) & (0.098) \end{array}$$

$$R^2 = 0.76, \; DW = 2.05, \; LM \, (6, 36) = 0.18$$

which has acceptable diagnostics. (LM is a Lagrange multiplier test statistic for up to sixth-order serial correlation.)

5.11   A maximum likelihood approach to cointegration

In sections 5.5 and 5.6 we outlined methods of testing for cointegration and estimating cointegrating vectors, based on ordinary least squares estimation. A major advantage of the least squares approach is that it is relatively simple and intuitive. It does, however, suffer from a number of disadvantages. One disadvantage is that the distribution of the test statistics discussed in section 5.6 will, in general, be slightly different in any particular application – they are not invariant with respect to the nuisance parameters which characterise any particular situation. Thus, the critical values given in Engle and Granger can be taken only as a rough guide.

A more fundamental problem concerns the *number* of cointegrating combinations which may exist between a set of variables. Consider two variables, each of which is integrated of order one $X_t \sim I(1)$ and $Y_t \sim I(1)$. Now, if (X_t, Y_t) cointegrates with parameter α then:

$$u_t = X_t - \alpha Y_t \sim I(0) \tag{5.13}$$

and α can be shown to be unique. To see this, suppose we had another cointegrating parameter, β:

$$\omega_t = X_t - \beta Y_t \sim I(0) \tag{5.14}$$

Adding and subtracting βY_t in (5.13):

$$u_t = X_t - (\alpha - \beta) \, Y_t - \beta Y_t$$

that is,

$$u_t = \omega_t - (\alpha - \beta)Y_t \tag{5.15}$$

By assumption, u_t and ω_t are both $I(0)$ while Y_t is $I(1)$. The latter three conditions can hold only if $\alpha = \beta$ that is, α is unique. Unfortunately, once we consider more than two variables, it is no longer possible to demonstrate the uniqueness of the cointegrating vector. Indeed, it turns out that if we have a vector of N variables, each integrated of the same order, then there can be up to $(N - 1)$ cointegrating vectors. (In the preceding paragraph, we merely demonstrate this for $N = 2$.)

Thus, if we cannot reject cointegration between a set of three or more variables, based on least squares methods, we have no guarantee that we have an estimate of a *unique* cointegrating vector. In a system with three variables, for example, it is quite possible that there are two statistically significant distinct cointegrating vectors and that our OLS estimate is a linear combination of them.

Johansen (1988) suggests a method for both estimating all the distinct cointegrating relationships which exist within a set of variables and for constructing a range of statistical tests. The method begins by expressing the data generation process of a vector of N variables X as an unrestricted vector autoregression in the levels of the variables:

$$X_t = \Pi_1 X_{t-1} + \ldots + \Pi_k X_{t-k} + e_t \tag{5.16}$$

where each of the Π_i is an $(N \times N)$ matrix of parameters. The system of equations (5.16) can be reparameterised in ECM form:

$$\Delta X_t = \Gamma_1 \Delta X_{t-1} + \Gamma_2 \Delta X_{t-2} + \ldots \Gamma_{k-1} \Delta X_{t-k+1}$$
$$+ \Gamma_K X_{t-k} + e_t \tag{5.17}$$

$$\Gamma_i = -I + \Pi_1 + \ldots \Pi_i, \qquad i = 1, \ldots, k.$$

Thus Γ_k now defines the *long run* 'levels solution' to (5.16).

Now, if X_t is a vector of $I(1)$ variables, we know that the left-hand side and the first $(k - 1)$ elements of (5.17) are $I(0)$ but that the last element of (5.17) is a linear combination of $I(1)$ variables. Johansen uses cannonical correlation methods to estimate all the distinct combinations of the levels of X which produce high correlations with the $I(0)$ elements in (5.17); these combinations are, of course, the cointegrating vectors. Johansen's approach is a maximum likelihood method of estimating *all* of the distinct cointegrating vectors which may exist between a set of variables. Johansen also shows how one can test which of these distinct cointegrating vectors are statistically significant, and also how to construct a likelihood ratio test for linear restrictions on the cointegrating parameters.

Consider an N-dimensional vector of variables X_t. Johansen starts by considering a kth order vector autoregression (VAR) for X_t (5.16) where e_t is an independent and identically (normally) distributed vector of disturbances, with zero mean and covariance matrix Δ. All terms on the right-hand side of (5.17) are clearly $I(0)$ except the final term. Thus, the last term on the right-hand side must also be $I(0)$: $\Gamma_K X_{t-k} \sim I(0)$, either X contains a number of cointegrating vectors or Γ_K must be a matrix of zeros.

Now consider an $N \times r$ matrix β such that

$$\beta' X_{t-k} \sim I(0)$$

If all the elements of X_t are $I(1)$, then the columns of β must form cointegrating parameter vectors for X_{t-k} and hence X_t. Since there can only be up to $(N - 1)$ cointegrating vectors, β must have r less than N. If, however, X_t is $I(1)$ but the elements are *not* cointegrated, β must be a null matrix. Now define another $(N \times r)$ matrix α such that:

$$-\Gamma_k = \alpha\beta' \tag{5.18}$$

The Johansen technique is based upon estimating the factorisation (5.18). Suppose, for example, that there was in fact only one cointegrating vector. Then we need consider only the first column of α and β, (5.16) could then be written:

$$\Delta X_t = \Gamma_1 X_{t-1} + \Gamma_2 \Delta X_{t-2} (-\alpha_1 Z_{t-k}) + e_t \tag{5.19}$$

where $Z_t = \beta_1 X_t \sim I(0)$.

The system (5.19) is directly analogous to (5.7). Indeed, it is the error correction representation of the system where the lag length k is assumed high enough to allow one to assume a white noise disturbance vector, e_t, and the error correction term enters with lag k. (It is in fact easy to show, by simply rearranging terms, that the error-correction term can enter at any lag.) Thus, Johansen provides a technique for estimating all possible cointegrating vectors, the β matrix as well as the corresponding set of error-correction coefficients, the α matrix. If the X_t vector does in fact cointegrate – one or more of the β_i vectors are statistically significant – then, by the Granger representation theorem, we know that α_i must contain at least one non-zero element. In general, considering all of the logically possible cointegrating vectors, (5.19) is written

$$\Delta X_t = \Gamma_1 X_{t-1} + \Gamma_2 \Delta X_{t-2} + \ldots (-\alpha\beta')X_{t-k} + e_t \quad \textbf{(5.20)}$$

A fuller discussion of the Johansen technique is given in the appendix. Here, we can consider the following sketch.

The likelihood function for the system (5.20) is proportional to

$$L(\alpha, \beta, \Delta; \Gamma, \ldots \Gamma_{k-1}) = |\Omega|^{-T/2} \exp\left\{-1/2 \sum_{t=1}^{T} (e_t \Omega^{-1} e_t)\right\}$$

Where T is the number of observations Ω is the covariance matrix of e. Rewrite the system (5.20) as

$$\Delta X_t + \alpha\beta' X_{t-k} = \Gamma_1 \Delta X_{t-1} + \ldots \Gamma_{k-1} \Delta X_{t-k+1} + e_t \quad \textbf{(5.21)}$$

If $(\alpha\beta')$ were known, maximum likelihood estimates of the Γ_i could be obtained by ordinary least squares. Consider therefore, correcting for the effect of the k *lags* of ΔX_t on ΔX_t and X_{t-k}. Correcting the right-hand side for ΔX_{t-j} ($j = 1, 2, \ldots$), i.e. taking out their effect, just leaves e_t. We can correct X_t and X_{t-k} for the effects of k lags of X_t by replacing ΔX_t and X_{t-k} with the residuals from regressing them individually on $\{\Delta X_{t-1}, \ldots \Delta X_{t-k}\}$. Note that this will not change their basic properties; X_{t-k} remains $I(1)$ and ΔX_t remains $I(0)$. Thus (5.21) becomes:

$$R_{ot} + \alpha\beta' R_{kt} = e_t \quad \textbf{(5.22)}$$

where R_{ot} is the vector of residuals from regressing ΔX_t on to $\Delta X_{t-1}, \ldots, \Delta X_{t-k}\}$ and R_{kt} is the corresponding residual vector for X_{t-k}. The expression for the likelihood function, (5.20), can now be written:

$$L_1(\alpha, \beta, \Omega)$$
$$= |\Delta|^{-T/2} \exp\left\{-1/2 \sum_{t=1}^{T} (R_{ot} + \alpha\beta' R_{Kt})' \Omega^{-1} (R_{ot} + \alpha\beta' R_{Kt})\right\} \quad \textbf{(5.23)}$$

If β were known, an estimate of α and of Δ could be obtained in the usual way from a regression of R_{ot} on $\beta' R_{Kt}$. Thus, $\hat{\alpha}$ and $\hat{\Delta}$ can be expressed as functions of β.

$$\hat{\alpha}(\beta) = -S_{ok}\beta(\beta' S_{kk}\beta)^{-1} \quad \textbf{(5.24)}$$

$$\hat{\Omega}(\beta) = S_{oo} - S_{ok}\beta(\beta' S_{kk}\beta)^{-1}\beta' S_{ko} \quad \textbf{(5.25)}$$

$$S_{ij} = T^{-1} \sum_{t=1}^{T} R_{it}R_{jt}', \quad i, j = o, k \quad \textbf{(5.26)}$$

After substituting (5.24) and (5.25) into (5.23), the concentrated likelihood function can be seen to be proportional to

$$L_2(\beta) = |\hat{\Omega}(\beta)|^{-T/2}$$

$$= |S_{oo} - S_{ok}\beta(\beta' S_{kk}\beta)^{-1}\beta' S_{ko}|^{-T/2} \qquad (5.27)$$

Thus, maximum likelihood estimation of the full set of possible cointegrating vectors, β, involves choosing β to minimise the function

$$F = |S_{oo} - S_{ok}\beta(\beta' S_{kk}\beta)^{-1}\beta' S_{ko}|^{-T/2} \qquad (5.28)$$

Johansen shows how this can be done by solving an eigenvalue problem. The matrix $\hat{\beta}$ is thus obtained as a set of eigenvectors together with a corresponding vector of $(N - 1)$ eigenvalues $\hat{\lambda}$. The columns of β are significant only if the corresponding eigenvalue is significantly different from zero. Let the elements of $\hat{\lambda}_i$ be ordered such that

$$\hat{\lambda}_1 > \hat{\lambda}_2 > \ldots \hat{\lambda}_{N-1}$$

and let the columns of β also be ordered accordingly (i.e. so that in the column of $\hat{\beta}$, $\hat{\beta}_i$, is the eigenvector corresponding to $\hat{\lambda}_i$). These eigenvalues are defined such that the maximum likelihood estimate of Ω is given by

$$\hat{\Omega}(\beta) = |S_{oo}| \prod_{i=1}^{N} (1 - \hat{\lambda}_i) \qquad (5.29)$$

Now suppose we wish to test the null hypothesis that there are at most r cointegrating vectors:

$$H_0: \lambda_i = 0, i = r + 1, \ldots, N - 1$$

where only the first r eigenvalues are non-zero. If these restrictions are imposed, the restricted estimate of Δ denoted $\tilde{\Delta}$ is:

$$\tilde{\Omega}(\beta) + |S_{oo}| \prod_{i=1}^{r} (1 - \lambda_i) \qquad (5.30)$$

Since the likelihood function can be expressed in terms of the estimate of Δ, equation (5.27), we can use (5.27), (5.29) and (5.30) to form a likelihood ratio statistic for the null hypothesis of at most r cointegrating vectors.

$$\text{LR}(N - r) = -2\ln(Q) = -T \sum_{i=r+1}^{N} \ln(1 - \hat{\lambda}_i) \qquad (5.31)$$

where

$$Q = \frac{\text{restricted maximised likelihood}}{\text{unrestricted maximised likelihood}}$$

$\text{LR}(N - r)$ has degrees of freedom equal to the number of restrictions, $(N - r)$. Note that for $\hat{\lambda}_i = 0$, $i = r + 1, \ldots N$, $\text{LR}(N - r)$ will be zero, and will tend to get large as one or more of the $\hat{\lambda}_i$ approach unity.

The likelihood ratio statistic defined in (5.31) does not, in fact, have a χ^2 distribution, even in large samples. Johansen does, however, find the asymptotic distribution of $\text{LR}(N - r)$ by applying some results in Brownian motion theory. This distribution does not vary with the particular model being estimated or other variable factors as in the case of the Dickey–Fuller tests for cointegration; however, it is not invariant to the assumption made about the underlying VAR model. In particular, there are three main assumptions which may be made:

1. The VAR may be as specified in (5.16) without any constant term.
2. The VAR has a restricted constant term which appears only as a part of the cointegrating vectors so that the ECM form (5.17) contains any constants within the term $\Gamma_K X_{t-K}$ only.
3. The VAR has an unrestricted constant. This means that if the ECM form of the VAR (5.17) has some equations which do not contain a cointegrating vector (so that they are purely difference equations) these equations will still contain constants. This is unlike assumption 2, where the constants were associated with the cointegrating vectors. So these variables will behave like generalised random walk variables but with a drift term and the data will contain deterministic trend terms. This assumption is therefore characterised by the presence of deterministic trend in some of the variables.

Johansen (1989) gives the critical values for all three cases for the test outlined in (5.31).

5.12 Testing linear restrictions on the cointegrating parameters

In section 5.11 we gave an outline of a maximum likelihood technique for testing for and estimating the set of unique cointegrating vectors. Johansen (1988) also demonstrates how the technique can be applied to test linear restrictions on the parameters of the cointegrating vectors.

Suppose that, after an initial application of the Johansen technique, we have decided that there are at most r cointegrating vectors among the N-dimensional vector X_t. Let the $(N \times r)$ matrix of cointegrating vectors be β. Johansen considers linear restrictions on β which reduce the number of *independent* cointegrating parameters from N to S, $S \leq N$.

For example, suppose we analysed a vector consisting of the exchange rate (e_t) and domestic and foreign prices, p_t^* and p_t respectively (all in logarithms). As in the example discussed in section 5.10, if $Z_t = (p_t e_t p_t^*)'$ was an $I(1)$ vector, then long-run purchasing power parity would suggest that

$$g_t = e_t - p_t + p_t^* \sim I(0) \tag{5.32}$$

Thus, if we found $r = 1$ statistically significant cointegrating vectors:

$$\beta_{i1} e_t + \beta_{i2} p_t + \beta_{i3} p_t^* = g_t, \quad i = 1, \ldots, r \tag{5.33}$$

Then, the restrictions in (5.32) involve reducing the number of independent cointegrating parameters from three to one. For the full $(N \times r)$ matrix β, they can be written:

$$\beta = \begin{bmatrix} 1 \\ -1 \\ 1 \end{bmatrix} \phi$$

where ϕ is a $(S \times r)$ (in this case 1×1) matrix of parameters.

In general, Johansen considers restrictions which can be written in the form

$$H_o: \beta = H\phi \tag{5.34}$$

where H is an $(N \times S)$ matrix of full rank $= S$ and ϕ is an $(S \times r)$ matrix of unknown parameters.

The method of obtaining the restricted estimates is straightforward. Since H is known, simply replace β with $H\phi$ in the procedure discussed in the previous section, to obtain an estimate ϕ^* say. The restricted estimate of β is then given by $\beta^* = H\phi^*$.

Along with the restricted estimates will be produced a set of eigenvalues, $\hat{\lambda}$, corresponding to the set produced in the unrestricted estimation, and similarly ordered such that $\lambda_1^* > \lambda_2^*, \ldots \lambda_r^*$. The relationship between these eigenvalues and the maximised value of the likelihood function, see (5.27), (5.29), (5.30), can then be exploited to yield a test of the hypothesis based on the first r cointegrating vectors:

$$\text{LR}^*[r(N - S)] = -2 \ln Q = T \sum_{i=1}^{r} \ln\{1 - \lambda_i^*)/(1 - \hat{\lambda}_i)\} \tag{5.35}$$

This will have an asymptotic chi-square distribution with $r(N - S)$ degrees of freedom. As is generally the case with likelihood ratio statistics, the number of degrees of freedom is equal to the number of restrictions $r(N - S)$ since $(N - S)$ fewer parameters are estimated in each of the r cointegrating parameters vectors.

5.13 Example: The demand for broad money during the Gold Standard

Taylor (1991) estimates a 'long-run' demand function for UK broad money for the period 1871–1913. He starts by testing for unit roots in a pre-specified set of variables – broad money (m_t), prices (p_t), real income (y_t), the long bond rate (RL_t) and the prime bill rate (RPB_t), (all data except interest rates in logarithms). The results are listed here as Table 5.1. Taylor uses the DF test and the Johansen statistic (5.31), where 'cointegration in one variable' simply implies that the variable is $I(0)$. Table 5.1 suggests that all of the 'levels variables' listed above correspond to $I(1)$. Table 5.2(a) then demonstrates that at a nominal significance level of 5% the hypothesis of zero cointegrating vectors is strongly rejected, while the hypothesis of one or more cointegrating vectors is not. Taylor thus concludes that there is a unique statistically significant cointegrating vector relating the variables. This is reported as the unrestricted equation 1 in Table 5.2(b), where the cointegrating parameters have been normalised on m_t.

Taylor then argues that, whilst the short interest rates RD_t and RPB_t may effect 'long run' or 'average' money demand, their long-run effect will be felt only through their constant means. He therefore tests for cointegration amongst, m_t, p_t, y_t and RL_t. He then estimates a VAR for these variables with lag length two (chosen on the basis of standard diagnostics, see Chapter 4) and applies the Johansen procedure. The results are given in Table 5.2.

Table 5.1 Unit root tests for money, prices, income and interest rates

Variable	Dickey–Fuller statistic	Johansen statistic
m_t	1.00	1.04
Δm_t	−4.21	16.80
p_t	−1.60	1.66
Δp_t	−5.03	22.97
y_t	−0.32	0.28
Δy_t	−3.82	21.82
RL_t	−0.68	2.24
ΔRL_t	−3.54	9.87
RD_t	−3.68	14.35
RPB_t	−3.30	11.69

Note: The null hypothesis in each case is that the variable in question is $I(1)$; the 5% rejection region for the Dickey–Fuller statistic is $\{\text{DF}\varepsilon R | \text{DF} < -2.93\}$ (Fuller 1976, p. 373); the 5% rejection region for the Johansen statistic is $\{J\varepsilon R | J > 9.094\}$ (Johansen 1989).

Table 5.2 Applying the Johansen procedure to money demand during the Gold Standard

(a) Tests for cointegration

Null hypothesis	Likelihood ratio statistic	5% critical value
Number of cointegrating vectors r		
$r \leqslant 3$	0.001	9.094
$r \leqslant 2$	5.12	20.168
$r \leqslant 1$	20.65	35.068
$r = 0$	60.21	53.347

(b) Estimated cointegrating vector (largest eigenvalue only)

1. Unrestricted: $m_t = 1.06p_t + 0.97y_t - 0.097\text{RL}_t$

2. With homogeneity restrictions: $m_t = p_t + y_t - 0.076\text{RL}_t$
   Likelihood ratio statistic: $\text{LR}(2) = 1.39 \ (0.50)$

3. With exclusion restriction on RL: $m_t = 0.78p_t + 1.01y_t$
   Likelihood ratio statistic: $\text{LR}(1) = 7.618(0.5E - 2)$

Note: Figures in parenthesis are marginal significance levels. The $\text{LR}(n)$ statistics are asymptotically $\chi^2(n)$ variates under the null hypothesis.

The likelihood ratio statistics

Given the cointegrating vector (non-normalised) from the Johansen procedure:

$$\beta_{11}m_t + \beta_{12}p_t + \beta_{13}y_t + \beta_{14}\text{RL}_t \sim I(0)$$

then equation 1 in Table 5.2(b) corresponds to

$$m_t = -(\beta_{12}/\beta_{11})p_t - (\beta_{13}/\beta_{11})y_t - (\beta_{14}/\beta_{11})\text{RL}_t$$

This equation clearly looks like a 'textbook' money demand function – it has a negative interest rate semi-elasticity and the coefficients on prices and income are positive and close to unity [Table 5.2(b), equation 1].

Taylor then tests for price and income homogeneity, i.e that the 'long-run' coefficients on prices and income are unity when normalised on money. In terms of (5.34), these restrictions are written:

$$\begin{bmatrix} \beta_{11} \\ \beta_{12} \\ \beta_{13} \\ \beta_{14} \end{bmatrix} = \begin{bmatrix} 1 & 0 \\ -1 & 0 \\ -1 & 0 \\ 0 & 1 \end{bmatrix} \begin{bmatrix} \phi_{11} \\ \phi_{12} \end{bmatrix}$$

so that

$$\beta_{11} = \phi_{11}, \ \beta_{12} = -\phi_{11}, \ \beta_{13} = -\phi_{11} \quad \text{and} \quad \beta_{14} = \phi_{12}$$

The restricted estimates are given as equation 2 in Table 5.2(b) and the likelihood ratio statistic (5.35) for the restrictions is LR(2) = 4.57. The restrictions are not rejected at the 5% level.

Finally, Taylor tests whether RL_t can be excluded from the co-integrating vector. The likelihood ratio statistic listed alongside the restricted equation 3 in Table 5.2(b) shows that this hypothesis is easily rejected at the 1% level.

5.14 Summary

Cointegration deals with the relationships between variables that have stochastic trends. If cointegration is not rejected then there exists one or more 'long-run' linear relationship between the variables. The economic interpretation of the these relationships requires an *a priori* economic theory. Cointegration implies the existence of a dynamic error correction model, which again must be interpreted with the aid of economic theory. Hypothesis testing on the cointegration para-meters, of $I(1)$ variables, is possible although not standard. Cointe-gration is currently one of the most active research areas in time series econometrics and innovative results are frequently appearing in journals. We have provided an overview of the basic ideas in this area that are likely to be of use to the applied economist.

Appendix: The Johansen procedure

Johansen (1988) sets his analysis within the following framework. Begin by defining a general polynomial distributed lag model of a vector of variables X as

$$X_t = \pi_1 X_{t-1} + \ldots + \pi_k X_{t-k} + \varepsilon_t \qquad t = 1, \ldots, T \qquad \text{(A1)}$$

where X_t is a vector of N variables of interest; π_i are NXN coeffi-cient matrices, and ε_t is an idependently identically distributed N-dimensional vector with zero mean and covariance matrix Ω. Within this framework the long-run, or cointegrating matrix is given by

$$I - \pi_1 - \pi_2 \ldots -\pi_k = \pi \tag{A2}$$

where I is the identity matrix.

π will therefore be an NXN matrix. The number, r, of distinct cointegrating vectors which exists between the variables of X, will be given by the rank of π. In general, if X consists of variables which must be differenced once in order to be stationary [integrated of order one of $I(1)$] then, at most, r must be equal to $N - 1$, so that $r \leqslant N - 1$. Now we define two matrices α, β both of which are $N \times r$ such that

$$\pi = \alpha\beta'$$

and so the rows of β form the r distinct cointegrating vectors.

Johansen then demonstrates the following theorem.

Theorem: The maximum likelihood estimate of the space spanned by β is the space spanned by the r canonical variates corresponding to the r largest squared canonical correlations between the residuals of X_{t-k} and ΔX_t corrected for the effect of the lagged differences of the X process. The likelihood ratio test statistic for the hypothesis that there are at most r cointegrating vectors is

$$-2 \ln Q = -T \sum_{i=r+1}^{N} \ln(1 - \hat{\lambda}_i) \tag{A3}$$

where $\hat{\lambda}_{r+1} \ldots \hat{\lambda}_N$ are the $(N - r)$ smallest squared canonical correlations. Johansen then goes on to demonstrate the properties of the maximum likelihood estimates and, more importantly, he shows that the likelihood ratio test has an asymptotic distribution which is a function of an $(N - r)$ dimensional Brownian motion which is independent of any nuisance parameters. This means that a set of critical values can be tabulated which will be correct for all models. He demonstrates that the space spanned by β is consistently estimated by the space spanned by $\hat{\beta}$.

In order to implement this theorem we begin by reparameterising (A1) into the error correction model:

$$\Delta X_t = \Gamma_i \Delta X_{t-1} + \ldots + \Gamma_{k-1} \Delta X_{t-k+1} + \Gamma_K X_{t-k} + \varepsilon_t \tag{A4}$$

where

$$\Gamma_i = -I + \pi_1 + \ldots \pi_i; \quad i = 1 \ldots k$$

The equilibrium matrix π is now clearly identified as $-\Gamma_k$.

Johansen's suggested procedure begins by regressing ΔX_t on the lagged differences of ΔX_t which yields a set of residuals R_{ot}. We then regress X_{t-k} on the lagged differences ΔX_{t-j} which yields residuals R_{kt}. The likelihood function, in terms of α, β and Ω is then proportional to

$$L(\alpha, \beta, \Omega) = |\Omega|^{-T/2} \exp\left[-1/2 \sum_{t=1}^{T} (R_{ot} + \alpha\beta' R_{kt})' \right. \tag{A5}$$

$$\Omega^{-1} (R_{ot} + \alpha\beta' R_{kt})]$$

If β were fixed we could maximise over α and Ω by a regression of R_{ot} on $-\beta' R_{kt}$ which gives

$$\hat{\alpha}(\beta) = - S_{ok}\beta(\beta' S_{kk}\beta)^{-1} \tag{A6}$$

and

$$\hat{\Omega}(\beta) = S_{oo} - S_{ok}\beta(\beta' S_{kk}\beta)^{-1}\beta' S_{ko} \tag{A7}$$

where

$$S_{ij} = T^{-1} \sum_{t=1}^{T} R_{it}R'_{jt} \qquad i, j = 0, k$$

and so maximising the likelihood function may be reduced to minimising

$$|S_{oo} - S_{ok}\beta(\beta' S_{kk}\beta)^{-1}\beta' S_{ko}| \tag{A8}$$

It may be shown that (A8) will be minimised when

$$|\beta' S_{kk}\beta - \beta' S_{ko}SS_{oo}^{-1}S_{ok}\beta|/|\beta' S_{kk}\beta| \tag{A9}$$

attains a minimum with respect to β.

We now define a diagonal matrix D which consists of the ordered eigenvalues $\lambda_1 > \ldots > \lambda_N$ of $(S_{ko}S_{oo}^{-1}S_{ok})$ with respect to S_{kk}. That is λ_i satisfies

$$|\lambda S_{kk} - S_{ko}S_{oo}^{-1}S_{ok}| = 0 \tag{A10}$$

Define E to be the corresponding matrix of eigenvectors so that

$$S_{kk}ED = S_{ko}S_{oo}^{-1}S_{ok}E \tag{A11}$$

where we normalise E such that $E' S_{kk}E = I$.

The maximum likelihood estimator of β is now given by the first r rows of E, that is, the first r eigenvectors of $(S_{ko}S_{oo}^{-1}S_{ok})$ with respect to S_{kk}. These are the canonical variates and the corresponding eigenvalues are the squared canonical correlations of R_{kt} with respect to R_{ot}. These eigenvalues may then be used in the test proposed in (A3) to test either for the existence of a cointegrating vector $r = 1$ or the number of cointegrating vectors $N > r > 1$.

Johansen (1988) calculates the critical values for the likelihood ratio test for the cases where $m \leqslant 5$, where $m = P - r$, and P is the number of variables in the set under consideration and r is the maximum number of cointegrating vectors being tested for.

6
Rational expectations

Over the last ten years the role of expectations formation in both theoretical and applied macroeconomics has been of central importance. New Classical models embody the assumption of rational expectations and clearing markets and may give rise to policy ineffectiveness, an issue which has influenced policy debates particularly in the US. In the UK, the treatment of expectations has been more pragmatic than in the US, but explicit modelling of expectations is now used in a wide range of large-scale macroeconometric models (see Wallis 1986 for a survey). Policy simulations of these models generally do not yield 'short-run' policy ineffectiveness but they do produce projections which differ substantially from conventional 'backward-looking' models.

At the applied level, relatively few practitioners have adopted the 'full' Muth-rational approach which requires specification of the complete macromodel. Such 'full information methods' have generally been confined to estimating 'small models' (e.g. Blake 1984, Taylor 1979). Much applied work has concentrated on estimating 'single equations' that contain expectations variables. For example, in the price expectations augmented Phillips curve (PEAPC), wage inflation depends on expected price inflation (and the excess demand for labour). The Life-Cycle hypothesis implies that consumption depends on some measure of expected future income. The risk aversion model has money and bond demand depending on expected capital gains.

The efficient markets literature is concerned with the proposition that agents use all available information to remove any known profitable opportunities in the market. For example, if uncovered interest parity holds then the interest differential in favour of the domestic currency should equal the *expected* depreciation of the domestic currency. To test such a proposition we need a framework for modelling the unobservable one-period-ahead expected spot rate of the domestic currency.

Estimation of single equations containing expectations terms has proved popular because they are more robust to potential misspecifications and simpler to estimate than full-information methods based on a 'complete' model. In this chapter we shall not be concerned with the latter case.

The literature on estimating expectations models is vast and can quickly become very complex. We have attempted to explain only the main (limited information) methods currently in use. We shall concentrate only on those problems introduced by expectations variables and shall leave 'other' problems that might also arise such as simultaneous equations problems and equations containing lagged dependent variables to be dealt with in other chapters.

The rational expectations, RE, hypothesis has featured widely in the literature and we begin in section 6.1 by discussing the basic axioms of RE which we later see are crucial in choosing an appropriate estimation procedure. We also examine equations that contain multi-period expectations. In section 6.2 we discuss the widely used errors in variables method (EVM) of estimating structural equations under the assumption that agents have rational expectations. The use of auxiliary equations (such as extrapolative predictions) to generate a suitable proxy variable for the unobservable expectations series, gives rise to two-step procedures and the pitfalls involved in such an approach are also examined in section 6.2.

In section 6.3 we highlight the problems which arise when the structural expectations equation has serially correlated errors. The generalised method of moments (GMM) estimator of Hansen (1982) and Hansen and Hodrick (1980) and the two-step two-stage least squares estimator (Cumby *et al*. 1983) provide solutions to this problem.

In sections 6.4 and 6.5 we provide illustrative empirical examples of the techniques discussed in earlier sections. We begin in section 6.4 with tests of the axioms of RE. We then discuss fixed-parameter forecasting schemes and then relax the assumption that agents have unchanged structural parameters in their model of the economy. Instead we assume that agents slowly *learn* about their economic environment and for example may utilise useful 'rules of thumb' in forming their expectations. We demonstrate how the Kalman filter and other 'variable parameter' approaches can be used to mimic simple learning processes. In section 6.5 we demonstrate how RE models give rise to testable cross-equation restrictions. The Barro (1978) policy ineffectiveness New Classical model, the Carr–Darby (1981) unanticipated money model and tests of the efficient markets hypothesis fall into this class. We discuss such tests in the context of one-period-ahead expectations and multi-period expectations. A final section concludes.

6.1 The economics of expectations models and the RE hypothesis

In this section we analyse the various ways in which expectations variables are utilised in the applied literature and the implications of the economic assumptions for the estimation issues discussed in a later section.

Usually the applied economist is interested in estimating the structural parameters of a single behavioural equation or set of equations containing expectations terms which forms a subset of a larger model. (In a 'full' Muth–RE model (Muth 1961) we would have to specify the whole model.) The simplest *structural expectations equation* can be represented:

$$y_{1t} = bx^e_{t+j} + u_{1t} \tag{6.1}$$

where

$$x^e_{t+j} = E(x_{t+j}|\Omega|_{t-j}) \quad j \geqslant 0 \tag{6.2}$$

and x^e_{t+j} is an exogenous expectations variable, E is the expectations operator conditional on the complete (relevant) information set available to the agent at time $_{t-j}$ (i.e. Ω_{t-j}). For example, in a purchasing power parity export price equation, Ex_{t+j} represents expected world prices and y_{1t} the domestic export price, both in a common currency. Also equation (6.1) could, for example, represent the wage-expected price element of the Phillips curve. In the absence of data on Ex_{t+j} (e.g. quantitative survey data) we must posit an auxiliary hypothesis for Ex_{t+j}. Whatever expectations scheme we choose, of key importance for the economics and econometrics of the model are (a) the forecast horizon, (b) the dating and content of the information set used in making the forecast, and (c) the relationship between the forecast error and the information set.

To develop these issues further it is useful to discuss the basic axioms of RE.

Basic axioms of RE

If agents have RE they act as if they know the structure of the complete model to within a set of white noise errors (i.e. the axiom of correct specification). Forecasts are unbiased on average, with constant variance and successive (one-step-ahead) forecast errors are uncorrelated with each other and with the information set used in making the forecast. Thus, the relationship between outturn x_{t+1} and the *one-step-ahead*, RE forecast $_t x^e_{t+1}$ using the complete information set Ω_t (or a subset Λ_t) is:

$$x_{t+1} = {}_t x^e_{t+1} + \omega_{t+1} \tag{6.3}$$

where

$$E(\omega_{t+1}|\Omega_t) = E(\omega_{t+1}|\Lambda_t) = 0 \tag{6.3a}$$

$$E(\omega^2_{t+1}|\Omega_t) = \sigma^2_\omega \tag{6.3b}$$

$$E(\omega_{t+1}\omega_{t+1-j}|\Omega_t) = 0 \qquad j = 1, 2 \ldots \infty \tag{6.3c}$$

The one-step-ahead rational expectations forecast error ω_{t+1} is 'white noise' and an 'innovation', conditional on the complete information set Ω_t and is orthogonal to a subset of the complete information set $(\Lambda_t \subset \Omega_t)$.

The *k-step-ahead* RE forecast errors $(k > 1)$ *are* serially correlated and are MA $(k - 1)$. To demonstrate this in a simple case assume x_t is AR(1).

$$x_{t+1} = \phi x_t + \omega_{t+1} \quad \text{and} \quad E(\omega_{t+1}|\Omega_t) = 0 \tag{6.4}$$

Hence

$$x_{t+j} = \phi^j x_t + \omega_{t+j} + \phi\omega_{t+j-1} + \phi^2\omega_{t+j-2} + \ldots \tag{6.5}$$

From (6.5) it is easy to see that

$$(x_{t+1} - {}_t x^e_{t+1}) = \omega_{t+1} \tag{6.6}$$

while the two-period-ahead forecast error is

$$(x_{t+2} - {}_t x^e_{t+2}) = (\phi\omega_{t+1} + \omega_{t+2}) \tag{6.7}$$

The *one-step*-ahead forecast error is an independent white-noise process, ω_{t+1} but the two-period-ahead forecast error is MA(1); similarly the *k*-step-ahead forecast error is MA($k - 1$). Note that *all* the multi-period forecast errors

$$(x_{t+j} - {}_t x^e_{t+j}) \qquad j \geqslant 1$$

are independent of (orthogonal to) the information set Ω_t (or Λ_t).

There is one further property of RE that is useful in analysing RE estimators, namely the form of revisions to expectations. The *one-period revision* to expectations

$$\left({}_{t+1}x^e_{t+j} - {}_tx^e_{t+j} \right)$$

depends only on new information arriving between t and $t + 1$ and hence from (6.5) is easily seen to be

$$\left({}_{t+1}x^e_{t+j} - {}_tx^e_{t+j} \right) = \phi^{j-1}\omega_{t+1} \tag{6.8}$$

The two-period revision to expectations

$$\left({}_{t+2}x^e_{t+j} - {}_tx^e_{t+j} \right)$$

will of course depend on ω_{t+1} and ω_{t+2} and be MA(1); one can generalise the result for k-period revisions to expectations.

Direct tests of RE

Direct tests of the basic axioms of RE may involve multi-period expectations and this immediately raises estimation problems. For example, *if monthly* quantitative survey data is available on the *one-year-ahead* expectation, ${}_tx^e_{t+12}$, a test of the axioms often involves a regression of the form:

$$x_{t+12} = \beta_0 + \beta_1({}_tx^e_{t+12}) + \beta_2 \Lambda_t + \eta_t \tag{6.9}$$

where

$$H_0: \beta_0 = \beta_2 = 0, \, \beta_1 = 1$$

Under the null, η_{t+12} is MA(11) and an immediate problem due to RE is the need to use some kind of generalised least squares (GLS) estimator if efficiency is to be achieved. Of course, for one-period-ahead expectations where data of the same frequency is available, the error term is white noise and independent of the regressors in (6.9); OLS therefore provides a BLUE.

An additional problem arises if the survey data on expectations is assumed to be measured with error. If the true RE expectation is ${}_tx^e_{t+12}$ and the survey data provides a measure ${}_t\tilde{x}^e_{t+12}$ where we assume a simple linear measurement model (Pesaran 1985):

$$_t\tilde{x}^e_{t+12} = \alpha_0 + \alpha_1({}_tx^e_{t+12}) + \varepsilon_t \tag{6.10}$$

Then substituting for ${}_tx^e_{t+12}$ from (6.10) in (6.9):

$$x_{t+12} = \lambda_0 + \lambda_1({}_t\tilde{x}^e_{t+12}) + \beta_2 \Lambda_t + \zeta_t \tag{6.11}$$

where

$$\lambda_0 = (\alpha_1\beta_0 - \beta_1\alpha_0)/\alpha_1$$
$$\lambda_1 = \beta_1/\alpha_1$$
$$\zeta_t = \eta_t - (\beta_1/\alpha_1)\varepsilon_t$$

The additional problem in (6.11) is that now $_t\tilde{x}^e_{t+12}$ is correlated with ζ_t; some form of generalised IV estimator is required for consistency and asymptotic efficiency. As we shall see the orthogonality property between the RE forecast error and the information set (Λ_t or Ω_t) is frequently used in finding a suitable instrument set. However, it is not always simply the case that Λ_t provides a valid instrument set for the problem at hand.

Multi-period expectations

Sargent's (1979) model where agents minimise a multi-period quadratic cost function provides a tractable expectations framework, much used in the applied literature. Agents are assumed to know the time-path of the 'long-run' choice variable y_t^* (as given by some static equilibrium theory) and then choose actual y_t to minimise costs of being out of equilibrium $(y_{t+i} - y_{t+i}^*)^2$ and costs of adjustment $(y_{t+i} - y_{t+i-1})^2$. The cost function C is

$$C = E_t\sum_{i=0}^{\infty} D^i(a_0(y_{t+i} - y_{t+i}^*)^2 + a_1(y_{t+i} - y_{t+i-1})^2)$$

(6.12)

where E_t is the expectation operator, D is a discount factor $0 < D < 1$ and a_0 and a_1 are weighting factors $(a_0, a_1 > 0)$.

The solution to this problem is

$$y_t = \lambda_1 y_{t-1} + (1 - \lambda_1)(1 - \lambda_1 D) \sum_{i=0}^{\infty} (\lambda_1 D)^i(k_t x^e_{t+i})$$ **(6.13)**

where we have assumed the static equilibrium relationship is

$$y_t^* = kx_t$$ **(6.13a)**

and λ_1 is the stable root of the Euler equation obtained from the first-order conditions $\partial C/\partial y_t = 0$.

Equation (6.13) has proved popular in the applied literature because it has the 'plausible' property that the weights on the future expected values of the 'forcing variables' $_t x^e_{t+i}$ decline, the further the expectations are into the future. In addition, it provides a rationale for the inclusion of a lagged dependent variable and many economic time series have a strong autoregressive component.

The model has been applied to the determination of employment (Hall *et al*. 1986, Hansen and Sargent 1981, 1982), export prices (Cuthbertson 1986, 1990) and the demand for money (Cuthbertson 1988a, Cuthbertson and Taylor 1987, Muscatelli 1988). A slight modification to the cost function leads to an additional lagged dependent variable (y_{t-2}) and more complex weights on the forward terms $_tx^e_{t+i}$ which has been used to model stockbuilding (Hall, Henry, Wren-Lewis 1986). In most of the above studies the information set is assumed to be dated at either t or $t-1$. A number of different estimation techniques have been used in applied studies utilising equation (6.13) and it is not always clear what assumptions are required to yield optimal estimators, or the relationship between the various estimation methods used. It is our aim to clarify these issues in the subsequent sections.

6.2   The EVM and extrapolative predictors

In order to motivate our discussion of the estimation problems in the next two sections it is useful at this stage to summarise some of the problems encountered when estimating a structural expectations model; problems that arise include serial correlation and correlation between regressors and the error term. For illustrative purposes assume the structural model of interest is

$$y_t = \delta_1(_tx^e_{t+1}) + \delta_2(_tx^e_{t+2}) + u_t \tag{6.14}$$

u_t is taken to be white noise and x_t is an exogenous expectations variable.

Under the assumption of RE we have

$$x_{t+j} = {}_tx^e_{t+j} + \omega_{t+j} \tag{6.15}$$

A method of estimation widely used (and one of the main ones discussed in this chapter) is the errors in variables method EVM, where we replace the unobservable $_tx^e_{t+j}$ by its realised value x_{t+j}. This method is consistent with agents being Muth–rational, but could also be taken as a condition of the relationship between outturn and forecast without invoking Muth–RE.

Substituting from (6.15) in (6.14):

$$y_t = \delta_1x_{t+1} + \delta_2x_{t+2} + \varepsilon_t \tag{6.16}$$

$$\varepsilon_t = u_t - \delta_1\omega_{t+1} - \delta_2\omega_{t+2} \tag{6.16a}$$

Clearly from (6.15), x_{t+j} and ω_{t+j} are correlated and hence:

$$\text{plim}\,(x'_{t+j}\varepsilon_t)/T \neq 0 \qquad (j = 1, 2)$$

and

$$E(\varepsilon\,\varepsilon') \neq \sigma_\varepsilon^2\,I$$

because of the moving average error introduced by the RE forecast errors, ω_{t+j}. Hence our RE model requires some form of instrumental variables estimation procedure with a correction for serial correlation. These two general problems form a main focus for this chapter.

Fixed coefficient *extrapolative* predictors are also used widely to proxy expectations terms. Here it is explicitly recognised that the econometrician may have a subset $\Lambda_t = \{x_{t-j}\}$, say, of the complete information set used by agents $\Omega_t = (x_{t-j}, y_{t-1})$, say. Hence the econometrician posits an expectations scheme

$$x_{t+1} = \phi(L)x_t + v_t = \phi_1 x_t + \phi_2 x_{t-1} + \phi_3 x_{t-3} + \ldots + v_t$$

$$\textbf{(6.17)}$$

Given an estimate of $\phi(L)$ we generate predictions with information at time t, using the *chain rule of forecasting*:

$$\tilde{x}_{t+1} = \hat{\phi}(L)x_t \qquad\qquad \textbf{(6.18a)}$$

$$\tilde{x}_{t+2} = \hat{\phi}_1[\hat{\phi}(L)x_t] + \sum_{j=2} \hat{\phi}_j\, x_{t+2-j} \qquad \textbf{(6.18b)}$$

and if these replace x^e_{t+j} in (6.14) we have a structural estimation equation

$$y_t = \delta_1\,\tilde{x}_{t+1} + \delta_2\,\tilde{x}_{t+2} + q_t \qquad\qquad \textbf{(6.19)}$$

$$q_t = \sum_1^2 \delta_i((x_{t+i} - \tilde{x}_{t+i}) - (x_{t+i} - x^e_{t+i})) + \varepsilon_t \qquad \textbf{(6.20)}$$

The error term q_t contains the MA(1), true forecast error of agents $\omega_{t+i} = (x_{t+i} - x^e_{t+i})$ as before but there is an extra term $(x_{t+i} - \tilde{x}_{t+i})$ which may cause additional estimation problems and these issues are discussed in the next section.

There is a logical problem in using a fixed coefficient expectations equation (6.17). *All* of the data is used in estimating $\phi(L)$, yet this fixed estimate is used to predict x_{t+1} at the beginning of the sample; part of the $\tilde{x}_{t+1}$ series therefore embodies sample information that the agent could not have had at the time his forecast was made. This may not matter asymptotically if $\phi(L)$ really is constant but clearly in small samples the assumption may yield incorrect predictions (see Friedman 1979).

We may wish to relax the assumption that agents act as if they use the 'true' fixed coefficient model in forming expectations. It may be the case either that the *true* model for x_t has some time varying parameters or that agents use a limited information set (of the true fixed parameter model) and update the changing estimates of the parameters of interest in some optimal fashion. In terms of a simplified AR(1) model with time-varying parameters we have:

$$x_{t+1} = \phi_{t+1}x_t + v_t \qquad (6.21)$$

The Kalman filter can be used in a wide variety of models with time-varying parameters (or unobservable components – see Chapter 7) to provide optimal estimators $\hat{\phi}_{t+1/t}$ based on information at time t. We can then generate predictors $_t\hat{x}_{t+j}$ to use in (6.14). Hence similar issues arise when using such 'learning models' to provide a proxy variable for $_tx^e_{t+j}$ in the structural equation (6.14), as in the fixed parameter model.

The precise method used in estimating single equations with expectations terms depends on whether the expectations terms are formed for the current period $_{t-1}x^e_t$ or for many future periods $_tx^e_{t+j}(j \geq 1)$ and whether the residuals are serially correlated or white noise. Serial correlation may arise because of 'omitted variables', or wrong functional form in the structural equation or the assumption of RE *per se* may induce serially correlated errors in the estimation equation. To delineate these cases and to avoid confusion we take them in turn. We can then ascertain precisely the source of the estimation problem for each case. We begin with a simple model with one-period expectations to illustrate the basic principles of the EVM, we then discuss extrapolative predictors.

The errors in variables method EVM

The EVM is a form of IV or 2SLS approach. Under RE, the unobservable expectations variable $_tx^e_{t+j}$ is determined by the full relevant information set Ω_t. In the EVM a subset of the true information set Λ_t ($\subset \Omega_t$) is sufficient to generate consistent estimates. However, we begin by demonstrating that OLS yields an inconsistent estimator (see section 1.6 (Chapter 1) for a more general exposition).

One-period-ahead expectations: white noise structural error

It is important to note that here we are dealing with a very specific expectations model. The simplest structural model embodying one-period-ahead expectations is

$$y_t = \beta x^e_{t+1} + u_t \tag{6.22}$$

where u_t is white noise and x^e_{t+1} is assumed to be uncorrelated in the limit with u_t:

$$\text{plim}(x^e_{t+1}u'_t)/T = 0 \tag{6.23}$$

If we assume rational expectations, then

$$x_{t+1} = x^e_{t+1} + \omega_{t+1} \tag{6.24}$$

and the RE forecast error ω_{t+1} is independent of the information set Ω_t (or Λ_t)

$$E\left(\Omega'_t\omega_{t+1}\right) = 0 \tag{6.25}$$

Substituting (6.24) in (6.22) we obtain

$$y_t = \beta x_{t+1} + q_t \tag{6.26}$$

$$q_t = (u_t - \beta\omega_{t+1}) \tag{6.26a}$$

Consider applying OLS to (6.26), we have:

$$\hat{\beta} = \beta + (x'_{t+1}x_{t+1})^{-1}(x'_{t+1}q_t) \tag{6.27}$$

From (6.24):

$$\text{plim}(x'_{t+1}\, x_{t+1})/T = \text{plim}(x^e_{t+1}{}'x^e_{t+1})/T + \text{plim}(\omega'_{t+1}\, \omega_{t+1})/T \tag{6.28}$$

or rewriting this more succinctly:

$$\sigma^2_x = \sigma^2_{xe} + \sigma^2_\omega \tag{6.28b}$$

From (6.24) and (6.29) and noting that x^e_{t+1} is uncorrelated in the limit with ω_{t+1}:

$$\text{plim}(x'_{t+1}q_t)/T = -\beta\,\text{plim}(\omega'_{t+1}\omega_{t+1})/T = -\beta\sigma^2_\omega \tag{6.29}$$

Substituting these expressions in (6.27):

$$\text{plim}\,\hat{\beta} = \beta\left[1 - \frac{\sigma^2_\omega}{\sigma^2_xe + \sigma^2_\omega}\right] \tag{6.30}$$

Thus the OLS estimator for β is inconsistent and is biased downwards. The bias is smaller the smaller the variance of the 'noise' element σ^2_ω in forming expectations. The above analysis is the basis of Friedman's (1957) view that if the permanent income hypothesis of consumption is correct but the latter is proxied by measured income, then OLS yields an underestimate of the true long-run marginal propensity to consume (out of permanent income). Similarly, many early studies of the price-expectations augmented Phillips curve used actual inflation as a proxy for expected inflation; OLS estimates are inconsistent and it was argued that the finding of the presence of money illusion and a non-vertical long-run Phillips curve is due to an inappropriate estimation technique in the presence of expectations variables.

Instrumental variables: 2SLS

OLS is inconsistent because of the correlation between the variable x_{t+1} and the error term q_t which 'contains' the RE forecast error, ω_{t+1}. The solution to this problem is to use instrumental variables, IV, on (6.26), (see Chapter 1). However, to illustrate some additional nuances when applying IV, consider the model:

$$y_t = \alpha x_{1t+1}^e + \beta x_{2t} + u_t = Q\delta + u_t \qquad (6.31)$$

$$Q = \{x_{1t+1}^e, x_{2t}\} \qquad \delta = (\alpha, \beta)' \qquad (6.31a)$$

where x_{1t+1}^e, x_{2t} are asymptotically uncorrelated with u_t.

Direct application of IV to (6.31) would require an instrument for x_{1t+1}^e and an obvious candidate are the OLS predictions from the regression of x_{1t+1} on a subset of the information set, Λ_t *but including* x_{2t}:

$$\hat{x}_{1t+1} = \Lambda_t \hat{\Pi} \qquad (6.32a)$$

$$\hat{\Pi} = (\Lambda_t'\Lambda_t)^{-1}(\Lambda_t'x_{1t+1}) \qquad (6.32b)$$

The researcher is now faced with two options. Direct application of IV would utilise the instrument matrix

$$W_1 = \{\hat{x}_{1t+1}, x_{2t}\} \qquad (6.33a)$$

where x_{2t} acts as its own instrument, giving

$$\delta_1 = (W_1'Q)(W_1'y) \qquad (6.33b)$$

$$\text{Var}(\hat{\delta}_1) = \sigma^2(W_1'Q)^{-1} \qquad (6.33c)$$

This is also the 2SLS estimator since in the first stage x_{1t+1} is regressed on *all* the predetermined (or exogenous variables) in (6.31) *and* the additional instruments in Λ_t.

An alternative is to *replace* x_{1t+1}^e in (6.31) by $\hat{x}_{1t+1}$ and apply OLS to:

$$y_t = \alpha\hat{x}_{1t+1} + \beta x_{2t} + q_t^* \qquad (6.34)$$

$$q_t^* = u_t - \alpha(x_{t+1} - x_{t+1}^e) - \alpha(\hat{x}_{t+1} - x_{t+1}) \qquad (6.34a)$$

This yields a 'two-step estimator' but as long as x_{1t+1} is regressed on *all* the predetermined variables, the OLS on (6.34) is *numerically* equivalent to the 2SLS estimator $\hat{\delta}_1$ and is therefore consistent.

However, there is a problem with the approach. The OLS residuals from (6.34) are

$$e = y_t - \hat{\alpha}\hat{x}_{1t+1} - \hat{\beta}x_{2t} \tag{6.35}$$

but the correct (IV/2SLS) residuals use x_{1t+1} and not $\hat{x}_{1t+1}$ and are:

$$e_1 = y - \hat{\alpha}x_{1t+1} - \hat{\beta}x_{2t} \tag{6.36}$$

Hence the variance–covariance matrix of parameters from OLS on (6.34) is incorrect since $s^2 = e'e/T$ is an incorrect (inconsistent) measure of σ^2 (Pagan 1984). The remedy is straightforward however; one merely amends the OLS program to produce the correct residuals e_1 in the second stage.

Extrapolative predictors

Extrapolative predictors are those where the information set utilised by the econometrician is restricted to be lagged values of the variable itself, that is an AR(ρ) model:

$$x_{1t+1} = \phi_1 x_{1t} + \phi_2 x_{1t-1} + \phi_2 x_{1t-2} + \ldots \phi_\rho x_{t-\rho} + \varepsilon_t \tag{6.37}$$

$$x_{1t+1} = \Phi(L)x_{1t} + \varepsilon_t \tag{6.37a}$$

The maximum value of ρ is usually chosen so that ε_t is white noise. OLS applied to (6.37a) yields one-step-ahead predictions

$$\hat{x}_{1t+1}^* = \hat{\Phi}(L)x_{1t} \tag{6.37b}$$

The use of extrapolative predictors has proved popular in models with multi-period expectations and in testing RE cross-equation restrictions. (In the latter procedure a VAR rather than an AR model is normally used.)

For the moment, consider using the extrapolative predictor either *as an instrument* for x_{1t+1}^e or to *replace* x_{1t+1}^e in (6.34). Using $\hat{x}_{1t+1}^*$ as an instrument for x_{1t+1}^e *and* x_{2t} as its own instrument yields a consistent estimate of δ since x_{1t-j} ($j \geqslant 0$) are uncorrelated with q_t^* and therefore so is $\hat{x}_{1t+1}$. This is all we need for IV/2SLS to be consistent, but note that in this case x_{2t} also appears in the instrument matrix W_1. The latter becomes important when we consider the two-step approach. Having obtained $\hat{x}_{1t+1}^*$ in the 'first stage', the second stage regression consists of OLS on:

$$y_t = \beta \hat{x}^*_{1t+1} + \gamma x_{2t} + q^*_t \tag{6.38a}$$

$$q_t = [u_t + \beta(x^e_{t+1} - x_{t+1}) - \beta(\hat{x}^*_{t+1} - x_{t+1})] \tag{6.38b}$$

Compared with the EVM/IV approach (see equations (6.26), (6.26a)), we have an additional term $(\hat{x}^*_{t+1} - x_{t+1})$ in the error term of our second-stage regression (6.38a). The term $(x_{t+1} - \hat{x}^*_{t+1})$ is the residual from the first stage regression (6.37b).

The variable x_{2t} is part of the agent's information set, at time t, and may therefore be used by the agent in predicting x_{1t+1}. If so, then $(x_{t+1} - \hat{x}^*_{t+1})$ and the 'omitted variable' from the first stage regression, namely x_{2t} are correlated. Thus in (6.38a) the correlation between the variable x_{2t} and a component of the error term q^*_t imply that OLS on (6.38a) yields inconsistent estimates of δ (Nelson 1975). This is usually expressed in the literature as follows: If x_{2t} Granger-causes x_{1t+1} then the two-step estimator is inconsistent.

This illustrates the danger in using extrapolative predictors and *replacing* x^e_{t+1} in the second stage OLS regression, rather than using $\hat{x}^*_{t+1}$ as an instrument and applying the IV formula. Viewed from the perspective of 2SLS, the inconsistency at the second stage (6.38a) arises because in the first stage regression the researcher does not use *all* the predetermined variables in the model; he erroneously excludes x_{2t}. Somewhat paradoxically then, even if x_{2t} is not used by agents in forecasting x_{1t+1} it must be included in the first stage regression if the two-step procedure is used, otherwise $(x_{1t+1} - \hat{x}_{1t+1})$ may be correlated with x_{2t}. Of course, if the two-step procedure is used and consistent estimates $(\hat{\alpha}, \hat{\beta})$ are obtained, the correct residuals calculated using x_{1t+1} and not $\hat{x}_{1t+1}$ (as in equation (6.36)) must be used in the calculation of standard errors.

6.3   Serially correlated errors and expectations variables

Up to this point in our discussion of appropriate estimators we have assumed white noise errors in the regression equation. We now relax this assumption. Serially correlated errors may arise because of multi-period expectations or because of serially correlated structural errors. In either case, we see below that two broad solutions to the problem are possible. The first method uses the generalised method of moments (GMM) approach of Hanson (1982) and 'corrects' the covariance matrix to take account of serially correlated errors. The second method is a form of generalised least squares estimator under IVS and is known as the *two-step, two-stage, least squares* estimator (2S-2SLS), (Cumby *et al.* 1983). These two solutions to the problem are by no means exhaustive but have been widely used in the literature. The estimator due to Hayashi–Sims (1983) is also briefly discussed.

The GMM approach

We demonstrate this approach by first considering serial correlation that arises in equations with multi-period expectations and then move on to consider serial correlation in the structural error.

Multi-period expectations

Suppose that the structural error u_t is white noise but we have multi-period expectations (we restrict ourselves to two-period-ahead expectations for ease of exposition):

$$y_t = \beta_1 x^e_{t+1} + \beta_2 x^e_{t+2} + u_t \tag{6.39}$$

$$x^e_{t+j} = E(x_{t+j}|\Omega_t) \quad j = 1, 2 \tag{6.39a}$$

RE implies:

$$x_{t+j} = x^e_{t+j} + \eta_{t+j} \quad (j = 1, 2) \tag{6.40}$$

and substituting (6.40) in (6.39) we have our estimating equation:

$$y_t = \beta_1 x_{t+1} + \beta_2 x_{t+2} + q_t \tag{6.41a}$$

$$q_t = u_t - \beta_1 \eta_{t+1} - \beta_2 \eta_{t+2} \tag{6.41b}$$

2SLS on (6.41a) with instrument set Λ_t will yield consistent estimates of β_1, β_2. However, the usual formula for the variance of the IV estimator is incorrect in the presence of serial correlation (see equation (1.73)) and q_t is MA(1). Hansen and Hodrick (1980) suggest a 'correction' to the formula for the variance of the usual 2SLS estimator. Putting (6.41a) in matrix notation:

$$y = X\beta + q \tag{6.42}$$

The 2SLS estimator for β is equivalent to OLS on

$$y = \hat{X}b^* + q \tag{6.43}$$

$$\hat{X} = (\hat{x}_{t+1}, \hat{x}_{t+2}) \tag{6.44}$$

and $\hat{x}_{t+j}$ are the predictions from the regression of x_{t+j} $(j = 1, 2)$ on Λ_t. The 2SLS estimator is:

$$b^* = (\hat{X}'\hat{X})^{-1} (\hat{X}'y) \tag{6.45}$$

with residuals:

$$e^* = y - Xb^* \tag{6.46}$$

Note that in the calculation of e^* we use X and not $\hat{X}$. To calculate the correct variance of β in the presence of an MA(1) error, note that the variance covariance matrix is

$$E(q \quad q') = \sigma_0^2 \begin{bmatrix} 1 & \rho_1 & 0 & \cdots & & 0 \\ \rho_1 & 1 & \rho_1 & 0 & \cdots & \vdots \\ 0 & \rho_1 & 1 & \rho_1 & & 0 \\ \vdots & & & \ddots & 1 & \rho_1 \\ 0 & & \cdots & 0 & \rho_1 & 1 \end{bmatrix} = \sigma_0^2 \Sigma$$

$$\tag{6.47}$$

where ρ_1 is the correlation coefficient between the error terms.

Since e_t^* are based on the consistent estimator b^*, then consistent estimators of σ_0^2, σ_1^2 and ρ are given by the following 'sample moments':

$$\hat{\sigma}_0^2 = (n^{-1}) \sum_1^n e_t^{*2} \tag{6.48a}$$

$$\hat{\sigma}_1^2 = (n^{-1}) \sum_2^n e_t^* e_{t-1}^* \tag{6.48b}$$

$$\hat{\rho}_1 = (\hat{\sigma}_1 / \hat{\sigma}_0)^2 \tag{6.48c}$$

Knowing Σ we can calculate the correct formula for Var (b^*) as follows. Substitute from (6.42) in (6.45):

$$b^* = \beta + (\hat{X}'\hat{X})^{-1}\hat{X}'q \tag{6.49}$$

Since $\text{plim}(T^{-1})(\hat{X}'q) = 0$, then b^* is consistent and the asymptotic variance of b^* is given by:

$$\text{Var}(b^*) = T^{-1} \text{plim}\,[(\hat{X}'\hat{X})^{-1}\hat{X}'(q\ q')\hat{X}(\hat{X}'\hat{X})^{-1}]$$
$$\text{Var}(b^*) = \sigma_0^2(\hat{X}'\hat{X})^{-1}(\hat{X}'\hat{\Sigma}\hat{X})(\hat{X}'\hat{X})^{-1} \tag{6.50}$$

Above we assume that the population moments are consistently estimated by their sample equivalents, e.g. $(\hat{X}'\hat{X})$. Note that Var (b^*), the Hansen–Hodrick correction to the covariance matrix for b^*, reduces to the usual 2SLS formula for the variance when there is no serial correlation (i.e. $\Sigma = \sigma^2 I$). The Hansen–Hodrick correction is easily generalised to the case where we have an MA(k) error; we merely have to calculate $\hat{\rho}_s(s = 1, 2, \ldots k)$ and substitute these estimates in Σ.

Serial correlation AR(1) in the structural error

Our model, in this case is

$$y_t = \beta x_t^e + u_t \tag{6.51}$$

or

$$y_t = \beta x_t + (u_t - \rho \eta_t) \tag{6.51a}$$

$$u_t = \rho u_{t-1} + \varepsilon_t \tag{6.51b}$$

IV applied to (6.51) using Λ_{t-1} as instruments yields a consistent estimate of β but the estimator is not asymptotically efficient because it ignores the serial correlation. In conventional models (i.e. those excluding expectations terms) the solution to this problem is to apply IV to the ρ-transformed equation (see Chapter 1):

$$(y_t - \rho y_{t-1}) = \beta(x_t - \rho x_{t-1}) + q_t \tag{6.52}$$

or

$$y_t^* = \beta \, x_t^* + q_t \tag{6.52a}$$

$$q_t = \varepsilon_t + \beta(\eta_t - \rho \eta_{t-1}) \tag{6.52b}$$

Although Λ_{t-1} is independent of ε_t (by assumption) and of η_t, it is *not* independent of the lagged RE forecast error η_{t-1}; information arising during $t-1$ 'causes' the forecast error between $t-2$ and $t-1$, that is, η_{t-1}. The GLS transformation has destroyed the orthogonality conditions between the error term in (6.51) and the information set Λ_{t-1}. This is because the GLS transformation introduces a moving average error, MA(1), in the RE forecast errors (the term, $\eta_t - \rho \eta_{t-1}$). We have 'removed' the serially correlated structural error u_t but have introduced another serially correlation error which is MA(1) and hence q_t is MA(1).

We wish to outline two methods that can be used to circumvent the above problems. Both methods utilise the Hansen–Hodrick procedure.

In the first method we apply IV to (6.51) using Λ_{t-1} as instruments to obtain a consistent estimator of b^*. The 'consistent' residuals u^* (as in the previous section) are used to obtain an estimate for ρ:

$$\hat{\rho} = (\Sigma u_t^* u_{t-1}^*)/\Sigma u_{t-1}^2 \tag{6.53}$$

which is used to form the transformed variables y_t^*, x_t^*. Λ_{t-1} and q_t in (6.52) are correlated, as noted above, but if we move the instrument set back one period, that is use Λ_{t-2} this is independent of η_t and η_{t-1}, asymptotically.

Using Λ_{t-2} as instruments for x_t^* yields a consistent estimator b^* for β and the residuals

$$e_t^* = y_t - x_t b^* \tag{6.54}$$

can be used to form the Σ matrix. The Hansen–Hodrick variance for b is then given by (6.50) with $\hat{X}^* = (x_t - \hat{\rho} x_{t-1})$ in place of $\hat{X}$.

The second method uses the insight of Hayashi–Sims. For example, suppose we have an MA(1) error $u_t = (1 + \phi L) \, \varepsilon_t$ in our original structural model. The backward filter $(1 - \phi L)^{-1}$ removes the serial correlation in u_t, but destroys the orthogonality condition between the information set and the error term. Hayashi–Sims suggest the '*forward filter*' on the variable x_t giving:

$$\tilde{x}_t = - \phi(1 - \phi L^{-1})^{-1} x_t \tag{6.55}$$

In this case any error terms η_t introduced by the EVM are transformed into terms in η_{t+j} $(j > 0)$ which are independent of the 'original' information set at time t, Λ_t.

A two-step, two-stage least squares (2S-2SLS) estimator

So far we have been able to obtain a consistent estimator of the structural parameter β_1 in (6.39) under RE by utilising IV/2SLS or EVM method. We have then 'corrected' the usual formula for the variance of the estimator using the Hansen–Hodrick formula. Although the Hansen–Hodrick correction yields a consistent estimator of the variance it is possible to obtain an asymptotically more efficient estimator which is also consistent. Cumby *et al.* (1983) provide such an estimator which is a *specific form* of the class of generalised instrumental variables estimators. The formulae for this estimator look rather formidable. If our structural expectations equation after replacing any expectations variables by their outturn values is:

$$y = X\beta + q \tag{6.56}$$

with $E(qq') = \sigma^2 \Sigma$ and plim $[T^{-1}(X'q)] \neq 0$ \quad (6.56a)

then the 2S-2SLS estimator is:

$$\hat{\beta}_{g2} = [X'\Lambda(\Lambda'\Sigma\Lambda)^{-1}\Lambda'X]^{-1}[X'\Lambda(\Lambda'\Sigma\Lambda)^{-1}\Lambda'y] \tag{6.57}$$

$$\text{var}(\hat{\beta}_{g2}) = \sigma^2[X'\Lambda(\Lambda'\Sigma\Lambda)^{-1}\Lambda'Q]^{-1} \tag{6.58}$$

where Λ is the information set available. Clearly to make this estimator operational we need a suitable instrument set Λ and an estimate of the variance-covariance matrix of error terms Σ. We have already discussed above how to choose an appropriate instrument set and how a 'consistent' set of residuals can be used to form Σ. The 'first stage' estimate of Σ can then be substituted in the above formulae, to complete the 'second stage' of the estimation procedure (see Cuthbertson 1990).

In small or moderate size samples we cannot say whether the Hansen–Hodrick correction is 'better than' the 2S-2SLS procedure since both rely on asymptotic results. Hence at present, in practical terms either method may be used. The one clear fact which emerges however, is that the normal 2SLS estimator for $\text{Var}(\hat{\beta})$ is incorrect and care must be taken in utilising Cochrane–Orcutt type transformations to eliminate AR errors since this may result in an inconsistent estimator for β.

Summary

There are two basic problems involved in estimating structural (single) equations involving expectations terms, such as equation (6.39), by the EVM. First correlation between the ex-post variables x_{t+j} and the error term which involves the use of IV (or 2SLS) estimation to obtain consistent estimates of the parameters. In addition, the error term is likely to be serially correlated, for example MA(1) in equation (6.41a), which means that the usual IV/2SLS formulae for the variances of the parameters are incorrect. Two avenues are then open. Either one can use the IV residuals to form the (non-scalar) covariance matrix $(\sigma^2 \Sigma)$ and apply the 'correct' IV formula for var (b^*), see equation (6.50). Alternatively, one can take the estimate of $\sigma^2 \Sigma$ and apply a variant of generalised least squares under IV, for example, the 2S-2SLS estimator var $(\hat{\beta}_{g2})$ of equation (6.58).

6.4   Empirical work on expectations models

In this section we provide examples of empirical work which illustrate some of the estimation issues outlined above. We begin with tests of the axioms of RE. Alternative expectations schemes are then discussed and their use in a forward-looking money demand function is examined.

Testing the axioms of rational expectations

There has been a large number of tests of the basic axioms of RE, using survey data. Here we illustrate the methodology using the results from Taylor (1988).

Survey data of people's expectations of key economic variables are often not in the form of numerical estimates but are collected as categorical responses (such as percentage of respondents expecting inflation to go 'up', 'down' or stay the 'same'). However these categorical responses can be converted using a variety of methods, into numerical data on expectations. Taylor (1988) converts *monthly* categorical data from UK investment managers into quantitative expectations series for expected annual price inflation $_tp^e_{t+12}$, annual wage inflation $_tw^e_{t+12}$, the annual percentage change in the FTA all share index $_tf_{t+12}$ and the US, Standard and Poors composite share index $_ts_{t+12}$.

The axioms of RE imply that the forecast errors are independent of the information set used in making the forecast. Consider the regression

$$(x_{t+12} - {}_tx^e_{t+12}) = \beta'\Lambda_t + q_t \qquad (6.59)$$

for $x = p, w, f, s$ and where Λ_t is a subset of the complete information set. If the orthogonality property of RE holds, we expect $\beta = 0$.

If *we assume no measurement error* in x^e_{t+12} then q_t is a moving average error of order 11 at most. OLS yields consistent estimates of β because Λ_t and q_t are uncorrelated asymtotically but the usual formula for the *covariance matrix* of β is incorrect. However the OLS residuals from (6.59) can be used to construct a consistent estimate of the variance–covariance matrix (White 1980) along the lines outlined in the previous section where we discussed the more general Hansen–Hodrick adjustment. In this case the OLS residuals e_t from (6.59) yield consistent estimates of the variance–covariance matrix (6.47) using (6.48a) to (6.48c), (with the OLS residuals not the 2SLS residuals). The correct OLS variance is then

$$\text{Var}(b) = \sigma_0^2(\Lambda'\Lambda)^{-1}(\Lambda'\hat{\Sigma}\Lambda)(\Lambda'\Lambda)^{-1} \qquad (6.60)$$

where $\quad \sigma_0^2 = T^{-1}\sum_1^n e_t^2 \qquad (6.60a)$

Equation (6.60) has the same form as the Hansen–Hodrick correction, equation (6.50) except that the OLS rather than IV residuals are used and we do not need to instrument the information set Λ_t.

The results of this procedure are given in Table 6.1 for the information set $\Lambda_t = (x_{t-1}, x_{t-2})$. For the price inflation, wage inflation and the FT share index, the standard errors on the own lagged variables indicate that all of these variables taken individually are not significantly different from zero. This is confirmed by the Wald test W(2), which indicates that the two RHS variables in each of the first

Table 6.1 Orthogonality regressions with small information sets 1981 (7)–1985 (7), ordinary least squares with adjusted covariance matrix. (See note)

Estimated equation			R^2	SEE	W(2)
$p_{t+12} - {}_tp^e_{t+12} =$	-0.155 (0.695)	$- 0.310p_{t-1} + 0.214p_{t-2}$ (0.255) (0.245)	0.06	1.131	2.96 (0.23)
$w_{t+12} - {}_tw^e_{t+12} =$	2.596 (1.918)	$- 0.492w_{t-1} + 0.109w_{t-2}$ (0.282) (0.204)	0.20	1.891	4.25 (0.12)
$f_{t+12} - {}_tf^e_{t+12} =$	9.842 (3.075)	$- 0.262f_{t-1} - 0.2227f_{t-2}$ (0.179) (0.226)	0.07	11.519	6.33 (0.04)
$s_{t+12} - {}_ts^e_{t+12} =$	15.747 (9.597)	$- 0.933s_{t-1} + 0.463s_{t-2}$ (0.233) (0.336)	0.21	24.17	19.99 (0.00)

Note: R^2 is the coefficient of determination, SEE the standard error of the equation; W(2) is a Wald test statistic for the coefficients of the two lagged regressors to be zero and is asymptotically central chi-square under the null of orthogonality, with two degrees of freedom; figures in parentheses denote estimated standard errors or marginal significance levels for W(2).

Source: Taylor (1988)

three equations are jointly not significantly different from zero. For the S&P index the lagged values are significantly different from zero, thus rejecting the RE orthogonality axiom.

If there are measurement errors in the expectations series, see equations (6.10), (6.11), we do not expect the coefficient on ${}_t\tilde{x}^e_{t+12}$ to be unity and there is a non-zero correlation between the variable ${}_t\tilde{x}^e_{t+12}$ and the error term. The latter requires the use of IV. Taylor uses p_t, f_t, w_t, s_t as instruments for the expectations variables, ${}_t\tilde{x}^e_{t+1}$, to yield consistent estimates of the parameters, residuals and covariance matrix, see equations (6.47) and (6.48). The variance of these parameters is then given by Hansen's GMM estimator, see equation (6.50).

$$\text{Var}(b) = \sigma_0^2(\Lambda'\Lambda)^{-1}(\Lambda' \Sigma \Lambda)(\Lambda'\Lambda)^{-1} \qquad (6.61)$$

Taylor's results using this estimator are given in Table 6.2. The results are similar to those in Table 6.1, except for the FT share price index f_{t+12}. Here the GMM estimator indicates that the forecast error for the FT share price index is not independent of the information set (W(2) = 46.9). This demonstrates that when testing the axioms of RE, correct inference may require careful choice of appropriate estimation technique.

Taylor repeats the above exercise using a larger information set:

$$\Lambda^* = (p_{t-j}, w_{t-j}, f_{t-j}, s_{t-j}); j = 1, 2.$$

With this extended information set the GMM estimator indicates that

Table 6.2 Orthogonality regressions with small information sets 1981 (7)–1985 (7), generalised method of moments. (See note)

Estimated equation				R^2	SEE	H(3)	W(2)
$p_{t+12} =$	$0.550_t p^e_{t+12} +$ (0.202)	$1.315 -$ (1.122)	$0.399 p_{t-1} +$ (0.286)	$0.488 p_{t-2}$ (0.270)	0.97	1.000	0.04 (0.99)	6.17 (0.05)
$w_{t+12} =$	$0.021_t w^e_{t+12} +$ (0.144)	$6.151 +$ (1.712)	$0.006 w_{t-1} +$ (0.075)	$0.185 w_{t-2}$ (0.122)	0.97	1.436	0.05 (0.99)	3.85 (0.15)
$f_{t+12} =$	$0.473_t f^e_{t+12} +$ (0.340)	$20.066 -$ (6.925)	$0.199 f_{t-1} -$ (0.125)	$0.124 f_{t-2}$ (0.175)	0.89	8.004	0.06 (0.99)	46.49 (0.00)
$s_{t+12} =$	$-0.725_t s^e_{t+12} +$ (0.468)	$62.658 -$ (16.716)	$0.614 s_{t-1} -$ (0.179)	$0.154 s_{t-2}$ (0.260)	0.66	19.761	0.04 (0.99)	18.86 (0.00)

Note: Instruments used for the expectations variable were p_t, w_t, f_t and s_t; H(3) is Hansen's (1982) test statistic for the instruments, and is asymptotically central chi-square with three degrees of freedom for three *valid* over-identifying instruments. See note to Table 6.1 for other definitions.

the orthogonality condition is decisively rejected for *all* four variables.

Fixed parameter AR and VAR schemes

Cuthbertson (1988) estimates a forward-looking model in the UK demand for narrow money (M1) using a two-step procedure. The structural demand for money function (simplified somewhat) is

$$m_t = \lambda m_{t-1} + (1 - \lambda D)(1 - \lambda)(c_p \, SP^e + c_y \, SY^e + c_R SR^e) \tag{6.62}$$

where

$$SX = \sum_{i=0}^{8} (\lambda D)^i (SX^e_{t+i}) \text{ and } X^e_t = (P^e, Y^e, R^e)_t \tag{6.62a}$$

The agent is assumed to have information dated $t - 1$ and earlier. In order to estimate the model a data series for the expectations terms is required. Cuthbertson uses two alternative schemes; namely, fixed-parameter AR and VAR models. The AR and VAR models are given in Tables 6.3 and 6.4. The chain rule of forecasting is then applied to generate multi-period forecasts $\hat{X}^e_{t+j}$ ($j = 0, 1, 2, \ldots 8$) for each variable. These then replace the expectations terms, X^e_{t+j} and OLS is applied to (6.62) to yield two-step estimates of the structural money demand function. Using the AR system for X^e_{t+j} yields:

$$M_t = - 0.86 + 0.89 \, M_{t-1} + 0.052 \, \hat{S}Y^e + 0.024 \, \hat{S}P^e$$
$$\quad\;\; (1.8) \quad\;\; (20.6) \qquad\quad (2.4) \qquad\qquad (2.0)$$

$$\quad - 0.176 \, \hat{S}R^e \tag{6.63}$$
$$\quad\;\; (3.3)$$

OLS, 64(3) − 79(4), SEE = 1.47(%), DW = 2.6, HF(12) = 13.6,

SALK(12) = 9.1, WK = 1.7.

Table 6.3 Autoregressive forecasting equations for *P, Y, R*

1 ΔP_t $\quad = \quad$ 0.0075 $\quad + \quad$ 0.83ΔP_{t-1} $\; - \;$ 0.22$\Delta^2 p_{t-3}$ $\; + \;$ 0.037(D793)
$\qquad\qquad\qquad\quad$ (4.0) $\qquad\quad$ (12.3) $\qquad\qquad$ (2.3) $\qquad\qquad$ (6.0)
$\quad$ OLS, 64(3)–79(4), SE = 0.82(%), DW = 1.9, LM4F = 0.67, LM4 = 2.9, F(5, 52) = 0.75

2 ΔY_t $\quad = \quad$ 0.0137 $\quad - \quad$ 0.12($\Delta^2 Y_{t-1} + \Delta^2 Y_{t-3}$) $\quad - \quad$ 0.024(D793)
$\qquad\qquad\qquad\quad$ (4.4) $\qquad\qquad$ (3.3) $\qquad\qquad\qquad\qquad$ (1.6)
$\quad$ OLS, 64(3)–79(4), SE = 21.1(%), DW = 2.0, LM4F = 0.23, LM4 = 1.1, F(6, 52) = 0.17

3 R_t $\qquad = \quad$ 1.00R_{t-1} $\; + \; u_t$ $\qquad\qquad u_t = $ 0.21u_{t-1} $\; + \; \varepsilon_{t-1}$
$\qquad\qquad\qquad\quad$ (42.8) $\qquad\qquad\qquad\qquad\qquad$ (1.65)
$\quad$ AR, 64(3)–74(4), SE = 0.013, DW = 2.0, LM4F = 0.59, LM4 = 2.5, F(5, 55) = 1.4

Notes:
   (i) SE = standard error of the regression, DW = Durbin–Watson statistic, AR = estimation subject to autoregressive errors.
   (ii) LM4 is the Langrange multiplier statistic for autocorrelation up to order 4, asymptotically distributed under the null of no serial correlation, as central chi-squared with four degrees of freedom. Critical value at 5% significance level is 9.5.
   (iii) LM4F is the Langrange multiplier test, expressed as an *F*-distribution.
   (iv) $F(n_1, n_2)$ is the *F*-test of the restrictions in moving from the general AR(6) equations, with n_1, n_2 degrees of freedom. The critical value at 5% significance level for the above equations is (approximately) 2.4.

Table 6.4 VAR forecasting equations for *Y, P, R* (See notes for Table 6.3)

1 ΔY_t $\quad = \quad$ −0.6 $\quad - \quad$ 0.32ΔY_{t-1} $\; + \;$ 0.06Y_{t-2} $\quad - \quad$ 0.64ΔP_{t-2} $\; - \;$ 0.82ΔR_{t-2}
$\qquad\qquad\qquad\quad$ (2.0) $\qquad\quad$ (3.1) $\qquad\qquad$ (2.0) $\qquad\qquad$ (2.7) $\qquad\qquad$ (4.1)
$\quad$ OLS, 64(3)–79(4), SE = 2.0(%), LM4F = 0.7, LM4 = 3.3

2 ΔP_t $\quad = \quad$ 0.008 $\quad + \quad$ 0.58ΔP_{t-1} $\; - \;$ 0.29ΔP_{t-3} $\; + \;$ 0.08ΔY_{t-1} $\; + \;$ 0.25ΔR_{t-1}
$\qquad\qquad\qquad\quad$ (2.7) $\qquad\quad$ (7.4) $\qquad\qquad$ (3.7) $\qquad\qquad$ (2.4) $\qquad\qquad$ (5.4)
$\qquad\qquad\qquad + $ 0.032(D793)
$\qquad\qquad\qquad\quad$ (6.5)
$\quad$ OLS, 64(3)–79(4), SE = 0.6(%), LM4F = 0.32, LM4 = 1.6

3 R_t $\qquad = \quad$ −0.86 $\quad + \quad$ 0.93R_{t-1} $\; - \;$ 0.23R_{t-2} $\; - \;$ 0.25ΔP_{t-3} $\; + \;$ 0.08Y_{t-1}
$\qquad\qquad\qquad\quad$ (4.4) $\qquad\quad$ (7.6) $\qquad\qquad$ (1.9) $\qquad\qquad$ (2.0) $\qquad\qquad$ (4.4)
$\quad$ OLS, 64(3)–79(4), SE = 0.011, LM4F = 1.2, LM4 = 5.2

A unit (expected) nominal income elasticity is accepted by the data (on a Wald test $W(2) = 1.2$, $\chi^2(2) = 6.0$), and the long-run semi-elasticity with respect to the interest rate is $- 4.2$. As we noted in section 6.2, the use of extrapolative AR or VAR forecasting equations and a two-step estimation procedure may result in inconsistent parameter estimates. This will occur if M_{t-1} in (6.63) Granger, causes either P_t, Y_t or R_t. Although widely used, the two-step procedure may be somewhat hazardous. Thus although the equation passes the Hendry parameter constancy test HF(12), it must be interpreted with caution.

If we apply the EVM technique to the above model, the terms SX^e must be *instrumented* and M_{t-1} acts as its 'own' instrument. Cuthbertson and Taylor (1991) employ the EVM in this forward-looking model which yields consistent parameter estimates. The instruments used for SX^e are four lagged values of P, Y, R and M. However they find serial correlation in the (IV) residuals of (6.63), of order 2 and 3. They therefore apply the Hayashi–Sims (1983) forward filter to all the variables of (6.62).

The residuals e_t^* from the IV regression (6.62), without the Hayashi–Sims correction are used to calculate consistent estimates of the 'unknown' autocorrelation coefficients ρ_j:

$$\rho_j = \sum_t e_t^* e_{t-j}^* \Big/ \sum_t e_{t-j}^* \qquad (j = 2, 3) \tag{6.64}$$

Because they employ the *forward* filter, the instrument set dated $t - 1$ and earlier is asymptotically uncorrelated with the error-term (see section 6.3). Hence we obtain consistent and asymptotically efficient estimators. When Cuthbertson and Taylor (1989) impose a unit long-run price level elasticity ($c_p = 1$) then representative estimates of the long-run (expected) income and interest rate elasticities (E_y, E_R, respectively) are:

$$E_y = \begin{array}{c} 1.8 \\ (2.8) \end{array} \qquad E_R = \begin{array}{c} - 4.9 \\ (3.0) \end{array} \tag{6.65}$$

over the period 1968(4)–1982(4)–asymptotic t-statistics in parenthesis. Although the point estimates of the expected income elasticity exceeds unity we can easily accept a unit coefficient on a t-test ($t = 1.2$). Thus, for this particular model the results from the two-step procedure and the EVM do not differ greatly, and hence any inconsistency in the former may not be too severe.

The Lucas critique: changing expectations schemes

One of the drawbacks in using fixed coefficient AR or VAR models is that forecasts made for the early part of the data set (using the chain rule) utilise information that was not available at the time the forecasts were made. This is because in obtaining the *estimated* parameters we use *all* of the data set. Clearly it may be more realistic to assume that agents update their view about the parameters of the expectations generating equations. This applies with stronger reason after major ('regime') changes in the economy; (for example, in the 1970s, the move from low to high inflation rates in the UK and the switch towards monetary targets in the USA).

Utilising a structural forward-looking demand for money function of the form (6.62), Cuthbertson and Taylor (1990) examine the 'case of the missing money' in the USA in the context of the Lucas (1976) critique. Around 1974, conventional (e.g. partial adjustment) money demand functions in the USA overpredicted the demand for money and this was interpreted as an inexplicable shift in the money demand function. Cuthbertson and Taylor (1990) put forward the hypothesis that the underlying forward-looking demand for money function (6.62) is stable over the whole of the 1970s, but a shift in the (VAR or AR) expectations formation scheme for Y, P or R caused estimated partial adjustment models to exhibit parameter instability (and serial correlation in the residuals). This is an example of the Lucas (1976) critique. To illustrate the Lucas critique in the context of our forward-looking demand for money function (6.62), simplify somewhat and assume:

$$M_t = \lambda M_{t-1} + (1 - \lambda)(1 - \lambda D)c_y \left[\sum_{i=0}^{\infty} (\lambda D)^i Y^e_{t+i+1} \right]$$

is a stable money demand function. Now assume agents forecast 'income' according to the AR(1) model:

$$Y_{t+1} = \phi Y_t + v_t \tag{6.67}$$

where v_t is white noise. Predictions from (6.67), with information dated t and earlier, are:

$$_tY^e_{t+j} = \phi^{j+1} Y_t \tag{6.68}$$

Substituting (6.68) in (6.66),

$$M_t = \lambda_1 M_{t-1} + [(1 - \lambda)c_y(1 - \lambda D)\phi/(1 - \lambda D\phi)]Y_t \tag{6.69}$$

Equation (6.69) may also be viewed as a conventional partial adjustment form of money demand function:

$$M_t = \pi_0 M_{t-1} + \pi_1 Y_t \qquad\qquad (6.70)$$

However if we estimate (6.70) but the way agents form their expectations alters (for example, undergoes a structural shift), then the 'conventional' partial adjustment demand function (6.70) will exhibit parameter 'shifts' even though the underlying (or 'deep') parameters λ, D and c_y of the 'true' forward-looking equation remain constant. This is the Lucas critique.

The above argument applies if the variables Y_t, P_t and R_t are assumed to be generated by a first-order vector autoregressive scheme, as assumed by Cuthbertson and Taylor (1990), when investigating the US demand function for narrow money (i.e. M1B). They find that the VAR scheme for (Y, P, R) does undergo a structural break around the 'missing money' period. They therefore estimate the ϕ parameter(s) for the pre- and post-1974 period. When these *two* separate VAR schemes are used to determine the variables SY^e, SP^e, SR^e in the forward demand for money function pre- and post-1974, they find that the demand function has relatively stable parameters and does not have serial correlation in the errors. However, if one ignores the shift in the VAR scheme then the 'solved out' form of the demand for money function, i.e. the analogue to (6.70), has 'poor' statistical and economic properties. Thus, Cuthbertson and Taylor 1990 provide some evidence that fixed parameter AR or VAR expectations schemes may be inadequate and that the Lucas critique may be of some practical relevance. (For an alternative account of the missing money episode see Baba *et al.* 1988.)

Hendry (1988) provides an interesting test to discriminate between the forward model (6.66) and the backward-looking model (6.70). Using our simple model, Hendry's argument is that if ϕ in (6.67) is found to be unstable (time varying) and the forward model (6.62) is correct, then π_1 in the 'backward-looking' model (6.70) should also be unstable. Hence a finding of a constant π_1 in (6.70) and time-varying ϕ in (6.67), leads to a refutation of the forward model (6.66) and (6.67), (and incidentally of the empirical relevance of the Lucas critique).

Another way of gaining an insight into Hendry's argument is to use the formula for the OLS estimator of the expectations model under EVM. Equation (6.30) indicates that plim $\hat{\beta}$ depends on σ_{xe}^2. The variance of x^e is given by the variances of ϕY_t in (6.67) in our money demand model. If ϕ is non-constant, then σ_{xe}^2 is also time-varying and hence we expect the OLS estimator, $\hat{\beta}$ to be non-constant. Hence Hendry's counterfactual argument is that a constant $\hat{\beta}$ and non-constant $\hat{\phi}$, are incompatible with the structural expectations model (6.66) and (6.67).

Cuthbertson (1991) argues that in finite samples Hendry's test does not rule out the structural forward model (6.66) and some other expectations generation equation like (6.67) that has constant parameters but which is, as yet, undiscovered by the econometrician. Also it is not clear how the Hendry's analysis deals with the issue of explicit time-varying parameters in (6.67) as discussed below. However, for any fixed parameter form for (6.67), for which it is hypothesised agents actually use in forecasting, Hendry's test is valid (even in small samples). In practice, proponents of the structural expectations model (6.66) will have to 'Hendrify' the expectations generating equation (6.67) in an attempt to obtain constant parameters in (6.67).

Variable parameter forecasting schemes

Instead of a series of discrete breaks in expectations equations, as in the above case, we may wish to assume agents *continually* update the parameters of their expectations generating equations as 'new' information becomes available. A simple yet tractable form of 'updating' is to assume agents update their AR or VAR forecasting schemes *as if* they applied recursive OLS to the model. Cuthbertson and Taylor (1991) apply a recursive VAR scheme to (Y, P, R) in the context of the forward demand for money function (6.62). At each point in time the VAR parameters are estimated (say using data from $t = 1$ to n). The chain-rule of forecasting is then applied to obtain k-period ahead forecasts for $n + 1$, $n + 2$, $n + k$ (with information and parameter estimates available only to period n). The VAR scheme is then re-estimated for period 1 to n_1 ($n_1 = n + 1$) and the next k period ahead forecasts obtained. These forecasts provide instruments for SX^e using information actually available to the agent at the time of the forecast. The forward demand function may then be estimated using the EVM (with appropriate adjustments for any serial correlation). Cuthbertson and Taylor (1991) using a recursive VAR obtain the following long-run elasticities for UK, M1 in the forward model (6.70); for the period 1968(4)–1979(4):

$$E_y = \quad 0.80 \qquad E_p = \quad 1.11 \qquad E_R = -\ 1.9$$
$$(2.3) \qquad\qquad (11.3) \qquad\qquad (2.2) \tag{6.71}$$

(asymptotic t-statistics in parentheses). Thus under an expectations scheme that embodies a simple form of updating, the forward demand for money function continues to yield sensible long-run elasticities (note that we can accept $E_p = 1$) which are also stable over the 1980(1)–1982(4) period.

Optimal updating schemes

A Muth–rational agent is assumed to act as if his forecasts are calculated using *the* true model of economy. In reality, for any real world economy there are a number of competing models and the agent may be uncertain as to what constitutes the 'true' model. In addition it is possible that the parameters of the true model may alter through time as the economy undergoes 'regime changes' (such as from low to high inflation periods). Also, agents acting on their predictions from a false model, generate data which later may have to be explained by the econometrician. Theoretical models that embody learning by agents are relatively new and do not provide a tractable alternative for the applied econometrician (see for example, Bray and Savin 1986). Hence the applied worker either has to utilise survey data (with its own limitations, see Pesaran 1985) or has to utilise 'plausible' expectations schemes. A reasonable compromise is to assume that although costs of information (and inherent uncertainty about the true model) force agents to use sensible 'rules of thumb', nevertheless they utilise whatever information they have, in an optimal fashion as they learn about their economic environment. This leaves considerable scope for the applied worker.

In Chapter 7 we demonstrate two models which embody learning by agents and we utilise the Kalman filter to estimate these models, which are known as 'systematically varying parameters' and the 'stochastic trend' model. Both types of model can be useful in generating expectations series.

For the varying parameter model we assume agents forecast the variable x_{t+1} using:

$$x_{t+1} = (\phi_{t+1/t})x_t \qquad (6.72)$$

where $\phi_{t+1/t}$ is their best guess of ϕ given information up to time, t. An explicit form of time variation in ϕ_t is assumed, the simplest being a random walk:

$$\phi_{t+1} = \phi_t + \varepsilon_{t+1} \qquad (6.73)$$

We defer further discussion of the estimation of this model until Chapter 7 but merely wish to note here that such models can be used in generating expectations series where the agent continually learns about his environment and as he does so, he updates his estimate of

ϕ. Clearly such a model is not a panacea for modelling expectations, since it can only mimic the way agents form expectations. However, it is a useful alternative to assuming agents continuously know the (constant parameter) true model.

In the 'unobservable components model' the econometrician has observations on y_t (e.g. measured income) but we wish to obtain an estimate of the unobservable permanent income π_t. Measured income is assumed to consist of permanent income and (zero mean) transitory income ε_t, hence:

$$y_t = \pi_t + \varepsilon_t \tag{6.74}$$

The agent faces a 'signal extraction problem'. He has to determine how much of a change in actual income y_t can be attributed to permanent income (the 'signal') and how much is merely 'transitory' (the noise). Lucas' (1972) New Classical supply curve is derived under similar assumptions, where the firm has to decide the increase in the *aggregate* price index based on information about prices in the industry ('local prices').

To 'solve' the above signal extraction problem we have to make some assumption about the behaviour of π_t. In the stochastic trend model (Harvey and Todd 1983) the growth in π_t is itself stochastic and the model reduces to one which may be interpreted in terms of a stochastic trend for y_t and π_t:

$$y_t = \alpha_0 + \alpha_t t + u_{1t} \tag{6.75}$$

$$\Pi_t = \alpha_0^* + \alpha_t^* t + u_{2t} \tag{6.76}$$

where t = time trend but the coefficient on this variable is time varying (i.e. α_t, α_t^*).

The reader need note at this point only that the Kalman filter can be used to estimate this model and it yields optimal predictions for y_{t+j} as more information on y_t becomes available. It therefore mimics 'learning' by agents.

Cuthbertson and Taylor (1990) use the stochastic trend model to generate multi-period forecasts for (Y_t, P_t, R_t) for the UK, assuming agents 'learn' from their past forecast errors. Using these predictions $X_t^e = (y^e, P^e, R)_t$ and the 'surprise' terms $(X_t - X_t^e)$ yield the following forward-looking demand function for UK, M1:

$$M_t = -\ 0.87 + \ 0.94\ M_{t-1} + \ 0.0066\,(\hat{S}P)$$
$$\quad\ (5.6) \qquad (34.1) \qquad\qquad (1.9)$$

$$+\ \ 0.014(\hat{S}Y) - \ 0.048(\hat{S}R) + \ 0.11(P - P^e)$$
$$\quad\ (2.8) \qquad\qquad (3.4) \qquad\qquad (0.7)$$

$$+ \quad {}_t0.20 \, (Y - Y^e) - \quad {}_t0.87(R - R^e)_t \qquad \textbf{(6.77)}$$
$$\quad (3.5) \qquad\qquad\quad (5.6)$$

1964(1)–1979(4), SEE = 1.41(%), Q(8) = 9.7, W(2) = 3.0, HF(12) = 17.1.

The Wald test W(2) = 3.0 is distributed as central chi-squared and indicates that a unit long-run price and real income elasticity is accepted by the data: the long-run interest rate semi-elasticity is − 7.1. The Hendry forecast test indicates parameter constancy over the period 1980 (1)–1982 (4). 'Surprises' in real income $(Y - Y^e)_t$ are added to money balances and unexpectedly high interest rates on alternative assets leads to a switch out of M1. The results on the demand for M1, utilising this particular optimal forecasting scheme are therefore encouraging. (Q(8) is the Ljung–Box statistic, and indicates the absence of serial correlation of up to order 8.)

6.5 Rational expectations: cross-equation restrictions

We have already noted that in order to estimate 'a structural model' containing expectations variables (such as a forward-looking demand for money function) we often require an ancillary 'weakly rational' *expectations generation equation*. However to obtain consistent estimates of the structural model we do not require knowledge of the full information set used by agents. Thus our expectations model often consists of *two* equations (even when we do *not* assume full Muth–rational expectations). So far we have used our expectations generation equation (often an AR or VAR model) to generate instruments for the unobservable expectations (for example, expected income in the demand for money). Broadly speaking, predictions from the expectations generation equation are used as 'proxy' variables for the unobservable expectations variables. In this section we show that our two-equation system, plus the assumption of rational expectations *often* implies testable *cross-equation* parameter restrictions. Cross-equation restrictions provide a test of the *joint* hypothesis of the structural model assumed and the assumption of RE. We inserted 'often' in the above sentence because in some cases cross-equation restrictions may not ensue – as in the case of 'observational equivalance'. Here, an RE model may be indistinguishable from a non-RE model. We do not discuss this aspect here (see Pesaran 1987 and Cuthbertson and Taylor 1988). In general, more efficient estimates of the parameters are obtained if the two equations that comprise our model are estimately jointly. (This applies *a fortiori* if the cross-equation restrictions *do* hold and are then imposed in estimation.)

Tests of cross-equation retrictions abound in the RE literature. For example, they have been used widely in testing (a) policy ineffectiveness and neutrality propositions (see below), (b) the efficient markets hypothesis in, for example, the foreign exchange, stock and bond markets, (c) in the Life Cycle/RE model of consumption, and (d) in forward-looking investment and employment equations (see, *inter alia*, Cuthbertson 1985, Cuthbertson and Taylor 1988, MacDonald 1988, Pesaran 1984, 1987, and Mishkin 1983, Lucas and Sargent 1981 for surveys/readings in this area). Here we only seek to illustrate the basic issues involved. Tests of the 'policy ineffectiveness model' have been widely reported (Barro 1978, Leiderman 1980) and summaries are readily available (including Mishkin 1983, Pesaran 1987). The underlying principles behind tests of cross-equation (rationality) restrictions are very similar even though the models considered may be rather disparate. Hence we demonstrate the basic principles using empirical results on the Carr–Darby (1981) shock-absorber hypothesis of the demand for money. We contrast results obtained from two-step estimation procedures and joint estimation subject to cross-equation restrictions. The model only has one-period-ahead expectations variables. Our second main empirical example of testing cross-equation RE restrictions utilises multi-period expectations. It is based on the work of Sargent (1979) and involves our forward-looking demand for money function.

The shock-absorber model of the demand for money

An important debate in monetary economics concerns the role of money as a buffer stock (for general discussions and surveys see Laidler 1984, Goodhart 1984, Cuthbertson and Taylor 1986a). An important theme in this literature is the notion that money balances act as a short-run 'shock absorber' or buffer to unanticipated shocks to the money supply. This ideas was advance by Carr and Darby (1981) and has been examined empirically by them and by MacKinnon and Milbourne (1984). Carr and Carby (CD) argue that a proportion of unanticipated changes in the nominal money supply are willingly held in the short run, whereas anticipated changes will be fully reflected in changes in the price level and so will be neutral with respect to the level of real money holdings. The CD shock-absorber hypothesis may be represented by the two equations:

$$(m - p)_t = \beta x_t + \alpha(m - m^a)_t + \delta m_t^a + u_t \qquad (6.78)$$

$$m_t^a = \gamma z_{t-1} + v_t \qquad (6.79)$$

where m_t is the logarithm of the nominal money stock at the time t, p_t is the logarithm of the price level, x_t is the vector of determining variables observed at time t (such as income, interest rates), which also includes lagged real money balances; β is a suitably dimensioned coefficient vector and u_t is a random disturbance. m_t^a is the anticipated component of money supply and is determined as the predictions from equation (6.79). z_{t-1} is a vector the components of which are considered by agents to have a systematic influence on money supply, γ is a stable coefficient vector and v_t is the non-systematic component of the money supply process. In the CD paper, equation (6.78) is a conventional demand for money function augmented by the monetary surprise term $(m - m^a)_t$, and anticipated money. CD argue that anticipated money is fully reflected in the current price level, that is $\delta = 0$, and a proportion $(0 < \alpha < 1)$ of unanticipated money accumulates as desired money holdings.

However, Cuthbertson and Taylor (1986b, 1988) argue that the shock-absorber hypothesis makes sense only if the aggregate 'money demand' equation is interpreted as an 'inverted' price equation. Rearranging (6.78):

$$p_t = -\beta x_t + (1 - \alpha)(m - m^a)_t + (1 - \delta) m_t^a + u_t \qquad (6.80)$$

Expressing (6.78) in the form of a price equation (6.80) makes clear the logic of the shock-absorber hypothesis. If $\delta = 0$, anticipated money has a proportional effect on the price level, so that unanticipated shocks lead to a rise in short-run real money holdings.

Cuthbertson and Taylor (1986b, 1988) initially estimate (6.78) (or equivalently 6.80) for UK and US narrow money using a two-step procedure. Alternative expectations generation equations (6.79) (e.g. AR(4), ARIMA, and the stochastic trend model for the money supply are used to generate predictions $\hat{m}_t$ and surprises $\hat{v}_t = m_t - \hat{m}_t$. These are then used in (6.78) in place of m^a, $(m - m^a)$ and OLS is applied to (6.78). (The variables z_{t-1} are used as instruments for $\hat{m}_t$ to obtain the correct standard errors for δ. Cuthbertson and Taylor find that broadly speaking the CD hypothesis is accepted using this two-step procedure; that is, $\hat{\alpha} > 0$ and $\hat{\delta} = 0$. (See also Cuthbertson and Taylor 1987b.)

Joint estimation, imposing rationality (but not neutrality; $\delta \neq 0$), implies running the equations:

$$(m - p)_t = \beta x_t + \alpha(m_t - \gamma z_{t-1}) + \delta\gamma z_{t-1} + u_t^R \qquad \textbf{(6.80a)}$$

$$m_t = \gamma z_{t-1} + v_t^R \qquad \textbf{(6.80b)}$$

Notice that the vector of parameters 'γ' appears in both equations; this is the cross-equation restriction implied by RE. These two equations without the RE restriction imposed are:

$$(m - p)_t = \beta x_t + \alpha(m - \gamma^* z_{t-1}) + \delta\gamma^* z_{t-1} + u_t \qquad \textbf{(6.81a)}$$

$$m_t = \gamma z_{t-1} + v_t \qquad \textbf{(6.81b)}$$

where $\gamma \neq \gamma^*$. Under the assumption that u_t, v_t are normally and independently distributed with zero mean and variances σ_u^2, σ_v^2, respectively, then the log-likelihood is:

$$L = \frac{-T}{2} \ln \sigma_u^2 - \frac{T}{2} \ln \sigma_v^2 - \frac{u'u}{\sigma_u^2} - \frac{v'v}{\sigma_v^2} \qquad \textbf{(6.82)}$$

A test of the RE cross-equation restrictions is provided by a likelihood ratio test between equations (6.80a)/(6.80b) and (6.81a)/(6.81b). (Note that here this test is conditional on neutrality *not* holding, $\delta \neq 0$.) Since we assume $\sigma_{uv} = 0$ then the determinant of the covariance matrix in the unrestricted model (6.80a) + (6.80b) is

$$\det(\Sigma) = \sigma_v^2 \sigma_u^2$$

Similarly, the determinant in the restricted model is obtained from the residuals u_t^R and v_t^R to give $\det(\Sigma_R)$. The likelihood ratio statistic is then:

$$\text{LR} = T \ln(\det \Sigma_R / \det \Sigma) \qquad \textbf{(6.83)}$$

which is distributed asymptotically as central chi-squared under the null that the cross-equation restrictions $\gamma = \gamma^*$ hold. (The number of degrees of freedom equals the number of independent restrictions in $\gamma = \gamma^*$.)

The above procedure is applicable to most tests of RE cross-equation restrictions and with appropriate variants (such as using instrumental variables) has been widely applied. One can also use a Wald test for $\gamma = \gamma^*$ which requires only an estimate of the unrestricted model, but we do not pursue that here (see for example Baillie *et al.* 1983).

By setting $\delta = 0$ in the above equations and repeating the LR test one can test rationality subject to neutrality. Similarly one can undertake a joint test of rationality *plus* neutrality (i.e. $\gamma = \gamma^*$ *and* $\delta = 0$) by comparing the likelihood from the completely unrestricted equations (6.81a) + (6.81b) with that from equations which impose both these restrictions. Cuthbertson and Taylor find both for UK and US (not reported) narrow money that the hypothesis of 'rationality without neutrality' and 'rationality plus neutrality' are decisively rejected by the data (see Table 6.5).

In the two-step procedure one tests the shock-absorber hypothesis while *implicitly imposing* the RE cross-equation restrictions (since $\hat{m} = \gamma Z_{t-1}$, replaces m^a in (6.78)); here Cuthbertson and Taylor find in favour of the shock-absorber hypothesis. However, joint estimation rejects the cross-equation restrictions. Hence, either the shock-absorber hypothesis or the assumption of RE does not hold – although we cannot determine from these tests which element of the joint hypothesis is incorrect.

Table 6.5   Results for UK, Narrow Money (See note)

Fully unconstrained model ($\gamma \neq \gamma^*$, $\delta \neq 0$)	
1. LR(8) = 24.34 (0.0020) Rationality imposed ($\gamma = \gamma^*$) Neutrality not imposed ($\delta = 0$)	2a. LR(9) = 29.87 (0.0005) Rationality imposed Neutrality imposed
1b. LR(1) = 5.53 (0.0187) Neutrality test	
	3. Fully restricted model Rationality imposed ($\gamma = \gamma^*$) Neutrality imposed ($\delta = 0$)

Note: Likelihood ratio test statistics for the jointly estimated model: LR(n) is the likelihood ratio statistic, asymptotically distributed as central chi-square with n degrees of freedom. Degrees of freedom are calculated as the number of identified parameters estimated in the unrestricted system, less those estimated in the restricted system, see Mishkin (1983). Figures in parenthesis below statistics values are marginal significance levels.

Forward-looking money demand function

We now address the question of how we can test cross-equation rationality restrictions when we have *multi-period* forward looking variables. The illustrative model is based on Hansen and Sargent (1982) and has been used widely elsewhere (e.g. Hall *et al.* 1986b, Kennan 1979, Cuthbertson 1988). Our forward-looking money demand function may be represented as:

$$M_t = \lambda M_{t-1} + (1 - \lambda)(1 - \lambda D) \sum_0^\infty (\lambda D)^i \gamma' Z_{t+i}^e \qquad \textbf{(6.84)}$$

where $Z_t^e = (P_t^e, Y_t^e, R_t^e)$ $\qquad$ **(6.84a)**

$\qquad$ $\gamma' = (c_p, c_y, c_R)$ $\qquad$ **(6.84b)**

Assuming agents have information up to and including $t - 1$, we can rearrange (6.84), (see Cuthbertson and Taylor 1987a), to yield

$$M_t = \gamma M_{t-1} + (1 - \lambda)\left[\gamma' Z_{t-1} + \sum_0^\infty (\gamma D)^i (\gamma' \Delta Z_{t+i}^e)\right] + u_t$$

(6.85)

Suppose ΔZ_{t+1} can be represented by an rth order vector Markov process

$$\Delta Z_{t+1} \Phi(L) = v_{t+1} \qquad \textbf{(6.86)}$$

where $\Phi(L)$ is a (3×3) rth order matrix polynominal in the lag operator L.

$$\Phi(L) = I - \sum_1^r \Phi_i L^i \qquad \textbf{(6.87)}$$

and each Φ is a deterministic 3×3 matrix and the roots of $\det[\Phi(x)] = 0$ lie outside the unit circle. Clearly, (6.86) could be used by agents to forecast future values of Z_{t+i} which then determine the demand for money, via (6.85). Using the chain rule of forecasting on (6.86) yields a very complex expression for say Z_{t+4}^e even when we have only a VAR(1) process for $Z = (Y, P, R)$ – try it by hand! However, such an expression is required if we are to substitute for ΔZ_{t+i} in (6.85) and hence test the implicit cross-equation restrictions between (6.85) and (6.86). Sargent 1979, using the Weiner–Kolmogorov prediction formula, is able to provide a solution to this problem which results in the following 'restricted' two-equation model

$$M_t = \lambda M_{t-1} + (1 - \lambda)(\gamma' Z_{t-1} + \gamma' \Pi(L)\Delta Z_t) + \zeta_t$$

(6.88a)

$$\Delta Z_{t+1} = \Phi'(L)\Delta Z_t + v_{t+1} \qquad \textbf{(6.88b)}$$

where

$$\Pi(L) = \Phi(\lambda D)^1 \left[I + \sum_{j=1}^{r-1} \sum_{k=j+1}^{r} (\lambda D)^{k-j} \Phi_k L^j\right] \qquad \textbf{(6.88c)}$$

Thus the Φ_k elements from the VAR process (6.88b) also appear in the (reformulated) money demand function (6.88a) via the term $\Pi(L)$ given in (6.88c). These non-linear restrictions must be coded into the appropriate software and then (6.88a) and (6.88b) can be estimated jointly. Releasing the cross-equation restrictions on (6.88), gives an autoregressive distributed lag (ADL) formulation of the money demand equation which can then be estimated with (6.88b) to yield the 'unrestricted' system. An appropriate test statistic (for example, likelihood ratio, or quasi-likelihood ratio if instruments are used), can then be used to test the cross-equation rationality restrictions.

The appropriate estimation technique in this case is also not straightforward. The error term ζ_t in (6.88a) may be shown to be

$$\zeta_t = (1 - \lambda) \sum_0^\infty (\lambda D)^i \{ E(\gamma' \Delta Z_{t+1}/\Omega_t)$$

$$- E(\gamma' \Delta Z_{t+1}/\Lambda_t) \} \qquad \textbf{(6.88d)}$$

where Ω_t = complete information set used by the agent and Λ_t = information set available to the econometrician. Because ζ_t is a *future* convolution it is independent of a subset of the information available at time t, namely Λ_t. Also by RE, v_{t+1} is independent of Λ_t. If ζ_t is *not* serially correlated then Λ_t provide valid instruments with which to estimate the joint system (6.88a) + (6.88b). However if, for whatever reason, ζ_t is serially correlated we cannot use 'conventional adjustments' (GLS) for serial correlation (section 6.2). One of the methods outlined in section 6.3 must be used. IV on the unrestricted ADL money demand equation using Λ_t as instruments yields consistent (but not efficient) estimates of the parameters and hence the residuals. The latter can be used to estimate the (low order) AR coefficients ρ_1, ρ_2, etc. on the residuals. If we use the ρ_i to 'forward filter' the *variables* in the restricted equation (6.88a), then we can continue to use the IV set Λ_t dated at time t (Hayashi–Sims 1983).

Cuthbertson and Taylor (1987a) test the RE cross-equation restriction in the forward demand for money equation using data on UK, M1. The (quasi)-likelihood ratio statistic QLR(3) = 4.36 and does not reject these restrictions. In the restricted system of equations the elasticity of the demand for money with respect to income and price level can be constrained to unity, W(2) = 2.0, and the semi-elasticity with respect to R is $- 4.3$. Therefore it appears as if the forward demand for money function together with the assumption of (weakly) rational expectations characterises the data reasonably well. Of course, this does not imply that other models of the demand for money might not perform better on purely statistical criteria (see the debate in Hendry 1988, Cuthbertson 1991, Muscatelli 1989, Cuthbertson and Taylor 1990). However, we hope we have demonstrated how cross-equation restrictions provide an additional test of the assumption of rational expectations (conditional in the assumed structural model) and in general provide a much more stringent test of the RE hypothesis than two-step procedures.

6.6 Summary

The implications of introducing expectations variables into both analytic and large-scale (econometric) models is now well established (see, for example, Lucas and Sargent 1981, Sargent 1979, Cuthbertson and Taylor 1988, Wallis *et al*. 1986, Fair 1979). However, there is much debate about how to model expectations variables and how important expectations actually are in influencing economic behaviour. We have presented a wide variety of econometric techniques for dealing with equations containing expectations terms. Although the rational expectations assumption has tended to dominate the applied (as well as the theoretical) literature we have also presented elementary 'learning' models of expectations formation which we believe will be of increasing importance. Also one must recognise that survey data on expectations can often be used directly in structural equations containing unobservable expectations (e.g. Pesaran 1985). Expectations variables are used widely in structural behavioural equations and we have analysed the main estimation methods used in the applied literature.

7
State-space models and the Kalman filter

State-space models were developed originally by control engineers (Wiener 1949, Kalman 1960) but are receiving increasing attention in the economics literature. There is a number of advantages in representing models in state-space form. We noted in Chapter 2 that the likelihood function can be written in terms of the one-step-ahead prediction errors $\tilde{v}_t$ and their variance f_t. The Kalman filter when applied to a model in state-space form provides an algorithm for producing $\tilde{v}_t$ and its variance. Since many models (for example all ARMA models) can be represented in state-space form, the Kalman filter provides a convenient general method of representing the likelihood function for what may be very complex models. Two types of model that are especially amenable to representation via the Kalman filter are *unobservable components* models and *time-varying parameter* models. In unobservable components models we *observe* y_t (say actual income) which we assume consists of an *unobserved* permanent component π_t plus a white noise error ε_t:

$$y_t = \pi_t + \varepsilon_t$$

The Kalman filter provides an optimal updating scheme for the unobservable π_t based on information about measured income, as it sequentially becomes available. With this interpretation the unobservable components model provides a method of generating an expectations series for permanent income π_t.

In time-varying parameter models we have

$$y_t = x_t \beta_t + \varepsilon_t$$

where (y_t, x_t) are observables. The problem is then to estimate β_t as

191

it varies through time. It is clear that the unobservable components model and time-varying parameter models are 'non-standard', that is, one cannot apply 'least squares' procedures (e.g. OLS, IV, GLS) *directly* to the above equations. However, each of the above models can be 'rewritten' in terms of two distinct types of equation (called the *measurement* and *transition* equations) which together are called *the state-space form*. The Kalman filter can be applied to the state-space form equations to yield a set of *recursive equations*; the latter are then used to generate a series for $\tilde{v}_t$ and its variance which will contain unknown parameters to be estimated. At this point, the Kalman filter recursive equations have completed the required task. Now standard maximum likelihood procedures are used to estimate the unknown parameters.

The Kalman filter is a rather versatile construct, but its derivation may involve unfamiliar concepts to some readers. Therefore we approach the issues involved from different standpoints. In section 7.1 we motivate our discussion of the state-space form and the Kalman filter recursive algorithms in terms of the modelling of expectations in a learning environment. The technical aspects are introduced via the Theil–Goldberger (1961) pure and mixed estimator in section 7.2 and the 'full' Kalman filter equations are then examined from the standpoint of Bayes theorem. Bayes theorem allows one to combine prior information with the data to yield an optimal posterior estimator. In fact, the Theil–Goldberger estimator is a special case of the 'general' updating formulae of Bayes theorem. In section 7.3 we examine how the unknown parameters in the Kalman-filter formulae can be estimated using maximum likelihood and in particular we consider time-varying parameter models. In section 7.4 we give some practical examples of the use of the Kalman filter in applied economics (see Note 1).

7.1   Expectations and learning and the state-space form

In this section we wish to motivate our discussion of the Kalman filter by interpreting it in terms of agents forming expectations. The predominant paradigm for modelling expectations is the rational expectations hypothesis REH, see Chapter 6. It assumes agents act 'as if' they know the true model of the economy (up to a set of white noise errors); a rather strong assumption that some may find a little implausible. As Friedman (1979) clearly points out, the *information exploitation* assumption of RE, namely that agents use efficiently whatever information is available, is largely uncontentious. It is the *information availability* assumption that many economists find objectionable. For agents that are (Muth, 1960) rational their predictions are equal to the conditional mathematical expectation of the model and hence their forecast errors are independent of any information available at the time the forecast is made; the latter is the error-orthogonality property of RE. In early New Classical models (e.g. Sargent and Wallace 1975) if the parameters of the model alter (usually taken to be the parameters of the monetary policy reaction function), agents are assumed to know the 'new' parameter values immediately. The latter also applies to changes in the functional form of behavioural equations. In later work (e.g. Cyert and De Groot 1974, Bray 1982), agents are assumed to know the true structure of the model but are initially ignorant of the true values of the one (or more) of the parameters.

The results of these studies broadly suggest that agents expectations do eventually converge on the Muth rational solution. However, where agents operate with a set of possible models, then even if one of them is the true model, there is no guarantee that the learning process converges to the true model (Blume and Easley 1982). One would expect this conclusion to apply *a fortiori* when agents are not allowed the luxury of having the true model in their set of models, or where the parameters of the model vary over time. In this type of situation we have the added complication that agents, during their learning process, generate outcomes which are contaminated with 'noise' from the learning process as well as 'noise' from the underlying true model.

Consideration of the information availability assumption has led critics of the REH to label it unrealistic. However, such critics have not been able to provide an alternative 'optimising' framework to RE, particularly one that is empirically tractable. Friedman (1979) goes some way along this route when he advocates that given the true model $y_t = x_t \beta + u_t$ (u_t, white noise), agents may sequentially update their estimate of the *fixed* true parameter vector β as more information on (y_t, x_t) becomes available (e.g. time-varying parameter models). Using the Kalman filter we extend Friedman's framework to include the case where (i) agents have some prior information about β (at time $t = 0$) and (ii) β is allowed to vary stochastically. Friedman alludes to the latter outcome (Friedman 1979, pp. 33–4) when he discusses the possibility that agents may perceive that a good approximation to the complex 'true' model may be a simple (linear) model but with time-varying parameters. Such a model may be analysed using the Kalman filter (Kalman 1960), and the familiar recursive least squares learning procedure is a special case of this more general procedure.

The Kalman filter, although widely used in certain branches of the engineering literature and by applied statisticians, is only just emerging as a possible useful tool of the applied economist (see, for example, Lawson 1980, Harvey *et al*. 1986, Cuthbertson and Taylor 1986). For certain models the Kalman filter may be viewed as mimicking a learning process by agents. For example, the Kalman filter may be interpreted as a form of adaptive expectations where the adjustment parameter is updated each period, based on new information. This formalises Flemming's (1976) idea of a 'change of gear' when forming expectations. It is well known that adaptive expectations is optimal (in the sense of producing unbiased forecasts) only when the data generation process is IMA(1, 1) or ARIMA(1, 1, 1). The Kalman filter, however, is optimal under more general conditions, and in fact produces minimum mean square estimators (MMSE) under normality. Therefore agents, *given the assumed information set*, do not make systematic forecast errors. The Kalman filter therefore confronts directly the question of how agents learn about the time series behaviour of economic variables; agents are not assumed to know instantaneously the 'true' model but they do use information optimally (or efficiently). The Kalman filter can also be applied to unobservable components models and it therefore formalises the 'signal extraction problem' presented in Lucas's (1972) derivation of the 'surprise supply function'. Note that the Kalman filter does not provide a panacea, it provides merely a tractable alternative to the 'extreme' information assumption of the REH, based on optimising behaviour in the face of uncertainty about the evolution of the parameters of the assumed model.

The rest of this chapter is organised as follows. We begin with a discussion of fixed coefficient adaptive expectations models that proved so popular in the empirical literature prior to the advent of rational expectations in the 1970s. We then present a simple adaptive expectations model in which the adaptive coefficient varies through time. Our final example utilises the signal extraction problem that an individual faces when trying to estimate his permanent income say, faced only with information on his measured income. This *stochastic trend model* embodies sequential learning in a time series context and allows us to demonstrate how this model is represented in *state-space* form: a prerequisite for understanding the application of the Kalman filter in more general situations.

Fixed coefficient-adaptive models

It is now well understood that if (the logarithm of) measured income y_t is accurately represented by an IMA$(1,1)$ process

$$y_t = y_{t-1} + \varepsilon_t - (1 - \Theta)\varepsilon_{t-1} \qquad (7.1)$$

then the optimal updating equation for expected income,

$$y^e_{t/t-1} = E(y_t|\Omega_{t-1}), \text{ where } \Omega_{t-1} \equiv \{y_{t-j}, \varepsilon_{t-j}\}_{j=1\ldots\infty}$$

is (see Note 2):

$$y^e_{t/t-1} - y^e_{t-1/t-2} = \Theta(y_{t-1} - y^e_{t-1/t-2}) \qquad (7.2)$$

This is nothing more than first-order adaptive expectations with the *fixed* updating coefficient related to the moving average parameter in the data generation process. The above approach is easily generalised to include a 'change-of-gear' (Flemming 1976). If the *growth* rather than the level of income is IMA$(1,1)$ then first-order adaptive expectations applied to the growth in income is optimal. 'Optimal' in this context is taken to mean that expectations are correct on average (and have minimum mean square prediction errors). Although Granger (1966) finds that a number of economic time series are adequately represented as IMA$(1,1)$ processes and therefore fixed coefficient adaptive expectations are optimal, nevertheless the model does not allow agents to learn slowly about their new environment as new information becomes available. For these adaptive models to be optimal, when the data generation process undergoes a 'change of gear', agents must instantaneously acquire knowledge of the 'new' moving average coefficient. Thus ironically, the above adaptive expectations model also requires a rather extreme information availability assumption when the stochastic behaviour of a variable alters.

Variable parameter adaptive expectations

Consider an agent who has sequential observations on his measured income (in logarithms) y_t which he views as consisting of an *unobserved* permanent component π_t and a zero mean (unobserved) 'surprise' element s_t. The agent has an initial or prior estimate of permanent income π_0 and wishes to update this estimate as information on measured income becomes available. Clearly to 'solve' this problem the agent must have some view (or model) of how permanent income varies over time. For expositional reasons we assume the *transition equation* describing the evolution of π_t is a random walk. Our final assumption is that the agent *perceives* that a fraction k_t of the surprise s_t in measured income, constitutes permanent income and $(1 - k_t)s_t$ is considered to be an addition to transitory income. Note that the coefficient k_t varies through time and for the moment we assume the value of k_t in each successive period is known by the agent. (The Kalman filter provides a method of estimating and optimally updating k_t as we see in section 7.2). The model assumed by the agent is therefore (see Note 3):

$$y_t = \pi_t + (1 - k_t)s_t \qquad \text{'measurement equation'} \qquad (7.3)$$

$$\pi_t = \pi_{t-1} + k_t s_t \qquad \text{'transition equation'} \qquad (7.4)$$

with

$$E_{t-1}s_t = s^e_{t/t-1} = 0; \qquad \text{and} \qquad E(\pi_t s_{t-j}) = 0 \quad (j = 0, \infty)$$

The measurement equation has measured income y_t as the sum of permanent π_t and transitory income $(1 - k_t)s_t$, while the transition equation represents the assumed evolution of π_t through time.

Substituting (7.4) in (7.3):

$$y_t = \pi_{t-1} + s_t \qquad (7.5)$$

Multiplying (7.5) by k_t and substituting from (7.4) for $k_t s_t$ we obtain the updating equation for π_t in the form of a variable parameter adaptive model:

$$\pi_t = \pi_{t-1} + k_t(y_t - \pi_{t-1}) \qquad (7.6)$$

Thus given an initial estimate of permanent income π_0, knowing k_t and y_t, the updating equation (7.6) can be used to give all future values of permanent income. The analogy with the fixed parameter adaptive model is completed by noting that the equations (7.3) and (7.4) may be written as an IMA(1, 1) model with a *time-varying moving average coefficient*. Equation (7.3) minus itself lagged one period yields:

$$\Delta y_t = \Delta \pi_t + (1 - k_t)s_t - (1 - k_{t-1})s_{t-1} \qquad (7.7a)$$

Substituting for $\Delta \pi_t$ from (7.4) we obtain our IMA(1, 1) representation:

$$\Delta y_t = s_t - (1 - k_{t-1})s_{t-1} \qquad (7.7b)$$

In using the updating equation (7.6) for π_t the key missing element is how the agent forms and updates the coefficient k_t which turns out to be analogous to the 'Kalman gain'. To demonstrate some preliminary intuitive insights into how agents estimate the Kalman gain we consider the example of the generalised stochastic trend (GST) model.

Generalised stochastic trend model

Instead of assuming that the agent knows k_t, the proportion of any surprise s_t that accrues as permanent income, we adopt the weaker assumption that the shocks to permanent and measured income are statistically independent. In addition we assume that the growth in permanent income $\Delta\pi_t$ is time varying with parameter γ_{t-1} which itself evolves as a random walk (Harvey and Todd 1983). Hence the agents best approximation to his stochastic environment is assumed to be characterised as:

$$y_t = \pi_t + \varepsilon_t \tag{7.8a}$$

$$\pi_t = \pi_{t-1} + \gamma_{t-1} + \zeta_t \tag{7.8b}$$

$$\gamma_t = \gamma_{t-1} + \omega_t \tag{7.8c}$$

which may be represented in matrix form (known as the *state-space form*) as:

$$y_t = x'\beta_t + \varepsilon_t \qquad \text{Measurement equation} \tag{7.9a}$$
$$(t = 1, 2, \ldots n)$$

$$\beta_t = T\beta_{t-1} + \eta_t \qquad \text{Transition equation} \tag{7.9b}$$

where

$$x' = [1, 0]$$
$$\beta_t = (\pi_t, \gamma_t)'$$

$$T = \begin{pmatrix} 1 & 1 \\ 0 & 1 \end{pmatrix}$$

$$\eta_t = (\zeta_t, \omega_t)'$$

$\varepsilon_t, \zeta_t, \omega_t$ are zero mean, error terms independent of each other and

$$\text{Var}(\varepsilon_t) = \sigma_\varepsilon^2; \ \text{Var}(\zeta_t) = \sigma_\zeta^2; \ \text{Var}(\omega_t) = \sigma_\omega^2$$

In the measurement equation, observed data on income y_t again consists of a permanent π_t and transitory component ε_t. The growth in permanent income $\Delta\pi_t$ is assumed to equal a stochastic growth coefficient γ_{t-1} (plus a random error term, ζ_t) and γ_{t-1} itself evolves as a random walk. The system (7.9a) and (7.9b) may appear a little strange to applied economists used to dealing with the usual fixed regression parameter model. In this unobservable components model *only* y_t is observed and the agent faces a 'signal extraction problem' to determine how much of any change in y_t can be attributed to a change in permanent income (the 'signal') and how much is due to transitory income ε_t (the 'noise'), (Lucas, 1972). However this particular unobservable components model may be given an intuitive interpretation in which y_t and π_t are perceived by the agent as being generated by a stochastic trend. This is easily seen by noting that given an initial estimate of π_0, successive substitution in (7.8b) yields

$$\pi_t = \pi_0 + \sum_{i=1}^{t} \gamma_{i-1} + \sum_{i=1}^{t} \zeta_i \tag{7.10}$$

and hence:

$$y_t = \left(\pi_0 + \sum_{i=1}^{t} \gamma_{i-1}\right) + u_t \tag{7.11}$$

where

$$u_t = \sum_{i=1}^{t} \zeta_i + \varepsilon_t = \zeta_t^* + \varepsilon_t$$

To see why (7.10) and (7.11) embody a stochastic trend, consider the special case where $\omega_t = 0$ (for all t). From (7.8c), $\gamma_t = \gamma_{t-1} = \gamma$ say, hence (7.10) and (7.11) reduce to:

$$y_t = \pi_0 + \gamma_t t + u_t \tag{7.12}$$

$$\pi_t = \pi_0 + \gamma_t t + \zeta_t^* \tag{7.13}$$

Equations (7.12) and (7.13) are global linear trend models with moving average error terms (see Note 4).

Returning to the signal extraction problem, assume for simplicity that $\omega_t = \sigma_\omega^2 = 0$ and that the agent knows the values of σ_ε^2 and σ_ζ^2. Assume also that with information on y up to period $t-1$ (which could be 'time zero') he has formed a prior estimate of the unobservable, permanent income for time t, namely $\pi_{t/t-1}$. The key question is how the agent optimally uses information to update his estimate of π when new information on y_t arrives. To gain some intuitive insights consider the two polar cases $\sigma_\varepsilon^2 = 0$ and $\sigma_\zeta^2 = 0$. In the first case there is no measurement noise ($y_t = \pi_t$) and we would expect all of his forecast error

$$\tilde{v}_t = (y_t - \tilde{y}_{t/t-1}) = (y_t - \pi_{t/t-1})$$

to be included in his estimate of permanent income, that is

$$\pi_t = \pi_{t/t-1} + (y_t - \tilde{y}_{t/t-1})$$

The converse applies for $\sigma_\zeta^2 = 0$, and here $\pi_t = \pi_{t/t-1}$. In the intermediate case (σ_ε^2, $\sigma_\zeta^2 \neq 0$) the proportion of the forecast error added to $\pi_{t/t-1}$ will depend upon the agents' perception of the *relative* variance of σ_ε^2 and $\text{Var}(\pi_{t/t-1})$. The latter is equal to the sum of his prior estimate of the variance of π (say, σ_0^2) and his sampling error for π, (i.e. σ_ζ^2). Hence, if the updating equation is

$$\pi_t = \pi_{t/t-1} + k_t(y_t - \tilde{y}_{t/t-1}) \tag{7.14}$$

then we might expect

$$k_t = (\sigma_0^2 + \sigma_\zeta^2)/(\sigma_\varepsilon^2 + (\sigma_0^2 + \sigma_\zeta^2)) \tag{7.15}$$

It is easily seen that $k = 1$ for $\sigma_\varepsilon^2 = 0$ and $k = 0$ for $\sigma_\zeta^2 = \sigma_0^2 = 0$. Thus our intuitive arguments have led us to interpret our model both in terms of a stochastic trend and as a variable parameter partial adjustment model. The adjustment parameter k_t is known as the Kalman gain and equation (7.14) will be seen to be the updating equation for the 'unobservable' permanent income variable. Given an initial estimate $\pi_{1/0}$ and knowing k_t, equation (7.14) provides a recursion formula for updating π_t as new information on y_t arrives.

Having provided an intuitive interpretation of our unobserved components model we now turn to our main task which is to derive the general equations for the Kalman filter. These equations provide a general formula for the Kalman gain and updating equations for a wide variety of possible models.

7.2 The econometrics of the Kalman filter

The econometrics of the Kalman filter can appear rather formidable to the applied economist when reading the engineering or statistical literature. One of our aims in this section is therefore to present the econometrics of the Kalman filter using conventional procedures. We begin by deriving the formulae for one-step-ahead prediction errors in the general linear model. These results are then used to reinterpret the Theil–Goldberger 'pure and mixed' estimator in terms of a 'one-shot' Kalman filter. The prior 'guesses' for the parameters and error variances are combined with the sample data to yield an 'optimal' 'posterior' estimator based on both sets of information. We then use the stochastic trend model as a concrete example with which to develop the general formulae used in the Kalman filter. The Kalman filter is then seen to be a *useful algorithm* to generate the variables needed in the (prediction error decomposition of the) likelihood function: the key variables are the one-step-ahead prediction errors

$\tilde{v}_t$ and their variance-covariance matrix (F_t or f_t). We then present an alternative derivation of the Kalman filter equations in terms of Bayes theorem and maximum likelihood, which will reinforce the (somewhat difficult) concepts involved, when dealing with the general formulation of the state-space model.

Prediction in the general linear model

Given the true fixed parameter model

$$Y = X\beta + \varepsilon \tag{7.16}$$

where we assume a scalar covariance matrix:

$$\varepsilon \sim N(0, V) = N(0, \sigma^2 I) \tag{7.17}$$

and $E(X'\varepsilon) = 0$, X is ($n \times k$); Y and ε are ($n \times 1$); β is ($k \times 1$).
  The OLS estimator b_0 is BLUE:

$$b_0 = (X'X)^{-1}X'Y \tag{7.18}$$

with variance–covariance matrix:

$$\text{Cov}(b_0) = P_0 = \sigma^2(X'X)^{-1} \tag{7.19}$$

and using (7.16) and (7.18) we obtain the familiar result

$$b_0 - \beta = (X'X)^{-1}X'\varepsilon \tag{7.20}$$

  Of particular interest given what follows is the problem of *predicting* q 'new' observations Y_1 based on *new* information on X_1, where X_1 is ($q \times k$), and the estimator b_0. We assume an *unchanged structural model* over the forecast horizon:

$$Y_1 = X_1\beta + \varepsilon_1 \tag{7.21}$$

$$\varepsilon_1 \sim N(0, V_1) = N(0\ \sigma^2 I_1) \tag{7.22}$$

where ε_1 is ($q \times 1$) uncorrelated with ε. The prediction $\tilde{Y}_1 = X_1 b_0$ is an unbiased predictor of the values of Y in the forecast period. The covariance matrix of the *one-step-ahead forecast errors* $\tilde{v}_1 = Y_1 - \tilde{Y}_1$ is:

$$F = \text{Cov}(\tilde{v}_1) = E(X_1(\beta - b_0) + \varepsilon_1)(X_1(\beta - b_0) + \varepsilon_1)' \tag{7.23}$$

where F is ($q \times q$). Substitute from (7.20) for ($\beta - b_0$):

$$F = E(X_1(\text{Cov}\,b_0)X_1' + \varepsilon_1\varepsilon_1') = \sigma^2(X_1(X'X)^{-1}X_1' + I) \tag{7.24a}$$

or $F = (X_1 P_0 X_1' + V_1)$ (7.24b)

The variance of Y_1 around $\tilde{Y}_1$ depends on the uncertainty in estimating the parameters in β $(\text{Cov}(b_0) = P_0)$ and also on the intrinsic uncertainty in equation (7.16), $V_1 = \sigma^2 I_1$.

If we have one additional observation on the x-variables, the X_1 is replaced by $x_1'(1 \times k)$ and Y_1, $\tilde{v}_1$ and F are scalars. Hence (7.24b) becomes:

$$f = [x_1' P_0 x_1 + \sigma^2]$$ (7.25)

which we will use in our discussion of the stochastic trend model later in this section.

Theil-Goldberger (T-G) estimation and the Kalman filter

The T-G pure and mixed estimator considers the problem of how best to combine prior information on the parameter vector β and information on β generated by our sample of observations. It is assumed that the agent (econometrician) makes an initial informed guess concerning the mean value of the true parameters β, denote this guess b_0^*. The *uncertainty* surrounding this prior 'guess' is summarised in the 'guess' about the prior covariance matrix, P_0^* Hence:

$$\beta = b_0^* + \omega_0^*$$ (7.26)

$$\omega_0^* \sim N(0, P_0^*)$$ (7.27)

where ω_0^* is a vector of 'prior' error terms and P_0^* is the (possibly non-scalar) non-diagonal prior covariance matrix. β is $(k \times 1)$, b_0^* is *known*, P_0^* is the *known* $(k \times k)$ covariance matrix (often assumed diagonal in practice (MacDonald 1988), or simplified in some way.

$$b_0^* \sim N(\beta, P_0^*)$$ (7.28)

Hence, the agent has both prior and sample information, the latter consists of Y which is $(n \times 1)$ and X which is $(n \times k)$, which may be represented:

$$\begin{pmatrix} Y \\ b_0^* \end{pmatrix} = \begin{pmatrix} X \\ I \end{pmatrix} \beta + \begin{pmatrix} \varepsilon \\ \omega_0^* \end{pmatrix} \qquad \begin{matrix} \varepsilon \sim N(0, V) \\ \omega_0^* \sim N(0, P_0^*) \end{matrix}$$ (7.29)

or $Y_* + X_* \beta + \varepsilon_*$ (7.30)

where $Y_* = \begin{pmatrix} Y \\ b_0^* \end{pmatrix}$

$$X_* = \begin{pmatrix} X \\ I \end{pmatrix}$$

$$V_* = E(\varepsilon_* \varepsilon_*') = \begin{pmatrix} E(\varepsilon\varepsilon') & 0 \\ 0 & E(\omega_0^* \omega_0^{*'}) \end{pmatrix} = \begin{pmatrix} V & 0 \\ 0 & P_0^* \end{pmatrix}$$

$$(7.31)$$

We have assumed zero covariance between the prior estimation error ω_0^* and the error term ε in the regression equation. (In addition we assume zero covariance between ω_0^* and X and ε and X.)

The Theil–Goldberger pure and mixed estimator may be viewed as 'one-shot' application of the Kalman filter which provides an updating equation for β and its covariance matrix based on the prior and sample information. The posterior estimates of β say b_1 is BLUE and its covariance matrix we denote $\mathrm{Cov}\,(b_1) = P_1$.

GLS applied to (7.30) yields:

$$b_1 = (X_*' V_*^{-1} X_*)^{-1} (X_*' V_*^{-1} Y_*)$$

$$(7.32)$$

with covariance matrix

$$\mathrm{Cov}\,(b_1) = P_1 = (X_*' V_*^{-1} X_*)^{-1}$$

$$(7.33)$$

Equations (7.32) and (7.33) may be interpreted as *updating equations* for β and its covariance matrix although this is not apparent from the normal textbook GLS formulae above. However, it is shown in the appendix that (7.32) and (7.33) can be rewritten in the intuitively appealing form:

$$P_1^{-1} = (P_0^*)^{-1} + (X' V^{-1} X)$$

$$(7.34a)$$

$$P_1 = (I - KX) P_0^*$$

$$(7.34b)$$

$$b_1 = b_0^* + K(Y - X b_0^*) = b_0^* + K \tilde{v}$$

$$(7.35)$$

where $K = P_0^* X' F^{-1}$

$$(7.36)$$

$$F = \mathrm{Cov}\,(\tilde{v}) = (V + X P_0^* X')$$

$$(7.37)$$

$$\tilde{v} = Y - \tilde{Y} = (Y - X b_0^*)$$

$$(7.38)$$

Equation (7.34a) is the updating equation for the inverse of the covariance of b_1. The $(k \times k)$ inverse of the posterior covariance, P_1^{-1}, is simply the sum of the inverse of the prior covariance $(P_0^*)^{-1}$ and the sample covariance (for the 'unrestricted' GLS estimator) that is $(X' V^{-1} X)$. Equation (7.3a) may be rewritten in terms of the Kalman gain and is given in (7.34b).

Equation (7.35), the updating equation for β, expresses the updated estimate b_1 as the sum of the prior estimate b_0^* and the product of the Kalman gain K and the error $\tilde{v}$ in forecasting Y using the prior estimate b_0^*. The Kalman gain depends upon 'relative variances' namely the variance of b_0^* ($= P_0^*$) relative to the variance of the 'one-step-ahead' prediction error $\text{Cov}(\tilde{v}) = F = (V + XP_0^*X')$.

We are now ready to present the complete state-space formulation which underlie most applications of the Kalman filter that are likely to be used by applied economists. The increased generality is provided by relaxing the assumption of fixed underlying true parameter vector β; the parameter vector is now assumed to vary through time but in a systematic way. It is this additional complexity that allows the Kalman filter to be used in estimating unobservable components and variable parameter models (which may be used to generate 'plausible' expectations variables without invoking the extreme RE, 'axiom of correct specification').

In the Theil–Goldberger model, β is non-stochastic and the estimator b_1 is 'optimal' where optimal is synonymous with BLUE. However, when β is stochastic in the sense that it is randomly drawn from a prior distribution before the observations on Y are generated, then b_1 retains its 'optimal' properties in that it is unbiased and is the minimum mean square estimator of β (given that Y is multi-variate normal). Thus with β stochastic, the Kalman filter will provide 'rational' predictions. The agent utilises information at time $t - 1$ to provide unbiased estimators of β, which have minimum variance. As new information on Y at time t arrives, the agent combines this with his current priors to optimally update his estimate of both the parameter vector β and its covariance. It is in this sense that the Kalman filter may be viewed as mimicking a sequential optimal learning process. The predictions are 'rational' in the sense that the agent optimally exploits current and past information when learning about his stochastic environment.

State-space formulation and Kalman filtering

In developing the Kalman filter recursion formulae, conceptually, we move from our 'one-shot' Theil-Goldberger formulation to one where the estimates are updated each time period. Thus, in place of b_0, P_0 we have prior estimates $b_{1/0}$ and $P_{1/0}$ based on information at $t = 0$ and we use these to provide updated estimates b_1, P_1 as information on the scalar y_t for $t = 1$ becomes available. The recursion formulae then provide estimates $b_{t/t-1}$, $P_{t/t-1}$ ($t = 1, \ldots n$). In order to update our estimate of the $(k \times 1)$ vector β in each period, we need to know the stochastic process by which β alters through time. This is given by the so called 'transition equation'. Our complete *state-space* model (see Note 5) is:

$$y_t = x'\beta_t + \varepsilon_t$$
$$(t = 1, 2, \ldots n) \quad \text{Measurement equation} \quad \text{(7.39)}$$

$$\beta_t = T\beta_{t-1} + R\eta_t \quad \text{Transition equation} \quad \text{(7.40)}$$

$$b_0 = \beta_0 + \psi_0 \quad \text{Prior estimate} \quad \text{(7.41)}$$

$$\varepsilon_t \sim N(0, \sigma^2)$$

$$\eta_t \sim N(0, Q)$$

$$\psi_0 \sim N(0, \Psi_0)$$

where x' is $(1 \times k)$, β_t is $(k \times 1)$: T, Q, Ψ_0, R are $(k \times k)$ and we take $V = \sigma^2 I$.

We have already demonstrated how the stochastic trend model (7.8a–7.8c) may be represented in state-space form (with $R = I$). Equation (7.41) represents our initial guesses (or starting values) for the parameter vector β and its covariance matrix Ψ_0.

It is important to keep in mind what information the agent is assumed to possess. At $t = 0$, he has an initial *fixed* estimate b_0 of the true parameter vector β_0 and its covariance matrix, that is $b_0 \sim N(\beta_0, \Psi_0)$. He knows the structure of the model in the form of the *fixed* vector x, fixed matrices Q, R, T and the fixed variance of the measurement equation σ^2. The problem the agent faces is to utilise the information contained in the sequential data y_t to update optimally his estimates of β_t and its covariance matrix.

If we can reduce the three equation system (7.39–7.41) to the Theil–Goldberger formulation then we can apply the appropriate GLS formulae to produce optimal posterior (or one-step-ahead) estimates of β and its covariance matrix; these constitute the Kalman filter updating equations.

Given b_0 the unbiased predictor of β_1 is

$$b_{1/0} = Tb_0 \quad \text{(7.42)}$$

The covariance of b_1 around the true value β_1 is defined as:

$$\text{Cov}(b_{1/0}) = P_{1/0} = E(b_{1/0} - \beta_1)(b_{1/0} - \beta_1)' \quad \text{(7.43)}$$

Substituting for β_0 from (7.41) in (7.40) and using (7.42):

$$(\beta_1 - b_{1/0}) = -T\psi_0 + R\eta_1 = \omega_1, \text{ say} \quad \text{(7.44)}$$

The prediction error in forecasting β_1, namely $(b_{1/0} - \beta_1)$ is a weighted average of the 'prior uncertainty', ψ_0, and the uncertainty in the transition equation for β, namely, η_1. From (7.43) and (7.44) the covariance of this prediction error is the $(k \times k)$ matrix $P_{1/0}$:

$$P_{1/0} = E(\omega_1 \omega_1') = (TP_0T' + RQR') \qquad (7.45)$$

Equations (7.42) and (7.45) are the *prediction equations* for $t = 1$, for the state vector β_1 and its covariance matrix, which may be calculated *without any reference to the observations* y_t. Suppose the agent now receives a single observation y_1. The sample and prior information may now be arranged as in the Theil–Goldberger model:

$$\begin{pmatrix} y_1 \\ b_{1/0} \end{pmatrix} = \begin{pmatrix} x' \\ I \end{pmatrix} \beta_1 + \begin{pmatrix} \varepsilon_1 \\ \omega_1 \end{pmatrix} \qquad (7.46)$$

where

$$\varepsilon_1 \sim N(0, \sigma^2)$$
$$\omega_1 \sim N(0, P_{1/0})$$

Comparing (7.46) with our Theil–Goldberger formulation (7.29) we have:

$$b_0^* = b_{1/0} \qquad (7.47a)$$

$$P_0^* = P_{1/0} \qquad (7.47b)$$

With the above substitutions, we can use the updating formulae (7.34) to (7.38) to calculate the $(k \times 1)$ vector for the Kalman gain for $t = 1$:

$$K_1 = P_{1/0}xF_1^{-1} = P_{1/0}xf_1^{-1} \qquad (7.48)$$

where in this model F_1 is a scalar, denoted f_1:

$$F_1 = f_1 = (x'P_{1/0}x + \sigma^2) \qquad (7.49)$$

The optimal updating equation for b_1 is:

$$b_1 = b_{1/0} + K_1(y_1 - x'b_{1/0}) \qquad (7.50)$$

with $(k \times k)$ covariance matrix:

$$P_1 = (I - K_1x')P_{1/0} \qquad (7.51)$$

The updated values b_1, P_1 are then used in equations (7.42) and (7.45) respectively, to generate new predictions $b_{2/1}$ and $P_{2/1}$. Estimates b_t and P_t are then updated sequentially using (7.48) and (7.51) as information on y_t becomes available. The Kalman filter also generates one-step-ahead prediction errors for y_t, that is, $\tilde{v}_t = y_t - y_{t/t-1}$ and their variance f_t (a matrix if we have a vector of observations on a *set* of variables at time t) which can be used directly in the prediction error decomposition form of the likelihood function and estimated by maximum likelihood (see section 7.3).

We have now demonstrated that the Kalman filter may be interpreted in terms of conventional least squares procedures. Furthermore, the updating equation for b may be interpreted as adaptive expectations with a time varying parameter K_t:

$$b_t = b_{t/t-1} + K_t(y_t - x'b_{t/t-1}) \qquad (7.52)$$

where

$$K_t = P_{t/t-1}xf_t^{-1} \qquad (7.53)$$

$$f_t = (x'P_{t/t-1}x + \sigma^2) \qquad (7.54)$$

K_t may be viewed as representing the degree of uncertainty surrounding the new information y_t. For any given forecast error $\tilde{v}_t = (y_t - x'b_{t/t-1})$ the adjustment to $b_{t/t-1}$ is smaller the larger the variance of past forecast errors, since

$$f_t^{-1} = (\text{Var}(\tilde{v}_t))^{-1}.$$

Throughout we have assumed that the variance–covariance matrices are known to the agent, and to the econometrician. In the practical implementation of the Kalman filter one can either assume 'plausible' values for these and conduct a sensitivity analysis (e.g. Lawson 1980) or the covariance matrices may be estimated (see below).

Two further points need to be mentioned. First, at any point in time the prediction equations (7.42) and (7.45) can be used to generate multi-period predictions based on information at t. For example

$$b_{t+n/t} = T^n b_t \quad \text{and} \quad \tilde{y}_{t+n/t} = x'b_{t+n/t}$$

and the latter can be used directly in multi-period, forward-looking models (e.g. Sargent 1979, Cuthbertson and Taylor 1986) of the form:

$$Z_t = \lambda_0 Z_{t-1} + \lambda_1 \sum_{i=1}^{m} \delta^i y_{t+i/t}^e \qquad (7.55)$$

where $\tilde{y}_{t+i/t}$ replaces $y_{t+i/t}^e$.

Second, an agent at time $t = T$ may wish to use *all* past sample information to provide a 'smoothed' estimate of the unobservable (permanent income) π_t (the first element of β_t) rather than utilising his current one-step-ahead prediction. The updating equations (7.50) and (7.51) can be used in reverse to obtain $b_{t/T}$ and $P_{t/T}$. These smoothed estimates of π_t could provide a proxy for permanent income (see below).

Some special cases

We now consider how recursive least squares and our intuitive results on the stochastic trend model may be viewed as special cases of the Kalman filter equations derived in the previous section.

Our simple *unobservable components model* (with $\gamma_{t-1} = 0$) is:

$$y_t = \pi_t + \varepsilon_t \tag{7.56}$$

$$\pi_t = \pi_{t-1} + \zeta_t \tag{7.57}$$

In state-space form, the model has

$$X = T = 1, \ \beta_t = \pi_t, \ V = \sigma_\varepsilon^2 I, \ Q = \sigma_\zeta^2 I, \ \Psi_0 = \sigma_0^2 I \tag{7.58}$$

Substituting (7.58) in the prediction equations (7.42) and (7.45):

$$\pi_t = \pi_{t/t-1} \tag{7.59}$$

$$P_{1/0} = \sigma_{t/t-1}^2 = \sigma_0^2 + \sigma_\zeta^2 \tag{7.60a}$$

and the updating equations using (7.48)–(7.51) are:

$$\pi_t = \pi_{t/t-1} + k_t(y_t - \pi_{t/t-1}) \tag{7.60b}$$

$$\sigma_t = (1 - k_t)\sigma_{t/t-1}^2 \tag{7.61}$$

where

$$k_t = \sigma_{t/t-1}^2(\sigma_{t/t-1}^2 + \sigma_\varepsilon^2)^{-1} = (\sigma_0^2 + \sigma_\zeta^2)((\sigma_0^2 + \sigma_\zeta^2) + \sigma_\varepsilon^2)^{-1} \tag{7.62}$$

which confirm our earlier intuitive ideas on the updating equation for π_t given in equations (7.14) and (7.15).

In *recursive least squares* an initial $t - 1 \ (> k)$ observations can be used to provide an initial estimate b_{t-1} with covariance matrix P_{t-1}:

$$b_{t-1} = (X'X)_{t-1}^{-1} (X'Y)_{t-1}$$

$$P_{t-1} = \sigma^2(X'X)_{t-1}^{-1}$$

The OLS model may then be represented in state-space form as

$$y_t \ = x_t'\beta_t + \varepsilon_t \quad (t = 1, 2, \ldots n)$$

$$\beta_t \ = T\beta_{t-1} + R\eta_t$$

with $\quad \varepsilon_t \ \sim N(0, \sigma^2)$

$$\eta_t \ = 0; \quad Q, R = 0$$

$$T \ = I$$

and $b_0 = b_{t-1} \sim N(\beta_{t-1}, P_{t-1})$

The prediction equations are then extremely straightforward:

$$b_{t/t-1} = b_{t-1}$$

$$P_{t/t-1} = P_{t-1} = \sigma^2 (X'X)^{-1}_{t-1}$$

while the updating equations, given the scalar y_t and the vector x_t are:

$$b_t = b_{t-1} + K_t(y_t - x'_t b_{t/t-1})$$

$$P_t = (I - K_t x'_t)P_{t/t-1}$$

where

$$K_t = (X'X)^{-1}_{t-1} x'_t f^{-1}_t$$

and

$$f_t = \text{Var}(\tilde{v}_t) = \sigma^2 (1 + x'_t(X'X)^{-1}_{t-1} x_t)$$

The series $\tilde{v}_t / f_t^{1/2}$ is also referred to as the 'recursive residuals' and forms the basis for the CUSUM and CUSUMSQ tests for parameter stability (see Chapter 4). Note that recursive least squares is *not* a variable parameter model since we do not assume a specific model of how β varies through time since we believe the *true β is constant*. The Kalman filter is merely an algorithm for 'repeating' OLS as we extend the sample. We expect to see β settle down to a constant value as more data is added, since the underlying 'true' model has β as a constant in the population.

General form of the Kalman filter using Bayes theorem

We now wish to generalise the equations for the Kalman filter and present the derivation in terms of Bayes theorem. Again it is important to focus on what is known (to the econometrician) and what is to be estimated. We have a set of m state variables = $(\beta_1, \beta_2 \ldots \beta_{mt})$ which are *not observed directly* and instead of a single series we have n measurement variables $y_t = (y_{1t} \ldots y_{nt})$ for time periods $t = 1, 2, 3 \ldots T$, which are observed directly. The model then has two distinct blocks.

The *measurement equation* for time t is:

$$y_t = X_t \beta_t + \varepsilon_t \qquad t = 1, 2 \ldots T \qquad (7.63)$$

$$\varepsilon_t \sim N(0, V_t)$$

where X_t is an $n \times m$ *known* matrix and ε_t is an $n \times 1$ vector of error terms with mean zero and covariance matrix V_t.

As mentioned above, while the values of β_t are assumed to be unobservable we do need to make some assumption about the mechanism which governs the generation of β_t. This takes the form of the *transition equation*:

$$\beta_t = T_t \beta_{t-1} + R_t \eta_t \tag{7.64}$$

$$\eta_t \sim N(0, Q_t)$$

where T_t and R_t are again *known* $m \times m$ matrices and η_t is an $m \times 1$ vector of disturbances with mean zero and covariance matrix Q_t.

We assume η_t and ε_t are uncorrelated (for all t), that β_{t-1} is independent of the error term η_t in the transition equation and finally that β_t is uncorrelated with the measurement error ε_t:

$$E(\eta_i \varepsilon_j) = 0 \text{ for all } i, j$$

$$E(\beta_{t-1}, \eta_t) = 0 \tag{7.65}$$

$$E(\beta_t \varepsilon_t) = 0$$

Equations (7.63) and (7.64) together make up the state-space model. At first sight these two equations look fairly standard but the time subscripts must be intepreted very precisely. Equation (7.63) contains only *current* dated values of β_t while (7.64) contains only a single lagged value, β_{t-1}. These restrictions do not rule out more complex dynamic models but they do mean that such models must be re-parameterised into the state-space form of (7.63) and (7.64).

Some simple examples may make this clearer. Suppose we have an AR(1) model in the scalar y_t.

$$y_t = \alpha y_{t-1} + \eta_t$$

Then the state-space form is:

$$y_t = \beta_t \qquad \text{(measurement equation)} \tag{7.66}$$

$$\beta_t = \alpha \beta_{t-1} + \eta_t \qquad \text{(transition equation)} \tag{7.67}$$

where $X_t = 1$, $T_t = \alpha$, an unknown scalar constant, $R_t = 1$, $\varepsilon_t = 0$.

Consider next the AR(2) model:

$$y_t = \alpha_1 y_{t-1} + \alpha_2 y_{t-2} + \eta_t$$

Here the reparameterisation requires the creation of an additional state variable and the state-space form is:

$$y_t = \beta_{1t} \qquad \text{(measurement equation)} \tag{7.68}$$

$$\beta_{1t} = \alpha_1\beta_{1t-1} + \alpha_2\beta_{2t-1} + \eta_{1t} \quad \text{(transition equation)} \quad \textbf{(7.69a)}$$

$$\beta_{2t} = \beta_{1t-1} \quad \text{(transition equation)} \quad \textbf{(7.69b)}$$

In matrix form we have:

$$X_t = (1, 0) \qquad \beta_t = (\beta_{1t}, \beta_{2t}) \qquad \eta_t = (\eta_{1t}, \eta_{2t})$$

$$T = \begin{pmatrix} \alpha_1 & \alpha_2 \\ 1 & 0 \end{pmatrix} \qquad R = \begin{pmatrix} 1 & 0 \\ 0 & 0 \end{pmatrix}$$

The above may appear a little strange but clearly such a reparameter-isation allows the model to be expressed in state-space form. In the second case note that extra lags (y_{t-2}) in the original model are dealt with simply by defining extra state variables, $\beta_t = (\beta_{1t}, \beta_{2t})$. Note that although T_t, R_t have time subscripts, in many econometric applications these are constant matrices/vectors. The Kalman filter assumes T is known; estimation of T which contains the unknown parameters (α_1, α_2) is discussed in section (7.3) on maximum likeli-hood estimation.

The state-space form which is a first-order dynamic system (equa-tion (7.64)) has quite wide relevance in mathematics generally. For example, the analysis of the stability of a dynamic system by the calculation of eigenvalues is carried out usually on the state-space form of a model. One final point which is worth bearing in mind when considering the relationship between structural economic mod-els and the state-space form is that the latter is essentially a type of reduced form of the structural model. However it does not allow *simultaneous* interactions between the observed variables and so if the structural form is over-identified it is not possible to use the state-space form to represent uniquely the structural parameters of the model.

The Kalman filter

The intuition behind the Kalman filter is fairly simple. We have an initial guess of β_0 and its covariance P_0. In (7.63) and (7.64) we know the values of T_t, X_t, R_t, V_t and Q_t and further, we have observations on y_t. With this information the Kalman filter provides an 'optimal' forecast of the *unobserved* β_t $(t = 1, 2, T)$. The notion of 'optimal' needs to be made a little more specific. Kalman and Bucy (1961) use the minimum mean square error (MMSE) criterion as their definition of optimality. However, if we make the additional assump-tion that the error terms (ε_t, η_t) are normally distributed, then the Kalman filter also provides the maximum likelihood estimator of β_t.

The latter approach is intuitively appealing and we present the derivation of the Kalman filter from the perspective of maximum likelihood using Bayes theorem.

We have an initial estimate of β_{t-1} namely b_{t-1} (at $t - 1 = 0$ say) and an initial estimate of its covariance matrix P_{t-1}. The unbiased *predictor* of β_t based on information at $t - 1$, that is $\beta_{t/t-1}$, is given by the transition equation

$$\beta_{t/t-1} = T_t \beta_{t-1} \tag{7.70a}$$

We discussed earlier, see equation (7.45), the estimate of the covariance matrix based on information at $t - 1$:

$$\mathrm{Cov}\,(\beta_{t/t-1}) = P_{t/t-1} = (T_t P_{t-1} T_t' + R_t Q_t R_t') \tag{7.70b}$$

Equations (7.70a) and (7.70b) are the *prediction equations* for the state vector β_t and its covariance which may be calculated without any reference to the observations y_t. We can use this information at $t - 1$ to *predict* y_t at time t, and the covariance matrix of the one-step-ahead prediction errors F_t:

$$y_{t/t-1} = X_t \beta_{t/t-1}$$

The one-step-ahead prediction error $\tilde{v}_t$ is

$$\tilde{v}_t = y_t - y_{t/t-1}$$

with covariance matrix:

$$F_t = \mathrm{Cov}\,(y_t) = (X_t P_{t/t-1} X_t' + V_t) \tag{7.70c}$$

We can now state the probability density functions for β_t, ε_t and y_t:

$$p_1(\beta_t) = C_1 \exp\left[-0.5(\beta_t - \beta_{t/t-1})'(P_{t/t-1})^{-1}(\beta_t - \beta_{t/t-1})\right] \tag{7.71}$$

$$p_2(\varepsilon_t) = C_2 \exp\left[-0.5(y_t - X_t \beta_t)V_t^{-1}(y_t - X_t \beta_t)\right] \tag{7.72}$$

$$p_3(y_t) = C_3 \exp\left[-0.5(y_t - X_t \beta_{t/t-1})' F_t^{-1}(y_t - X_t \beta_{t/t-1})\right] \tag{7.73}$$

where C_1, C_2 and C_3 can be evaluated but are complex and add nothing to the present exposition.

Now the 'optimal' estimate of β_t is taken to be that value which maximises the conditional probability of β_t, given the observed values of y_t. As β_t and ε_t are uncorrelated their joint probability density function is simply

$$p_4(\beta_t, \varepsilon_t) = p_1(\beta_t).p_2(\varepsilon_t) \tag{7.74}$$

It is also possible to show that the joint probability density function of β_t and y_t is

$$p_5(\beta_t, y_t) = p_4(\beta_t, \varepsilon_t) = p_1(\beta_t) \cdot p_2(y_t - X_t\beta_t) \qquad (7.75)$$

Finally using Bayes' decision rule we can state the probability density function of β_t conditional on y_t as:

$$p_6(\beta_t/y_t) = p(\beta_t, y_t)/Pr(y_t)$$
$$= p_1(\beta_t) \cdot p_2(y_t - X_t\beta_t)/p_3(y_t) \qquad (7.76)$$

and it is this quantity which we wish to maximise by a suitable 'estimate' of β_t, which we denote b_t. The first- and second-order conditions for a maximum are that

$$\frac{\partial p_6(\beta_t|y_t)}{\partial \beta_t} = 0 \quad \text{and} \quad \frac{\partial}{\partial \beta_t}\left[\frac{\partial p_6(\beta_t|y_t)}{\partial \beta_t}\right] \text{ is negative definite.}$$

Now differentiating (7.76):

$$\frac{\partial p_6}{\partial \beta_t} = \frac{p_1(\beta_t)\dfrac{\partial}{\partial \beta_t}[p_2(y_t - X_t\beta_t)] + \left[\dfrac{\partial}{\partial \beta_t} p_1(\beta_t)\right]p_2(y_t - X_t\beta_t)}{p_3(y_t)}$$

$$= 0 \qquad (7.77)$$

which implies that

$$[p_1(\beta_t)] \frac{\partial}{\partial \beta_t} [p_2(y_t - X_t\beta_t)]$$

$$= -\frac{\partial}{\partial \beta_t} [p_1(\beta_t)][p_2(y_t - X_t\beta_t)]$$

$$(7.78)$$

Using (7.71) and (7.72) respectively we have:

$$\partial[p_1(\beta_t)]/\partial \beta_t = -P_{t|t-1}^{-1}(\beta_t - \beta_{t|t-1})p_1(\beta_t) \qquad (7.79a)$$

$$\partial[p_2(y_t - X_t\beta_t)]/\partial \beta_t = X_t'V_t'(y_t - x_t\beta_t)[p_2(y_t - X_t\beta_t)] \qquad (7.79b)$$

Substituting (7.79a) and (7.79b) in (7.78) and rearranging:

$$X_t'V_t^{-1}(y_t - X_tb_{t|t-1}) = P_{t|t-1}(b_t - b_{t|t-1}) \qquad (7.80)$$

Rearranging terms we get

$$b_t = b_{t|t-1} + [P_{t|t-1}^{-1} + X_t'V_t^{-1}X_t]^{-1}X_t'V_t^{-1}(y_t - X_tb_{t|t-1})$$

$$(7.81)$$

or by defining an updating matrix P_t as

$$P_t = (P_{t|t-1}^{-1} + X_t'V_t^{-1}X_t)^{-1} \tag{7.82}$$

then (7.81) is rewritten as

$$b_t = b_{t|t-1} + P_tX_t'V_t(y_t - X_tb_{t|t-1}) \tag{7.83}$$

Equation (7.82) may be put into a slightly more convenient form by using the matrix inversion lemma (see Harvey (1983) page 118) to yield an equivalent formula:

$$P_t = P_{t|t-1} - P_{t|t-1}X_t'F_t^{-1}X_tP_{t|t-1} \tag{7.84}$$

and this may be substituted into (7.83) which upon rearranging gives

$$b_t = b_{t|t-1} + P_{t|t-1}X_t'F_t^{-1}(y_t - X_tb_{t|t-1}) \tag{7.85}$$

Equations (7.84) and (7.85) are the standard *updating equations* of the Kalman filter. The filter works recursively through time: given an initial estimate of the state β_{t-1} and the covariance matrix P_{t-1} we can form predictions of β_t and P_t as new information on y_t becomes available. The one-step-ahead prediction errors $\tilde{v}_t = (y_t - X_tb_{t|t-1})$ and their covariance F_t, can then be used as an input into the prediction error decomposition of the likelihood function.

7.3 Maximum likelihood and the Kalman filter

Let us turn now to a specific practical example. Consider using the Kalman filter and the state-space form to estimate the AR(2) model above. When we derive the prediction and updating equations for the Kalman filter we assume the covariance matrices (Q_t, V_t) are known as are the matrices X_t, T_t and R_t and we have observations on y_t. In our AR(2) example we will assume Q and V are fixed scalar covariance matrices $Q = \sigma_q^2 I$, $V = \sigma_\varepsilon^2 I$, and we noted that $T = (\alpha_1, \alpha_2)$. Clearly, σ_q^2, σ_ε^2 and T are *not* known, these are precisely what we wish to estimate. (Note that X_t and R_t *are* fixed and known.) However, in using the Kalman filter we can assume any initial values for α_1, α_2, σ_q^2 and σ_ε^2 and derive recursive values for b_t, P_t and $\tilde{v}_t$, *conditional on these initial guesses*. Hence, these $\tilde{v}_t$, F_t, Q_t, V_t and of course y_t can be fed into the prediction error decomposition of the likelihood function and a suitable maximisation routine used to choose that combination of α_1, α_2, σ_q^2, σ_ε^2 that maximises the likelihood. The Kalman filter here merely acts as a useful *algorithm* to yield the likelihood function. This procedure is summarised in Figure 7.1 for our AR(2) model.

What is known and fixed (e.g. X_t, R_t for our AR(2) model) throughout the maximisation procedure and what is to be maximised (i.e. $Q_t = \sigma_q^2 I$, $\Omega_t = \sigma_\varepsilon^2 I$, $T_t = f(\alpha_1, \alpha_2)$) varies depending on the problem under consideration. But the procedure remains the same. Once the model is cast in state-space form and starting values provided, the Kalman filter generates the inputs to the likelihood function which can then be maximised by the numerical optimisation procedures described in Chapter 2. This makes the Kalman filter a particularly powerful tool, as it is possible to estimate both the unobserved part of a model (such as a time-varying parameter) or an expectations variable (e.g. stochastic trend) plus the parameters of the system, (e.g. the variances) in one operation.

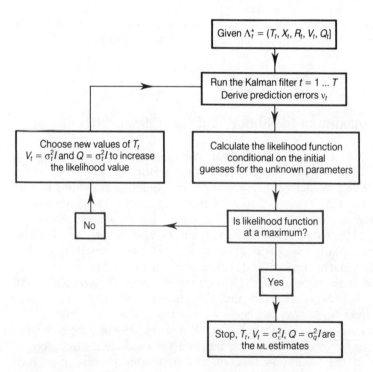

Figure 7.1 The logical structure of maximum likelihood estimation with the Kalman filter.

Smoothing

We have discussed how the Kalman filter yields 'optimal' predictors of the state vector $b_{t+n|t-1}$ based on information at $t-1$. The Kalman filter may also be used to produce *smoothed estimates*. These are the best estimates of β_t, given *all information*, $t = 1, 2, \ldots T$ in the sample. 'Smoothing' is a process whereby we 'look back' from $t = T$, to obtain best estimates for $T - 1$, $T - 2$, etc. On the last 'round' of the Kalman filter we obtain b_T and its covariance matrix P_T (at $t = T$). The smoothing equations are recursive equations that work backwards from b_T, P_T. If $b_{t|T}$ and $P_{t|T}$ denote the smoothed estimator and its covariance then the smoothing equations are:

$$b_{t|T} = b_t + P_t^*(b_{t+1|T} - T_{t+1}b_t) \tag{7.86}$$

and

$$P_{t|T} = P_t + P_t^*(P_{t+1|T} - P_{t+1|t})P_t^* \tag{7.87}$$

where

$$P_t^* = P_t T'_{t+1|t} P_{t+1|t}^{-1} \qquad t = T - 1, T - 2, \ldots 1$$

and $b_{T|T} = b_T$ and $P_{T|T} = P_T$. There is little or no 'intuitive feel' one can give to these smoothing recursions. However, in terms of the stochastic trend model, say for income y_t, then smoothed estimates of π_t may be viewed as a measure of permanent income. In the case of time-varying parameters, the smoothed estimates may be interpreted as the best estimates obtainable with all the data available, even though the parameters are still assumed to vary over time.

Time-varying parameter models and the state-space form

It is possible to cast many models in state-space form. We have already demonstrated this for some ARMA models, the unobservable components/stochastic trend model and for recursive least squares. We now analyse how two forms of time-varying parameter model may be cast in state-space form. The Kalman filter and the prediction error decomposition of the likelihood function may then be used to estimate these models.

The state-space formulation (7.3) and (7.4) provides a very general form of time-varying parameter model and in fact this may be further generalised by adding a matrix of constant terms to the transition equation. In practical applications such a general model will usually prove unmanageable and some simplification is required. Consider first, the *random coefficient model*. Here the parameters have a constant mean value but are allowed to stochastically deviate around the mean. The state-space form is:

Random coefficient model

(a) *Measurement equation*

$$y_t = X_t \beta_t + \varepsilon_t \tag{7.88}$$

where β_t is an $(m \times 1)$ unknown state vector: $\beta_t = (\beta_{1t}, \ \beta_{2t}, \ \ldots \ \beta_{mt})$, X_t is $(T \times m)$ data matrix.

(b) *Transition equations*

$$\beta_{1t} = \phi_1 + \eta_{1t}$$
$$\vdots \tag{7.89}$$
$$\beta_{mt} = \phi_2 + \eta_{mt}$$

Note that $\phi_i = (i = 1, 2, \ldots m)$ are constants and $\varepsilon_t, \eta_{1t} \ldots \eta_{mt}$ are normally distributed error terms with zero mean, constant variance (and are independent of each other). This formulation allows the parameters to depart from their expected values of $\beta_i (i = 1, 2, \ldots m)$, but this departure is temporary, as at any point in time the expected value of β_{it} is ϕ_i, a constant. So trend-like behaviour in the parameters is ruled out. The transition equation is straightforward and for $m = 2$ is:

$$\beta_t = T\beta_{t-1} + \phi + \eta_t$$

where

$$T = \begin{pmatrix} 0 & 0 \\ 0 & 0 \end{pmatrix}, \quad \beta_t = (\beta_{1t}, \beta_{2t}), \quad \phi = (\phi_1, \phi_2)$$

Our second-time varying parameter model might be referred to as a *'systematically varying parameter model'*. In this case the parameters follow a random walk, which is much less restrictive than the random coefficient model. We have:

Systematically varying parameters

(a) *Measurement equation*

$$y_t = X_t \beta_t + \varepsilon_t \tag{7.90}$$

(b) *Transition equation*

$$\beta_{1t} = \beta_{1t-1} + \eta_{1t}$$
$$\vdots \qquad\qquad (7.91)$$
$$\beta_{mt} = \beta_{mt-1} + \eta_{mt}$$

This model allows considerable scope for systematic variation in the parameters but note that β_{it-1} does not affect β_{jt} $(i \neq j)$, so the T matrix in (7.4) is assumed to be diagonal. It is also usual to assume that Q_t is diagonal. The assumption of diagonality may be easily relaxed, although it is often not wise to do so. A further restriction in (7.91) is that the variation in β_t is random rather than being caused by some observed variable. If for example we have a prior belief that the random parameter β_{1t} is related to some observed variable y_{2t} then we should build this into the estimation process. This can be done by making one of the measurement equations non-stochastic. A simple two-variable example will demonstrate this.

Measurement equation

$$y_{1t} = X_{1t}\beta_{1t} + \varepsilon_t$$
$$y_{2t} = \beta_{2t} \qquad\qquad (7.92)$$

Transition equation

$$\beta_{1t} = T_1\beta_{2t-1} + \eta_{1t}$$
$$\beta_{2t} = \beta_{2t-1} + \eta_{2t} \qquad\qquad (7.93)$$

Note that the second measurement equation in (7.92) has no error term (or its variance is zero) so $\beta_{2t} = y_{2t}$. In (7.93) β_{1t} is a function of β_{2t-1}, so by including the extra measurement equation we are able to build the prior information about the dependence of β_{1t} on y_{2t} (i.e. $\beta_{1t} = T_1 y_{2t-1} + \eta_{1t}$) into the transition equation.

7.4 Applied work using the Kalman filter

A model of the exchange rate

Our first example of estimation using time-varying parameters is a model of the exchange rate. Hall (1987) presents a structural equation for the log of the real exchange rate:

$$E_t = A_1 E_{t+1}^e + A_2 E_{t-1} + A_3 r_t + A_4 r_{t-1}$$
$$+ A_5 TB_t + A_6 TB_{t-1} \tag{7.94}$$

where E_t is the log of the real (Sterling) effective exchange rate, r_t is the real interest rate differential between UK short-term rates and world rates (proxied by the real three-month Eurodollar rate and the real three-month Treasury Bill rate) and TB the log of the ratio of exports to imports which is a measure of the real trade balance. The theoretical derivation of this equation will not be repeated here, it may be derived in a number of ways. For example, Hall (1987b) uses a stock equilibrium model with government intervention whereas Curry and Hall (1989) use a model which characterises capital markets as exhibiting both stock and flow elements in equilibrium. At a pragmatic level it may even be thought of as a general encompassing model of a wide range of models, for example if $A_6 = A_5 = A_2 = 0$, then the model reduces to the open arbitrage model (see Cuthbertson and Taylor 1987, Chapter 5, or Cuthbertson and Gripaios 1992 Chapters 5 and 6).

Earlier work estimated (7.94) under the Rational Expectations Hypothesis (REH) using the errors in variables (IV) methods described in Chapter 6 for the expectations variable E_{t+1}^e. Here we concentrate on constructing a learning model for the expected exchange rate which has time-varying parameters. We can then use the forecasts of E_{t+1} as inputs into the structural exchange rate equation (7.94).

We may rearrange (7.94) to give

$$E_{t+1}^e = B_1 E_t + B_2 E_{t-1} + B_3 r_t + B_4 r_{t-1}$$
$$+ B_5 TB_t + B_6 TB_{t-1} \tag{7.95}$$

Hall (1987) assumes that the reduced form equations for r_t and T_t are:

$$r_t = C_1(L) r_{t-1} + C_2(L) \text{GDP}_{t-1} + C_3(L) P_{t-1} \tag{7.96}$$

$$TB_t = D_1(L) TB_{t-1} + D_2(L) \text{GDP}_{t-1} + D_3(L) OP_{t-1}$$
$$+ D_4(L) E_{t-1} \tag{7.97}$$

where OP is the log of real oil prices, P is the rate of domestic inflation (i.e. the change in the log of the RPI) and GDP is the log of the real output measurement of GDP. C_i, D_i are polynomial lag operators.

Hall (1987) then demonstrates that equations (7.95)–(7.97) yield the following equation for the evolution of the exchange rate:

$$(E_t - E_{t-1}) = B_{ot} + B_{it}(OP_{t-2} - OP_{t-3}) + B_{2t}(r_{t-2})$$

$$+ B_{3t}(\dot{P}_{t-2} - \dot{P}_{t-3}) + B_{4t}(\text{GDP}_{t-2} - \text{GDP}_{t-3})$$
$$+ B_{5t}(T_{t-2} - T_{t-3}) + B_{7t}E_{t-2} \tag{7.98}$$

Because equations (7.96) and (7.97) are 'rules of thumb' used by agents when forecasting τ_t and TB_t, Hall assumes the parameters are likely to be time-varying and hence the B_i coefficients in (7.98) have 't' subscripts.

Note that all lagged information is dated $t - 2$ or greater so that when we forecast E_{t+1} in (7.95) the information set will be dated at $t-1$. The time-varying parameters are assumed to be generated by a random walk:

$$B_{it} = B_{it-1} + \eta_{it} \tag{7.99}$$

The measurement equation is (7.98) with $y_t = (E_t - E_{t-1})$ as the dependent variable and the known X_t matrix consisting of the RHS variables in (7.98). The state vector β_t is the vector of time varying parameters B_i ($i = 0, 1, 2, \ldots 7$) and the transition equation(s) are given in (7.93).

As demonstrated in equations (7.84) and (7.85) above we can apply the Kalman filter to (7.98) and (7.99), conditional on the variance of the error term in (7.98) and the covariance matrix for (7.99) which is assumed to be diagonal. In fact the likelihood function may be concentrated so that only the *ratio* of the variance of (each of) the state equation(s) to the measurement equation is estimated. Hall finds that the residuals from the measurement equation (7.98) are reasonably well behaved, the Ljung–Box tests for serial correlation are $\text{LB}(1) = 0.1$, $\text{LB}(2) = 2.4$, $\text{LB}(4) = 2.5$, $\text{LB}(8) = 5.6$, $\text{LB}(16) = 17.3$ which indicates a lack of serial correlation in the error process. The latter suggests that there are no important variables omitted from (7.98).

Hall (1987) shows the graphs of some of the time-varying parameters which will not be included here to save space. The overall conclusions are that all the parameters exhibit marked variation over time with no strong tendency to converge on a stable parameter value; they also show a tendency to jump markedly in 1978. Interpreting the movement in the parameter values is not straightforward as we must remember that they reflect market expectations not underlying structural parameters. For example, in the early part of the period a positive interest rate differential seems to be associated with an expected rise in the exchange rate; this effect seems to disappear during the 1980s. Part of the explanation for this may be given by a corresponding movement in the coefficient on the lagged exchange rate from zero to nearly minus one. When this coefficient is zero the exchange rate is a first difference formulation so that it is essentially a random walk. When it is minus one the equation determines the level of the exchange rate rather than its change. An intepretation of these coefficients movements is as follows. As the commitment of the government towards controlling inflation strengthened in the 1980s then the foreign exchange (FOREX) market interpreted this as a change in the exchange rate regime such that a particular level of the exchange rate was seen as a target, in order to aid the fight against inflation stemming from exchange rate changes.

The fact that there is no serial correlation in the errors is clearly one requirement for the forecast from the learning model to be weakly rational, but we clearly need to check that the expectations series generated by the model is not consistently biased. We may do this by first generating the one-step-ahead forecast of the model and then testing this for biasedness relative to the outturn. The one-step-ahead forecast of the model is generated as:

$$E_{t+1}^e = E_{t-1} + \sum_{i=1}^{7} B_{it} X_{it-i} + B_{ot} \tag{7.100}$$

where the X_i are all the variables given in (7.98). This series for E_{t+1}^e was then subject to the following tests:

$$E_{t+1} = 1.000898 \ E_{t+1}^e \tag{7.101}$$
$$(0.0017)$$

$$E_{t+1} - E_{t+1}^e = 0.00451 \tag{7.102}$$
$$(0.0080)$$

$$E_{t+1} = 1.49 + 0.678 \ E_{t+1}^e \tag{7.103}$$
$$(0.45) \ (0.098)$$

where () = standard error of the coefficient. Equations (7.101) and (7.102) are simple tests of unbiasedness. In (7.101) the coefficient is not significantly different from one and hence we do not reject unbiasedness. The latter conclusion is reinforced by (7.102) where the constant is not significantly different from zero. Equation (7.103) is a little more complex under the null hypothesis that E_{t+1}^e is an unbiased *and* efficient forecast of E_{t+1}; the constant in (7.103) should equal zero and the coefficient on E_{t+1}^e should equal unity (Wallis 1989, Mincer and Zarnowitz 1969). Both of these conditions are statistically rejected so we may conclude that while the learning model is unbiased it is not fully efficient. This is a satisfactory result since weak REH requires unbiasedness but only the strong form of REH implies efficiency. It is therefore not surprising that a '*partial information'* learning model as used here would fail to meet the efficiency requirement.

Having derived the expectations series from our 'learning model', the structural exchange rate equation (7.94) is estimated. This is done by estimating a three-equation system using three-stage least squares where the three equations are the exchange rate equation itself, the interest rate (r) and trade balance equation (T). In addition, E^e_{t+1} is specified as endogenous in the estimation. The trade balance and interest rate equations are not a central concern of this paper so they will not be discussed here, they should rather be thought of as instrumenting equations which help to give consistent and efficient estimates of the exchange rate parameters. Applying this system estimation technique then gives the parameter estimates shown in Table 7.1 for the exchange rate equation: a restricted and an unrestricted model are presented.

The two restrictions on the model, $A_2 = 1 - A_1$ and $A_3 = 0$ are accepted easily with a quasi likelihood rate test statistic of 1.32 (distributed as $\chi^2(2)$). Both the interest rate effect (A_4) and the trade effect $(A_5 + A_6)$ are correctly signed and significant. The summary statistics indicate an absence of serial correlation and heteroscedasticity in the error process. Structural stability is clearly an important

Table 7.1 Estimation of a structural model of the exchange rate

	Unrestricted model	Restricted model
A_1	0.55 (4.8)	0.53 (4.8)
A_2	0.45 (3.9)	$(1 - A_1)$
A_3	−0.14 (0.4)	− −
A_4	0.73 (2.8)	0.66 (3.8)
A_5	0.35 (3.3)	$(T_{-2} - T_{-3})$
		0.35 (3.6)
A_6	−0.20 (1.9)	0.16 (2.9)
σ	0.022	0.017
DW	1.92	2.06
BP(1)[1]	0.03	0.07
BP(2)[1]	2.8	2.0
BP(4)[1]	4.5	4.0
BP(8)[1]	12.9	11.5
BP(1)[2]	0.8	0.8
BP(2)[2]	1.6	1.2
BP(4)[2]	2.9	2.7
BP(8)[2]	4.2	5.0
		Data period: 1978 Q2–1988 Q1

Note: BP(.)[1] is the Box–Pierce test carried out on the residuals of the equation. BP(.)[2] is the Box–Pierce test carried out on the squared residuals of the equation.

requirement of any equation although it is not often found in exchange rate models. Assessing structural stability is not straightforward when the estimation process is 3SLS and the number of observations is fairly limited. In order to gain some insight into the stability of the model recursive 3SLS estimation is performed over the period 1985 Q1–1988 Q1. The overall impression is that the model is reasonably stable, with the parameter estimates never moving outside their standard error bounds.

Thus the use of a learning model based on a time-varying parameter model for the exchange rate yields reasonable results when incorporated in a structural exchange-rate equation.

7.5   Summary

The Kalman filter involves some specialist terminology and concepts which have been discussed widely in this section and are sumarised below. The Kalman filter recursive algorithms may be interpreted in a number of ways because they constitute an optimal updating procedure for a wide class of models. The Kalman filter itself consists of a set of convenient recursive formulae which allow one to calculate the one-step-ahead prediction errors $\tilde{v}_t$ and their variance-covariance matrix F_t (or scalar, $\sigma^2 f_t$). However, to apply these recursive algorithms (i.e. updating and prediction equations) one must be able to express the model in state-space form (the measurement and transition equations). The Kalman filter itself does not estimate the unknown parameters of the model; it merely provides $\tilde{v}_t$ and F_t *conditional on* these unknown parameters. However, the prediction error decomposition of the likelihood function utilises $\tilde{v}_t$ and F_t and hence conventional maximisation routines can then be used to determine the unknown parameters. For certain models (for example generalised stochastic trend model) the Kalman filter recursive algorithms also provide an intuitive insight into the working of the statistical model.

The procedure used when estimating a model with the *aid of* the Kalman filter is (a) express the model in state-space form, (b) generate $\tilde{v}_t$ and F_t using the Kalman filter recursions, (c) use $\tilde{v}_t$ and F_t to set up the prediction error decomposition of the likelihood functions, and (d) maximise the latter with respect to the unknown parameters. We have seen that the Kalman filter is useful in estimating variable parameter models, unobservable components, standard ARMA and least squares problems.

Notes

1. Our aim is to bring together different strands of a diverse literature, so that applied economists can understand and utilise the Kalman filter. The main results are all available in the technical literature, indeed the Kalman filter first appeared as early as 1960 (Kalman 1960). The basic 'source material' for this chapter is to be found in Lawson (1980, 1984), Athans (1974), Duncan and Horn (1972), Diderrich (1985), Harrison and Stevens (1976), Harvey and Todd (1983), Harvey (1984a, 1984b), and, most notably, Harvey (1984c).

2. The proof is as follows:

$$\Delta y_t = \varepsilon_t - (1 - \theta)\varepsilon_{t-1} \tag{i}$$

Taking expectations of (i):

$$y^e_{t/t-1} = y_{t-1} - (1 - \theta)\varepsilon_{t-1} \tag{ii}$$

Rearranging (i) using the lag operator L:

$$\varepsilon_t = \Delta y_t/[1 - (1 - \theta)L] \tag{iii}$$

Substituting for ε_{t-1} from (iii) in (ii) and rearranging:

$$y^e_{t/t-1} = y_{t-1} - (1 - \theta)\Delta y_{t-1}/[1 - (1 - \theta)L]$$

or

$$y^e_{t/t-1} - y^e_{t-1/t-2} = \theta(y_{t-1} - y^e_{t-1/t-2})$$

3. This example is taken directly from Lawson (1984).
4. An alternative method of illustrating the stochastic trend nature of the model is to take first differences of (7.8a) and substitute for $\Delta \pi_t$ from (7.8b), yielding:

$$\Delta y_t = \gamma_{t-1} + (\zeta_t + \varepsilon_t)$$

where γ_{t-1} is the stochastic trend growth in y.
5. In the most general form of the Kalman filter the matrices X, T, R, V and Q may be time-varying. This makes little difference to the analytics of the derivation of the Kalman filter as will be seen in section (7.2).

Appendix

Lemma 1

To show:

$$P_1^{-1} = (P_0^*)^{-1} + (X'V^{-1}X) \tag{A1}$$

$$b_1 = b_0^* + K(Y - Xb_0^*) \tag{A2}$$

Given:

$$K = P_1 X' V^{-1} \tag{A3}$$

$$P_1 = (X'_* V_*^{-1} X_*)^{-1} \tag{A4}$$

$$b_1 = P_1(X'_* V_*^{-1} Y_*) \tag{A5}$$

$$\begin{pmatrix} Y \\ b_0^* \end{pmatrix} = \begin{pmatrix} X \\ I \end{pmatrix} \beta + \begin{pmatrix} \varepsilon \\ \omega_0 \end{pmatrix} \tag{A6}$$

or

$$Y_* = X_* \beta + \varepsilon_* \tag{A7}$$

where

$$V_* = \begin{pmatrix} V & O \\ O & P_0^* \end{pmatrix} \tag{A8}$$

Given (A4) and the definitions (A6)–(A8), the (A1) is easily derived:

$$P_1 = \left((X', I') \begin{pmatrix} V^{-1} & O \\ O & P_0^{*-1} \end{pmatrix} \begin{pmatrix} X \\ I \end{pmatrix} \right)^{-1}$$

$$= (X' V^{-1} X + P_0^{*-1})^{-1} \tag{A9}$$

To derive (A2), note that using (A5) and the definitions (A3), (A4) and (A6)–(A8) we have:

$$b_1 = P_1(X', I') \begin{pmatrix} V^{-1} & O \\ O & P_0^{*-1} \end{pmatrix} \begin{pmatrix} Y \\ b_0^* \end{pmatrix}$$

$$= (P_1 X' V^{-1}) Y + P_1 P_0^{*-1} b_0^*$$

$$= KY - P_1 P_0^{*-1} b_0^* \tag{A10}$$

Concentrating on the term $P_1 P_0^{*-1}$, using (A1) and (A3):

$$P_1 P_0^{*-1} = P_1(P_1^{-1} - X'V^{-1}X) = (I - KX) \tag{A11}$$

Substituting (A11) in (A10) completes the proof:

$$b_1 = KY - (I - KX) b_0^* = b_0^* + K(Y - X b_0^*) \tag{A12}$$

Lemma 2

To show:

$$K = P_1 X' V^{-1} = P_0^* X'(V + X P_0^* X') \tag{A13}$$

From (A11):

$$P_1 = (I - KX)P_0^*$$ (A14)

Substitute (A14) in (A3):

$$K = (I - KX)P_0^* X' V^{-1}$$
$$K (I + XP_0^* X' V^{-1}) = P_0^* X' V^{-1}$$ (A15)

Rearranging (A15) completes the proof:

$$K = P_0^* X' (V + XP_0^* X')^{-1} = P_0^* X' F^{-1}$$

where

$$F = (V + XP_0^* X')$$

8
Using large non-linear models

One of the main practical applications of econometric work is the construction and use of systems of equations in the form of econometric models. The earlier parts of this book are typical of econometric theory generally in that it concentrates largely on linear systems and equations. So suppose we have the following set of simultaneous equations.

$$AY = BX + u \tag{8.1}$$

where Y is a vector of N endogenous variables, X is a vector of M exogenous variable, u is a vector of N independently normally distributed error terms with zero mean, A is an $N \times N$ matrix of parameters, and B is an $N \times M$ matrix of parameters. This model can be solved analytically to give

$$Y = A^{-1}BX + \varepsilon \tag{8.2}$$

where

$$\varepsilon = (A^{-1})u$$

ε will be normally distributed with $E(\varepsilon) = 0$ and a covariance matrix we denote S.

The simulation properties of the model may easily be calculated as

$$\frac{\partial Y_i}{\partial x_j} = a_{ij}$$

where a_{ij} is the i, j element of $A^{-1}B$.

If the parameter matrices A, B are estimated then the uncertainty attached to a given simulation is given by the standard error of the reduced form coefficient a_{ij} and this may be calculated directly from the covariance matrices of A and B.

For a linear system we can therefore derive analytical solutions for the model and its simulation properties, as well as fully defining the stochastic nature of the model solution. Unfortunately almost all models which are designed for practical use are non-linear and do not fall within the scope of the analysis outlined above. Even when the modeller restricts himself to using standard linear estimation techniques the use of data transformations in estimation inevitably produces a final model which cannot be put into a linear framework. Often linear estimation is carried out on logarithms of the variables for a number of valid reasons. For example, it may reduce heteroscedasticity, or a constant elasticity relationship may often be regarded as more theoretically reasonable than a linear formulation, etc. However it is not generally possible to specify the whole model in logarithmic form. For example, we cannot express linear identities in this form (e.g. the GDP identity). Thus there is no transformation of the whole model which allows it to be put in the form of equation (8.1).

Once the linear form is abandoned then we must also abandon the whole range of solution techniques described above. It is no longer possible to derive explicit general solutions to the model or explicit results about the simulation or stochastic properties of the model. Instead, a range of numerical techniques has grown up for the solution and analysis of non-linear models. In this Chapter we outline a number of these techniques. In section 8.1 we examine the solution methods for deterministic models; section 8.2 considers deterministic simulation methodology; and in section 8.3 we deal with problems posed by rational expectations. The consequences of the stochastic nature of models are addressed in section 8.4 and in section 8.5 we give a brief description of optimal control.

8.1 Model solution procedures

Most econometric models which are used either for forecasting or for simulation are both large and non-linear. It is therefore necessary to resort to a numerical procedure in order to determine the solution to the model. There are two main types of solution technique which are available, Newton and Gauss–Seidel (see Froeberg 1981 for a general mathematical exposition). Of these two approaches Gauss–Seidel has been almost universally adopted as the most practical for large econometric models and will be the only method discussed here.

In this section we will discuss the solution of what might be termed 'conventional' econometric models, that is, those which do not include explicit expectations of future endogenous variables. In section 8.3 we will discuss extensions of the standard solution techniques to allow for full model consistent expectations.

The Gauss–Seidel solution technique

We represent an n-equation model in the following notation where a linear form is adopted for convenience without loss of generality.

$$Y_i = A_i Y + B_i X \qquad i = 1, 2, \ldots, n \qquad (8.3)$$

so that there are n endogenous variables (Y) and m exogenous or predetermined variables (X) and A_i, B_i are suitably dimensioned matrices. The Gauss–Seidel method proceeds by first assigning a starting value to the Y vector. In practice this is often the actual values of the Ys in the previous period. It then uses these values to solve the equations, *one at a time*. After each single equation is solved, that solution value is used to replace the initial guess for that variable. So if $\bar{Y}$ is the initial guess and Y^* is the new value, then for any equation:

$$Y_j^* = A_{Kj} Y^* + A_{Mj} \bar{Y} + B_j X \qquad (8.4)$$

Where

$$A_{Kj} = \begin{cases} A_{Kj} & K < j \\ 0 & K > j \end{cases}$$

$$A_{Mj} = \begin{cases} 0 & M > j \\ A_{Mj} & M > j \end{cases}$$

That is to say, we work our way through the model equations sequentially solving each in turn. Any other endogenous variables in a specific equation take either their original starting value $\bar{Y}$ if they are higher in the ordering (and so have not yet been solved) or they take their new solution values Y^* if they are lower in the ordering (i.e. they have already been solved). This process of continual updating distinguishes the Gauss–Seidel technique from other schemes such as the Jacobi method where the whole model is solved before any updating takes place.

When all the equations have been solved, a check is made according to some convergence criteria on $|\bar{Y}_i - Y_i^*|$. If the two estimates of each Y are satisfactorily close a solution to the model has been found; if not, then the Y^* are redefined as $\bar{Y}$ and the process is repeated for another iteration. A more complete exposition of the Gauss–Seidel method may be found in Faddeev and Faddeva (1963), and an early example of its application to econometric models is Norman (1967).

In the linear case described above we know that if a solution exists it is unique and that a solution will exist if all the equations are linearly independent. The Gauss–Seidel technique in practice is not guaranteed to find such a solution even when it exists and is unique. The crucial factors in the success of the Gauss–Seidel approach is the order in which the equations are solved (this is referred to as 'the ordering' of the model) and the normalisation of the equations (that is, which variables are chosen as being the dependent variable for a particular equation).

There are a number of variants on the Gauss–Seidel technique which have received attention. A good survey of the recent literature may be found in Hughes-Hallett (1981). If we restate (8.3) in a more compact form as

$$AY = B \tag{8.5}$$

then the iteration procedure may be characterised as

$$Y^{S+1} = GY^S + C \tag{8.6}$$

with some arbitrary starting value Y^0. The various iteration procedures may be nested within this framework by varying the construction of G and C. If we define $A = (P - Q)$ then $G = P^{-1}Q$ and $C = P^{-1}b$. The way the A matrix is split determines the exact form of the iteration procedure. The simplest procedure is the Jacobi iteration which defines

$$P = \begin{cases} A_{iJ} & \text{if } I = J \\ O & \text{if } I \neq J \end{cases} \tag{8.7}$$

The Gauss–Seidel iteration is produced by setting

$$P = (D - E)$$

$$D = \begin{cases} A_{ij} & \text{if } i = J \\ O & \text{if } i \neq J \end{cases} \quad \text{and} \quad E = \begin{cases} -A_{ij} & \text{if } i < J \\ O & \text{if } i > J \end{cases}$$

$$\tag{8.8}$$

The successive over-relaxation iterative method is defined by

$$P = \frac{1}{\alpha} D(I - \alpha D^{-1}E) \tag{8.9}$$

where D and E are defined above.

A particularly important variant on these techniques allows for the incorporation of a damping factor γ in the following way:

$$Y^{(S+1)} = \gamma(GY^{(S)} + C) + (1 - \gamma)Y^S \qquad (8.10)$$

When this is applied to the Gauss–Seidel iteration (8.8), the resulting technique is often called 'fast' Gauss–Seidel. The importance of this development is that while (8.6) can be shown to converge only if the spectral radius of $G < 1$ (see Young 1971), (8.10) can be shown to converge on the much weaker assumption that the real parts of the eigenvalues of G are all greater ($\gamma < 0$) or less ($\gamma > 0$) than one (see Hughes-Hallett 1981).

To make some of these ideas a little clearer, a simple two-dimensional example of the Gauss–Seidel technique is given in Figure 8.1. An initial value is assigned to x_2 of x_2^A; the first equation is then solved for x_1 using x_2^A; this yields x_1^A. This value is used to solve the second equation to yield x_2^B. The new value of x_2^B is then used to solve the first equation again and this finds x_1^B. The solution procedure then converges in the direction of the arrows towards the solution. If the equations had been normalised arbitrarily in the reverse way so that equation 2 had been solved first for x_1, the algorithm would have moved away from the solution and would have diverged indefinitely.

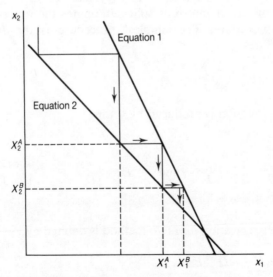

Figure 8.1   The Gauss–Seidel solution procedure.

8.2   Types of deterministic model solution

Users of large models have developed a range of different types of model solutions which are useful both in analysing a model and in using models in an applied framework. These techniques have not been discussed widely in the literature and so we will provide a summary of the more basic procedures here.

Suppose we write an N equation model in the following notation (again linearity is used for simplicity without loss of generality).

$$Y = B(L)Y + \gamma(L)Y + CZ \qquad (8.11)$$

where Y is the vector of N endogenous variables, $B(L)$ is a matrix lag polynomial $(L = 0, 1, 2, \ldots)$ where all the leading diagonals are zero, $\gamma(L)$ is a matrix lag polynomial $(L = 1, 2, \ldots)$ where all off diagonal elements are zero and C is an $N \times M$ vector of coefficients on the M exogenous variable Z. In the notation $\gamma(L)Y$ will contain all the lagged dependent variables in each equation and $B(L)Y$ will contain all the lagged and contemporaneous endogenous (but not dependent) variables. This split simply isolates the lagged dependent variables in each equation in the γ matrix.

We may then define a dynamic solution to this model as Y^1 where

$$Y^1 = B(L)Y^1 + \gamma(L)Y^1 + CZ \qquad (8.12)$$

That is, all lagged and contemporaneous endogenous variables take their solution values.

A very useful form of solution is defined as:

$$Y^2 = B(L)\bar{Y} + \gamma(L)\bar{Y} + CZ \qquad (8.13)$$

where $\bar{Y}$ is a given value of Y, usually an historical realisation. A model solution such as (8.13) is often referred to as a single-equation residual solution, all the inputs to each equation take some known value. Each equation is therefore treated in isolation and $Y - Y^2$ will define a vector of single equation residuals which are exactly analogous to the residuals produced during estimation of a linear model.

A single-equation residual solution is particularly useful in assessing the recent performance of a model equation and it is a useful guide in tracking down the sources of errors which occur during a dynamic solution. If we define the dynamic residuals produced by a solution such as (8.12) as $U^D = Y - Y^1$ and the single equation residual as $U^S = Y - Y^2$ then it may easily be shown that for a linear model the information in U^D and U^S is identical. Each presents the same information in a different form; it is however, often much easier to deal with one than the other.

An important use for the single equation residuals U^S is in constructing a model simulation. Suppose we wish to increase Z by Δ then the solution outlined in (8.12) will become

$$Y^3 = B(L)Y^3 + \gamma(L)Y^3 + C(Z + \Delta)$$

The simulation effect will therefore be

$$Y^3 - Y^1 = B(L)(Y^3 - Y^1) + \gamma(L)(Y^3 - Y^1) + C\Delta$$

and the effect of Δ may be expressed as

$$Y^3 - Y^1 = [I - B(L) - \gamma(L)]^{-1}C\Delta \tag{8.14}$$

In the linear case defined above the simulation effect is a constant value and does not depend on the initial condition Y^1. For a general non-linear model this will not be true and so it is often desirable to calculate a simulation from a base which is particularly relevant, perhaps the actual historical data. In order to do this, Y^1, the model solution, must exactly reproduce the base data Y, which can be done by adding the *single-equation* residuals (U^S) to the dynamic model solution. This can be seen as:

$$Y = B(L)Y^* + \gamma(L)Y^* + CZ + U^S$$

$$Y = B(L)Y^* + \gamma(L)Y^* + CZ + Y - Y^2 \tag{8.15}$$

and by the substituting for Y^2 from (8.13) and rearranging, we get

$$(Y^* - Y) = B(L)(Y^* - Y) + \gamma(L)(Y^* - Y)$$

The solution to the equation is obviously $Y^* = Y$ and so the dynamic solution to the model with U^S added is Y (the base values used to calculate the single-equation residual). This result holds for both the linear and the non-linear case, the only problem being that in the non-linear case the solution to the model may not be unique.

A final solution method which is sometimes used as a model diagnostic is the *single-equation dynamic* solution, which may be characterised by

$$Y^4 = B(L)\bar{Y} + \gamma(L)Y^4 + CZ \tag{8.16}$$

where $\gamma(L)$ is a matrix lag polynomial with zero off diagonal terms and $B(L)$ is a matrix lag polynomial with zeros on the diagonal. This is exactly analogous to the dynamic forecast produced by a single equation. Each equation is treated in isolation and equation solution values are entered as lagged values only in the 'own' equation (but not in other equations). This may be a useful way of isolating dynamic instability in a model or detecting the source of a particularly bad dynamic performance.

8.3 Rational expectations and non-linear models

In this section we examine some of the special problems which arise when a model includes explicit expectations terms and when we wish to solve the model on the basis of model consistent or 'rational' expectations. The introduction of such terms raises both conceptual and practical problems. We will first discuss some of the conceptual problems of using expectations in non-linear models and will then examine some of the practical suggestions for dealing with the solution problem and the need for terminal conditions.

Before embarking on the details of model simulation and solution, there is an important conceptual problem which must be considered. The theoretical literature about rational expectations has evolved almost solely within a framework of small linear models. Within this framework it is accepted as axiomatic that a rational individual is interested in forming an estimate of the expected values of *all* relevant variables. That is to say, he will try to arrive at an estimate of the conditional mean of the probability distribution. Now, as the *deterministic* forecast of a linear model with normally distributed error processes coincides with the conditional mean of the probability distributor of the model, there is no conflict and the deterministic model solution may be used. Unfortunately (as discussed below) this is not the case for a non-linear model. The deterministic forecast of a stochastic non-linear model is not the mean of the probability distribution of the model. If the model represents a non-linear mapping from the error terms to the endogenous variables then the deterministic forecast may have no well-defined place on the probability distribution. This train of reasoning leads us towards carrying out stochastic simulations so as to *estimate* the *mean forecast* of the model. There is, however, a further complication; the expected values of any non-linear *identities* in the model are not given by the expected values of their component parts. Thus the expected real exchange rate will not equal the expected nominal exchange rate deflated by some expected relative price.

Of course, it does not follow that a set of expectations has to be consistent. If individuals have a quadratic loss function in their forecast errors and they use a non-linear model and are fully rational, then they should act on the basis of a *mutually inconsistent* set of expectations. Indeed, as we are dealing with many individuals, it may well be reasonable to think of these individuals as being different groups which hold inconsistent expectations about a number of variables. An exporting firm may form expectations about the real exchange rate while individuals hold price expectations and agents in financial markets have an expectation of the nominal exchange rate. All these expectations can be optimal, based on the same model and information set, and yet be inconsistent with each other.

These problems are perhaps most easily presented by stating a general non-linear model in the following form. Let

$$Y_t = f(Y_i, Y_j^e, X_k, B, \Omega) \tag{8.17}$$

$$i = 0, 1, \ldots t, \; j = t + 1, \ldots, T, \; k = 0, 1, \ldots, T$$

where Y_t is a set of N endogenous variables, X is a set of M exogenous variables, B is the full parameter set of the model and Ω is the variance–covariance matrix of all stochastic terms in the model (both parameters and error terms). In traditional macromodels the terms Y_j^e, future expected endogenous variables, may be viewed as having been substituted out of the model by some explicit expectations generating submodel:

$$Y_j^e = g(Y_i, X_k, \gamma, \phi) \tag{8.18}$$

$$i = 0, 1, 2 \ldots t, \; j = t + 1, \ldots, T, \; k = 0, 1, \ldots, t$$

where γ are parameters and ϕ is a covariance matrix of stochastic terms. We may substitute (8.18) into (8.17) to eliminate the future terms in the endogenous variables, Y_j. The model may then be solved in the traditional way. However, this procedure fails to identify explicitly the expectations formation procedure (8.18) so there is a loss of estimation efficiency. Further, if due to some regime change there is a shift in either the functional form of (8.18) or in its parameters, then, in the reduced form, of (8.17) and (8.18), the parameters will alter as the parameters in (8.18) alter under the new regime. However, if we deal with (8.17) and (8.18) *separately*, any change in the expectations formation mechanism is isolated in (8.18) and the structure (8.17) will be invariant to this form of structural change. This is the Lucas (1976) critique discussed in Chapter 6, but here in a whole model context.

Perhaps the simplest form of solution to this problem would be to derive an explicit model for expectations formation (8.18) and then use a complete structural model in the form of the set of equations (8.17) and (8.18) taken together. Certainly if we had a good idea of how expectations are actually formed the ideal situation would consist of explicit models of (8.18). However, in the absence of such information practitioners often invoke the rational expectations hypothesis. Under this assumption it is assumed that the expectations will coincide with the expected value of the actual forecast of the model:

$$Y_h^e = f(Y_i, Y_j^e, X_k, \beta, \Omega) \tag{8.19}$$

$$h = i, \ldots, T, i = 0, \ldots, h, j = h + 1, \ldots, T,$$

$$k = 1, \ldots, T$$

In fact, most implementations on large models do not conform fully to (8.19) as the solution is carried out in a deterministic fashion so that Ω is ignored. It is well known that for a non-linear model the deterministic forecast will differ from the mean (or expected value) of the model's density function. So under the REH assumption the usual procedure is to define

$$Y_h^e = f(Y_0, Y_j^e, X_k, \beta) \tag{8.20}$$

$$h = 1, 2, \ldots, T, i = 0, 1, \ldots, h, j = h + 1, \ldots, T,$$

$$k = 1, 2, \ldots, T$$

We will call an *explicit* expectations mechanism such as (8.18) an 'expectations model' solution. The deterministic model solution such as (8.14) we refer to as a 'consistent solution' and a stochastic solution such as (8.19) a 'rational solution'.

Carrying out a specific explicit expectations model solution involves no special problems, as the standard model solution procedures outlined above are quite able to cope with these models. The problems raised by the consistent solution have been the subject of recent attention in the literature. Very little attention has been paid to the rational solution of non-linear models, although Hall and Henry (1988) are an exception to this. The rest of this section will concentrate on the work which has dealt with consistent solution techniques.

There are currently a number of techniques in use for solving models with consistent expectations; the first to be used widely was the Fair (1979), Anderson (1979) iterative technique. A more recent approach using optimal control is the Holly and Zarrop (1983) penalty function method. An approach from the engineering literature is the multiple shooting technique. Finally there is the iterative technique outlined in Hall (1985b). All these techniques address the same problem, although the relationship between them is not always clear.

We will discuss the problem of model solution within a linear framework. This is done so that matrix notation may be used; none of the conclusions to be drawn are dependent on the assumption of linearity.

We begin by stating a general linear deterministic simultaneous model as

$$\alpha(L)Y_t = \beta(L)X_t \tag{8.21}$$

where $\alpha(L)$ and $\beta(L)$ are matrix lag polynomials (which may include lead terms), Y is a vector of N endogenous variables and X is a vector of M exogenous variables. Now, if we want to solve this model over a fixed time period, $1 \ldots T$, subject to suitable initial and terminal conditions Z, we may restate the problem, in a more explicit framework, as

$$AY' = BX' + CZ' \tag{8.22}$$

where Y and X are stacked vectors over all the time periods $1 \ldots T$ and CZ' is the initial and terminal conditions, that is, any lags which need values before the start of the solution (period 0) or expectations beyond the end of the solution (period T). It is worth actually writing out in full the left-hand side of (8.16):

$$
\begin{bmatrix}
\alpha & \alpha(L^{-1}) & \alpha(L^{-2}) & & & \alpha(L^{-(T-1)}) \\
\alpha(L) & \alpha & \alpha(L^{-1}) & & & \cdot \\
\alpha(L^2) & \alpha(L) & \alpha & & & \cdot \\
\alpha(L^3) & \alpha(L^2) & \alpha(L) & \alpha & & \cdot \\
\alpha(L^4) & \alpha(L^3) & \alpha(L^2) & \alpha(L) & \alpha & \\
\vdots & & & & \ddots & \\
\alpha(L^{T-1}) & & & \cdot & & \alpha
\end{bmatrix}
\begin{bmatrix}
y_1 \\
y_2 \\
y_3 \\
\cdot \\
\cdot \\
\cdot \\
y_T
\end{bmatrix}
$$

$$\tag{8.23}$$

If the full A matrix is actually lower triangular, having only zeros above the leading diagonal, then the model contains no consistent expectation terms and it may be solved in the usual way, one period at a time. When the upper triangle is not empty, one of the special approaches mentioned earlier must be employed.

The approach outlined in Hall (1985b) is simply to deal directly with the equation system set out in (8.22) and (8.23). So we may normalise the model by defining $A = D - E$ and then use any of the standard iterative techniques (Gauss–Seidel, Fast, Gauss–Seidel, etc.) to solve the model.

Both the Fair–Anderson and the penalty function techniques make use of a separate split in the A matrix before the normalisation procedure is made. Both techniques begin by defining $A = (P - U)$, where P is the principal diagonal and all the lower triangular elements of A and U are minus the upper triangular elements of A. We can then rewrite (8.22) as

$$PY' = UY' + BX' + CZ' \tag{8.24}$$

This isolates all the lead terms and they can then be treated separately. This is done by defining a new vector, Y^e, where the consistent solution is defined by $Y^e = Y$. The model may then be written as

$$PY' = UY^{e'} + BX' + CZ' \qquad (8.25)$$

The Fair–Anderson procedure begins by setting arbitrary values for Y^e, solving (8.25), as a model without consistent expectations, and then updating the estimate of Y^e with the solution values. This procedure iterates until $Y = Y^e$.

The penalty function method proceeds in a similar fashion to achieve consistency by viewing the variables Y^e as control variables and then minimising a function $\Omega = \Sigma(Y - Y^e)^2$ using standard optimal control algorithms. This function has a minimum when $Y = Y^e$ and consistency is achieved.

The advantage of both these techniques is that the actual model solution procedure is reduced to a period-by-period problem without any consistent expectation terms entering. The added cost of this is obviously the cost of the extra iteration procedure in the Fair–Anderson technique and the cost of the optimal control exercise in the case of the penalty function approach. In effect these are both very sensible procedures to adopt while the upper triangle of A is very sparse. As A becomes more dense the costs can rise enormously.

The relationship between (8.23) and the multiple shooting techniques is a little less obvious. Any of the above techniques would proceed by normalising the model on the principal diagonal and then proceeding from there. The multiple shooting technique however first normalises the model on any lead terms. In terms of (8.23) this is rather like moving any rows with non-zero upper triangular elements down the model until the non-zero elements are on the diagonal. The model is then normalised on this new leading diagonal, which leads to some variables being determined twice. The initial period variables are then chosen so as to make the terminal values of the endogenous variables conform with the terminal conditions.

A simple example makes this more clear. Suppose we have an equation

$$E_t = E_{t+1} + \alpha X_t \qquad (8.26)$$

where $E_T = \Sigma$. We renormalise this equation to give

$$E_{t+1} = E_t - \alpha X_t \qquad (8.27)$$

This equation can now be used to solve the whole path of E_t, given E_0 and X_t. We search over alternative values of E_0 so that the solution for E_T, the terminal value, is equal to the (pre-set) terminal condition (see below).

The advantage of the multiple shooting technique is that it emphasises the importance of model normalisation and suggests ways in which the normalisation can be improved. The disadvantage is that it is in only very special cases where renormalisation is actually possible. If a single equation can be renormalised as a single unit, as in the case of (8.26), then the approach is quite straightforward. However, most cases would involve renormalising whole blocks of the model and this would not generally be feasible. An employment equation which includes expected output cannot be renormalised as a single unit, for example.

Specifying terminal conditions for a model with consistent expectation

Before one can solve a model which involves future expectations to yield a consistent solution, a suitable set of terminal conditions must be supplied. There has for some time been confusion over the distinction between terminal conditions and transversality conditions, in fact the two are quite different. This may be appreciated best by the following example, suppose we wish to minimise the following intertemporal cost function, where X_t^* is the desired, or target, value:

$$C = \sum_{t=1}^{\infty} \frac{a}{2} (X_t - X_t^*)^2 + \frac{b}{2} (X_t - X_{t-1})^2 \qquad (8.28)$$

which implies the following Euler equation (i.e. set $\delta C/\delta X_t = 0$)

$$aX_t^* = (a + 2b)X_t - b(X_{t+1} + X_{t-1}) \qquad (8.29)$$

A suitable transversality condition for this problem is

$$\lim_{t \to \infty} (X_t - X_t^*) = 0 \qquad (8.30)$$

However a finite-time horizon problem does not require a transversality condition. Instead, the Euler equations take on a special form as they approach the terminal date. For example, consider the three-period problem:

$$C = \sum_{t=1}^{3} (a/2)(X_t - X_t^*)^2 + (b/2)(X_t - X_{t-1})^2 \qquad (8.31)$$

The three first-order conditions are

$$aX_1^* = (a + 2b)X_1 - b(X_0 - X_2) \qquad (8.32a)$$

$$aX_2^* = (a + 2b)X_2 - b(X_1 + X_3) \qquad (8.32b)$$

$$aX_3^* = (a + b)X_3 - bX_2 \qquad (8.32c)$$

The transversality condition (8.30) may be derived by letting 't' in (8.32) go to infinity. But in the finite horizon case no transversality condition is necessary; instead the problem is dealt with by special equations appearing towards the terminal period.

The proper analogy for a macromodel would seem to be that we may interpret terminal conditions as transversality conditions if we solve the model over an infinite horizon. This is obviously impractical. It is wrong, however, to view the finite solution to the model with a terminal condition as being a version of (8.32) unless we recognize that this implies that all planning horizons end at the terminal period, as in (8.31) above.

A better interpretation of the terminal condition is that they should force the model solution to be on the infinite time horizon solution path at period T. Let us define $\bar{Y}$ to be the solution path of the model solved over an infinite time horizon subject to a set of transversality conditions derived by driving the model's own equations to infinity. Then, if we solve the model over the finite period 1, 2, .., T subject to $Y_T = \bar{Y}_T$, the finite solution Y_i, $i = 1, \ldots, T$ will be equal to the infinite solution path for the first T periods. So we may achieve part of the infinite horizon solution path without solving the model to infinity.

The obvious difficulty here is that we cannot know what $\bar{Y}$ is until after an infinite model solution has been achieved. However, bearing this interpretation of the terminal conditions in mind we are able to make a more precise interpretation of the various suggestions which have been made. In particular, the Minford and Mathews (1978) suggestion that equilibrium values should be used, is based on the idea that they are using a market clearing model which quickly moves towards its equilibrium. So after a few initial periods have been passed, the infinite time solution path should be the steady-state equilibrium. Similarly the Holly and Beenstock (1980) suggestion of projecting constant growth rates as a terminal condition may be seen as a suggestion that the infinite time solution path is characterised by steady growth rates. The Fair (1979) idea of testing the terminal condition by extending the solution period until no significant change occurs in the early part of the solution period may also be seen as a way of fixing the terminal conditions on the infinite time solution path.

8.4 The analysis of stochastic models

By their very nature models are stochastic simply because no description of the world can ever be so complete that the models fit the data perfectly. So the full specification of an econometric model must include a set of error terms on the behavioural equations. For a linear model, as long as the error terms are normally distributed with zero mean, the stochastic part of the model is largely redundant. Ignoring the error terms completely gives rise to a deterministic forecast which is identical to the mean forecast of the stochastic model and which is optimal on almost any criterion. However, as soon as the model becomes non-linear this is no longer the case. There is then no general analytical relationship between the deterministic solution and the solution to the full stochastic model. In this section we explore the consequences of the stochastic nature of large models and discuss some of the numerical techniques for analysing non-linear models.

Stochastic simulation is a numerical computer technique which allows us to investigate the uncertainty which is associated inevitably with any large econometric model. Because such models are generally non-linear and highly complex, an analytic investigation of the effects and importance of their stochastic nature is impossible. Stochastic simulations bypass the analytic problems by simply performing large numbers of model simulations; each simulation differs from the others because of the different set of 'shocks' administered to the model. These shocks may be added to the equations, the parameters, or even the exogenous variables; the shocks are random drawings from a particular distribution. Given this repeated experiment it is then possible to calculate a range of statistics such as the mean, the standard deviation and the higher moments of the solution of the model variables. As the number of simulations undertaken increases, these summary statistics should provide a good guide to the stochastic performance of the whole model.

For any behavioural equation of a macromodel there is always some degree of uncertainty about its general specification, the actual values of its parameters and the importance of any error term. Typically, when an econometric model is used either for forecasting or simulation the stochastic nature of the model will be ignored. All error terms will be set, at least initially, to zero and the parameter estimates will be taken as known with certainty. It is natural to ask what the standard error of the deterministic forecast is and stochastic simulation can provide this answer. However, a much more important problem lies in the meaning of the deterministic forecast itself. It is well known that if the model is non-linear then the mean of the forecast will differ from the deterministic solution value. It has recently been pointed out (Hall 1984, Wallis 1984) that for some types of non-linearity the deterministic forecast may be quite meaningless and highly misleading as to the model's true forecast. A simple example can demonstrate this:

Let $\quad Y = \alpha X + u$

$$W = \beta Y + v \tag{8.33}$$

$$Z = Y.W$$

where u, v are stochastic error processes, α, β are parameters and X, Y, W, Z are variables. The reduced form solution is

$$Z = \beta \alpha^2 X^2 + 2\alpha\beta Xu + Xv + \beta u^2 + uv$$

$$Y = \alpha X + u \tag{8.34}$$

$$W = \alpha\beta X + \beta u + v$$

The equations for Y and W are simple linear equations, so assuming $E(u) = E(v) = 0$, the expected value of Y and W will be equal to the deterministic model forecast. This is not true for Z however, as the term in $E(u^2)$ will be positive. So the deterministic forecast, which sets $u^2 = 0$ will be an extreme point on the probability distribution of the random variable u^2. Any error at all will make $u^2 > 0$ and so the deterministic forecast is a highly biased and misleading indication of the stochastic model forecast.

It will be shown below that there are three broad classes of model. First, there are linear models and the deterministic forecast of such models is equal to the mean of the stochastic linear model, and all endogenous variables are normally distributed around this point (assuming normal error processes). Second, there are non-linear models which represent bijective mapping from the error terms on to the endogenous variables. A bijective mapping is a unique one-to-one mapping in both the function and its inverse. (The quadratic term discussed above is not bijective as its inverse is not a true one-to-one function.) The deterministic forecast of such a model can be shown to be the median of a (generally) skewed probability distribution. In this case the median, the mode and the mean of the probability density functions of the model are different. Forecasting the median seems a reasonable option especially considering some undesirable properties of the mean and the mode, discussed below. Finally, the third category is a non-linear model which is also non-bijective; in this case the deterministic forecast has no well-defined place on the probability density functions of the model. It can even lie at some highly unrepresentative extreme point, as shown above.

The example given above shows that a fairly simple form of non-linearity, which certainly exists in most large models, can give rise to non-bijective terms in the reduced form. So unless considerable work is undertaken to define and investigate the shape of the probability function of such models we have great difficulty interpreting any deterministic model results.

Stochastic simulations are useful therefore in defining and quantifying the uncertainty associated with a model forecast or simulation. But far more importantly they allow us to have a firm basis for interpreting the results of a deterministic model solution. If we know that the deterministic forecast is close to the mean value and that the probability distribution is near to being normal, then the model may be used in deterministic solution mode with some confidence. Until we have that information a serious problem of interpretation exists.

Interpreting the deterministic solution

When we are faced with the problem of having to choose a single point forecast from a skewed probability distribution there is no single point on the distribution which should be chosen in all circumstances. Instead, the optimal predictor will depend on the specific loss function of the forecaster (see Dunham Jackson 1921). For example, with a quadratic loss function and if a_i $(i = 1, \ldots N)$ is a set of real numbers:

$$S_1 = \sum_{i=1}^{N} (x - a_i)^2 \tag{8.35}$$

then S_1 may be minimised with respect to x by setting x equal to the arithmetic mean of the a_i. In a forecasting context, if x is a point forecast and the a_i are all possible outcomes, then the optimal forecast is the mean of the probability distribution of the a_i.

The quadratic loss function is perhaps the most immediately appealing choice but it is by no means the only one. A clear alternative is to minimise the absolute error of the forecast:

$$S_2 = \sum_{i=1}^{N} |(x - a_i)| \tag{8.36}$$

S_2 will take a minimum value when x is equal to the median of the distribution of a_i.

Both of the above loss functions consider the whole set of possible errors. A more restrictive loss function might be to maximise the probability of picking the correct value:

$$S_3 = -|\text{Max} \, PR(x - a_i) = 0| \tag{8.37}$$

This function will be minimised when x is set equal to the mode of the a_i.

Clearly, in the case of a normal distribution all three loss functions will deliver the same point estimate. The final function (S_3) is in general unappealing as it gives no weight to the shape of the density function and in a highly perverse case could lead to extreme forecasts on the boundary of the density function. When considering the other two functions it may be argued that it is desirable to penalise large errors with a proportionately greater weight than small errors, so at first sight we may prefer the quadratic function.

There is, however, only highly undesirable property of the mean which makes it difficult to accept as a coherent forecast. This is that the mean forecast of the model is likely to violate any non-linear identities in the model. We can see quite easily that linear identities will hold in the mean forecast as

$$E(\Sigma x_i) = \Sigma E(x_i) \tag{8.38}$$

But we know that

$$E(XY) = E(X).E(Y) + \text{Cov}(XY) \tag{8.39}$$

So any relationships which involve deriving a variable from the product of two other endogenous variables which are not independent of each other will not hold in expected values. This is not a trivial problem as most large macro models have many such identities, in particular the nominal value of a variable is often derived as the product of the real quantity of the variable and its price (for example, real disposable income, real wages or the real exchange rate). In general we would not expect the price (P) of a good to be independent of the quantity (Q) traded. The covariance of the two must therefore be non-zero and the mean value of revenue ($R = PQ$) will not equal the mean quantity multiplied by the mean price.

There are, of course, several alternatives which could be used to derive a coherent forecast based on the expected values of the model. One would be to derive the expected values of the behavioural equations, $E(X)$ and $E(Y)$, and then calculate any identities on the basis of these values, i.e. set arbitrarily $E(XY) = E(X)E(Y)$. There are two objections to this. First, if the identity feeds back into the model then the value calculated will not be the same as the value used in the model. Second, if we report the means because our loss function is quadratic, then to impose the identities is to behave sub-optimally. This point raises the second major objection to requiring coherency; it may be that rather than abandon the mean forecast we should actually abandon the coherency requirement. Part of the popular appeal of large models among forecasters is that they ensure that a large number of accounting identities are observed simultaneously. This may, however, be a mistake if the forecaster is simply interested in minimising his squared forecast error. However, if a forecasting group places some weight on the coherency of its forecast then it may well be that the use of mean forecasts is simply too simplistic.

The importance of the non-linearities present in large econometric models should not be underestimated. The interpretation of the stochastic nature of the endogenous variable is rendered particularly difficult by this problem. While we appear to have a good deal of information about the density function of the error terms of the model, the only information usually available on the endogenous variables is the deterministic forecast. Generally we have no way of even knowing where the deterministic solution lies on the density function.

Hall (1989) provides an analysis of this question and he establishes a proof for an important class of models that the deterministic solution is in fact the median of the distribution of the endogenous variables. When the distribution of the endogenous variables is skewed the normal measures of central tendency (the mean, the mode and the median) will of course differ and there is no strong reason to chose one measure over another. Indeed each can be justified as the optimal choice for a particular loss function. So establishing that the deterministic solution is the median of the distribution is an important justification for the use of non-stochastic model solutions, although clearly only a stochastic solution procedure can provide information on the overall shape of the distribution.

The numerical procedure of stochastic simulation

In this section we discuss a range of techniques which are known generally as stochastic simulation. Conceptually this is a very simple procedure. Suppose we have a non-linear model expressed in a general non-linear final form as

$$Y = Y(X, A, U) \tag{8.40}$$

where Y is a vector of endogenous variables, X is a vector of exogenous variables, A is a set of parameters and U is a set of stochastic error terms. If both A and U are stochastic with mean zero and covariance matrix Σ_A and Σ_U then Y will also be stochastic with a vector of means Y' and a covariance matrix Σ_Y. Unfortunately the analytical calculation of Σ_Y and Y' is impossible for anything but the most simple form of non-linearities and even in these cases the size of a large model would often render the problem intractable.

The technique of stochastic simulation avoids the analytical calculation of Σ_Y and Y' by constructing a numerical approximation which is asymptotically equivalent to the true density function of Y. This approximation is carried out simply by repeatedly simulating (8.40) with values of A and U drawn from their distributions, defined above. The solution values for Y are then collected together and the moments of the distribution may be calculated. As the number of repetitions becomes very large the estimates of the moments of the distribution converge on Σ_Y and Y'. Further details and application of this approach may be found in Hall and Henry (1988), Fair (1984), Bianch and Calzolari (1982). We will now discuss a few of the details of the application of this technique.

Structural errors and additive errors

Despite the fact that most large models are non-linear they are generally estimated by single equation linear techniques, typically OLS. This is done by subjecting the variables to various transformations, for example, by taking the log of a variable, $\ln X$. When the equations are coded into the actual computer model the dependent variable is always transformed back into the 'pure' variable, X. This means that a random error added to the end of such an equation will not play the same role, or have the same properties as the estimated residual. An example will make this clear. If an equation of the form

$$\Delta \log (Y) = \alpha \Delta \log (X) + U$$

is estimated, then this will often be coded as

$$Y = \exp \left[\log Y_{t-1} + \alpha \Delta \log (X) + B \right] + A \qquad (8.41)$$

A is an additional 'residual' used for shocking the equation. B is the structural error term, normally set to zero, which will be a transformation of the estimation error U. Other forms of non-linearity are treated analogously. It is possible therefore to apply random shocks to either the A- or the B-residuals. The B or structural residuals depend on the estimation assumption of normality but there is no general reason to expect the B-residuals to be normally distributed, rather than the A-residuals.

Univariate and multivariate residual shocks

The distinction between structural (B) and additive (A) residuals has been made above but when we apply shocks to either of these sets of residuals we must also decide whether these shocks are to be univariate or multivariate ones. Univariate shocks are simply random, normally distributed shocks which have a given variance but are completely independent of each other.

Multivariate shocks will also generally be distributed normally with a given variance but they will also have some covariance structure between the individual shocks. In its simplest form we may allow for the fact that the error terms of different equations have some non-zero contemporaneous covariances. As an extension we may allow also for the covariance of the error terms in different equations to be related over different time periods.

The main argument for considering the covariances of the error terms in a model which has been estimated by OLS on the assumption of zero covariance in the equation error terms is that often the estimation assumptions are not actually fulfilled. An equation may be subject either to simultaneous equation bias or to omitted variable bias, or both, and the covariance structure of the error terms across equations may contain a great deal of information on this misspecification. For example, if current income were incorrectly omitted from the consumption function, then the covariance of the error term in the consumption equation and the other income-generating equations should pick up this omission.

There are currently three main techniques used to generate additive residual shocks which follow the covariance structure of the error terms of the whole model. Only one of these techniques can be used for large models however. The simplest technique is the Mariano and Brown (1981) approach; they use observed residuals from an N period model solution to carry out N static, one-period replications. This limits the number of replications to thirty or forty at the most as well as allowing the calculation of only the one-quarter-ahead static error bounds. A more useful technique is Nagar (1969); this uses an estimate of the full covariance structure of the model to apply shocks to the residuals. The problem here is that the covariance matrix must be estimated from observed residuals so that there must be more data points available than equation residuals. This will not generally be the case for a large model and so the initial covariance matrix cannot be defined. The final, and more useful, technique is the McCarthy algorithm (1972). This approach generates a vector of shocks by using the formula:

$$S = T^{0.5} rU$$

where S is the vector of random shocks, r is a $1 \times T$ vector of random numbers which are distributed $N(0, 1)$ and U is a $T \times M$

matrix of disturbances from T observations of M true structural equations.

This technique therefore only requires a set of equation errors over T periods; T may be any length although the properties of S only tend to those of the true structural errors as T tends to infinity. Therefore this gives an asymptotic estimate of the true covariance matrix. The McCarthy technique has been extended to take account also of serial correlation in the error terms, although this extension will not be discussed here.

Handling parameter uncertainty

The variance of the forecast errors is made up from two sources, the variance of the true error term (U) and the parameter uncertainty, represented by the covariance matrix of the parameters. In stochastic simulation exercises it is relatively easy to take account of the variance of U but it is extremely difficult to make proper allowance for the variance of A in a satisfactory manner when the model is large. It is, of course, easy to shock the parameters by applying random shocks which are normal and have the parameters' estimated standard error. This procedure is, however, not satisfactory as it ignores the covariances between the parameters in any given equation as well as the covariances of the parameters across different equations. When these covariances are ignored there is a significant possibility that all the shocks in a given equation may be applied in the same direction, causing the dependent variable to change by an enormous amount, even changing sign. This need happen to only one equation in any run for the model to fail. Making allowance for the parameter covariance is therefore vital as this will mean that, on average, if one parameter falls then another will move in a compensating fashion so that the level of the dependent variable is maintained within 'sensible' bounds.

Three main techniques are used to deal with the problem of stochastic parameters, none of them being entirely satisfactory. These techniques are:

1. *Stochastic simulation and re-estimation (see Schink 1971)* Random shocks are added to the error term of the model so as to generate new values for the endogenous variables. These new values are then used to re-estimate the entire model and carry out a forecast run. The process is repeated many times so that the forecast errors can be

calculated. This technique is almost completely satisfactory in the sense that it generates sets of parameter values which take full account of all the covariances between the parameters themselves and between the parameters and the error terms. The disadvantage is, of course, that it is almost infeasible to consider 500 or 1000 replications of this technique for a large model.

2. *Monte Carlo on coefficients (see Cooper and Fisher 1974)* Shocks are applied to the parameters as well as to the random errors of each equation. The disadvantage here is that in the case of a large model where system estimation techniques are impractical, it is very hard, if not impossible, to carry out the necessary decomposition of the parameter covariance matrix. The normal technique used here when dealing with a large model is simply to ignore the cross-equation covariances and deal only with variance of the parameters. This clearly represents an important loss of information.

3. *Analytical simulation of coefficients (see Bianchi and Calzolari 1980)* An analytical formula is involved for the parameter uncertainty term which concerns the partial derivative of the parameters with respect to the endogenous variables. These partial derivatives are evaluated by using finite difference which involves many model simulations. The analytical formula also involves using an estimate of the variance–covariance matrix of the parameters.

It seems that the only feasible method in the case of a large model is to use procedure 2 and follow the assumption of Cooper and Fisher (1974), Fair (1980), Haitovsky and Wallace (1972) and assume the cross-equation covariances are all zero.

Variance reduction techniques

The main procedure used to reduce the uncertainty of the estimate of the mean of the distribution is the technique of antithetic errors. This means that the sets of residual errors to be applied in each simulation are not completely independent of the other sets, but instead are generated in pairs, where the second set of each pair is minus the first set. This produces a group of errors which are perfectly symmetric around the mean of the error process. A substantial increase is given in the efficiency of the estimate of the mean of the endogenous variables but it does not increase the efficiency of the estimate of the variance.

Estimating the uncertainty of a model's simulation properties

From the point of view of economic policy formation, the main interest in any macro model is its simulation properties. It is these properties which determine the policy prescriptions which are given by the model, no matter whether a simple set of policy alternatives is examined or if a complex analysis involving optimal control is used. When evaluating a large model an important aspect of its properties, which is often ignored, is the density function of the simulation effects. To say that the deterministic effect of a rise in government expenditure is to raise GDP is of little use until we are able to say what the margin of error surrounding this estimate is.

The original work in this area was undertaken by Fair (1980) and the approach is summarised in Fair (1984).

An analytical framework

Let Y_{it} be the set of i endogenous variables in a general non-linear model, X_{nt} be a set of n exogenous variables, Ω represents the variance–covariance matrix of all stochastic elements in the model (error terms and parameters) and B is a vector of parameter estimates. It is then possible to state the model in reduced form as

$$Y_{it} = Y_{it}(\Omega, B, X) \tag{8.42}$$

The deterministic model solution would be given by ignoring the stochastic parts of the model as:

$$Y_{it}^{D} = Y_{it}(B, X) \tag{8.43}$$

Conventional stochastic simulation techniques allow us to estimate the expected value of the endogenous variables conditional on an estimate of the variance–covariance matrix.

$$Y_{it}^{e} = Y_{it}(\hat{\Omega}, B, X) \tag{8.44}$$

A model simulation exercise consists of solving the model for some base set of exogenous values (X^{I}) and then comparing this with another solution carried out on the basis of a different set of exogenous variables (X^{II}). So the effect of the deterministic simulation will be

$$d_{it}^{D} = Y_{it}(B, X^{II}) - Y_{it}(B, X^{I}) \tag{8.45}$$

and similarly the difference in expected values of the stochastic simulation will be

$$d_{it}^e = Y_{it}^e(\Omega, B, X^{II}) - Y_{it}^e(\Omega, B, X^I) \tag{8.46}$$

In order to assess the uncertainty of a model's simulation properties we need to investigate the probability density function of d_{it}. As with conventional stochastic simulations, if the model is non-linear we will generally expect d_{it}^D to differ from d_{it}^e. Also it is clear that when we are dealing with non-linear models the variance of d_{it} will depend on both the stochastic parameters and the stochastic error terms. It is only in the case of a linear model that the variance of d_{it} is due to only the parameter uncertainty. This point can be appreciated easily by referring back to the simple model of (8.33). The reduced form equation for W, a linear part of the model, is

$$W = \alpha\beta X + \beta U + V \tag{8.47}$$

A simulation on X would give

$$d^W = \alpha\beta(X^{II} - X^I) \tag{8.48}$$

the error terms U, V drop out, and the density function of d^W is due solely to the stochastic nature of α and β. However, the situation is different for Z, the reduced form equation here is

$$Z = \beta\alpha^2 X^2 + 2\alpha\beta XU + \alpha XV + \beta U^2 + UV \tag{8.49}$$

So

$$d^Z = \beta\alpha^2((X^{II})^2 - (X^I)^2) + 2\alpha\beta U(X^{II} - X^I) \\ + \alpha V(X^{II} - X^I) \tag{8.50}$$

Here both the second and third term include the stochastic variables U and V, so the density function of d^Z depends in part on the density function of U and V.

Calculating the uncertainty of a model's simulation properties

Here we present the algorithm of Hall (1985) which efficiently provides estimates of the density function of a model's simulation properties.

1. Given the covariance matrices of the parameters and the error terms, draw a set of random parameters B^* and a set of residuals U^*.
2. Using the set of parameters and errors (B^*, U^*), solve the model for a base set of exogenous variables X^I to give $\hat{Y}^I$. The outcome of the model conditional on B^*, U^* and X^I.

3. Using the same set of parameters and errors (B^*, U^*), solve the model for a simulation set of exogenous variables X^{II} to give $\hat{Y}^{II}$, the outcome of the model conditional on B^*, U^* and X^{II}.
4. Compute $\hat{d}^J = \hat{Y}^{II} - \hat{Y}^I$
5. Repeat steps 1 to 4, J times, when J is the desired number of trials.
6. Given the J values of d, compute the mean and variance of d.

8.5 Optimal control of non-linear models

Wherever a model is used for policy analysis we are essentially trying to find the best setting for some group of instruments, given our understanding of the economy which is formalised in the model. The formal framework for any such analysis is clearly that of optimal control, even if in practice the analysis is conducted in a less formal way using only simulation methodology. The problem statement in its most general form is quite straightforward; let the model be

$$f_i(Y, X, A, \Omega) = 0 \qquad (8.51)$$

where Y is a vector of endogenous variables, X are the exogenous variables, A the parameters and Ω is the full covariance matrix of the stochastic elements (from both the error terms and parameter estimates). The problem statement then simply involves specifying an objective function which is to be minimised.

$$\text{Min } E(J) = E[J(Y, X, \Omega)] \qquad (8.52)$$

Note that we are minimising the expectation of some general function (J) of the stochastic model. We then minimise (8.52) subject to the model (8.51) with respect to a set of control variables C which are some subset of the exogenous variables X such that $(X) = (Z, C)$ where Z is all the exogenous variables not under the control of the policy maker.

For the case where the model is linear and the objective function is quadratic, a well-defined analytical solution exists which is detailed in a number of books, Intriligator (1971) or Hall and Henry (1988), and will not be discussed here. When the model is non-linear however, analytical solutions no longer exist and we must again resort to numerical procedures. The deterministic case is relatively easy to deal with, if we normalise (8.51) with fixed parameters such that

$$Y_i = h_i(Y, X) \qquad (8.53)$$

and then state the reduced form of the system (assuming that this exists) as

$$Y_i = h'_i(X) \tag{8.54}$$

We may then state the problem (8.52) as the unconstrained minimisation problem

$$\text{Min} = J[h'_i(X), X]$$

or

$$\text{Min } J = g[h'_i(Z, C), Z, C] = g'(Z, C)$$

which is simply a problem of minimising a non-linear function with respect to a set of variables C; this problem was dealt with earlier when we considered maximum likelihood procedures. In practice because although many econometric models are large they are also fairly simple systems and so a number of particularly efficient algorithms have been developed (for example, Fair 1984, Holly *et al.* 1979 discuss such algorithms). Conceptually however we are simply maximising a non-linear function and any of the standard techniques could be used.

The problem takes on a different order of complexity when the non-linear model is stochastic. In this case there is no widely accepted procedure for calculating the optimal solution. This problem has been addressed by Chow (1976) from a theoretical standpoint and he outlines an algorithm which calculates optimal control rules for stochastic non-linear models. The Chow algorithm, in essence, works by iterating over a number of linearisations of the stochastic model using standard dynamic control theory to optimise the stochastic linearised model at each iteration. The key feature of the algorithm is that it is the stochastic model which is linearised not the deterministic model. To linearise a large stochastic model once would be enormously difficult and to include this as part of an iteration procedure would be an order of magnitude more complex, and as far as we know the Chow (1976) algorithm has never been implemented in its full form.

A few applications exists of stochastic optimal control of fairly small models, such as Bray (1975), but this work has generally proceeded by linearising the deterministic model rather than the full stochastic model. These applications then tend to produce solutions close to the deterministic solution (as we would expect) – indeed, if they were performed using fixed parameters and only error term uncertainty this algorithm converges on the deterministic solution.

Hall and Stephenson (1989) propose an algorithm which combines the technique of stochastic simulation with optimal control. It enables one to calculate a very close approximation to the full stochastic optimal control solution. Their algorithm has the following form.

If the model has the general form of (8.51) then we may define Y^* to be the solution to (8.51) subject to the full stochastic processes of the model.

$$E[f_i(Y^*, X, \Omega, A, U)] = 0 \qquad i = I, N \qquad (8.55)$$

and Y^* will be the mathematical expectation of Y, and U is a vector of error terms. Now define $\hat{Y}$ to be the deterministic model solution,

$$f = [\hat{Y}, X, 0, E(A), 0] = 0 \qquad i = 1, N \qquad (8.56)$$

That is the variance–covariance matrix if the parameters are set to zero and the error terms take their mean value, which is assumed to be zero without loss of generality.

We know that, when the model is not linear:

$$\hat{Y} \neq Y^* \qquad ?$$

We may extend this framework to include optimal control by splitting the X vector into two sections Z, a vector of exogenous variables and C a vector of control variables. We then need only to specify a suitable objective function which is to be minimised.

We will examine the standard case of a conventional quadratic objective function:

$$E(J) = E\left[\sum_{i=1}^{n} A_i(Y_i - \bar{Y}_i)^2\right] \qquad (8.57)$$

where $\bar{Y}_i$ is the desired value for variable Y_i and (8.57) is to be minimised subject to the model.

$$f(Y, Z, C, \Omega, A, U) = 0 \qquad (8.58)$$

with respect to the control variables C. Again without loss of generality, we assume a one-period time horizon so as to simplify the notation, the multi-period extension is trivial.

Now we may rewrite (8.57) in the following way:

$$E(J) = \sum_{i=1}^{N} A_i E(Y_i^2 + \bar{Y}_i^2 - 2Y_i\bar{Y}_i) \qquad (8.59)$$

$$= \sum_{i=1}^{N} A_i[E(Y_i^2) + \bar{Y}_i^2 - 2\bar{Y}E(Y_i)] \qquad (8.60)$$

and given that $E(Y_i)^2 = E(Y_i)E(Y_i) + \text{Var}(Y_i)$

$$E(J) = \sum_{i=1}^{N} A_i[E(Y_i)E(Y_i) + \text{Var}(Y_i) + \bar{Y}_i^2 - 2\bar{Y}_i E(Y_i)] \qquad (8.61)$$

and we may define $E(Y_i) = \hat{Y}_i + E(d_i)$, the expected value of Y_i equals the deterministic model solution $\hat{Y}_i$ plus the expected deviation of the deterministic value from the mean value $E(d_i)$. Then, substituting this into (8.61) gives:

$$E(J) = \sum_{i=1}^{N} A_i[\hat{Y}_i\hat{Y}_i + E(d_i)E(d_i) + 2\hat{Y}_iE(d_i)$$
$$+ \text{Var}(Y_i) + \bar{Y}_i^2 - 2\bar{Y}_i\hat{Y}_i - 2\bar{Y}_iE(d_i)] \tag{8.62}$$

The advantage of (8.62) over (8.57) is that the stochastic elements of the solution have been isolated in the terms $\text{Var}(Y_i)$ and $E(d_i)$ and we are able to provide numerical estimates for both of these terms through the use of stochastic simulation. This suggests the possibility of an algorithm to solve the stochastic problem which has the following step-by-step form:

1. Calculate the optimal solution to the deterministic problem given by (8.57) subject to (8.51), let the solution be C^*.
2. Perform a set of stochastic simulation around the base given by C^* to produce estimates of $\text{Var}(Y_i)$ and d_i ($i = 1, 2, \ldots, N$).
3. Using these estimates of d_i and $\text{Var}(Y_i)$ we can now minimise (8.62) subject to (8.51) to produce a new optimal solution C'. If C' is within a convergence criteria of $C^*(|C' - C^*| < \text{EPS})$ for EPS suitably small then stop; if the convergence criteria is not met then set $C^* = C'$ and return to step 2.

This algorithm, at convergence will, still entail a small degree of approximation although this will be much less than the usual method of producing a linear approximation to the non-linear model. The conventional procedure of linearising the deterministic model, discussed in Kendrick (1981) would involve producing a linear approximation to the model and then appealing to the certainty equivalence theorem to solve the resulting deterministic quadratic–linear model. The problem with this approach is that when the objective function is quadratic and the parameters are known this procedure simply reproduces the deterministic solution.

We can see the source of the above approximation by noting that in general $\text{Var}(Y_i)$ and d_i are both functions of the control variables C. We may simplify the notation by considering an example with only one control variable (C) and one state variable Y. Then, following the notation in (8.62) we may define

$$\hat{Y} = f(C) \tag{8.63}$$

$$\text{Var}(Y) = g(C) \tag{8.64}$$

$$E(d) = h(C) \tag{8.65}$$

These terms may then be substituted into (8.62) to give

$$E(J) = f(C)f(C) + h(C)h(C) + 2f(C)h(C) + g(C)$$
$$+ \bar{Y}^2 - 2\bar{Y}f(C) - 2\bar{Y}h(C) \tag{8.66}$$

This is now an unconstrained function in C which will be minimised when the following FOC is met:

$$2f(C)f' + 2h(C)h' + 2f(C)h' + 2h(C)f'$$
$$+ g' - 2Yf' - 2Yh' = 0 \tag{8.67}$$

In the algorithm given above during the calculation of the optimal solution the partial derivatives g' and h' are set to zero so the solution which is calculated will be characterised by

$$2f(C)f' + 2h(C)f' - 2\bar{Y}f' = 0$$

The standard technique of linearising the model would also set $h(C) = 0$ and so this term would also be lost in the approximation. It must be appreciated at this point that $h(C)$, the deviation between the deterministic value of Y and its expected value, is of a quite different order of magnitude to g' and h', the derivatives of the deviation and the variance with respect to C. For most model applications g' and h' are likely to be so small that ignoring them is a reasonable approximation to make. However, if it is felt that a particular model is so non-linear that this is a damaging assumption then it is possible to reduce this level of approximation by estimating a simple linear approximation of $g(C)$ and $h(C)$. Two sets of stochastic simulation could be performed for different levels of C and a simple linear function for $g(C)$ and $h(C)$ could be calculated. Under normal circumstances however the main effect of the stochastic parts of the model will be captured by the term $h(C)$.

Finally, it is perhaps worth noting that the well-known certainty equivalence theorem can be demonstrated via equations (8.62) and (8.67). Certainty equivalence states that if the objective function is quadratic and the model is linear then the optimal and control trajectory for the stochastic problem is identical to the solution to the deterministic problem when all stochastic terms take their expected value. When the model is linear, $h(C) = g' = h' = 0$ and so (8.67) reduces to

$$2f(C)f' - 2\bar{Y}f' = 0 \tag{8.68}$$

which is identical to the FOC for the deterministic model.

8.6 Summary

This chapter has reviewed a range of techniques which allow large non-linear models to be analysed in much the same way that we are familiar with for small linear models. We have shown how model solutions can be obtained, how the stochastic properties of models can be investigated and how various forms of simulation and optimal control procedures may be defined. While these procedures may often be extremely complex from a numerical perspective, modern computers bring such techniques within the realms of feasibility even for very large models.

References

Aitchison, J. and Silvey, S. D. (1960), 'Maximum likelihood estimation procedures and associated tests of significance', *Journal of the Royal Statistical Society*, series B, 134–74.

Amemiya, T. (1981), 'Qualitative response models: a survey', *Journal of Economic Literature*, **19**, 1483–1536.

Anderson, B. D. O. and Moore, J. B. (1979), *Optimal Filtering*, Englewood Cliffs, N. J.: Prentice Hall.

Anderson, G. and Hendry, D. F. (1984), 'An econometric model of United Kingdom building societies', *Oxford Bulletin of Economics and Statistics,* **46** (3), 185–210.

Anderson, P. A. (1979), 'Rational expectations forecasts from non-rational models', *Journal of Monetary Economics*, **5**, 67–80.

Armijo, L. (1966), 'Minimization of functions having continuous partial derivatives', *Pacific Journal of Mathematics,* **16**, 1–3.

Athans, M. (1974), 'The importance of Kalman Filtering Methods for Economic Systems', *Annals of Economic and Social Measurement,* **3** (1), 49–63.

Baba, Y., Hendry, D. F. and Starr, R. M. (1985), 'A stable US money demand function, 1960–1984', Mimeo, Oxford: Nuffield College.

Baba, Y., Hendry, D.F. and Starr, R. M. (1988), 'US money demand 1960–1984', Oxford: Nuffield College, Discussion Paper no. 27.

Banerjee, A., Dolado, J. J., Hendry, D. F. and Smyth, G. W. (1986), 'Exploring equilibrium relationships in econometrics through state models: some Monte Carlo evidence', *Oxford Bulletin of Economics and Statistics,* **42** (3).

Barr, D. G. and Cuthbertson, K. (1990), 'Neoclassical consumer demand theory for the demand for money', *Economic Journal*, **101**, (407), July, 855–76.

Barr, D. G. and Cuthbertson, K. (1991), 'An interdependent error feedback model of UK company sector asset demands', *Oxford Economic Papers,* November.

Barro, R. J. (1978), 'Unanticipated money, output and the price level in the

United States', *Journal of Political Economy*, **86** (4), 549–81.

Becker, R. G., Dwolatzky, E. and Rustem, B. (1986), 'The simultaneous use of rival models in policy optimisation', *Economic Journal*, **96** (382), 425–48.

Bera, A. K. and Jarque, C. M. (1982), 'Model specification tests: a simultaneous approach', *Journal of Econometrics*, **20**, 59–82.

Berndt, E. R. and Savin, N. E. (1977), 'Conflict among criteria for testing hypotheses in the multivariate linear regression model', *Econometrica*, **45**, 1263–78.

Bhargava, A. (1983), 'On the theory of testing for unit roots in observed linear regression time series', LSE, ICERD no. 67.

Bianchi, C. and Calzolari, G. (1982), 'Evaluating forecast uncertainty due to errors in estimated coefficients' empirical comparison of alternative methods', in Chow, G. C. and Corsi, P. (eds), *Evaluating the Reliability of Macro-Economic Models*, London: Wiley.

Blake, D. (1984), 'Complete systems methods of estimating models with rational and adaptive expectations: a case study', *European Economic Review*, **24**, 137–50.

Blume, L. E. and Easley, D. (1982), 'Learning to be rational', *Journal of Economic Theory*, **26** (2), 340–51.

Bollerslev, T. (1986), 'Generalized autoregressive conditional heteroskedasticity', *Journal of Econometrics*, **31**, 307–28.

Boughton, J. M. (1979), 'Demand for money in major OECD countries', *OECD Economic Outlook Occasional Studies*, January.

Box, G. E. P. and Cox, D. R. (1964), 'An Analysis of Transformations', *Journal of the Royal Statistical Society*, **B 26**, 211–43.

Bray, J. (1975), 'Optimal control of noisy economy with the US as an example', *Journal of the Royal Statistical Society*, Series A, **138**, 339–73.

Bray, M. (1982), 'Learning, estimation and the stability of rational expectations', *Journal of Economic Theory*, **26** (2), 318–39.

Bray, M. M. (1983), 'Convergence to rational expectations equilibrium' in Frydman, R. and Phelps, E. S. (eds), *Industrial Forecasting and Aggregate Outcomes*, Cambridge: Cambridge University Press.

Bray, M. M. and Kreps, C. (1984), 'Rational learning and rational expectations', mimeo, Cambridge University.

Bray, M. M. and Savin, N. E. (1986), 'Rational expectations equilibria, learning and model specification', *Econometrica*, **54**, 1129–60.

Breusch, T. S. and Godfrey, L. (1981), 'A review of recent work on testing for auto-correlation in dynamic simultaneous models, in D. Currie, R. Nobay and D. Peel (eds), *Macroeconomic Analysis: Essays in Macroeconomics and Econometrics'*, London: Croom Helm.

Breusch, T. S. and Pagan, A. R. (1979), 'A simple test for heteroskedasticity and random coefficient variation', *Econometrica*, **50**, 1287–94.

Breusch, T. S. and Pagan, A. R. (1980), 'The Lagrange multiplier test and its application to model specification in econometrics', *Review of Economic Studies*, **47**, 239–54.

Brown, R. L., Durbin, J. and Evans, J. M. (1975), 'Techniques for testing the constancy of regression relationships over time', *Journal of the Royal Statistical Society* Series B, **37** (2), 149–92.

Buse, A. (1982), 'The likelihood ratio, Wald and Lagrange multiplier test: an expository note', *American Statistician*, **36** (3), 153–57.

Carr, J. and Darby, M. R. (1981), 'The role of money supply shocks in the short run demand for money', *Journal of Monetary Economics*, **8**, 183–200.

Chou, R. Y. (1988), 'Volatility, persistence and stock valuations: some empirical evidence using GARCH', *Journal of Applied Econometrics*, **3**, 279–94.

Chow, G. C. (1960), 'Tests of equality between sets of coefficients in two linear regressions', *Econometrica*, **28**, 591–605.

Chow, G. C. (1975), *Analysis and Control of Dynamic Economic Systems*, New York: Wiley.

Chow, G. C. (1976), 'The control of non-linear econometric systems with unknown parameters', *Econometrica*, **44**, 685–95.

Cochrane, D. and Orcutt, G. H. (1949), 'Application of least squares regression to relationships containing autocorrelated terms', *Journal of the American Statistical Association*, **44** (245), 32–61.

Cooper, J. P. and Fisher, S. (1972), 'Stochastic simulation of monetary rules in two macro-econometric models', *Journal of the American Statistical Association*, **67**.

Cooper, J. P. and Fisher, S. (1974), 'Monetary and fiscal policy in the fully stochastic St. Louis econometric model', *Journal of Money Credit and Banking*, (6), 1–22.

Cumby, R. E., Huizinga, J. and Obstfeld, M. (1983), 'Two-step two-stage least squares estimation in models with rational expectations', *Journal of Econometrics*, **21**, 333–55.

Currie, D. A. and Hall, S. G. (1989), 'A stock/flow model of the determination of the UK effective exchange rate', in M. P. Taylor and R. McDonald (eds), *The Exchange Rate*, London: Macmillan.

Currie, D. A. and Levine, P. (1985), 'Simple macroeconomic policy rules in an open economy', *Economic Journal*, **85**, 60–70.

Cuthbertson, K. (1985), *The Supply and Demand for Money*, Oxford: Basil Blackwell.

Cuthbertson, K. (1986), 'The behaviour of UK export prices of manufactured goods 1970–1983', *Journal of Applied Econometrics*, **1**, 255–75.

Cuthbertson, K. (1988a), 'The demand for M1: a forward looking buffer stock model', *Oxford Economic papers*, **40**, 110–31.

Cuthbertson, K. (1988b), 'Expectations, learning and the Kalman filter', *Manchester School*, **LVI** (3), 223–46.

Cuthbertson, K. (1990), 'Modelling expectations: a review of limited information estimation methods', *Bulletin of Economic Research*, **42** (1), 1–34.

Cuthbertson, K. (1991), 'The encompassing implications of feedforward versus feedback mechanisms: a reply to Hendry', *Oxford Economic Papers* **43** (2), 344–30.

Cuthbertson, K. and Barlow, D. (1989), 'The determination of liquid asset holdings of the UK personal sector', Manchester School, **LVIII** (4), 348–60.

Cuthbertson, K. and Gripaois, P. (1992), *The Macro Economy: A Guide for Business,* (2nd edn), London: Simon & Schuster.

Cuthbertson, K. (1985), *The Supply and Demand for Money*, Oxford: Basil Blackwell.

Cuthbertson, K. and Taylor, M. P. (1986a), 'Buffer stock money: an assessment', in Currie, D. A., Goodhart, C. A. E. and Llewellyn, D. (eds), *The Operation and Regulation of Financial Markets,* London: Macmillan.

Cuthbertson, K. and Taylor, M. P. (1986b), 'Monetary anticipations and the demand for money in the UK: testing the rationality of buffer-stock money', *Journal of Applied Econometrics*, **1** (4), 355–65.

Cuthbertson, K. and Taylor, M. P. (1987), *Macroeconomic Systems,* Oxford: Basil Blackwell.

Cuthbertson, K. and Taylor, M. P. (1987a), 'The demand for money: a dynamic rational expectations model', *Economic Journal*, **97**, (supplement), 65–76.

Cuthbertson, K. and Taylor, M. P. (1986), 'Anticipated and unanticipated variables in the demand for M1 in the UK', *Manchester School*, **57** (4), 319–39.

Cuthbertson, K. and Taylor, M. P. (1988), 'Monetary anticipations and the demand for money in the US: further results', *Southern Economic Journal*, **55** (2), 326–35.

Cuthbertson, K. and Taylor, M. P. (1990), 'The case of the missing money and the Lucas critique', *Journal of Macroeconomics*, **12** (3), 437–52.

Cuthbertson, K. and Taylor, M. P. (1991), 'A comparison of rational expectation and the general to specific approach to modelling the demand for M1', *Manchester School*, forthcoming.

Cyert, R. M. and De Groot, H. M. (1974), 'Rational expectations and Bayesian analysis', *Journal of Political Economy*, **82** (3), 521–36.

Davidson, J, Hendry, D. F. Srba, F. and Yeo, S. (1978), 'Econometric modelling of the aggregate time series relationships between consumers expenditure and income in the United Kingdom', *Economic Journal*, **88**, 661–92.

Davidson, J. and Hendry, D. F. (1981), 'Interpreting econometric evidence: the behaviour of consumers' expenditure in the UK', *European Economic Review*, **16**, 177–592.

Davidson, R. and MacKinnon, J. G. (1981), 'Several tests of model specification in the presence of alternative hypothesis', *Econometrica*, **49**, 781–93.

Davis, T. E, (1952), 'The consumption function as a tool for prediction', *Review of Economics and Statistics*, **34**, 270–77.

De Canio, S. J. (1979), 'Rational expectations and learning from experience', *Quarterly Journal of Economics*, **93**, 47–57.

Den Butter, and Fase, M. M. G. (1981), 'The demand for money in EEC countries', *Journal of Monetary Economics*, **8**, 201–30.

Dickey, D. A. and Pantula, S. G. (1988), 'Determining the order of differencing in autoregressive processes', *Journal of Business and Economic Statistics*, **5**, 455–61.

Didderich, G. T. (1985), 'The Kalman filter from the perspective of Goldberger–Theil estimators', *The American Statistician*, **39** (3), 193–7.

Doan, T. A. and Litterman, R. B. (1986), *Users Manual, RATS,* Minneapolis: VAR Econometrics.

Domowitz, I. and Hakkio, C. S. (1985), 'Conditional variance and the risk premium in the foreign exchange market', *Journal of International Economics*, **18**, 47–66.

Duncan, D. B. and Horn, S. D. (1972), 'Linear dynamic recursive estimation from the viewpoint of regression analysis', *Journal of the American Statistical Association*, **67** (340), 815–21.

Dunham, J. (1921), 'Note on the median of a set of numbers', *Bulletin of the American Mathematics Society*, **27**, 160.

Durbin, J. and Watson, G. S. (1950), 'Testing for serial correlation in least square regressions *I'Biometrica*, **38**, 159–78.

Edison, H. Miller, M. and Williamson, J. (1988), 'On evaluating and extending the target zone proposal', *Journal of Policy Modelling*, **9**, 199–224.

Engle, R. F. (1982), 'Autoregressive conditional heteroskedasticity with estimates of the variance of the UK inflation', *Econometrica*, **50**, 987–1007.

Engle, R. F. and Granger, C. W. J. (1987), 'Co-integration and error corrections representation, estimation and testing', *Econometrica*, **55**, 251–76.

Engle, R. F., Lilien, D. M. and Robins, R. P. (1987), 'Estimating time varying risk premia in the term structure: the ARCH-M Model' *Econometrica*, **55**, 391–407.

Engle, R. F. and Yoo, S. (1989), *A Survey of Cointegration*, mimeo, San Diego: University of California.

Faddeev, D. K. and Faddeva, V. N. (1963), *Computational Methods of Linear Algebra*, New York: Freeman.

Fair, R. C. (1979), 'An analysis of a macro-econometric model with rational expectations in the bond and stock market', *American Economic Review*, **69**, 539–52.

Fair, R. C. (1980), 'Estimating the uncertainty of policy effects in non-linear models', *Econometrica*, **48**, 1381–91.

Fair, R. C. (1984), *Specification, Estimation and Analysis of Macroeconometric Models*, Harvard University Press.

Fair, R. C. and Jaffee, D. M. (1972), 'Methods of estimation for markets in disequilibrium', *Econometrica*, **40**(3), 497–514.

Fama, F. (1984), 'Forward and spot exchange rates', *Journal of Monetary Economics*, **14**, 319–88.

Flemming, J. S. (1976), *Inflation*, Oxford: Oxford University Press.

Frankel, J. A. (1982), 'In search of the exchange risk premia: a six-currency test assuming mean-variance optimisation', *Journal of International Money and Finance*, **1**, 255–74.

Frenkel, J. A. and Johnson, H. G. (1976), *The Monetary Approach to the Balance of Payments*, London: Allen & Unwin.

Friedman, M. (1953), 'The Methodology of Positive Economics', in *Essays in Positive Economics*, Chicago: University of Chicago Press.

Friedman, B. M. (1975), 'Rational expectations are really adaptive after all', Howard Institute of Economic Research Discussion Paper No. 430.

Friedman, B. M. (1979), ''Optimal expectations and the extreme information assumptions of 'rational expectations' macro models', *Journal of Monetary Economics*, **5** (1), 23–41.

Friedman, B. M. and Roley, V. V. (1979), 'Investors' portfolio behaviour under alternative models of long-term interest rate expectations, unitary, rational or autoregresive', *Econometrica*, **47** (6), 1475–97.

Frisch, R. and Waugh, F. V. (1933), 'Control time regression as compared with individual trends', *Econometrica*, **1**, 221–3.

Froeberg, C. (1981), *Introduction to Numerical Analysis*, London: Addison-Wesley.

Fuller, W. A. [1976], (1978), *Introduction to Statistical Time Series*, New York: Wiley.

Frydman, R. (1982), 'Towards an understanding of market processes, individual expectations: learning and convergence to rational expectations equilibrium', *American Economic Review*, **72**, 652–68.

Gallant, A. R. and Holly, A. (1984) 'Statistical inference in an implicit nonlinear simultaneous equation model in the context of maximum likelihood estimation', *Econometrica*, **48**, 697–720.

Goldfeld, S. Quandt, R. and Trotter, H. (1966), 'Maximization by quadratic hill climbing', *Econometrica*, **34**, 541–51.

Goodhart, C. A. E. (1984), *Monetary Theory and Practice: The UK Experience*, London: Macmillan.

Granger, C. W. J. (1966), 'The typical spectral shape of an economic variable', *Econometrica*, **34** (1), 150–61.

Granger, C. W. J. (1983), 'Co-integrated variables and error correcting models', *UCSD Discussion Paper*.

Granger, C. W. J. (1986), 'Developments in the study of co-integrated economic variables', *Oxford Bulletin of Economics and Statistics*, **48** (3), 213–18.

Grauer, F. L. A., Litzenberger, R. H. and Stehlf, R. E. (1976), 'Sharing rules and equilibrium in an international capital market under uncertainty', *Journal of Financial Economics*, **3**, 233–56.

Hahn, F. H. (1982), *Money and Inflation*, Oxford: Basil Blackwell.

Haitovsky, B. and Wallace, N. (1972), 'A study of discretionary and non-discretionary monetary and fiscal policies in the context of stochastic macro-econometric models' in V. Zarnowitz (1972), (ed), *The Business Cycle Today*, National Bureau of Economic Research, New York.

Hakkio, C. S. (1981), 'Expectation and the forward exchange rate', *International Economic Review*, **22**, 663–78.

Haldane, J. B. S. (1948), 'Note on the median of a multivariate distribution', *Biometrica*, **35**, 414.

Hall, S. G. (1985a), 'The application of stochastic simulation techniques to the national institute's model 7', *Manchester School*, **LIV**, 180–201.

Hall, S. G. (1985b), 'Estimating the uncertainty of the simulation properties of large non-linear econometric models', *Applied Economics*, **18** (9), 985–94.

Hall, S. G. (1985c), 'On the solution of large economic models with consistent expectations', *Bulletin of Economic Research*, **37** (2), 137–61.

Hall, S. G. (1986), 'An application of the Granger and Engle two-step estimation procedure to United Kingdom aggregate wage data', *Oxford Bulletin of Economics and Statistics*, **48** (3), 229–40.

Hall, S. G. (1987a), 'Analyzing economic behaviour 1975–85 with a model incorporating consistent expectations', *National Institute Economic Review*, **120**, May.

Hall, S. G. (1987b), 'A forward looking model of the exchange rate', *Journal of Applied Econometrics*, **2**, 47–60.

Hall, S. G. and Henry, S. G. B. (1988), *Macroeconomic Modelling*, Amsterdam: North Holland.

Hall, S. G., Miles, D. K. and Taylor, M. P. (1989), 'Modelling asset prices with time varying betas', *Manchester School*. **LVII** (4), 340–56.

Hall, S. G., Henry, S. G. B. and Wren-Lewis, S. (1986), 'Manufacturing stocks and forward-looking expectations in the UK', *Economica*, **53**, 447–66.

Hall, S. G., Henry, S. G. B., Payne, J. and Wren-Lewis, S. (1986a), 'Forecasting employment: the role of forward looking behaviour', *International Journal of Forecasting*, **2**, 435–45.

Hall, S. G., Henry, S. G. B. and Pemberton, M. (1991), 'Testing a discreet switching disequilibrium model of the UK labour market', *Journal of Applied Econometrics*, forthcoming.

Hall, S. G. and Stephenson, M. J. (1989), 'An algorithm for the solution of stochastic optimal control problems for large non-linear econometric models', *Journal of Applied Econometrics*, **5**, 393–99.

Hall, S. G. and Urwin, R. A. (1989), 'A disequilibrium model of mortgage lending', Bank of England Discussion Paper.

Hansen, L. P. (1982), 'Large sample properties of generalised method of moments estimators', *Econometrica*, **50**, 1029–54.

Hansen, L. P., Hodrick, R. J. (1980), 'Forward exchange rates as optimal predictions of future spot rates: an econometric analysis, *Journal of Political Economy*, **88** (5), 829–53.

Hansen, L. P. and Sargent, T. J. (1980), 'Formulating and estimating dynamic linear rational expectations models', *Journal of Economic Dynamics and Control*, **2**, 7–46.

Hansen, L. P. and Sargent, T. J. (1981), 'Linear rational expectations models for dynamically inter-related variables' in Lucas, R. E. and Sargent, T. J. (eds), *Rational Expectations and Econometric Practice*, London: Allen & Unwin.

Hansen, L. P. and Sargent, T. J. (1982), 'Instrumental variables procedures for estimating linear rational expectations models', *Journal of Monetary Economics*, **9**, 263–96.

Harrison, P. J. and Stevens, C. F. (1976), 'Bayesian Forecasting', in *Journal of Royal Statistical Society, Series B*, **38** (3), 205–27.

Harvey, A. C. (1981a), *The Econometric Analysis of Time Series*, Hemel Hempstead: Philip Allan.

Harvey, A. C. (1981b), *Time Series Models*, Hemel Hempstead: Philip Allan.

Harvey, A. C. (1983), 'The formation of structural time series models in discrete and continuance time', QUESTITO 7, 563–75.

Harvey, A. C. (1984a), 'Dynamic models, the prediction error decomposition and state space', in D. F. Hendry and K. F. Wallis (eds), *Econometrics and Quantitative Economics*, Oxford: Basil Blackwell.

Harvey, A. C. (1984b), 'A unified view of statistical forecasting procedures', *Journal of Forecasting*, **3** (2), 245–75.

Harvey, A. C. (1987), 'Application of the Kalman Filter in econometrics', in *Advances in Econometrics*, **1**, 285–313, T. F. Bewley (ed), Cambridge: Cambridge University Press.

Harvey, A. C. and Todd, P. (1983), 'Forecasting economic time series with structural and Box–Jenkins models: A case study', *Journal of Business and Economic Statistics*, **1** (2), 299–315.

Harvey, A. C., Henry, S. G. B., Peters, S. and Wren-Lewis, S. (1986), 'Stochastic trends in dynamic regression models: an application to the employment-output equations', *Economic Journal*, **96** (384), 975–85.

Hausman, J. A. (1978), 'Specification tests in econometrics', *Econometrica*, **46**, 1251–72.

Hayashi, F. and Sims, C. A. (1983), 'Nearly efficient estimation of the time series models with predetermining but not exogenous instruments', *Econometrica*, **51**, 782–98.

Hendry, D. F. (1976), 'The structure of simultaneous equations estimators', *Journal of Econometrics*, **4**, 51–85.

Hendry, D. F. (1980), 'Predictive failure and econometric modelling in macroeconomics: the transactions demand for money', in Ormerod, P. (ed), *Economic Modelling*, London: Heinemann.

Hendry, D. F. (1983), Econometric modelling: the consumption function in retrospect, *Scottish Journal of Political Economy*, **30** (3), 193–220.

Hendry, D. F. (1986), *PC-GIVE*, Nuffield College, Oxford.

Hendry, D. F. (1988), 'The encompassing implications of feedback versus feedforward mechanisms in econometrics', *Oxford Economic Papers*, **40**, 132–9.

Hendry, D. F. and Mizon, G. E. (1978), 'Serial correlation as a convenient simplification not a nuisance: a comment on a study of the demand for money by the Bank of England', *Economic Journal*, **88**, 549–63.

Hendry, D. F. and Neale, A. J. (1989), 'The impact of structural breaks on unit root tests', Mimeo, Nuffield College Oxford.

Hendry, D. F., Pagan, A. R. and Sargan, J. D. (1984), 'Dynamic specification', in Griliches, Z. And Intriligator, M. D. (eds), *Handbook of Econometrics*, Amsterdam: North Holland.

Hendry, D. F. and Richard, J. F. (1987), 'Recent developments in the theory of encompassing', CORE Discussion paper no. 8722.

Hendry, D. F. and von Ungern-Sternberg, T. (1981), 'Liquidity and inflation effects on consumers' expenditure', in Deaton, A. S. (ed.), *Essays in the Theory and Measurement of Consumer Behaviour*, Cambridge: Cambridge University Press.

Hendry, S. G. B. and Wren-Lewis, S. (1984), 'The aggregate labour market in the UK: some experiments with RE models', in P. Malgrange and P. Muett (eds), *Contemporary Macro modelling*, Oxford: Basil Blackwell.

Himmelblau, D. M. (1972), *Applied Non-Linear Programming*, New York: McGraw-Hill.

Hodrick, R. J. and Srivastava, S. (1984), 'The co-variation of risk premiums and expected future spot exchange rates', Working Paper, Columbia Business School, no. 97.

Hoel, P. G. (1962), *Introduction to Mathematical Statistics*, New York: Wiley.

Holly, S. and Beenstock, M. (1980), 'The implications of rational expectations for the forecasting and the simulation of econometric models', LBS Discussion Paper.

Holly, S. Rustem, B. and Zarrop, M. (1979), *Optimal Control for Econometric Models*, London: Macmillan.

Holly, S. and Zarrop, M. B. (1983), 'An optimal and time consistency when expectations are rational', *European Economic Review*, February, 270–93.

Hughes-Hallett, A. J. (1981), 'Some extensions and comparisons in the theory of Gauss–Seidel literature techniques for solving large equation systems', in Proceedings of the 1979 Econometric Society Meeting, *Essays in Honour of Stephen Nalavani*, E. G. Charatsis (ed), Amsterdam: North Holland.

Intriligator, M. D. (1971), *Mathematical Optimisation and Economic Theory*, Englewood Cliffs: Prentice Hall.

Johansen, L. (1988), 'Production functions: an integration of micro and macro, short run and long run aspects', *Economica*, **55**, 220–35.

Johansen, S. (1988) 'Statistical analysis of cointegrating vectors', *Journal of Economic Dynamics and Control*, **12**, 231–54.

Johanson, S. (1989), 'Likelihood based inference on cointegration theory and application', Centro Studi Sorelle Clarke, Bagni Di Lucca, Italy.

Johnson, H. G (1983), '*Towards a General Theory of the Balance of Payments in International Trade and Economic Growth*, London: Allen & Uwin.

Judge, G. G., Carter-Hill, R., Griffiths, W. E., Lutkepohl, H. and Lee, T.

C. (1982), *Introduction to the Theory and Practice of Econometrics*, New York: Wiley.

Kalman, R. E. (1960), 'A new approach to linear filtering and prediction problems', *Transactions of ASME Series D, Journal of Basic Engineering*, **82**, 35–45.

Kalman, R. E. (1960), 'A new approach to linear filtering and prediction problems', *Journal of Basic Engineering*, March, 1, 35–45.

Kalman, R. E. and Bucy, R. S. (1961), 'New results in linear filtering and prediction theory', *Journal of Basic Engineering*, Transactions of the ASME, **83**, 95–108.

Kearney, C. and MacDonald, R. (1985), 'Public sector borrowing, the money supply and interest rates', *Oxford Bulletin of Economics and Statistics*, **47** (3), 249–73.

Kementa, J. (1971), *Elements of Econometrics*, New York: Macmillan.

Kendall, M. G. and Stuart, A. (1969), *The Advanced Theory of Statistics*, London: Charles Griffin.

Kennan, J. (1979), 'The estimation of partial adjustment models with rational expectations', *Econometrica*, **47** (6), 1441–55.

Kendrick, D. (1981), *Stochastic Control for Economic Models*, New York: McGraw-Hill.

Keynes, J. M. (1936), 'General theory of employment, interest and money', London: Macmillan.

Kiviet, J. F. (1985), 'Model selection test procedures in a single equation of a dynamic simultaneous system and their defects in small samples', *Journal of Econometrics*, **28**(3), 3227–362.

Kouri, P. J. K. and Porter, M. G. (1974), 'International capital flows and portfolio equilibrium', *Journal of Political Economy*, **82**, 443–67.

Laidler, D. E. W. (1984), 'The buffer stock notion in monetary econometrics', *Economic Journal*, (Supplement), **94**, 17–34.

Lawson, T. (1980), 'Adaptive expectations and uncertainty', *Review of Economic Studies*, **XLVII** (2), 305–20.

Lawson, T. (1984), 'Generalized adaptive expectations, in F. van der Ploeg (ed), *Mathematical Methods in Economics*, New York: Wiley.

Leamer, E. E. (1978), *Specification Searches: Ad Hoc Inference with Non-Experimental Data*, New York: Wiley.

Leiderman, L. (1980), 'Macroeconometric testing of the rational expectations and structural neutrality hypothesis for the United States', *Journal of Monetary Economics*, **6**, 69–82.

Lucas, R. E., Jnr (1972), 'Expectations and the neutrality of money', *Journal of Economic Theory*, **4** (2), 103–24.

Lucas, R. E. (1976), 'Econometric policy evaluation: a critique', in K. Brunner and A. H. Meltzer (eds), *The Phillips Curve and Labour Markets*, Amsterdam: North Holland.

Lucas, R. E. Jnr. and Sargent, T. J. (eds), (1981), *Rational Expectations and Econometric Practice*, London: Allen and Unwin.

MacCallum, B. T. (1976), 'Rational expectations and the natural rate hypothesis: some consistent estimates', *Econometrica*, **44**, (1), 43–52.

McCarthy, M. D. (1972), 'Some notes on the generation of pseudo errors for use in stochastic simulation studies', in Hickman, B. G. (1972), (ed), *Econometric Models of Cyclical Behaviour*, Columbia University Press.

MacDonald, R. (1988), *Floating Exchange Rates: Theories and Evidence*, London: Unwin-Hyman.

MacKinnon, J. G. (1990). *Critical values for cointegrating tests*, mimeo, Queens University, Ontario.

MacKinnon, J. G. and Milbourne, R. D. (1984), 'Monetary anticipations and the demand for money', *Journal of Monetary Economics*, **13**(4), 263–74.

Maddala, G. S. and Nelson, F. D. (1974), 'Maximum likelihood methods for models of markets in disequilibrium', *Econometrica*, **42**, 1013–30.

Malinvaud, E. (1970), *Statistical Methods of Econometrics*, Amsterdam: North Holland.

Mariano, R. S. and Brown, B. W. (1981), 'Non parametric stochastic prediction in a non-linear simultaneous system', presented at the North American Meeting of the Econometric Society.

Mincer, J. and Zarnowitz, V. (1969). 'The evolution of economic forecasts', in *Economic Forecasts and Expectations*, National Bureau of Economic Research Studies in Business Cycles, no. 19, J. Mincer (ed), p. 3–46, New York: Columbia University Press.

Minford, A. P. and Mathews, S. K. (1978), 'A note on terminal conditions and the analytical solution of rational expectations models', Liverpool Working Paper no. 7805, Department of Economics, University of Liverpool.

Mishkin, F. (1983), *A Rational Expectations Approach to Macroeconometrics*, Chicago: University of Chicago Press, for NBER.

Mizon, G. E. and Richard, J. F. (1986), 'The encompassing principle and its application to testing non-nested hypothesis', *Econometrica*, **54** (3), 657–78.

Mundell, R. A. (1968), *International Economics*, New York: Macmillan.

Muscatelli, V. (1988), 'Alternative models of buffer stock money: an empirical investigation', *Scottish Journal of Political Economy*, **35**(1), 1–21.

Muscatelli, V. (1989), 'A comparison of the rational expectations and the general to specific approach', *Oxford Bulletin of Economics and Statistics*, **51** (4), 353–75.

Muth, J. F. (1960), 'Optimal properties of exponentially weighted forecasts', *Journal of the American Statistical Association*, **55**, 299–305.

Muth, J. F. (1961), 'Rational expectations and the theory of price movements', *Econometrica*, **29** (3), 315–35.

Muth, J. F. (1961), 'Rational expectations and the theory of price movements', reprinted in R. E. Lucas and T. J. Sargent (eds), *Rational Expectations and Econometric Practice*, (1981), London: Allen & Unwin.

Nagar, A. L. (1969), 'Stochastic simulation of the Brookings econometric model', in Duessenbery, Fromm, Klein and Kuh (eds), *The Brookings Model: Some Further Results*, Amsterdam: North Holland.

Nelson, C. R. (1975), 'Rational expectations and the estimation of econometric models', *International Economic Review*, **16**, 555–61.

Nelson, M. C. (1985), 'On time varying risk premia in the foreign exchange market', *Journal of Monetary Economics*, **11**, 3–18.

Neyman, J. and Pearson, E. S. (1928), 'On the use and interpretation of certain test criteria for the purpose of statistical inference', *Biometrica*, **20A**, 173–263.

Nickell, S. J. (1985), 'Error correction, partial adjustment and all that: an expositional note', *Oxford Bulletin of Economics and Statistics*, **47**, 119–29.

Norman, M. (1967), 'Solving a non-linear econometric model by the Gauss–

Seidel literature method', paper presented at the Econometric Society meeting.

Obstfeld, M. (1982), 'Can we sterilize? Theory and evidence', *American Economic Association*, Papers and Proceedings, **72**, 45–55.

Pagan, S. (1984), 'Eonometric issues in the analysis of regressions with generated regressors', *International Economic Review* **25**(25), 221–47.

Pagan, A. R. and Nicholls, D. F. (1984) 'Heteroskedasticity in models with lagged dependent variables, *Econometrica*, **51**(4) 1233–42.

Park, J. Y. and Phillips, P. C. P. (1988), 'Statistical inference in regressions with integrated processes: part I', *Economic Theory*, **4**, 468–497.

Park, J. Y. and Phillips, P. C. P. (1989) 'Statistical inference in regressions with integrated processes: part II', *Econometric Theory*, **5**, 95–131.

Pesaran, M. H. (1984), 'The new classical macroeconomics: a critical exposition', in F. van der Ploeg (ed), *Mathematical Methods in Economics*, New York: Wiley.

Pesaran, M. H. (1985), 'Formation of inflation expectations in British manufacturing industries', *Economic Journal*, **95**, 948–75.

Pesaran, M. H. (1987), *The Limits of Rational Expectations*, Oxford: Basil Blackwell.

Polak, E. (1972), 'A survey of methods of feasible directions for the solution of optimal control problems', *IEEE Transaction on Automatic Control*, **AC-17**, 591–6.

Powell, M. J. D. (1964), 'An effective method for finding the minimum of a function of several variables without calculating derivatives', *The Computer Journal*, **7**, 155–62.

Radner, R. (1982), 'Equilibrium under uncertainty', in Arrow, K. J. and Intriligator, M. D. (eds), *Handbook of Mathematical Economics Vol. 2*, Amsterdam: North Holland.

Ramsey, J. B. (1974), 'Classical model selection through specification error tests', in P. Zarembka (ed), *Frontiers in Econometrics*, New York: Academic Press.

Rao, C. R. (1948), 'Large sample tests of statistical hypothesis concerning several parameters with applications to problems of estimation', *Proceedings of the Cambridge Philosphical Society*, **44**, 50–57.

Salkever, D. S. (1976), 'The use of dummy variables to compute predictions, prediction errors and confidence intervals', *Journal of Econometrics*, **4**, 393–7.

Sargan, J. D. (1964), 'Wages and prices in the United Kingdom: a study of econometric methodology', in P. E. Hart and J. K. Whittaker (eds), *Econometric Analysis for Natural Economic Planning*, London: Butterworths.

Sargan, J. D. and Bhargava, A. (1983), 'Testing residuals from least squares regression for being generated by the Gaussian random walk', *Econometrica*, **51**, 153–74.

Sargent, T. J. (1979), *Macroeconomic Theory*, New York: Academic Press.

Sargent, T. J. (1981), 'Interpreting economic time series', *Journal of Political Economy*, **89**, 213–48.

Sargent, T. J. and Wallace, N. (1975), 'Rational expectations, the optimal monetary instrument and the optimal money supply rule', *Journal of Political Economy*, **83** (2), 241–54.

Schink, G. R. (1971), 'Small example estimates of the variance-covariance matrix of forecast errors for large econometric models: the stochastic simulation techniques', University of Pennsylvania PhD dissertation.

Sims, C. A. (1980), 'Macroeconomics and Reality', *Econometrica*, **48**, 1–48.

Sims, C., Stock, J. H. and Watson, M. W. (1986) 'Inference in linear time series models with some unit roots', Hoover Institute, Stanford University, Working paper.

Spanos, A. (1986), *Statistical Foundations of Econometric Modelling*, Cambridge: Cambridge University Press.

Spendley, W. Hext, G. R. and Himsworth, F. R. (1962), 'Sequential application of simplex designs in optimisation and evolutionary operation', *Techometrics*, **4**, 441–61.

Stock, J. H. (1987), 'Asymptotic properties of least squares estimators of co-integrating vectors', *Econometrica*, **55**, 1035–56.

Stockman, A. C. (1978), 'Risk information and forward exchange rates', in *The Economics of Exchange Rates: Selected Studies*, Frenkel, J. A. and Johnson, H. G. (eds), London: Basil Blackwell.

Struth, F. K. (1984), 'Modelling expectations with parameter-adaptive filters: an empirical application to the Livingston forecasts', *Oxford Bulletin of Economics and Statistics*, **46** (3), 211–39.

Taylor, M. P. (1984) 'A varying parameter empirical model of balance of payments determination under fixed exchange rates: results for the UK and West Germany', *Applied Economics*, **18**(6), 567–82.

Taylor, M. P. (1986), 'From the general to the specific: the demand for M2 in three European countries', *Empirical Economics*, **11**, 242–61.

Taylor, M. P. (1987a), 'On the long run solution to dynamic econometric equations under rational epectations', *Economic Journal*, March, **97**, 215–218.

Taylor, M. P. (1987b), 'Expectations, risk and uncertainty in the foreign exchange markets: some results based on survey data' Bank of England discussion paper No. 29, *Manchester School*, **57**(2), 142–53.

Taylor, M. P. (1988), 'What do investment managers know? An empirical study of practitioners predictions', *Economica*, **55**, 185–202.

Taylor, M. P. (1991), 'Modelling the demand for UK broad money, 1871–1913', forthcoming, *Review of Economics and Statistics*, 1991.

Taylor, M. P. and McMahon, P. (1988), 'Long run purchasing power parity in the 1920s', *European Economic Review*, **32**, 179–97.

Theil, H. and Goldberger, A. S. (1961), 'Pure and mixed statistical estimation in economics', *International Economic Review*, **2** (1), 65–78.

Tobin, J. (1958), 'Estimation of relationships for limited dependent variables', *Econometrica*, **26**, 24–36.

Tobin, J. (1969), 'A general equilibrium approach to monetary theory', *Journal of Money Credit and Banking*, **1**, 15–29.

Townsend, R. M. (1978), 'Market anticipation, rational expectation and Bayesian analysis', *International Economic Review*, **19**, 481–94.

Townsend, R. M. (1983), 'Forecasting the forecast of others', *Journal of Political Economy*, **91**, 546–88.

Vjiie, J. (1978), 'A stock adjustment approach to monetary policy and the balance of payments', in *The Economics of Exchange Rates*, J. A. Frankel and H. G. Johnson (eds), London: Addison-Wesley.

Wald, A. (1943), 'A note on the consistency of the maximum likelihood estimator', *Annals of Mathematical Statistics*, **20**, 595–601.

Wallis, K. F. (1972), 'Testing for fourth-order serial correlation in quarterly regression models', *Econometrica*, **40**, 617–36.
Wallis, K. F. (1980), 'Econometric implications of the rational expectations hypothesis', *Econometrica*, **48** (1), 49–73.
Wallis, K. F. (ed), (1986), *Models of the UK Economy: II*, Oxford: Oxford University Press.
Wallis, K. F. (1989), 'Macroeconomic forecasting: a survey', *Economic Journal*, **99**(394), March, 28–61.
West, K. D. (1988), 'Asymptotic normality, when regressors have a unit root', *Econometrica*, **56** (6), 1397–1417.
White, H. (1980), 'A heteroskedasticity – consistent covariance matrix estimator and a direct test for heteroskedasticity', *Econometrica*, **48**, 55–68.
Wickens, M. R. (1982a), 'The efficient estimation of econometric models with rational expectations', *Review of Economic Studies*, **49**, 55–68.
Wickens, M. R. (1982b), 'The efficient estimation of econometric models with rational expectations', *Review of Economic Studies*, **XLIX** (1), 55–67.
Wiener, N. (1982), *The Extrapolation, Interpolation and Smoothing of Stationary Time Series*, New York: Wiley.
Wilcox, J. B. (1985) 'A model of the building society sector', Bank of England Discussion paper no. 23.
Wolff, C. C. P. (1987), 'Forward foreign exchange rates, expected spot rates and premia: a signal extraction approach', *Journal of Finance*, **42**(2), 395–406.
Young, D. N. (1971), *Iterative Solution of Large Linear Systems*, New York: Academic Press.
Zellner, A. (1971), *An Introduction to Bayesian Inference in Econometrics*, New York: Wiley.

Index